ESTHER

BHHB

Baylor Handbook on the Hebrew Bible

General Editor

W. Dennis Tucker Jr.

ESTHER
A Handbook on the Hebrew Text

John Screnock
Robert D. Holmstedt

BAYLOR UNIVERSITY PRESS

Cover Design by Pamela Poll
Cover photograph by Bruce and Kenneth Zuckerman, West Semitic Research, in collaboration with the Ancient Biblical Manuscript Center. Courtesy Russian National Library (Saltykov-Shchedrin).

Library of Congress Cataloging-in-Publication Data

Screnock, John, author.
Esther / John Screnock with Robert D. Holmstedt.
303 pages cm. — (Baylor handbook on the Hebrew Bible)
Includes bibliographical references and index.
ISBN 978-1-60258-678-9 (pbk. : alk. paper)
1. Bible. Esther—Criticism, interpretation, etc. I. Holmstedt, Robert D., coauthor. II. Title.
BS1375.52.H65 2015
222'.90446—dc23

2015006714

Printed in the United States of America on acid-free paper with a minimum of 30 percent post-consumer waste recycled content.

TABLE OF CONTENTS

ACKNOWLEDGMENTS

I would like to thank my advisor, Sarianna Metso, for allowing and supporting this major "side project" in the middle of my doctoral work. I am also grateful to Michael Wise, who first gave me an interest in the Hebrew language and the book of Esther. My wife, Charlotte, has been very patient and understanding as I invested countless hours into what must have seemed like an endless project. Finally, I want to dedicate this book to my parents, in thanks for their support and encouragement; I couldn't have done it without them.

—J.S.
Toronto, August 14, 2014

I am indebted to the graduate students who provided feedback on the drafts of this work as we read Esther together in my course on ancient Hebrew philology—Mark Graham, Jean-Philippe Delorme, and Daniel Sarlo. I am grateful to Dennis Tucker and the Baylor University Press for another opportunity to contribute to the BHHB series, which I consider to be an invaluable endeavor. And I thank my wife, Rachel, and our children, Avigayil, Benjamin, Eliana, Miryam, Noah, and Zechariah. They graciously accepted my adding another item to my long list of projects.

—R.D.H.
Toronto, August 14, 2014

INTRODUCTION

The story of Esther in her eponymous book is artistic, well crafted, and entertaining. The interplay of characters—from Esther's concealed Jewishness and Mordecai's lack of compromise to Haman's pompous egotism and King Ahashverosh's general cluelessness—is delightful and often humorous, even when the humor is dark and the result is tragic. Bush examines the careful plot structure in his thorough commentary and Fox (2001) analyzes how each of the story's actors are characterized and what this suggests for understanding the ideology of the author, and thus the book. Various other commentaries and monographs focus on the book's theology, historical setting, place in the early Jewish canon, textual history, relationship to Purim, etc. Few works, however, have been dedicated to the Hebrew language of the book, especially concerning grammar (rather than, for instance, intertextual cues): the few exceptions are the doctoral thesis of R. L. Bergey (1983), a small variety of shorter studies (e.g., Striedl, Bergey 1984), and passing treatment within studies of "late" biblical Hebrew (e.g., Bendavid; Polzin; Young, Rezetko, and Ehrensvärd).

Our goal with this volume is to address this surprising lack of attention to the grammar of the book of Esther. Before moving to our verse-by-verse commentary, it is important to contextualize our commentary with this introduction. In the following sections, we present the background and terminology necessary for understanding our grammatical analyses ("Linguistic Background," Appendix A, and Appendix C), summaries of the *Qere-Ketiv* in the book ("*Qere-Ketiv*") and the Greek Alpha text ("The Alpha Text of Esther"), before concluding with a discussion of diachronic features in the book and linguistic dating ("Dating Esther Linguistically" and Appendix B).

Linguistic Background

In our grammatical analysis we follow the approach taken in the Ruth volume of this series (Holmstedt 2010) as well as numerous subsequent studies by Holmstedt. In this section, we briefly describe the concepts by which we analyze the grammar of Ruth (we also suggest the reader consult the linguistic glossary and index at the end of the volume).

Syntactic Components: Constituency

The basic components of syntax are **constituents** and the ways in which they relate to one other. "Constituents are groups of words that function as units with respect to grammatical processes" (Carnie 2008:18). There are a number of "constituent tests" to isolate whether a given item or sequence of items qualifies as a constituent. Pronoun replacement is one such test—if a word or group of words can be replaced in a given phrase or clause by a pronoun, that word or group qualifies as a constituent (see Carnie 2006:86–87). For example, in (1) the group of words *the man with the green hat* can be replaced by the pronoun *he*, as we have done in (2). The grammatical acceptability of this replacement suggests that the group *the man with the green hat* is one constituent

(1) [The man with the green hat] walked to the bank.
(2) [He] walked to the bank.

Constituents combine with other constituents to create increasingly larger units, or phrases. Phrases are fundamentally hierarchical in structure. That is, one item in a phrase gives the entire phrase its identity and is thus the phrasal **head**. For instance, in the phrase *man with the green hat* above in (1), the noun *man* is the phrasal head, thereby making the phrase a **noun phrase (NP)**.

Just as a noun phrase has a noun as its head, so all phrasal types have one constituent that is hierarchically dominant. Verbs produce **verb phrases (VP)**, adjectives produce **adjective phrases (AP)**, and so on with other lexical categories: adverbs (>**AdvP**), prepositions (>**PP**), determiners (>**DP**).

Constituents continue to combine until they form the highest phrasal level—the clause. Returning to the example in (1) above, we can work our way backwards from the end of the clause and describe each head combining with other items to produce increasingly larger phrasal levels. The noun *bank*, which has no modifiers, becomes an NP by itself and then combines with the determiner *the* to produce a larger NP (or a DP in some theories), which in turn combines with the preposition *to* to create the PP that merges with the verb *walked* to produce a VP. The noun *hat* and the adjective *green* form an NP, to which the determiner *the* is added to produce a larger NP (or DP). This larger NP is combined with the preposition *with*, resulting in a PP, which itself is combined with the noun *man* and then the determiner *the*, all of which is a large NP. Each constituent and its nested, hierarchical position relative to the other constituents are represented by brackets in the modified example in (3).

(3) $[_{\text{CLAUSE}}$ $[_{\text{NP}}$ The $[_{\text{NP}}$ man $[_{\text{PP}}$ with $[_{\text{NP}}$ the $[_{\text{AP}}$ green] hat]]]]] $[_{\text{VP}}$ walked $[_{\text{PP}}$ to $[_{\text{NP}}$ the $[_{\text{NP}}$ bank]]]].

The combination of the two halves, the larger NP *the man with the green hat* and the VP *walked to the bank*, creates a clause, the first half functioning as the subject NP and the second as the VP predicate.

Syntactic Roles

Within the hierarchy of the clause, the two most prominent constituent roles are the subject and predicate. Subjects are nominal (i.e., have noun-like status), whether a simple noun or a complex clause that is "nominalized" (e.g., by אשר or כי). The predicate is coextensive with the VP. Within the VP, the head is a verb, whether finite (*yiqtol*, *qatal*, the past narrative *yiqtol* in the *wayyiqtol* complex, or a null copula), non-finite (infinitive construct or infinitive absolute), or imperative.

For the nonverbal constituents within the VP, rather than using the traditional transitivity terms of direct object, indirect object, etc., or the Latinate case-based terms of accusative, genitive, or dative, we use two terms to cover all the syntactic roles within the VP: **complement** and **adjunct**. A complement is a constituent that is required by the semantics of the head of the phrase in which it is located. Thus, in the VP *hit the ball*, the NP *the ball* is required by the verb *hit*, which would be semantically incomplete without an NP complement. In contrast, an adjunct is an optional constituent that provides information (regarding manner, time, location, instrument, etc.) about its phrasal head. For instance, in the VP *hit the ball hard*, the adjective *hard* functions as a verbal adjunct, providing an informative but nonobligatory feature about its phrasal head, the verb *hit*.

Even for modern spoken languages, determining whether a given verb requires a complement or not, or whether a given NP, PP, AP, or AdvP is a complement or adjunct can be challenging. How much more so, then, for an ancient language like Hebrew in the book of Esther. Making such semantic judgments requires rigorous philological work, consulting lexica and working through dozens, if not many more, examples for each verb, to determine the verbal *valency*.

Valency

A verb's valency is part of its lexical composition and refers to the number of arguments the verb requires in order to be semantically "complete." Constituents that either relate to the verb or are located within the verb phrase are available to fulfill the verbal valency requirements. Depending on the number of arguments a verb requires, it may be avalent (no arguments), monovalent (one argument—a subject), bivalent (two arguments—a subject and a complement), or trivalent (three arguments—a subject and two complements) (cf. Carnie 2006:51–53). Hebrew verbs are only monovalent, bivalent, or trivalent, as illustrated in the following chart.

	Monovalent	*Bivalent*	*Trivalent*
Arguments	A subject	A subject plus one of the following complements: NP, PP, direct speech, or infinitive clause	A subject plus two of the following complements: NP, PP, direct speech, or infinitive clause
Examples	Stative Qal; Niphal; Pual; Hophal	Many Qal, Piel; few Hiphil (the "internal" Hiphil)	Qal נתן, שׂים; some Piel[1]; many Hiphil

Verbal *binyanim* interact with valency requirements. The relationships among the *binyanim* often concern the increase or decrease of valency. Thus, for a bivalent Qal verb (e.g., *X hit Y*), decreasing the valency typically results in the passive Niphal, in which the complement of the bivalent assertion becomes the subject of the monovalent assertion (e.g., *Y was hit*). Increasing the valency of a bivalent Qal, in contrast, typically results in a causative Hiphil (e.g., *X caused Y to hit Z*), in which the former complement becomes a second agent (though still a syntactic complement) and a second complement is added as the patient, or thing affected.

[1] When the Piel is "causative" it is trivalent, whereas when it is "intensive" it is bivalent.

Although the set of terminology involving "transitivity" has some overlap with valency, transitivity deals primarily with the number of "direct objects" and "indirect objects" rather than complements. We consider valency to be better suited to the description of Hebrew grammar.

Verbal Semantics

For a full discussion of verbal semantics in biblical Hebrew (BH) that covers the history of interpretation and provides a linguistically grounded analysis that we both agree with and utilize in this volume, we direct the reader to John Cook's recent monograph (2012; see also 2005; 2006; 2008; 2013). Below we provide a brief summary of the Hebrew verbal system in Esther.

Verbal systems in different languages communicate three elements to varying degree; these elements are tense, "the time at which the action of the verb took place" (Crystal 2008:479), aspect, "the duration or type of temporal activity denoted by the verb" (38), and mood, which typically involves "attitudes on the part of the speaker toward the factual content of the utterance" (312). The bundle of these features in a verb is often referred to as *tense-aspect-mood* (TAM).

The verbal system in BH is aspect-prominent, with the primary opposition between the viewpoint aspects of perfective and imperfective (Cook 2012:268–71). The *qatal* is perfective, which refers to the temporal unfolding of a situation as an undifferentiated whole, while the *yiqtol* is imperfective, which refers to the temporal unfolding of a situation as in progress (see 199–201). A second semantic layer of information that the BH verbal system expresses is modality, or mood: the perfective *qatal* and imperfective *yiqtol* have both realis (indicative) and irrealis (subjunctive, volitive) functions as well (233–56). The distinction between realis and irrealis is often signaled by word order (subject-verb is the basic realis order; inversion to verb-subject word order typifies the irrealis; see below). Morphologically irrealis forms are the jussive (which is not always distinguished from the imperfective *yiqtol*) and the imperative. The *yiqtol* inside the *wayyiqtol* complex form, which is used mostly in narrative (though there are important exceptions), is not aspectual but a holdover of an older tense system and functions as a simple past or preterite verb.

The BH participle is fundamentally an adjective that encodes an activity or event rather than a quality (Cook 2008; 2012:223–33). As event-encoding items, participles may govern their own complements and adjuncts, as finite verbs do (e.g., מְבַקְשֵׁי רָעָתָם in 9:2). As adjectives, participles are always the complement of a copular verb, mostly null but occasionally overt (e.g., וַיְהִי אֹמֵן אֶת־הֲדַסָּה in 2:7). Semantically the BH participle is associated with progressive aspect, which can be extended for durative, habitual, and gnomic statements.

The expression of the time, or the temporal setting of a given action or event, is not an inherent feature of the verbs, though the perfective *qatal* is typically used in past settings and the imperfective *yiqtol* is typically used in nonpast setting. Clues drawn from the context, such as temporal adverbs and the literary genre, are what establish the temporal frame.

Another use of Hebrew verbs is for generic statements, whether gnomic (*all dogs pant*) or habitual (*my dog pants heavily whenever he is excited*) (Cook 2005; 2012:214–15, 222, 232–33, 252). Generic statements in BH are an area of overlap between the perfective *qatal,* imperfective *yiqtol*, and participle—all three may be used to express genericity (see, e.g., the participle in 2:3, שֹׁמֵר הַנָּשִׁים, the *yiqtol* verbs in 2:13, אֵת כָּל־אֲשֶׁר תֹּאמַר יִנָּתֵן לָהּ, and the *qatal* in 3:4, לֹא שָׁמַע אֲלֵיהֶם).

The Venn diagram below summarizes the semantics of the BH verbs, including the overlap between the conjugations (Cook 2012:270; see also Holmstedt and Cook, 123). The two darker circles in the middle highlight the centrality of the aspectual contrast between the *qatal* and *yiqtol.*

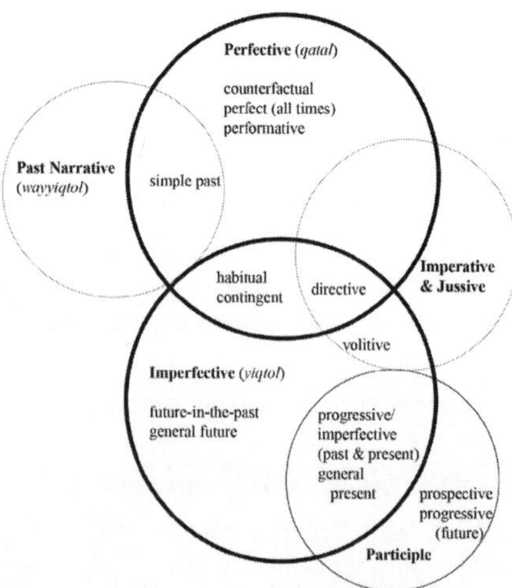

Finally, the use of the verbal system in narrative texts deserves specific comment. The conventions of BH narrative are fairly straightforward: the *wayyiqtol* carries the weight of the narrative progression, while clauses without a *wayyiqtol* are predominantly used to fill in the background, circumstantial narrative gaps. This narrative convention interacts with word order only coincidentally, since the *wayyiqtol* necessarily requires verb-subject order while the non-*wayyiqtol* clauses may exhibit the full range of Hebrew word order variation (see "Word Order" below). Verbal semantics within subordinate clause contexts is a significant desideratum in the study of BH grammar; however, our observations on the use of verbs within relative clauses suggests that the *qatal* and *yiqtol* both default to their basic temporal associations, past and nonpast, respectively, unless some contextual feature forces another semantic quality.

Word Order

Syntax

Although the basic word order of BH is traditionally understood to be verb-subject (VS) (see, e.g., Ewald 306b; GKC 142a; Davidson 105; WO 8.3b; JM 155k), we maintain that the general shift in Semitic languages from verb-subject to subject-verb (SV) order had occurred in Hebrew by the time most of the Hebrew Bible was written down (Holmstedt 2005; 2009a; 2013d; cf. Joüon 1947:155). While it is accurate to say that the word order one will most often encounter in BH texts, particularly narrative texts, is VS, it is incorrect to contend that the *basic* word order of the language (written *and* spoken) is VS. Rather, the basic order is SV, while a variety of grammatical factors—the placement of a constituent or certain grammatical words at the beginning of the clause, the use of a modal verb, the use of the past narrative verb—trigger the inversion to VS order. The list below summarizes the most common SV-to-VS triggers:

1. subordination (most commonly with אִם, אֲשֶׁר, כִּי, לְמַעַן, פֶּן)
2. clausal negation
3. irrealis verbs (irrealis *yiqtol* or *qatal*, jussives, cohortatives, imperatives)
4. Topic or Focus-fronting of a nonsubject constituent

The likely explanation for the marked difference between the basic SV order of main clauses and the dominant VS order in subordinate and negated clauses is diachronic. Cross-linguistic studies have demonstrated that syntactic change occurs first in nonembedded (i.e., main clause) structures and then only later spreads to embedded structures (Holmstedt 2013d:21). One indication that Hebrew continued to change during the span in which the Hebrew Bible was written is the different word order profiles we can detect in the different books. For example, finding a greater frequency of SV order infiltrating subordinate, negated, and/or irrealis contexts within a given book (e.g., the S-Neg-V clause in Esth 9:28b) strongly suggests a diachronically later linguistic stage (Holmstedt 2013d:21–23; see "Salient Grammatical Features").

Null copula clauses (so-called verbless or nominal clauses) also have the basic order SV. However, these clauses do not invert to VS order. Thus, the only variation in the word order of null copula clauses is when some constituent, whether subject, complement, or adjunct, is fronted for Topic or Focus. Note that we take the BH participle to be the complement of a copula (most often null, though occasionally overt); see "Verbal Semantics" above. The word order implication is that participles should also have a basic SV (or more accurately, subject-copula-complement [participle]) order. And this is, indeed, the case.

Finally, as copular items, we might expect יֵשׁ (positive) and אֵין (negative) to exhibit SV (or, subject-copula-complement) word order. While this order does occur (e.g., כְּתָב ... אֵין לְהָשִׁיב in 8:8), there are more cases where the copular particle is followed by the subject and then copular complement (e.g., אֵין אֶסְתֵּר מַגֶּדֶת מוֹלַדְתָּהּ in 2:20, and the single יֵשׁ occurrence in 3:8), or יֵשׁ or אֵין followed by the copular complement with the subject coming last (see, e.g., אֵין לָהּ אָב וָאֵם in 2:7). The syntax of יֵשׁ and אֵין copular phrase structure has not yet adequately been studied and so remains an important desideratum in BH grammar.

Pragmatics

When constituents are moved from their default position (e.g., subject-verb-complement-adjunct), the reasons are syntax (i.e., triggered inversion due to subordinating particles), semantics (i.e., irrealis verbs, negation), or pragmatics. Pragmatically motivated constituent movement in BH occurs for two primary reasons—to signal that a constituent carries **Topic** and **Focus** information. Though it is possible for a Topic-marked or Focus-marked constituent to reside in its default position (where it would be marked by an item like Focus גַּם or prosody) or to be moved to the end of the clause (e.g., extraposition and right-dislocation;

see Holmstedt 2014a), by far the dominant strategy to signal such discourse information is to raise the marked constituent to the front of the clause (see Holmstedt 2009a:126–29; and 2011:21–24).

Topic-fronting is used to signal a shift of "aboutness" (i.e., what the following assertions are "about"; the Topic is also typically the syntactic subject) between known discourse entities or to set the scene using circumstantial information, such as temporal or spatial PPs. An example of a scene-setting Topic is the temporal phrase PP בַּיּוֹם הַשְּׁבִיעִי in Esth 1:10. An example of Topic for "aboutness" is the subject הָמָן in the clause כִּי הָמָן ... חָשַׁב עַל־הַיְּהוּדִים in Esth 9:24. We can tell that הָמָן is Topic-fronted not only from the context (the previous verse had הַיְּהוּדִים and מָרְדֳּכַי as syntactic subjects and no mention has been made of הָמָן since 8:5) but also because the use of כִּי would normally cause VS word order. But here, after VS order is triggered by the כִּי, the subject הָמָן is raised back in front of the verb as the Topic.

Focus-fronting serves to establish a set of related items either from the discourse context or from shared knowledge of the world and then to set the Focus constituent over against the other members of the set. The result is often associated with a sense of contrast, illustrated in Esth 1:11b:

לְהַרְאוֹת הָֽעַמִּים וְהַשָּׂרִים אֶת־יָפְיָהּ כִּי־טוֹבַת מַרְאֶה הִיא

"to show the peoples and nobles her (Vashti's) beauty, because she was pleasing of appearance."

Within the null copula כִּי clause at the end of v. 11, the subject is the pronoun הִיא, but the copular complement טוֹבַת מַרְאֶה is fronted in the clause. This Focus-fronting establishes that of all Vashti's qualities (which are unlisted, and thus unknown to the reader, though other potential qualities could easily be imagined), it is her good looks that motivated the king's request to have her appear at his feast.

Both Topic and Focus constituents may be fronted in the same clause, with the Topic always preceding the Focus, as the tree diagram below illustrates. Additionally, it is possible for there to be more than one of each type, which is what the asterisk (*) in the tree diagram below represents. Note that the tree also shows where subordinators fit in non-main clauses, as well as the position to which "extreme" Topic-fronted constituents raise (see Holmstedt 2014a for further discussion).

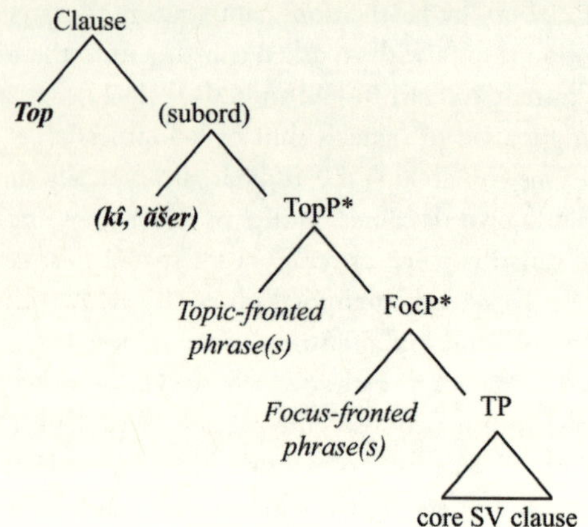

Subordinate Clauses

Subordinate clauses are adjuncts to a verb in the higher clause within which the subordinate clause resides (see Holmstedt 2013b). BH subordination is signaled by two methods: the use of subordinators or the type of verb (or both together). The subordinators used in BH fall into two categories, subordinating conjunction (e.g., כי) or the combination of a preposition and conjunction (כאשר), and they appear at the front of the subordinate clause. The most commonly used Hebrew subordinators are listed below.

'after' אַחֲרֵי
'if' אִם, לוּ
'if not' לוּלֵי
'that/which' אֲשֶׁר, שֶׁ, הַ
'when, just as' כַּאֲשֶׁר
'because, when, if, that' כִּי
'therefore' לָכֵן
'so that, in order to' לְמַ֫עַן
'before' לִפְנֵי
'while, until' עַד
'lest, so that not' פֶּן

The verb type typically associated with subordination is the BH infinitive. The "infinitive construct" is often the clitic host (and complement) for a preposition that overtly marks the infinitival clause as an adjunct of the verb in the higher clause (see, e.g., כְּשֶׁ֫בֶת in 1:2). These infinitives provide a wide range of subordinate clauses, such as temporal, purpose, and complement. The "infinitive absolute" takes its tense-aspect-mood value from its governing verb and is used to present its clause both as subordinate and as Focus-marked (see, e.g., נָת֫וֹן in 2:3).

Two frequently used types of subordinate clauses are relative and nominalized. Besides being subordinate—meaning they are subsumed within a larger matrix clause—both types of clauses are related because they can occur with אשר. In what follows, we explain the nature of relative and nominalized clauses by discussing the functions of אשר. Following this discussion, we note some additional important types of relative and nominalized clauses: nominalized clauses marked by כי, relatives marked by ה, and relatives that are unmarked. For a fuller treatment of relative clauses, see Holmstedt 2013a.

In grammars of BH there is typically a distinction made between "dependent" (or "attributive") relatives and "independent" (or "substantivized") relatives (Holmstedt 2002:20–21), but in fact there is only a small difference between these two; both are well within the normal function of אשר as a relative/nominalizing pronoun. The only difference between "substantivized" and "attributive" relatives is that the head (the word[s] modified by the relative) is overt in the latter and covert (null) in the former. As an example, consider a portion of Esth 2:1, זָכַר אֶת־וַשְׁתִּי וְאֵת אֲשֶׁר־עָשָׂתָה ("he remembered Vashti and what she had done"). The relative clause אֲשֶׁר־עָשָׂתָה is headless, but could be modified (by the addition of הַדָּבָר) to belong to a specific head:

זָכַר הַדָּבָר אֲשֶׁר עָשָׂתָה

"he remembered *the thing* which she did"

The head of the relative fills two syntactic roles, one within the relative clause and one in the larger matrix clause. In this example, הַדָּבָר is the complement of עָשָׂתָה in the relative clause (עָשָׂתָה הַדָּבָר, "she did *the thing*") and the complement of זָכַר in the matrix clause (זָכַר הַדָּבָר, "he remembered *the thing*"). In a headless relative, the modified constituent is null, but still fulfills the same syntactic roles:

זָכַר אֲשֶׁר עָשָׂתָה

"he remembered *[it]* which she did"

The null head, represented by "[it]" in the English translation, is the complement of עָשָׂתָה in the relative clause (עָשָׂתָה, "she did *[it]*") and the complement of זָכַר in the matrix clause (זָכַר, "he remembered [*it*]"). The only difference between these two relatives is the presence or absence of the relative head. Note that in either of these relative clause structures, resumption may be used to indicate the syntactic role of the relative head within the relative (e.g., זָכַר הַדָּבָר אֲשֶׁר עָשָׂתוֹ, "he remembered the thing which she did *it*" [unattested but grammatical]; Holmstedt 2013a:351).

The third use of אשר, however, has greater dissimilarity with both the above structures, and is best referred to as "nominalizing." When אשר acts as a nominalizer, there is no relative head, whether overt or covert; the entire אשר clause as a unit has one syntactic role in the matrix clause, and within the אשר clause itself there is no syntactic role to be fulfilled by a relative head. An example of a nominalized אשר clause is found in Esth 1:19.

וְלֹא יַעֲבוֹר אֲשֶׁר לֹא־תָבוֹא וַשְׁתִּי לִפְנֵי הַמֶּלֶךְ אֲחַשְׁוֵרוֹשׁ

"That Vashti did not enter before King Ahashverosh will not pass away."

The entire clause functions as the subject of יַעֲבוֹר in the matrix clause. Moreover, the אשר clause has all of its syntactic roles fulfilled by the words in the clause—the subject is וַשְׁתִּי, the verb is תָבוֹא, and the complement to the verb is לִפְנֵי הַמֶּלֶךְ אֲחַשְׁוֵרוֹשׁ. An analysis of this clause as a relative simply does not work:

*וְלֹא יַעֲבוֹר [null head] אֲשֶׁר לֹא־תָבוֹא וַשְׁתִּי לִפְנֵי הַמֶּלֶךְ אֲחַשְׁוֵרוֹשׁ

"[The thing] which Vashti did not enter before King Ahashverosh will not pass away."

This analysis does not work because the supposed relative head cannot have a syntactic role inside the אשר clause (Vashti cannot "enter the thing before King Ahashverosh," unless we incorrectly import part of the range of meaning of English "enter" onto the Hebrew בוא). There is no constituent (whether null or overt) that has a syntactic role in the matrix clause, that is modified by the אשר clause, and that has a syntactic role inside the אשר clause.

An easy way to remember these three types of אשר clauses is as follows. The first two, which are essentially the same with the minor difference of whether the head is null or overt, can be glossed with English "which" when the head is overt and "what" when the head is null. We refer to both of these as "relatives." The third type of אשר clause, which is significantly different from the first two, we refer to as a nominalized clause, and can be glossed with the English word "that."

Headed Relative: "I saw the book which my brother bought."
Headless Relative: "I saw what my brother bought."
Nominalized Clause: "I saw that my sister had arrived."

Note that the English gloss "that which" also works well for a headless relative, with the pronoun "that" supplied for the null head (e.g., "I saw that which my brother bought"). Note also that the word "that" in English can be used as a nominalizer *or* as a relative (e.g., "I saw the book that my brother bought"); in this duality of possible functions, English "that" shares some (but not all!) of the semantics of Hebrew אשר.

In the examples above, the syntactic structure of both the matrix and אשר clauses involved verbal predication; we should note that the structures of relative and nominalized clauses work in the same way with copular clauses as well. For example, in Esth 1:2, we read עַל כִּסֵּא מַלְכוּתוֹ אֲשֶׁר בְּשׁוּשַׁן הַבִּירָה, "on the throne of his kingdom which was in Susa, the citadel." The syntactic role of כִּסֵּא in the relative clause is as subject of the null copula clause ("the throne was in Susa"). Within the matrix clause, its role is complement of עַל ("on the throne").

In addition to אשר, the particle כי can be used to nominalize a clause (MNK 40.9; Aejmelaeus). For example, Esth 3:5 reads וַיַּרְא הָמָן כִּי־אֵין מָרְדֳּכַי כֹּרֵעַ וּמִשְׁתַּחֲוֶה לוֹ, "And Haman saw that Mordecai was not bowing or prostrating himself before him." The clause אֵין מָרְדֳּכַי כֹּרֵעַ וּמִשְׁתַּחֲוֶה לוֹ, "he was not bowing or prostrating himself before him" is transformed by כי into a single constituent, which serves as the complement of the verb ראה.

Relative clauses, too, can be introduced by means other than אשר. The cliticized article ש is not used in Esther; however, the cliticized article ה is used often as a relativizer, for example, in Esth 6:10: מָרְדֳּכַי הַיְּהוּדִי הַיּוֹשֵׁב בְּשַׁעַר הַמֶּלֶךְ, "Mordecai the Jew, *who* is sitting in the gate of the king." Finally, a relative clause may not be marked by a relative word of any sort; such unmarked relatives are found throughout Esther, for example in 3:8: יֶשְׁנוֹ עַם־אֶחָד מְפֻזָּר וּמְפֹרָד בֵּין הָעַמִּים, "There is a certain people *which* is scattered and divided from the (other) peoples." The syntactical structure of unmarked relatives is the same as marked relatives, with the exception of the null relative; the preceding example is essentially the same as the unattested but grammatical יֶשְׁנוֹ עַם־אֶחָד אֲשֶׁר מְפֻזָּר וּמְפֹרָד בֵּין הָעַמִּים. Note that unmarked relatives may also be headless relatives, as in Esth 3:11, כַּטּוֹב בְּעֵינֶיךָ "according to (*the thing*) *which* is good in your eyes" (with the addition of אשר).

Numeral Syntax in Esther

In the book of Esther, there are ten cases of ordinal numbers and fifty-four cases of cardinal numbers. The normal order of compound numerals is generally taken to go from higher digits to lower digits, for example, hundreds, tens, ones (WO 15.2.5d; Hetzron, 169), with the exception of numbers 11–19 where the "ones" numeral precedes the "-teen" numeral (Hetzron, 169–70). In Esther, however, compound numerals are always given in the opposite direction, beginning with the lowest digits and preceding to the highest (e.g., שֶׁבַע וְעֶשְׂרִים וּמֵאָה מְדִינָה in 1:1, 8:9, and 9:30; חֲמִשָּׁה וְשִׁבְעִים אָלֶף in 9:16), regardless of whether a "-teen" numeral is involved. See Appendix A for a full account of the data in Esther.

Ordinal numerals function as adjectives, typically agreeing with the words they modify in definiteness (cf. WO 14.2a). This is normally true in Esther, but in one case (2:14, בֵּית הַנָּשִׁים שֵׁנִי), the ordinal does not agree in definiteness (see comment on 2:14). Cardinal numbers have a different syntactic relationship to the modified noun: they are found in either a bound relationship or an appositional relationship (see discussion below). Regardless of syntax, the cardinal numbers 3–10 have an abnormal pattern of agreement with the modified noun, often referred to as "chiastic concord." The gender of these cardinals is opposite the gender of the modified noun (JM 100d; WO 15.2.2a). We find chiastic concord throughout Esther. The cardinal 10 shows chiastic concord only when it is used alone (e.g., 9:10, 12); when it means "-teen," it agrees in gender with the modified noun (WO 15.2.3b).

According to Waltke and O'Connor, the cardinal numbers 1–19 typically appear before the noun they modify, either bound to the noun or (in free form) in apposition to the noun (WO 15.2.2b, 15.2.3a; cf. also JM 142a–e); the higher cardinals sometimes appear before the noun and sometimes after (WO 15.2.4a, 15.2.5a). Some argue that there was a linguistic shift from early biblical Hebrew (EBH), where the numeral often precedes the noun, to late biblical Hebrew (LBH), where the noun precedes the numeral. Given the presence of examples of postnominal numerals in early texts and the preference for prenominal numerals in much later texts (1QS and 1QM), this argument is incorrect (Weitzman). In Esther we see clear examples of three of the four options: (1) the number preceding the noun in appositional relationship (e.g., שִׁשָּׁה חֳדָשִׁים in 2:12); (2) the number bound to the noun (e.g., שִׁבְעַת יָמִים in 1:5); and (3) the noun bound to the number (e.g., בִּשְׁנַת שְׁתֵּים עֶשְׂרֵה in 3:7). The fourth possibility—the noun preceding the number in appositional relationship—may occur, but the form of the noun is always ambiguous, such that it could be bound or in apposition (e.g., לְחֹדֶשׁ שְׁנֵים־עָשָׂר in 3:13; and בְּיוֹם אַרְבָּעָה עָשָׂר in 9:15). JM states that יוֹם in such constructions is "in the cst. state [= bound], of course, like שְׁנַת" (142o), but the form is always ambiguous. The parallel construction using bound שְׁנַת suggests that such phrases with חֹדֶשׁ and יוֹם utilize a bound construction, however the similarities with the syntax of ordinals (see discussion below), where the noun is not bound to the numeral (and the adjective is essentially in apposition to the noun it modifies), suggests that חֹדֶשׁ and יוֹם are in apposition to the numeral. These ambiguous cases appear in Esth 3:7, 13 (2×); 8:12; 9:15, 17, 19, 21 (2×).

The syntax of cardinal numerals in Esther is greatly clarified when a particular use of cardinals is considered. Because there are no ordinals above "tenth," when a higher number is needed for what would typically be an ordinal, a cardinal number is used (WO 15.3.1; JM 142o). This happens often in dating formulas (e.g., 9:15: בְּיוֹם אַרְבָּעָה עָשָׂר, "on the *fourteenth* day"; cf. also 3:7, 12, 13; 8:9, 12; 9:1, 17, 18, 19, 21). Similarly, with the word שנה, "year," cardinal numbers are always used with an ordinal sense, instead of ordinals (WO 15.3.2; JM 142o; cf. Esth 1:3, 2:16, 3:7). In eleven of the fourteen cases where a cardinal is used with an ordinal sense, the order is noun-number. When these fourteen cases are excluded, thirty-seven of the remaining forty cardinals in Esther have the order number-noun. The three exceptions are found in 3:8, 3:13, and 8:12, where אחד is used with the adjectival sense meaning "certain" (e.g., 3:8: עַם־אֶחָד, "a certain people"; cf. HALOT אחד; BDB אחד; GKC 125b; WO 15.2.1a; cf. WO 15.2.1b, f). It seems, then, that the normal syntax of cardinal numerals always has the number first, either number bound to noun, or number followed by noun in apposition (the first two options given above). The use of cardinals with an ordinal sense is similar to adjectival constructions, in that the noun precedes the numeral (the third and fourth options given above).

Type of numeral	*Order*
Ordinals	noun-number (adjectival)
Adjectival אחד	noun-number (adjectival)
Cardinals as ordinals	noun-number (adjectival)
Regularly functioning cardinals	number-noun

Qere-Ketiv

The coupled terms *Qere-Ketiv* refer to a phenomenon in the Masoretic Text where the Masoretes indicated that the letters as written should actually be read in a different manner. JM 16e: "The [*Qere*] is the reading which, according to the [Masoretes], must be read, or which is current; the [*Ketiv*] is the reading which emerges from the consonantal text. […] [The] vowels of the *Qere* are those of the text. The [*Ketiv*] is represented only by the consonants of the text, whereas the vowels are not indicated, and need to be reconstructed from the form of the word and the context."

In this volume, cases of *Qere-Ketiv* are treated as follows: the *Ketiv* is used without vocalization, and the *Qere* is noted in the comment on the verse. Readers can identify instances of *Qere-Ketiv* in the text simply by looking for unvocalized words. There are thirteen cases of *Qere-Ketiv* in the Leningrad Codex (B19a) of Esther, as represented in the following chart.

	Form in body of text	*Form in margin*	*Reconstructed Ketiv*	*Vocalized Ketiv*	*Vocalized Qere*
1:16	מְומֻכָן	ממוכן	מומכן	מוּמְכָן	מְמוּכָן
3:4	בְּאָמְרָם	כאמרם	באמרם	בְּאָמְרָם	כְּאָמְרָם
4:4	וַתָּבוֹאינָה	-	ותבואינה	וַתְּבוֹאֶינָה	וַתָּבוֹאנָה
4:7	בַּיְּהוּדִיים	-	ביהודיים	בַּיְּהוּדִיִּים	בַּיְּהוּדִים
8:1	הַיְּהוּדִיים	היהודים	היהודיים	הַיְּהוּדִיִּים	הַיְּהוּדִים
8:7	בַּיְּהוּדִיים	ביהודים	ביהודיים	בַּיְּהוּדִיִּים	בַּיְּהוּדִים
8:13	הַיְּהוּדִיים	היהודים	היהודיים	הַיְּהוּדִיִּים	הַיְּהוּדִים
8:13	עֲתִודִים	עתידים	עתודים	עֲתוּדִים	עֲתִידִים
9:15	הַיְּהוּדִיים	דים	היהודיים	הַיְּהוּדִיִּים	הַיְּהוּדִים
9:18	וְהַיְּהוּדִיים	והיהודים	והיהודיים	וְהַיְּהוּדִיִּים	וְהַיְּהוּדִים
9:19	הַפְּרַוזִים	הפרזים	הפרוזים	הַפְּרוּזִים	הַפְּרָזִים
9:27	וְקִבֵּל	וקבלו	וקבל	וְקִבֵּל	וְקִבְּלוּ
10:1	אֲחָשְׁרֵשׁ	אחשורוש	אחשרש	אֲחָשְׁרֵשׁ	אֲחַשְׁוֵרוֹשׁ

The Alpha Text of Esther

The Alpha Text of Esther is a Greek version of Esther that differs in significant ways from the Septuagint. The additions to Esther—found in the Septuagint but not in the MT (thus the term "additions")—are present in the Alpha Text. These additions are very close between the Septuagint and the Alpha Text, suggesting that the Alpha Text adopted them from the Septuagint. When the Alpha Text is considered without the additions, a core story remains that is significantly different from the versions found in the MT and in the Septuagint. Many scholars term this the "proto-AT" and argue that it is based on a Hebrew text that differs from, and is earlier than, the MT (see Moore 1967; 1971:lxii–lxiii; Clines 1984a:71–92; Bush, 281–84; cf. Jobes 1996).

Given the scope and purpose of the BHHB series, our comments rarely interact with the Alpha Text. However, at a few points the contents of the Alpha Text are relevant for our discussion. For a summary of the shape and character of the proto-AT, see Fox 2001:155–261 (and cf. Bush, 284–92; Clines 1984a:93–114).

The Linguistic Dating of Esther

A challenge in situating the book of Esther concerns the book's language: is it clearly "late" biblical Hebrew like that of Chronicles, Ezra, and Nehemiah (see e.g., Moore 1971), or is it more like the later language of the Mishnah (see e.g., Rabin; Sáenz-Badillos, 126–27)? On top of that, is the language also intentionally archaizing in an attempt to mimic the earlier "standard" biblical Hebrew of the Torah (e.g., Polzin)—and if so, why? The questions go on.

Categorizing the language of the book of Esther is both provocative and elusive. The questions we asked a moment ago hint at how the phonological, morphological, syntactic, semantic, and lexical features challenge our ability to classify the book. And yet, that is precisely what we offer in this study, an initial linguistic profile of this odd book. To do this, we present an explicitly methodological investigation, taking our cues from two sources: the discussions of Hebrew diachrony in recent years (see e.g., Miller-Naudé and Zevit) and an insightful doctoral thesis on the language of Esther, which Ronald Bergey completed thirty years ago (1983).

Previous Research and Methodological Issues

In his 1983 doctoral thesis on the language of Esther, Bergey based his analysis of the linguistic data upon the four criteria most often associated with Avi Hurvitz (1995; 2000): opposition, distribution, extra-biblical attestation, and accumulation.

He determined that while the book exhibited affinities with both earlier and later biblical Hebrew works, it also showed significant affinities with Mishnaic Hebrew. Saénz-Badillos' assertion that Esther is "one of the latest biblical writings" (125–26) attests to the influence of Bergey's study.

Bergey's impressive thesis notwithstanding, the elephant in the room is the distinction between cause and effect. Bergey focuses entirely on describing the effects of the supposed linguistic changes, with no attempt to explain if they are linguistically and historically plausible *as changes* and, if so, what the causes and mechanisms might have been. A second elephant, which Bergey introduces but does not dwell on, is the relative paucity of data. He admits that his analysis is "restricted to a narrow spectrum of linguistic potential," but provides no criteria by which to evaluate this potential (169). And a third elephant is the possibility of other explanations for the variation that are not specifically diachronic, such as dialect and style. It is time to face the herd of elephants in the room.

An explicit methodology is critical for any study carried out in the spirit of scientific inquiry. Hebrew studies have not been short on articulated methodology. However, for ancient language analysis, it is not enough to detail the criteria by which data are categorized and the steps by which the analysis proceeds. To avoid creating ad hoc, and potentially irrelevant procedures, it is essential that we use the established principles of historical-comparative linguistic investigation. Above all, this requires that we isolate the salient linguistic variation and then determine if the pattern of distribution matches known patterns outside Hebrew studies, whether diachronic or otherwise.

Diachronic Change

Any study of linguistic variation that proposes diachronic change as the explanation must address three core issues: *cause*, *mechanism*, and *effect*.

Identifying the effect is typically the easiest task, since it concerns the resulting sound, shape, sequence, or word that arises from the induced change. Cause and mechanism are more challenging to isolate, particularly since they are closely related. The cause of a given change falls into one of two categories that identify the source of the motivation: external and internal. The mechanisms by which changes occur fit into three broad categories: borrowing (externally motivated), reanalysis (internally motivated), and extension (internally motivated).

Externally Motivated Change: Borrowing

Languages borrow words from other languages for two primary reasons: need and prestige (Campbell, 64–65). For Esther, the fact of borrowed words is not the question—everyone admits the presence of both Persian and Aramaic loanwords in the book. Rather, the questions concern the likely reasons and their implications. For example, it makes sense that the author needed to borrow words like אֲחַשְׁדַּרְפָּן and כַּרְפַּס, since the former refers to an administrative role specific to the Persian period, and the latter refers to a type of linen that did not exist in ancient Israel. Other borrowed words in Esther, however, stand for concepts that have perfectly good Hebrew manifestations, such as פַּרְתְּמִים [// שָׂרִים], דָּת [// חֹק, מִשְׁפָּט, or תּוֹרָה], and פִּתְגָם [// מִשְׁפָּט or דָּבָר].

While both types of borrowing give insight into the source language and the general context of language contact, the prestige-based borrowings are a potential source of additional information about rhetorical design. Foreign words that are not need-based may, as Berlin suggests, "lend authenticity" or be "for showing off, adding to the snobbery of the court" (xxvii). Or such foreign items may signal political or social agendas.

Critically, borrowing and the closely related phenomenon of code-switching presume a necessary level of "intensity of contact." That is, if nonnative items are identified and they are not need-based lexical items, they must reflect intense contact between the language in question and the other language that is the source of the borrowed feature. Notably, among the factors that contribute to this contact intensity is "a high level of bilingualism" (Thomason, 689)—the use of prestige-based borrowing or code-switching presumes that *both* the *author* and the *audience* understood such elements.[2]

The use, or even avoidance, of features perceived to be non-native may serve as boundary-leveling or boundary-maintaining strategies, creating "in groups" and "out groups," based on religious, ethnic, or nationalistic concerns (Gordon and Williams, 80–81). The book of Esther may reflect the use of borrowing in order to create a group boundary that effectively encompasses only a Jewish audience (defined by the primary use of Hebrew) that also spoke Persian and had some familiarity with life in the Persian capital and even the royal court (defined by the use of the Persian loanwords and customs).[3]

Internally Motivated Change: Reanalysis and Extension

While borrowing has an external cause in language contact, internally motivated changes are responses to some perceived internal pressure on the language and are associated with the mechanisms of *reanalysis* and *extension.* Although it is not a hard and fast division, borrowing mostly concerns lexical items while reanalysis and extension affect grammatical structure or meaning. For the linguistic changes we have identified as operative in the language of Esther, reanalysis is the primary mechanism.[4]

---

[2] For Hebrew texts in the Bible, this raises an important issue: unless some texts were aimed only at the highly educated, the increasing presence of Aramaic words or the use of any Persian words presupposes a multilingual environment for the Hebrew-speaking audience. If the audience were not actually multilingual, they would at least have had to be passively familiar with the source languages of the borrowed items (see Thomason 2003:699 on passive familiarity as a mechanism of "interference"). General contact, political or economic, would not necessarily create a sufficient level of intensity of contact for prestige-based borrowing. It is only when Jews were living in exile in Babylonia or Persia that a Hebrew-speaking group would have experienced the sufficient intensity of contact for significant Persian borrowing to occur. For instance, we see from the Murashu and Al-Yahudu archives that the exilic communities in the neo-Babylonian and Persian periods became sufficiently enculturated that they began adopting non-Hebrew names (see Pearce; Zadok; Abraham; Beaulieu).

[3] A likely example of resistance to borrowing, and the related phenomenon of code-switching as a boundary-creating strategy is the case of the sectarian Qumran scrolls. In the context of general bilingualism (Hebrew and Aramaic) and in the face of significant linguistic pressure, the majority of the sectarian Qumran scrolls as a whole (excepting, e.g., 4QMMT and the Copper Scroll) appear to reflect the avoidance of perceived non-native elements in a concerted effort to mimic the language of the texts they considered authoritative, or their "Scripture."

[4] Extension is the opposite of reanalysis: it is a change to the surface pattern without any underlying modification (Harris and Campbell, 51). Paradigm leveling

Reanalysis is the change of the underlying structure or meaning of a linguistic phenomenon without any structural change to the surface manifestation (Harris and Campbell, 50). An example of reanalysis in Hebrew involves the conditional אִם in the oath formula. In the full formula, the אִם introduces a conditional clause, as it often does: "Thus shall God to you and thus shall he add, if (אִם) you do/do not …" (see 1 Sam 3:17). In many cases, though, the oath formula was abbreviated, with the initial threat omitted, leaving only the אִם clause. In the abbreviated examples, the אִם takes on a negative connotation, i.e., "(you will be cursed) *if* you do it" > "don't do it!" and אִם לֹא is interpreted positively, i.e., "(you will be cursed), *if* you do *not* do it" > "do it!" The negative אִם and positive אִם לֹא were then later used in nonoath contexts (e.g., Isa 22:14 and 1 Kgs 20:23, respectively; see JM 2006:165).

The Diffusion of Linguistic Change

One of the significant advances in Hebrew historical linguistics in the last five years is a more robust understanding of the process by which change spreads through time within a speech community. Critically, while the process unfolds, both the old and the new forms coexist, often for hundreds of years (Wolfram and Schilling-Estes, 715–16). Linguists have observed that the diachronic spread of a given change follows a Sigmoid ("S"-shaped) curve, an idealized example of which is provided in Figure 1 below.

As a new linguistic entity (e.g., lexeme, syntactic pattern) enters usage, it is a minority form alongside the previously existing entity. Over time, the usage of the new entity gains ground on the older entity, with increasing speed. As the new entity becomes dominant, the speed by which it pushes the older entity out of usage slows and the older entity never entirely disappears (Bailey, 77; Kroch 1989, 2001; Pintzuk).[5] Note

(or analogical change) is a classic example of extension. E.g., there is no good evidence that the second vowel of the Hiphil was a long /i/ before Hebrew, which suggests that Hebrew did not inherit the long /i/, but developed it. A likely source for this long vowel is the II-*w/y* verb class, in which the middle glide (*w* or *y*) assimilated to the adjacent vowel, producing a "long vowel" (e.g., **yaqwim* → **yaqyim* → **yaqiim* = **yaqîm*). This long vowel was then extended throughout the Hiphil paradigm, resulting in the pattern with which all Hebrew students are familiar, יַשְׁמִיד and הִשְׁמִיד.

[5] This S-curve model effectively replaces Hurvitz's principles of opposition and distribution. Though few real language variations match the idealized S-curve in figure 1, this model provides us with a statistically grounded pattern to use as a baseline for comparison in discerning whether a given variant pair likely reflects a diachronic

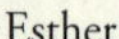

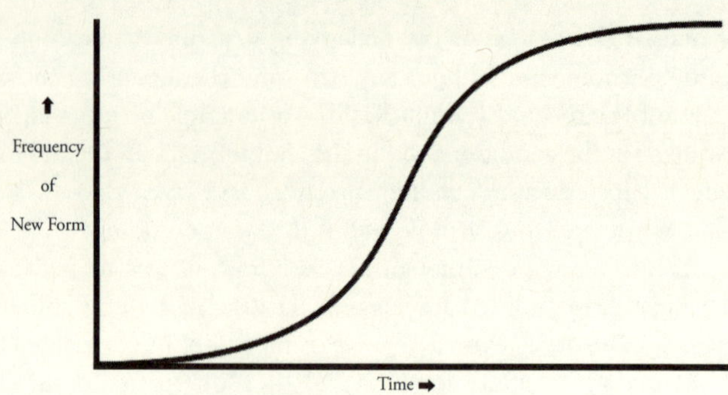

FIGURE 1: The S-Curve of Diffusion

that while we see great potential in using the S-curve model for BH diachrony, let us be crystal clear: one, two, or even ten S-curves (even using valid data sets) do not suffice to establish relative dating from a statistical perspective—dozens of rigorous and careful S-curve analyses must be performed before any results could approach statistical legitimacy. We hope that other researchers will be inspired by our initial studies below to carry out such work.

Change versus Style or Dialect

We do not doubt that some variation in the Hebrew Bible is on account of either dialectal differences or style rather than diachrony. The challenge is determining which is the likeliest answer. As a basic methodological principle to use in moving carefully forward, we follow the linguist David Crystal. In his discussion of stylistics, Crystal asserts that before "style" can be discussed, all historical and dialectal factors must be eliminated (1970:100–101; 1987:201, 205–6). We thus begin with a diachronic analysis, assuming that if the variation between two features aligns with the S-curve of diffusion, it is unlikely to be coincidental. We move beyond diachrony only if the tokens are too few for statistically valid analysis or if the pattern of variation does not fit the S-curve model of diffusion.

---

change or not. See Forbes 2014 for valuable criticism of the use of S-curves in language diachrony from a statistician's perspective. We thank Dean Forbes for giving us access to his insightful paper in prepublication form.

Statistical Analysis and Ancient Language Data

As a final methodological point, we submit that the cogency of any explanation is directly related to the size of the data set. First, to study a change and its chronological diffusion requires a clear variant pair—an "older" form and a "newer" form. Second, both features must be well attested in the identified corpus: one, two, or even a dozen examples of a given lexical or grammatical feature are not nearly enough from which to draw statistically valid conclusions about the nature of the variation being studied. Dozens, preferably hundreds, of "tokens" are required to approach a statistically valid analysis (on statistical analysis applied to BH, see Forbes 2012, 2014; Forbes and Andersen). This methodological principle casts a dark shadow over a great deal of the data previously used in historical Hebrew studies and guides our filtering of potential variant pairs from Esther.

Linguistic Change in Esther

Of the fifty-eight features that Bergey cited, all but fourteen must be excluded due to low attestation, resulting in an inability to draw statistically valid conclusions. (See appendix B for Bergey's list of features, modified to show which ones we consider salient.) On a more positive note, we can add four significant grammatical features to the list, which we will discuss below in "Salient Grammatical Features."

Salient Lexical Features

The most obvious features in Esther that signal language contact are lexical—the Persian and Aramaic loanwords. The Persian and Aramaic items borrowed into the language of Esther are important for establishing a general time period (i.e., when the linguistic contact situation was appropriate) and cultural influence, if not setting. It is easy for modern readers, who have access to lexica and commentaries, to undervalue the use of Persian borrowings and therefore miss the implications for reconstructing the compositional setting of the book of Esther. However we label the book in terms of genre and relation to history, the fact remains that the amount and type of Persian loanwords require that the intended audience had to have known some Persian as well as some basic information about Persian administrative and court practices.

In table 1 we list Persian loanwords in Esther, dividing them according to whether they reflect need- or prestige-based borrowing.

TABLE 1: Persian Loanwords in Esther

Persian (need-borrowed)	*Persian (prestige-borrowed)*
כַּרְפַּס, CN, "fine fabric; linen"; 1:6; not attested for Israel, HALOT s.v.; borrowing of the Persian *kirpās* < Sanskrit *karpāsa*. אֲחַשְׁדַּרְפְּן, CN, "satrap"; 3:12, 8:9, and 9:3, also once in Dan 8:36 and 9 times in Aramaic Daniel; borrowing of Persian *ḫšatra pāvan*, "protector of the land." אֲחַשְׁוֵרוֹשׁ, PN, "Ahashverosh"; 1:1. הֹדּוּ, PN, "India"; 1:1; borrowing of Old Persian and Avestan *Hindu*; Babylonian *Indū* suggests presence in Hebrew might have been a secondary borrowing through Babylonian. וַשְׁתִּי, PN, "Vashti"; 1:9. מְהוּמָן, PN, "Mehuman"; בִּזְּתָא, PN, "Biztha"; חַרְבוֹנָא, PN, "Harbona"; בִּגְתָא, PN, "Bigtha"; זֵתַר, PN, "Zethar"; 1:10. כַּרְשְׁנָא, PN, "Karshena"; שֵׁתָר, PN, "Shetar"; מֶרֶס, PN, "Meres"; מַרְסְנָא, PN, "Marsena"; מְמוּכָן, PN, "Memucan"; 1:.14. אֶסְתֵּר, PN, "Esther"; 2:7. פַּרְשַׁנְדָּתָא, PN, "Parshendatha"; פּוֹרָתָא, PN, "Poratha"; 9:7. אֲדַלְיָא, PN, "Adalya"; 9:8. פַּרְמַשְׁתָּא, PN, "Parmashta"; אֲרִיסַי, PN, "Arisay"; אֲרִדַי, PN, "Ariday"; וַיְזָתָא PN, "Vayzatha"; 9:9.	הַפַּרְתְּמִים, n.mp, "aristocrat" or "noble"; 1:3 and 6:9, also once in Dan 1:3; borrowing of Persian *fratama*. // HB שַׂר (see Esth 6:9, where פרתמים is in apposition to שׂרים). דָּת, n.ms, "order, decree" or "regulation, law"; 1:8+33x; borrowing of Persian *dāta*. דָּת is never found in the Hebrew DSS, and it is found only 5× in the Mishnah (Yoma 5:1; Sheqal 4:7; Ketub 7:6). // BH מִשְׁפָּט or תּוֹרָה (depending on nuance). פִּתְגָם, n.ms, "decision" or "announcement"; 1:20, also once in Qoh 8:11; borrowing of Persian *patigāma*. פִּתְגָם is used in fragmentary context in 4Q161 and 4Q420, and it is not found in the Mishnah or rabbinic texts. // BH מִצְוָה or דָּבָר (depending on nuance). פַּתְשֶׁגֶן, n.ms, "copy"; 3:14, 4:8, and 8:13, also in Ezra 4:11, 23; 5:6; 7:11 (as פַּרְשֶׁגֶן); borrowing of Persian *patšagn*. פַּתְשֶׁגֶן is possibly used once in the Hebrew DSS, in 4Q465 (פר]שגן האגר[ת), and never in the Mishnah. // BH מִשְׁנֶה or תַּבְנִית? אֲחַשְׁתְּרָן, adj.ms, "royal"; 8:10 and 8:14. // BH מַמְלָכוּת as the second, qualifying item in a bound phrase.

Though the Persian loanwords provide some information about the setting of the intended audience, neither they nor the Aramaic loanwords (e.g., זְמָן, יְקָר, כְּתָב) allow us to situate Esther more precisely in the rather broad chronological window in which Persian and Aramaic borrowing would likely have occurred—i.e., the entire second half of the first millennium B.C.E. The best solution that linguistic analysis can provide is to situate Esther relative to other books on the basis of the diffusion of the new form using data from well-attested loanwords that have "older" variants.

Beyond the demonstrable Persian and Aramaic loanwords, we identify a handful of additional lexical items in Esther as suggestive indicators of change: לָשׁוֹן ("language"), שִׁנָּה ("to change"), כָּנַס ("to gather"), זוּעַ ("to tremble"), שְׁאָר ("remainder"), קִבֵּל ("to receive"), and מַלְכוּת ("kingdom"). Bergey discusses each of these and we have fundamentally nothing to add. However, we will demonstrate how the variation should be analyzed for each pair.

Consider the distribution of the well-known variant pair מַמְלָכָה and מַלְכוּת. Dresher (2012) performed the most recent, and linguistically sophisticated analysis of this variation. He admitted only books, biblical and extra-biblical, that had at least three occurrences of one or the other of the words and concluded that the distribution of the words, and therefore the diffusion of the newer form, fits "quite well the conventional division of books into [early, middle, and late] periods" (31). In table 2 below, we present the occurrences of מַמְלָכָה and מַלְכוּת, with Dresher's periodization and some further modification (i.e., the division of Isaiah and raising the minimum to five occurrences, though even that is undesirably low). Note where Esther lies in table 2.

Since table 2 presents the diffusion of but one lexical item, the results are anything but secure, since each word has its own diffusion history. Combining this word with as many other salient variations would provide a much more accurate picture. Critically, with the study of each of the words that occur with enough frequency to give us a statistical toehold, Esther falls in the late period—toward the middle to end of the late period—in each case. Therefore, taking all the lexical evidence together situates Esther where the majority of biblical scholars date it using nonlinguistic means.

TABLE 2: The Diffusion of מַלְכוּת

Book	מַמְלָכָה	מַלְכוּת	*% new* (מַלְכוּת)	*Period*
Deut	7	0	0	
2 Sam	6	0	0	*Early*
Isa 1–39[6]	12	0	0	
1 Kgs	12	1	8	
1 Sam	6	1	14	*Middle*
Jer	17	3	15	
2 Chr	19	17	47	
Pss	6	6	50	
Qum	36	52	59	
1 Chr	3	11	79	*Late*
Ezra (Heb)	1	6	86	
Esth	0	26	100	
Dan (Heb)	0	16	100	
Mish	0	20	100	

Salient Grammatical Features

Grammatical variation is no less important than lexical variation, though the latter is simpler to identify and analyze. Because of this, though, grammatical variation has been underutilized (and sometimes misconstrued) in analyzing diachronic development in ancient Hebrew. We have determined that two semantic features and two syntactic features occur with sufficient frequency and with a sufficiently clear variant pair as to be good candidates for fuller analysis.

Both semantic changes involve the verbal system and its manifestation in Esther. These changes suggest that the position of Esther's language was well along in the multifaceted development of the Hebrew verbal system. The first change is an increase in the frequency of *qatal* instead of *wayyiqtol* in contexts in which *wayyiqtol* could have been used, such as following a fronted temporal clause (cf. Gen 22:4 and Esth 1:3). In fact, though the decreasing use of the *wayyiqtol* in Hellenistic period texts has

[6] Of 14 total occurrences, 12 occur in Isa 1–39 (9:6; 10:10; 13:4, 19; 14:16; 17:3; 19:2; 23:11, 17; 37:16, 20) and 2 in Isa 40–66 (47:5; 60:12).

long been noted, when we consider this from a change-and-diffusion perspective, given in table 3, the narrative text data are highly suggestive.

TABLE 3: wayyiqtol to qatal

Book	*All verbs*	*wayyiqtol (=old)*	*qatal (=new)*	*% new-to-old*
Jonah	200	84 (42%)	38 (19%)	31.1%
Judg	2552	1139 (44.6%)	552 (21.6%)	32.7%
Gen	5040	2105 (41.7%)	1105 (21.9%)	34.4%
2Sam	2728	1056 (38.7%)	618 (22.7%)	37.0%
2Kgs	3023	1216 (40.2%)	764 (25.3%)	38.6%
1Sam	3511	1318 (37.5%)	840 (23.9%)	39.0%
Ruth	414	138 (33.3%)	94 (22.7%)	40.5%
2Chr	2831	982 (34.7%)	735 (26%)	42.8%
1Kgs	3031	1041 (34.3%)	842 (27.8%)	44.7%
1Chr	1455	469 (32.2%)	429 (29.5%)	47.8%
Neh	973	264 (27.1%)	257 (26.4%)	49.3%
Esth	640	159 (24.8%)	165 (25.8%)	50.9%
Josh	1930	592 (30.7%)	618 (32.0%)	51.1%
Ezra (Heb)	363	86 (23.7%)	95 (26.2%)	52.5%
Qumran	21375	708 (3.3%)	5712 (26.7%)	89.0%
Mishnah	46202	32 (.007%)	14758 (32%)	99.8%

The second change is the replacement of *yiqtol* by the participle for generic expressions (gnomic and habitual statements) (see Cook 2013). We did an initial pass of the *yiqtol* and participle frequency in the Hebrew Bible and the results suggest that this may be another highly fruitful path for identifying a semantic change-and-diffusion that could be used to date texts relatively. Table 4 below presents the data, with books that attest 166 or more occurrences of both verb types (i.e., using Esther as our minimum).

TABLE 4: yiqtol to participle

Book	*All verbs*	*yiqtol (=old)*	*Ptcp (=new)*	*% new-to-old*
Job	2531	1242 (49.1%)	187 (7.4%)	13.1%
Lev	2501	895 (35.8%)	197 (7.9%)	18.0%
Hos	687	262 (38.1%)	60 (8.7%)	18.6%
Deut	3515	1023 (29.1%)	363 (10.3%)	26.2%
Exod	3714	820 (22.1%)	293 (7.9%)	26.3%
Num	3154	683 (21.7%)	254 (8%)	27.1%
Pss	5727	2089 (36.5%)	801 (14.0%)	27.7%
Mic	379	146 (38.5%)	59 (15.7%)	28.8%
Gen	5040	685 (13.6%)	321 (6.4%)	31.9%
Isa	4919	1541 (31.3%)	764 (15.5%)	33.1%
Eccl	698	222 (31.9%)	117 (16.8%)	34.5%
Ezek	4315	877 (20.3%)	467 (10.8%)	34.7%
2 Sam	2728	375 (13.7%)	217 (8.0%)	36.7%
Amos	523	134 (25.6%)	80 (15.3%)	37.4%
1 Sam	3511	462 (13.2%)	282 (8.0%)	37.9%
Prov	1900	820 (43.2%)	512 (26.9%)	38.4%
1 Kgs	3031	361 (11.9%)	230 (7.6%)	38.9%
Jer	5360	1139 (21.3%)	726 (13.5%)	38.9%
Judg	2552	261 (10.2%)	206 (8.1%)	44.1%
Zech	812	169 (20.8%)	137 (16.9%)	44.8%
Josh	1930	198 (10.3%)	163 (8.4%)	45.2%
2 Kgs	3023	295 (9.8%)	247 (8.2%)	45.6%
Dan (Heb)	1463	330 (22.6%)	329 (22.5%)	49.9%
Ezra (Heb)	549	79 (14.4%)	91 (16.6%)	53.5%
2 Chr	2831	239 (8.4%)	308 (10.9%)	56.3%
Esth	640	71 (11.1%)	95 (14.8%)	57.2%
1 Chr	1455	110 (7.6%)	168 (11.5%)	60.4%
Neh	973	115 (11.8%)	181 (18.6%)	61.1%
Qumran*	21375	8975 (42%)	4527 (21.2%)	33.5%
*4Q394-99	220	29 (13.2%)	72 (32.7%)	71.3%
Mishnah	46202	4429 (9.6%)	21203 (45.9%)	82.7%

Our two sets of verb data do require refinement to get completely accurate contrastive pairs. The next analytical step is to isolate the instances of realis *qatal* to contrast with *wayyiqtol* for table 3, and then to isolate generic *yiqtol* and generic participle for table 4. However, even with the squish we have allowed for this preliminary study, it is highly unlikely that, for example, the 31.9 percent "new" participle over *yiqtol* frequency in Genesis versus the 61.1 percent "new" participle over *yiqtol* frequency in Nehemiah is random. We are confident that refined analysis would confirm the conclusions we have drawn concerning these examples of change-and-diffusion.

The first syntactic feature concerns the syntax of object marking. Bergey, following many others (e.g, Kropat, 35–36; Polzin, 28–31), notes the variation between the use of the direct object marker אֵת with a clitic pronoun and the attachment of the clitic pronoun directly to a verb (1983:85–89). In table 5 we present the relevant data for the Bible, Ben Sira, Qumran, and the Mishnah.

TABLE 5: אֵת+pronoun(obj) to verb+pronoun(obj)

Book	אֵת *+ Pron (=old)*	*Verb + Pron (=new)*	*% new-to-old*
Lev	132	106	44.5%
Num	118	139	54.1%
Exod	140	210	60.0%
Josh	62	124	66.7%
Gen	127	319	71.5%
Judg	56	166	74.8%
2 Kgs	59	184	75.7%
1 Sam	43	238	84.7%
Deut	70	396	85.0%
1 Kgs	30	173	85.2%
2 Chr	30	187	86.2%
2 Sam	24	158	86.9%
Esth	1	17	94.4%
Neh	5	93	94.9%
Eccl	1	23	95.8%
1 Chr	3	78	96.3%
Ezra (Heb)	1	28	96.6%

TABLE 5 (cont.)

Book	*אֵת + Pron (=old)*	*Verb + Pron (=new)*	*% new-to-old*
Jonah	0	10	100%
Ruth	0	19	100%
Dan (Heb)	0	33	100%
Qumran	132	1272	90.6%
Ben Sira	10	197	95.2%
Mishnah	35	1763	98.1%

The list of biblical books covered in table 5 includes only narrative books, since the use of אֵת in biblical poetic books is a well-known issue that is a complicating variable for this study (see Andersen and Forbes). Additionally, we limited the verbs to finite verbs, since the clitic pronouns attached to participles and infinitives may represent non–direct object constituents. Finally, we limited the אֵת data to cases in which the אֵת+pronoun follows the verb, since pragmatic fronting of a pronominal object requires the use of אֵת+pronoun instead of the pronoun attached directly to the verb. The resulting frequency of usage supports previous scholarship on the decreasing frequency of אֵת+object pronoun. The cause of this change is not yet clear, nor is the mechanism (though reanalysis seems likely, given the development of אֵת+pronoun into a proleptic demonstrative in early rabbinic Hebrew; Pérez Fernández, 23). What is very clear, though, is Esther's position toward the end of this diffusion pattern.

A second potential syntactic change relevant to Esther is the general shift from verb-subject to subject-verb basic word order in BH (see Holmstedt 2013d). The cause and mechanism for word order changes are often difficult to untangle, and this is the case for the proposed VS-to-SV shift in BH. It is conceivable that the shift to SV was due to language contact; however, since this shift occurred over hundreds of years, it is more likely that it reflects a long-term reanalysis. In particular, it is plausible and supported cross-linguistically that the Topic- and Focus-fronted subjects in the earlier basic VS language were reanalyzed by successive generations of child learners as non-Topic and non-Focus constituents, resulting in an acquired basic SV pattern. As each generation reanalyzed the role of the subject in SV clauses, Hebrew moved through a series of word order profiles: strong VS → weak VS → weak SV → strong SV.

Although the study of this word order shift in ancient Hebrew is not yet complete—to be complete it must ultimately include all Hebrew syntactic data up to and including the Mishnah—the preliminary data collection from selections of the Hebrew Bible, which we present in table 6, is suggestive.

TABLE 6: "Basic" SV vs. VS

Book	*Verb-Subject (=old)*	*Subject-Verb (=new)*	*% new-to-old*
Amos	8	5	38.5%
Hab	11	8	42%
Joel	11	11	50%
Hag	2	2	50%
Dan (Heb)	21	23	52%
1 Sam	68	101	56%
Nah	9	13	59%
Gen	26	47	64%
Eccl	6	19	76%
Ruth	3	10	77%
Jonah	2	7	78%
Obad	1	4	80%
Mal	1	4	80%
Zeph	1	6	86%
Esth	5	30	86%
Ezra (Heb)	1	7	88%
Neh	1	16	94%

From the data and simple statistical analysis in table 6 we may draw two conclusions: first, there is a noticeable increase in the preference for SV order in these texts; and, second, Esther patterns towards the end of the diffusion within the biblical corpus.

Conclusion: Finding Esther

In conclusion, we concur with Elias Bickerman that Esther appears to be a strange book, though our reasons are different than Bickerman's. On first, and second, and even third glances, the language of the book presents a confusing profile: does it represent an earlier "standard" dialect, like Genesis, a slightly later dialect, like Nehemiah, or a much later dialect, like the Mishnah?

In our study, we found that Esther shares a number of features with the dialects of both earlier and later biblical texts. The former is not surprising, since strong linguistic continuity is a prerequisite for identifying a later stage of a language as the same essential language as earlier forms. What precisely, then, do the "later" features tell us about the book? For instance, the Persian words tell us that the book was not composed before the Persian period, but these data do not exclude a Hellenistic period origin. Moreover, the use of Persian words appears to reflect the author's intended audience and the creation of a realistic Persian court setting. Beyond the specific lexical items, though, there do not appear to be any further contact-induced changes, such as evidence of influence on the grammatical structure, or idioms that reflect a Persian linguistic origin. So, the book is firmly Hebrew but with a Persian "bouquet."

Similarly, with regard to Aramaic, we see clear loanwords and so evidence of contact-induced change. But given the history of the Levant and the Aramean kingdoms to the north of Israel in addition to the status of Aramaic in the neo-Babylonian and Persian empires, we expect to see some Aramaic loanwords. However, the number of Aramaic loanwords suggests a situation of highly intense language contact, which obliquely confirms the book's origin in a diaspora setting.

The grammatical evidence for change, while much less than Bergey (1983) proposed, still points to a relative position of Esther as one of the later texts in the biblical corpus. The book is often situated near Nehemiah and the nonbiblical books, Ben Sira, sometimes Qumran, and even the Mishnah. At the same time, the word order features suggest that the grammar of Esther was not quite as developed as early rabbinic Hebrew and patterns not too much differently than a number of postexilic biblical books. All in all, Esther simply stands in the natural linguistic sequence of Hebrew as it continued to change in the Second Temple period.

Ours is not a provocative conclusion, but when theoretically grounded and methodologically rigorous analysis refines, but does not invalidate, the conclusions of past scholarship, we increase our confidence that Hebrew studies has not totally been misguided, as some recent challenges have suggested.

PART I
Esther Becomes Queen of Persia (1:1–2:23)

Chapters 1–2 of Esther set the stage for the page-turning action of chapters 3–9, concluding in the post-action wrap up in 9:20–10:3 (see Fox 2001:155 for discussion of the time element of the three stages of the story). This prologue is neatly divided into two sections: chapter 1 (consisting of two episodes) describes Vashti's downfall and chapter 2 (consisting of three episodes) describes Esther's rise (with the third episode, in 2:21-23, an aside critical for chap. 6). A chiastic structure reinforces the unity of this two-chapter section:

1:1-9//2:18—In chapter 1, the king throws banquets for subjects from his entire empire, establishing the scale of the arena in which Esther and Mordecai will operate. Correspondingly, in chapter 2, after making Esther the new queen, the king celebrates by throwing a great banquet. The chiastic correspondences between the two chapters are not simply thematic; note the very similar language used in 1:3 and 2:18:

Esther 1:3 עָשָׂה מִשְׁתֶּה לְכָל־שָׂרָיו וַעֲבָדָיו
Esther 2:18 וַיַּעַשׂ הַמֶּלֶךְ מִשְׁתֶּה גָדוֹל לְכָל־שָׂרָיו וַעֲבָדָיו

1:10-12//2:16-17—In chapter 1, Vashti refuses to come before the king, infuriating him. In contrast, Esther pleases the king more than all the other eligible women in chapter 2.

1:13-14//2:12—In chapter 1, the action is suspended by a lengthy parenthesis explaining the king's practice of consulting his cabinet. Correspondingly, in chapter 2 the action is broken up when a lengthy parenthesis explains the beautification process of the eligible women. Both parentheses are introduced by the explanatory כִּי כֵּן.

1:15-22//2:1-4—At the end of chapter 1, the king requests advice on what to do about Vashti's disobedience; Memukan gives his advice, the king deems it good, and so acts in accordance. At the beginning of chapter 2, the king remembers the issue of finding a new queen, and is advised on how to proceed; after hearing his servants' advice, the king deems it good, and so acts in accordance. Note the verbal parallels:

Esther 1:21	וַיִּיטַב הַדָּבָר בְּעֵינֵי הַמֶּלֶךְ וְהַשָּׂרִים וַיַּעַשׂ הַמֶּלֶךְ כִּדְבַר מְמוּכָן
Esther 2:4	וַיִּיטַב הַדָּבָר בְּעֵינֵי הַמֶּלֶךְ וַיַּעַשׂ כֵּן

This sort of mirroring is utilized in several passages in chapters 3–9 as an intentional structuring device used to contrast characters (cf. Fox 2001:162). The point of the chiastic structure in chapters 1–2 is not to emphasize any one point of the mini-story, but to set Esther up as the heroine and so the antitype to Vashti.

Episode 1—Vashti's Downfall (1:1-22)

§1: The King's Banquet (1:1-9)

[1]And so it was, in the days of Ahashverosh—he was the Ahashverosh who ruled, from India to Cush, 127 provinces—[2]in those days, as King Ahashverosh sat on his royal throne, which was in Susa, the citadel, [3]in the third year of his reigning, he prepared a banquet for all his rulers and his servants. The army of Persia and Media, the nobles, and the rulers of the provinces were before him, [4]when he showed (them) the riches of the glory of his kingdom and the worth of the beauty of his greatness, (for) many days, 180 days. [5]When these days were completed, the king prepared a banquet for all the people who were found in Susa, the citadel, for both great and small, over seven days, in the courtyard of the king's pavilion garden. [6]White linen and violet (linen) were fastened with ropes of fine linen and purple upon rings of silver and columns of alabaster. Beds of gold and silver were upon floorings of porphyry and alabaster, pearl, and precious stone. [7]Drink-serving was in vessels of gold, that is, vessels differing from each other. And royal wine was abundant, according to the hand of the king. [8]The drinking was according to the regulation "No Constraint!" because thus the king established upon every chief of his palace: to act according to the desire of each man. [9]Moreover Vashti, the queen, prepared a banquet for women, in the royal palace, which belonged to King Ahashverosh.

1:1 וַיְהִי בִּימֵי אֲחַשְׁוֵרוֹשׁ הוּא אֲחַשְׁוֵרוֹשׁ הַמֹּלֵךְ מֵהֹדּוּ
וְעַד־כּוּשׁ שֶׁבַע וְעֶשְׂרִים וּמֵאָה מְדִינָה׃

Verses 1-2 establish the basic setting of the book of Esther, telling us when and where the story takes place: during the reign of Ahashverosh, in one of the royal cities of his kingdom, Susa.

וַיְהִי. *Wayyiqtol* 3ms Qal √היה. The 3ms ויהי and והיה exhibit two functions in biblical Hebrew: in certain cases they fill the expected clause-level role of a copular verb, linking a subject and a copular complement (in traditional terms, the predicate nominative) both by indicating an equative/identifying or predicative/classifying relationship and by providing a landing site for Tense-Aspect-Mood (TAM) marking (Cook 2012:309). However, in many cases in BH narrative, ויהי and והיה function as a "discourse-level TAM signal, often at the opening or closing of a scene or episode" (310). The ויהי here is just such a discourse marker, opening the book by establishing this story to be, at the outset, about something in the past. See also 2:8; 3:4; 5:1, 2. Note the absence of *dagesh* in the י of *wayyiqtol* וַיְהִי. The omission of the *dagesh* often affects the consonants ק, נ, מ, ל, י, ו, and the sibilants when they occur with a *sheva* (see JM 18m; GKC 20m).

בִּימֵי אֲחַשְׁוֵרוֹשׁ. Although it is tempting to take this PP with the preceding ויהי "and so it was in the days of Ahashverosh," discourse ויהי does not take any modifiers but stands alone in its own clause. This ב-PP is thus the first in a series of temporal adjuncts preceding the main verb, which is עשה in v. 3.

הוּא אֲחַשְׁוֵרוֹשׁ הַמֹּלֵךְ מֵהֹדּוּ וְעַד־כּוּשׁ. Null copula clause with subject הוא and NP complement. This clause is a parenthesis. Parenthetical clauses interrupt the flow of the narrative to fill in information that is helpful or necessary for understanding the sequence of events or the identities of the characters. Here the parenthesis further specifies who this Ahashverosh is—the king "who was ruling from Hodu to Cush." Parentheses are identifiable by (1) the departure from the syntax and verbal sequences used in the surrounding clauses and (2) maintaining a referential connection to some constituent in the preceding clause. In this case, the proper name אחשורוש provides the link to the preceding clause while the shift from the narrative TAM established by the discourse ויהי to a null copula clause signals the syntactic and narrative break. Parentheses occur often in Esther (e.g., 1:8, 1:14, 1:20, 3:7,

8:12, and 9:24). אחשורוש is the Hebrew version of Persian *ḫšayāršā* (rendered Ξερξης in Greek, and thus "Xerxes" in English; HALOT s.v.; BDB s.v.; cf. Gehman, 322; Stiehl, 10–12; Moore 1971:3–4; Bush, 345).

הַמֹּלֵךְ. The initial ה introduces the following as a relative clause (Holmstedt 2010:28–30; 2013a:352; cf. WO 19.7). Relative clauses are either restrictive and so identify or define the head of the relative clause from among a group of possible referents (e.g. "the man that you saw yesterday," identifies a particular man among a group of men—i.e., that you know but that you did not see yesterday), or nonrestrictive and so add discourse salient but nonidentifying information (see Holmstedt 2008:65, esp. n. 16). The relative clause המלך מהדו ועד כוש is restrictive, identifying Ahashverosh to an audience who apparently no longer knew who he was (which is why we have included "the" in our translation).

מֹלֵךְ. Participle ms Qal √מלך. Elsewhere in the Hebrew Bible, מלך is either monovalent ("to be king") or bivalent with an על-PP complement ("to rule over X"). The usage here, with the number phrase שבע ועשׂרים ומאה מדינה as its complement, is unique to the language of Esther. The BH participle has long been understood as an intermediate form between verbs and nouns, since sometimes it appears verbal, e.g., it takes complements, while other times it appears nominal, e.g., it takes possessive pronouns (GKC 116; see WO 37; JM 121). It is best understood as an adjective that encodes an activity or event rather than a quality (Cook 2008). Participles are thus complements of a copular verb, which is mostly null but is occasionally manifested as the lexical copula היה. The core semantics of the BH participle is progressive aspect, which can be extended for durative, habitual, and gnomic statements. Thus, here מלך could be a (past) progressive ("who was ruling"), durative/habitual ("who ruled") or gnomic (also "who ruled"; cf. "Verbal Semantics" in the Introduction). The first option fits the context the best: Ahashverosh was not in the habit of ruling, nor was it an enduring truth that he ruled; rather, at the time specified at the outset of the story, he was in the middle of his activity as ruler of the Persian Empire.

מֵהֹ֥דּוּ וְעַד־כּ֔וּשׁ. The collocation of מן ... ועד is a strategy for specifying extent, such as the two poles of a cline, e.g., "youngest to oldest" (3:13) or "smallest to largest" (Gen 19:11; 1 Sam 5:9; 30:2; 2 Kgs 25:26; Jer 8:10; 42:1; 44:12; 2 Chr 24:30). Here the phrase specifies the furthest points of the Persian Empire on an East-to-West line (see also 8:9). The PN הדו ("India") is derived from Old Persian and Avestan Hindu.

But note Babylonian *Indū* and Arabic *Al-Hind*: these Semitic cognates suggest that if the word had entered Hebrew by way of, say, Babylonian, the form would have been **hiddū* הִדּוּ (the asterisk [*] indicates a reconstructed, and thus formally unattested, word). The existing form, which may have entered Hebrew directly from Persian during the exilic period, appears to reflect the assimilation of the first vowel to the second ("vowel harmony"), with subsequent stress-induced lowering of the /u/ to /o/: **hindū* > **hundū* > **huddū* > *hóddū*. The word כוש could refer to a variety of locations, but probably refers to "the lands of the Nile in southern Egypt, meaning Nubia and northern Sudan" (HALOT s.v.; cf. BDB s.v.; Moore 1971:4).

שֶׁ֛בַע וְעֶשְׂרִ֥ים וּמֵאָ֖ה מְדִינָֽה. Note the form of the clitic conjunction ו—when attached to words beginning with ב, מ, or פ or with a *sheva*, the normal וְ becomes וּ (GKC 104e; JM 104c). There are several good examples of Hebrew numeral syntax in chapter 1. Here, מאה is not bound, which indicates that the syntactic relationship between the numeral and the quantified noun מדינה is appositional. Compare v. 4, where מאה is bound (מאת יום). For a full discussion of numeral syntax, see "Numeral Syntax in Esther" in the Introduction. Note that מדינה does exist in the plural (see 1:3), but that often with the higher cardinal numerals, the quantified noun is presented as a collective singular (WO 15.2.5a).

1:2 בַּיָּמִ֖ים הָהֵ֑ם כְּשֶׁ֣בֶת ׀ הַמֶּ֣לֶךְ אֲחַשְׁוֵר֗וֹשׁ עַ֚ל כִּסֵּ֣א מַלְכוּת֔וֹ אֲשֶׁ֖ר בְּשׁוּשַׁ֥ן הַבִּירָֽה׃

Verse 2 establishes, with v. 1, that the events occur during the reign of Ahashverosh, and moreover that the story takes place "in Susa."

בַּיָּמִ֖ים הָהֵ֑ם. This PP is appositive to בִּימֵ֖י אֲחַשְׁוֵר֑וֹשׁ in v. 1; the appositive does not so much clarify the initial PP but rather picks it up again after a large interruptive element. The *qameṣ* (BH [a:] > Masoretic [ɔ]) in the article of ההם reflects the lengthening (or in Masoretic phonology, backing) of the *pataḥ*, the base vowel of the article. This is motivated by the resistance of the so-called guttural consonants (א, ה, ח, ע) and ר to lengthening in cases where the cliticization of a proclitic (e.g., מִן when attached to the following word) results in the assimilation of a consonant at the syllable juncture (e.g., *min* + *melek* > *mimmelek*, but *min* + *ʿim* > *mēʿim*, not **miʿʿim*). Though the second consonant of the article remains a mystery, its attachment normally results in the lengthening of the initial consonant of the host word (e.g., *haʔ+melek* > *hammelek*). In words beginning with the consonants listed above, though, the attachment of the article changes not the initial consonant but the length (or quality, in the Masoretic phonology) of the vowel of the article (see also GKC 35c; JM 35d).

כְּשֶׁ֣בֶת ... עַ֚ל. Inf constr Qal √ישׁב. The bivalent verb ישׁב takes a locative PP complement in Esther (1:2; 2:19, 21; 5:1, 13; 6:10; 9:19; and arguably 3:15), as it typically does elsewhere in BH. The complement indicates where the person sat, either with ב (e.g., "in the gate") or על, as here.

הַמֶּ֣לֶךְ אֲחַשְׁוֵר֗וֹשׁ. It is possible that the proper name אחשורוש is in apposition to המלך, "the king, Ahashverosh." Like relative clauses, appositives can be restrictive (the appositive defines the head noun) or nonrestrictive (the appositive adds nondefinitional information that the author/speaker deems otherwise important for the discourse). In nonrestrictive apposition, the relationship between the head and appositive can represent equivalence ("X, that is/namely Y"), attribution ("X, being Y") or inclusion ("X, for example/especially Y"). In the case of המלך אחשורוש, because the identity of המלך within the story is clearly established as אחשורוש in v. 1, the appositive אחשורוש would be nonrestrictive and so represent an equivalence relationship: "the king, namely Ahashverosh." However, it is also possible, and perhaps more likely, that the phrase "the king PN" is a titling convention, much like "President Lincoln" or "Emperor Constantine" (more accurately called "pseudotitles" in Meyer 1992:47–48; contra WO 12.3e). For more on this, see the comment on ושתי המלכה in v. 9.

כִּסֵּ֣א מַלְכוּת֔וֹ אֲשֶׁ֖ר בְּשׁוּשַׁ֥ן הַבִּירָֽה. Within the אשר the null copula clause has a null subject and the ב-PP בשושן הבירה as the copular complement (on null subjects, see Holmstedt 2013c). Note the NP מלכות, which is one of two primary words for "kingdom" used in the Hebrew Bible. מלכות, used here and throughout Esther (26×), appears to be a term used in later books (Esther, Chronicles, Daniel, Ezra-Nehemiah; BDB s.v.; HALOT s.v.). The semantics of the bound relationship in כסא מלכותו is such that מלכות indicates the type or category that defines the כסא (the "genitive of species" in WO 9.5.3g). The other term, מַמְלָכָה, is used in earlier works (BDB s.v.; HALOT s.v.; Moore 1971:5; see also Dresher 2012; see "Salient Lexical Features" in the Introduction and Appendix B). Although the clitic host and embedded NP מלכות immediately precede the אשר relative clause, interpretative sense suggests that the slightly farther phrasal head כסא is the relative head: "the throne ... that was in Susa." The PN שׁושן is modified appositionally by הבירה, a nonrestrictive appositive of attribution (i.e., Susa is the citadel). The word בירה is a loanword from Akkadian (*birtu*) via Aramaic meaning "fortified town, citadel" (HALOT s.v.; cf. BDB s.v.; DCH s.v.; Paton, 134). Translating בירה as "the capital" (e.g., NRSV) without qualification is a bit misleading—while Darius I did build a royal residence there, his central project was making Persepolis into his primary royal city, a status it retained two hundred years after Darius (Brosius, 20). Moreover, it is inappropriate to apply the concept of a "capital" city, that is, a single city in which administration and the head of state are located, to the Achaemenids; the "capital" was wherever the king resided at any given time and the court often moved from one major city to another (P.-A. Beaulieu, private correspondence).

1:3 בִּשְׁנַ֤ת שָׁלוֹשׁ֙ לְמָלְכ֔וֹ עָשָׂ֣ה מִשְׁתֶּ֔ה לְכָל־שָׂרָ֖יו
וַעֲבָדָ֑יו חֵ֣יל ׀ פָּרַ֣ס וּמָדַ֗י הַֽפַּרְתְּמִ֛ים וְשָׂרֵ֥י
הַמְּדִינ֖וֹת לְפָנָֽיו׃

After briefly establishing even more specifically the timeframe of the story (the third year of Ahashverosh's reign), v. 3 moves to the actual story: Ahashverosh throws a party for some select individuals while his great army is paraded before him.

בִּשְׁנַ֤ת שָׁלוֹשׁ֙ לְמָלְכ֔וֹ. Inf constr Qal √מלך with 3ms clitic pronoun indicating the syntactic subject. The numeral syntax in this PP (שׁנת שׁלושׁ "third year") is not appositional as in v. 1; instead, the noun שׁנת is bound to the numeral, lit., "year of three" (see "Numeral Syntax in Esther" in the Introduction). The use of a ל-PP is typical for dating formulas ("in the third year *[belonging] to* his reigning"; cf. also 3:7 and 9:15). Note that the ל-PP in these formulas is not an adjunct to a verb, but to the nominal item it follows; these are known as "NP-internal" PPs. Here the nuance the ל-PP communicates is possession. The complement to the ל-PP in such dating formulas is usually a noun (Gen 7:11; 1–2 Kgs throughout [e.g., 15:9], Jeremiah throughout [e.g., 25:1], Hag 1:1; Zech 7:1; Dan 1:1; Ezra 6:3; Samaria Ostraca 1.1-2, 2.1-2; etc.), not an infinitive as here (though infinitives are not altogether unattested in other texts; e.g., 1 Kgs 6:1; 2 Kgs 24:12; Jer 1:2; cf. comment on 2:16).

עָשָׂה מִשְׁתֶּה. *Qatal* 3ms Qal √עשה. The fourth word of v. 3, the verb עָשָׂה provides the first main clause verb with lexical content in the book (the only preceding main clause verb is the discourse ויהי). Hebrew (similar to English) allows an indefinite number of temporal phrase Topics to be fronted before the main verb (see Gen 7:11, where three temporal PPs, all of which are then modified by an appositive PP, precede the main verb). Even so, the complexity of vv. 1-3 here, with four temporal PP adjuncts and a parenthesis preceding the main verb, exceeds even that of Gen 1:1 (see Holmstedt 2014a). The range of meaning for the verb עשה is large, extending well beyond the meanings of English "to do." Possible meanings, depending on the immediate context and the arguments used with the verb, include "to do," "to make," "to create," "to manufacture," "to treat," "to act/behave," "to produce," and "to observe, carry out" (HALOT s.v.; DCH s.v.; BDB s.v.). With the complement משתה, we should understand something like English "to prepare X" (HALOT s.v.; DCH s.v.; BDB s.v.). משתה is a *maqtal* noun built off the root שתה "to drink" (**maštay > mištê*); although its root suggests that its meaning originated in a specifically drink-oriented setting, the biblical noun refers to more than drinking, including eating, socializing, and merry-making, i.e., a banquet.

לְכָל־שָׂרָיו וַעֲבָדָיו חֵיל | פָּרַס וּמָדַי הַפַּרְתְּמִים וְשָׂרֵי הַמְּדִינוֹת לְפָנָיו. Note the form of the clitic conjunction ו—when attached to words beginning with a *ḥatef sheva* (normally a א, ה, ח, and ע), the normal וְ takes the full vowel corresponding to the *ḥatef*, thus here וַ (GKC 104e; JM 104c). Beginning at חיל, there is a null copula clause with compound NP subject (חיל ... המדינות) and PP complement (לפניו). The larger segment of text (לכל ... לפניו) is typically understood as one PP specifying the people for whom Ahashverosh prepared a banquet: "for all his rulers and his servants, the *ḥayil* of Persia and Media, the aristocrats and rulers of the provinces before him." Such an understanding demands that we take חַיִל (the free form of the bound חֵיל), as referring to the "chiefs of the army" (so RSV; cf. Levenson, 42), or to "nobility, aristocracy, upper classes" (Bush, 347). However, taking חיל in either of these ways is somewhat doubtful: "chiefs of the army" is unattested, and there is only one possible example of "nobility" (Neh 3:4; HALOT s.v.; Bush, 347). Although various attempts to emend the text have been made (see Moore 1971:6 and BHS), these are doubtful (Fox 2001:274;

Bush, 347). Instead, we suggest that a new clause begins with חיל (so Keil, 322; NRSV): "The army of Persia and Media, the nobles, and the rulers of the provinces (were) before him." Note that our analysis does not follow the Masoretic verse division, since this null copula clause begins in the middle of v. 3 and continues into v. 4 (where it is modified by a temporal infinitive).

הַֽפַּרְתְּמִ֛ים. This is a Persian loanword meaning "aristocrat" or "noble" (HALOT s.v.; DCH s.v.; BDB s.v.); it appears twice in Esther (here and 6:9) and once in Daniel (1:3). On the use of Persian loanwords, see "Salient Lexical Features" in the Introduction.

1:4 בְּהַרְאֹת֗וֹ אֶת־עֹ֨שֶׁר֙ כְּב֣וֹד מַלְכוּת֔וֹ וְאֶ֨ת־יְקָ֔ר
תִּפְאֶ֖רֶת גְּדוּלָּת֑וֹ יָמִ֣ים רַבִּ֔ים שְׁמוֹנִ֥ים וּמְאַ֖ת יֽוֹם׃

Verse 4 hints at the extravagance of the first banquet, by which Ahashverosh showed off his wealth and power. The details of such extravagance are described in greater detail for the second banquet, in vv. 6-8.

בְּהַרְאֹת֗וֹ אֶת־עֹ֨שֶׁר֙ כְּב֣וֹד מַלְכוּת֔וֹ. Inf constr Hiph √ראה. The Qal ראה is bivalent ("X sees Y"), whereas the Hiphil, as a causative, increases the valency ("X causes Y to see Z"). Besides a subject, which is the agent of the action—the one doing the showing (here the 3ms clitic pronoun ו referring to Ahashverosh), the trivalent Hiphil of ראה normally takes two complements: a recipient (the one being shown) and a patient (the thing being shown). However the occurrence here has only one overt complement: patient (the thing shown), expressed by the compound NP את־עשר כבוד מלכותו ואת־יקר תפארת גדולתו "riches ... and preciousness ..." As a result, some interpreters understand the verb to be bivalent "X displays Y" (NRSV; Moore 1971:1; Fox 2001:14; Bush, 339; Levenson, 42): "while he displayed the great wealth of his kingdom"; alternatively (but for similar reasons), BHS suggests the reading בְּהַרְאֹתָם instead of בְּהַרְאֹתוֹ. But since ראה is trivalent elsewhere (see, e.g., 1:11), and since the recipient is clear from context (the people listed at the end of v. 3 are those to whom the wealth is being shown), it is simpler and more consistent to understand the clause to include a null complement for the recipient: "while he showed [them] the riches of his glory." Hebrew often allows easily identifiable constituents to be unexpressed; and yet, such constituents, known as null or covert constituents, are syntactically real and should be represented overtly in a language like

English, which does not allow for the same null patterns (Holmstedt 2013c; cf. Creason).

וְאֶת־יְקָר תִּפְאֶרֶת גְּדוּלָּתוֹ. This sequence of words is a complex chain of bound nouns, lit., "the preciousness of the beauty of his greatness." Though the bound forms of יקר and תפארת are homophonous with their respective free forms, the lack of an article on either one along with the definiteness encoded by the 3ms clitic pronoun on the last NP, גדולתו, indicate that this complex bound phrase analysis is correct. Interestingly, the disjunctive accents over יקר and תפארת (*zaqef-qaṭon* and *ṭifḥa*, respectively) may indicate that the Masoretes heard and so signaled a pause on each of the three words, perhaps to highlight the extraordinary show of wealth and power. יְקָר is not the adjective יָקָר "rare," "precious," or "noble" (HALOT s.v.; DCH s.v.; BDB s.v.), but the noun יְקָר "preciousness," "price," or "honor," used in Esther (10 of 17 occurrences in the Hebrew Bible; DCH s.v.; HALOT s.v.; BDB s.v.). The form of this noun, with the *qameṣ* in the final, closed and unstressed syllable, does not reflect the paradigmatic form of bound nouns in BH, but rather that of Aramaic, in which the *qameṣ* reflects a long vowel, /ā/, which does not reduce like the BH lengthened /a/ the *qameṣ* typically represents (JM 88Ef, 96Dd). On the use of Aramaic words in Esther, see "Salient Lexical Features" in the Introduction; cf. Bergey, 93.

יָמִים רַבִּים. This NP is a temporal adjunct to the verb בהראותו and indicates the duration of the activity. The use of an NP as a verbal adjunct without a preposition introducing the phrase is sometimes referred to as the "adverbial accusative" (WO 10.2.2).

שְׁמוֹנִים וּמְאַת יוֹם. This number phrase is in apposition to the preceding NP ימים רבים. Similar to שנת שלוש in v. 3, the compound numeral שמונים ומאת and the quantified noun יום are in a bound relationship. However, with שנת שלוש the quantified noun is bound to the numeral, whereas here the numeral is bound to the quantified noun (cf. JM 142g; see "Numeral Syntax in Esther" in the Introduction). On the collective singular use of יום, see comment on מדינה in v. 1.

1:5 וּבִמְלוֹאת ׀ הַיָּמִים הָאֵלֶּה עָשָׂה הַמֶּלֶךְ לְכָל־
הָעָם הַנִּמְצְאִים בְּשׁוּשַׁן הַבִּירָה לְמִגָּדוֹל וְעַד־קָטָן
מִשְׁתֶּה שִׁבְעַת יָמִים בַּחֲצַר גִּנַּת בִּיתַן הַמֶּלֶךְ׃

After the completion of the first banquet, the king throws another banquet, not equal to the first in length (seven days compared to 180), but surpassing the first in the size of its guest list (everyone in Susa). The sheer size and length of these two banquets establishes the monumental stage on which the ensuing drama will unfold.

וּבִמְלוֹאת | הַיָּמִים הָאֵלֶּה. Inf constr Qal √מלא. The verb מלא can be monovalent (stative, "to be full, fulfilled, accomplished, completed") or bivalent ("to fill," taking a complement of the thing filled) (HALOT s.v.; BDB s.v.; DCH s.v.); it may even be trivalent in rare occasions (1 Kgs 18:34; Isa 14:21), where an NP designates the material with which something is filled (see 7:5). Here מלא is monovalent, with the NP הימים האלה "these days" the subject. Note the form of the ו conjunction; see comment on v. 1.

עָשָׂה הַמֶּלֶךְ לְכָל־הָעָם ... מִשְׁתֶּה. *Qatal* 3ms Qal √עשׂה. As in v. 3, Qal עשׂה takes an NP complement (משתה) and here also has a PP adjunct (... לכל־העם). The verb עשה with the preposition ל can be trivalent, but in that case the meaning of the verb is "make something *into* (ל) something else" (e.g., "make him king"); since that meaning is not possible here (the banquet is not made or transformed into people), the verb is bivalent and the ל-PP an adjunct. The long adjunct PP before the short complement is unexpected, since longer constituents are typically moved toward the end of the sentence. Hebrew follows the cross-linguistically common pattern referred to as "heavy noun phrase shift" (HNPS), that is, all other things being equal, phrases with fewer items ("light" constituents) will precede those with more items ("heavy" constituents). A departure from the pattern typically signals some sort of discourse-pragmatic marking on the one or both of the constituents in question. Here it is possible that the expansive guest list is being highlighted and so this very heavy PP is placed in front of the very light NP complement משתה. With regard to the position of the verb and subject, the initial temporal phrase (... במלואת) triggers inversion from basic subject-verb order to verb-subject (see "Word Order" in the Introduction).

הַנִּמְצְאִים בְּשׁוּשַׁן הַבִּירָה. Participle mp Niph √מצא. The participle stands within a ה relative clause that modifies עם "the people who were found." Within the relative, the PP בשושן is an adjunct to the passive נמצאים. The NP בירה is appositional to שושן, as in v. 2.

לְמִגָּדוֹל וְעַד־קָטָן. The ל preposition takes as its complement the compound PP, מגדול ועד קטן "from great unto small" (on מן ... ועד, see comment on v. 1). This complex PP is either appositional to the PP לכל־העם, "for all the people ..., (that is,) for great to small," or it modifies the NP כל העם and the ל has the general nuance of relationship, "with regard to" (see MNK 39.11), thus, "for all the people ..., with regard to great unto small." We consider the former (appositional) analysis to be more likely and have translated accordingly.

שִׁבְעַ֥ת יָמִֽים. Here the numeral is bound to the noun (see "Numeral Syntax in Esther" in the Introduction). The number phrase as a whole is a verbal adjunct (see v. 4 on NPs as adjuncts without an introductory preposition).

בַּחֲצַ֕ר גִּנַּ֥ת בִּיתַ֖ן הַמֶּֽלֶךְ. Hebrew ביתן is derived (by borrowing) from Akkadian *bītānu* and refers to the inner parts of a palace or temple (HALOT s.v.). Within the Hebrew Bible it is used only in Esther (see also 7:7, 8). Although it is often translated simply as "palace" (and so גנת ביתן as "the garden of the palace"), the noun ביתן does not refer to the palace as a whole or in general; rather it refers to an interior pavilion within the palace (Subtelny, 18–19 n. 61, and 20 n. 68).

1:6 ח֣וּר ׀ כַּרְפַּ֣ס וּתְכֵ֗לֶת אָחוּז֙ בְּחַבְלֵי־ב֣וּץ וְאַרְגָּמָ֔ן
עַל־גְּלִ֥ילֵי כֶ֖סֶף וְעַמּ֣וּדֵי שֵׁ֑שׁ מִטּ֣וֹת ׀ זָהָ֣ב וָכֶ֗סֶף עַ֛ל
רִֽצְפַ֥ת בַּהַט־וָשֵׁ֖שׁ וְדַ֥ר וְסֹחָֽרֶת׃

In v. 6, the furnishings of the courtyard are described, heightening the sense of extravagance (Keil, 325; Moore 1971:7). It is possible that this verse and its two null copula clauses (and also v. 7) are intended as an exclamation in amazement about the richness of the furnishings, "And, oh, the white and violet …!" (Bush, 339, 347; also, e.g., Moore 1971:7; Fox 2001:274). But without an obvious grammatical indicator, such as an initial presentative הִנֵּה, an exclamative force for the verse is speculative and the more natural reading is simply descriptive. The lack of finite verbs in this verse creates some interpretive confusion: Bush suggests that the verse contains two "incomplete sentences" (347), while Fox calls the verse a "long string of nouns ... used as a way of predicating existence" (2001:274; also pp. 16–17) and Moore says that the verse is "syntactically unrelated to the preceding material" (1971:7; cf. Paton, 138). The simplest analysis is to read the verse as two null copula clauses.

חֻ֣ור ׀ כַּרְפַּ֣ס וּתְכֵ֗לֶת אָחוּז֙ בְּחַבְלֵי־ב֣וּץ וְאַרְגָּמָ֔ן עַל־גְּלִ֥ילֵי כֶ֖סֶף וְעַמּ֣וּדֵי שֵׁ֑שׁ. A null copula clause with the passive participle ms Qal √אחז as the copular complement. The NPs חור כרפס ותכלת ("white linen material and violet") are part of a compound subject with a null copula and אחוז ("fastened") as its complement: "white linen material and violet (were) fastened ..."

חֻ֣ור ׀ כַּרְפַּ֣ס וּתְכֵ֗לֶת. The words חור and תכלת are nouns, not adjectives as suggested by the English glosses. חור ("white-ness," i.e., "white fabric" or "white material") appears in the Hebrew Bible only in Esther (here and 8:15); similarly, כרפס appears only here. Derived from the Persian kirpās, כרפס referring to a "fine fabric" (HALOT s.v.; BDB s.v.; cf. DCH s.v.). The use of several rare words in v. 6 (חור, כרפס, שׁשׁ, בהט, דַּר, סחרת) to describe the king's palace is a stylistic feature—rare words better portray exoticness of the foreign palace. The noun כרפס is appositive to חור (contra Paton, 144), lit., "white material, linen." The relationship communicated by the apposition is attribution ("white material, being linen"), specifying the material with which the "white stuff" is made. Thus חור כרפס is functionally equivalent to "white linen" (Bush, 348). Although כרפס is not repeated after תכלת "violet," it must be assumed, thus "and violet (linen)."

אָחוּז֙ בְּחַבְלֵי־ב֣וּץ וְאַרְגָּמָ֔ן. The passive participle אחוז means "being grasped" or "fastened." The noun בוץ appears only in Chronicles and Ezekiel, and refers to a "fine, costly, white fabric" (HALOT s.v.; cf. DCH s.v.; BDB s.v.). The PP בחבלי בוץ וארגמן ("with ropes of fine linen and purple material") is an adjunct to the participle אחוז, and refers to the instrument of fastening, not the agent (WO 11.2.5d). The NPs בוץ and ארגמן combine to form a compound clitic host for the bound head חבלי and specifies the material from which the חבלי are made (WO 9.5.3d; on a coordinate phrase as the host for a single bound word, see WO 9.3b). Alternatively, ארגמן could be understood as a second complement to ב: "with ropes of fine linen and with purple material" (WO 11.4.2). Not only is there no syntactic test to determine which option is correct, the semantic difference between "with ropes of fine linen and (with) purple material" and "with ropes of fine linen and (ropes of) purpose material" is negligible.

עַל־גְּלִ֥ילֵי כֶ֖סֶף וְעַמּ֣וּדֵי שֵׁ֑שׁ. This על-PP is an adjunct to the participle אחוז and indicates the things upon which the חור כרפס ותכלת were fastened. The coordinated NPs גלילי כסף and עמודי שׁשׁ are the compound complement of the על preposition. Both כסף and שׁשׁ are clitic hosts specifying the material out of which the bound גלילי and עמודי, respectively, are made (WO 9.5.3d). The noun גליל appears only ten times in the Hebrew Bible. Derived from the root גלל ("to roll"), גליל refers to a "cylinder," "rod," or "ring" (HALOT s.v.; DCH s.v.; BDB s.v.). Here it probably means "ring," although a round pole is also possible (parallel to עמודים, "columns," to which the ropes are also fastened; cf. Paton, 145). The noun שׁשׁ, "alabaster, marble," is used in this verse twice and once in Song of Songs (1:15). It is a loanword from Egyptian (šś), which, depending on whether the stone-determinative or the clothing-determinative is used, can mean "alabaster" or "fine linen," respectively (HALOT s.v.; DCH שֵׁשׁ II, שֵׁשׁ III; cf. BDB s.v.; Bush, 348).

מִטּ֣וֹת ׀ זָהָ֣ב וָכֶ֗סֶף עַ֛ל רִֽצְפַ֥ת בַּהַט־וָשֵׁ֖שׁ וְדַ֥ר וְסֹחָֽרֶת. Both the syntax and the accents suggest we begin a new clause here. The subject is מטות זהב וכסף and is followed by a null copula and its complement, the PP על רצפת בהט ושש ודר וסחרת. Within the subject NP, the compound clitic host זהב וכסף specifies the material from which the bound noun מטות are made.

רִֽצְפַ֥ת בַּהַט־וָשֵׁ֖שׁ וְדַ֥ר וְסֹחָֽרֶת. The רצפת, "pavement," is made of four materials, but syntactically there are three constituents to which רצפת is bound, because the *maqqef* and the *qameṣ* under the ו conjunction signal that בהט ושש is to be taken as a single prosodic constituent (WO 39.2.1b, ex. 8; cf., e.g., Gen 1:2 תֹהוּ וָבֹהוּ and Ps 1:2 יוֹמָם וָלָיְלָה). The syntax of the complex phrase is similar to English "sandwiches of peanut-butter and jelly and ham and tuna-salad," in which the compound "of" phrase modifying sandwiches falls into the three prosodically marked constituents: [peanut-butter and jelly] and [ham] and [tuna-salad].

רִֽצְפַ֥ת. The noun רצפה, "pavement, stone flooring" (BDB s.v.; HALOT s.v.; DCH s.v.), appears only here and in Ezekiel and Chronicles. Note the lack of the expected *dageš qal* in the פ at a syllable onset (cf. מִדְבָּר). Bauer and Leander (603) propose two possible explanations: either the *sheva* represents a reduced vowel, implying that the pattern is not a feminine *qatl-a(t)* as is appears, but a bisyllabic base such as *qatal+a(t)*, or the spirantization of the second root consonant is due to analogy with the *qatal+a(t)* pattern (though the motivation for this analogy is unclear).

בַּהַט. This noun appears, from context, to refer to a kind of stone, although the precise type remains unknown. This is a *hapax legomenon* (a one-time occurring word) in the Hebrew Bible. It may be related to Arabic *baht*, "aetite" (HALOT s.v.) or it may be a loanword from Egyptian *ʾbhti*, "porphyry" (HALOT s.v.; BDB s.v.; cf. also Bush, 348). Both of these suggestions are difficult, however, because the typical Hebrew phonological correspondence to /t/ in other Semitic languages is also /t/ ת, not /ṭ/ ט (Lambdin, 147; HALOT s.v.).

דַּר. This is another *hapax legomenon*. Comparison with Arabic *durr* suggests that דר means "pearl" (HALOT s.v.; Bush, 348; cf. BDB s.v.). With *hapax legomena* like בהט, דר, and סחרת (see below) it often makes sense to look to the Septuagint's understanding for guidance. However the Septuagint of v. 6 does not present a one-to-one equivalence for the Hebrew (cf. Tov and Polak on 1:6). As a result, we cannot rely on the Septuagint here, and the meaning "mother of pearl" (LXX πιννίνου … λίθου) should not be ascribed to דַּר.

סֹחָרֶת. This pausal form noun (contextual form: סֹחֶרֶת) is yet another *hapax legomenon*. Like בהט, there is little evidence with which to reconstruct the meaning of this word. It may be related to Arabic *šuḥḥār*, "blackish earth" (HALOT s.v.), Akkadian *siḫru* (BDB s.v.), or Egyptian *sḥrt*, a "mineral used to make figurines and amulets" (HALOT s.v.). It is possibly related to the verbal root סחר, "to pass through" (HALOT s.v.) or "go around" (DCH s.v.; BDB s.v.), but it is unclear what the derived noun would mean. Bush argues that סחרת (as well as בהט and דר) cannot refer to a precious stone, as is typically assumed, because precious stones are not suitable for pavement (they are not hard enough; 348). However, the extreme value of the materials used, perhaps *because of* their unsuitability for pavement, is part of the lavish description of the king's banquet. Moreover, these precious stones need not be the primary material out of which the floor is made; rather, they could be adornment in the form of edging.

1:7 הַשְׁקוֹת בִּכְלֵי זָהָב וְכֵלִים מִכֵּלִים שׁוֹנִים וְיֵין
מַלְכוּת רָב כְּיַד הַמֶּלֶךְ׃

In v. 7, the utensils of the banquet are described, adding to the opulent description of the banquet in v. 6. As with v. 6, the simplest analysis of this verse is as two null copula clauses.

וְהַשְׁקוֹת בִּכְלֵי זָהָב וְכֵלִים מִכֵּלִים שׁוֹנִים. Inf constr Hiph √שקה. The Hiphil שקה "to water" or "to give drink," is the suppletive causative of the morphologically unrelated Qal שתה "to drink" (JM 85a). Here the infinitive functions as an event noun, "giving drink" or "drink-giving" (Bush, 348; cf. Paton, 146) and is the subject of a null copula with the ב-PP as complement: "drink-giving was in gold vessels."

כְלֵי זָהָב. The word כלי denotes very generally an "article" or "object" made of any material (BDB s.v.; cf. HALOT s.v.; DCH s.v.); given the context here, it means "vessel" (HALOT s.v.; DCH s.v.; BDB s.v.). Since the infinitive השקות refers to "drink-serving," not "drinking," כלי probably refers to the large containers (e.g., pitchers) from which liquid was dispensed into smaller drinking vessels, such as cups, flagons, or chalices (cf. Bush, 348).

בִּכְלֵי זָהָב וְכֵלִים מִכֵּלִים שׁוֹנִים. The seemingly awkward phrase כלים מכלים שונים only appears so due to the order of the second and third words. Flipping the words, i.e., כלים שונים מכלים, not only removes the difficulty but also points toward the correct syntactic analysis. The NP כלים is modified by an unmarked relative clause in which the participle שונים is the complement of the null copula and the PP מכלים is an adjunct to the participle: "vessels (that) differ from (other) vessels." The verb שנה means "to change" or "to differ" (see also comments on 2:9 and 3:8) and the repetition of כלים serves a distributive function, indicating that the object of the comparison was the same group from which the standard was drawn: "vessels differing from each other," i.e., all the vessels were unique (Bush, 348; see Moore's translation "no two alike" (1971:1); cf. Levenson, 43; Paton, 141). Within the larger context, the complex NP כלים מכלים שונים is in apposition to כלי זהב, not conjoined to it, and the ו is the so-called epexegetical ו, which often introduces appositives (WO 39.2.4): "vessels of gold, i.e., each a unique vessel."

וְיֵין מַלְכוּת רָב כְּיַד הַמֶּלֶךְ. On the meaning of מלכות as a clitic host, see comment on 1:2. The PP כיד המלך builds on the metaphorical meaning of יד as "power" and results the idiom, "according to royal power." That is, the king provided wine in quality and quantity as only the king could do. The same phrase is used in 2:18 and 1 Kgs 10:13.

1:8 **וְהַשְּׁתִיָּה כַדָּת אֵין אֹנֵס כִּי־כֵן ׀ יִסַּד הַמֶּלֶךְ עַל**
כָּל־רַב בֵּיתוֹ לַעֲשׂוֹת כִּרְצוֹן אִישׁ־וָאִישׁ׃

In v. 8 the king's extravagance in throwing banquets is described in one final way. Besides being extreme in duration (v. 4), size of guest-list (v. 5), furnishings and utensils (vv. 6-7), the king's banquets are said to place no limitations on the attendees with regard to drinking. In other words, the entire city of Susa has an open bar at the king's expense.

וְהַשְּׁתִיָּה כַדָּת אֵין אֹנֵס. This is a null copula clause, with the NP שׁתיה the subject and the כ-PP the copular complement. The noun שׁתיה, "manner of drinking, time for drinking" (HALOT s.v.; cf. DCH s.v.; BDB s.v.) derives from √שׁתה "to drink" and appears only here in the Hebrew Bible. The word echoes the infinitive השקות "drink-serving" in the preceding verse. The form שְׁתִיָּה reflects the III-ה form (*qətiyy-*) of the deverbal noun pattern קְטִילָה used in rabbinic Hebrew for actions relating to Qal verbs (see Pérez-Fernández, 57). See Appendix B.

דָּת אֵין אֹנֵס. The noun דת is a borrowing of Persian *dāta* and refers to an "order, decree" or "regulation, law" (HALOT s.v.; DCH s.v.). The clause אין אנס may be appositive to דת, giving the content of דת: "The drinking was according to the regulation 'There is no constraint!'" Alternatively, we could understand a new clause at this point: "The drinking was according to regulation. There was no constraint, because ..." Finally, we could understand אין אנס as parenthetical: "The drinking was according to regulation (no constraint existed), because the king ..." Regardless which option we choose, we should understand the דת not as a legal precept established in Persia at the time, but rather as a regulation the king has given solely for this banquet; the implied content of the דת is filled out by the statements "there was no constraint" and "the king had established to do as each man wished."

אֹנֵס. Participle ms Qal √אנס. The Hebrew root אנס appears only here in the Hebrew Bible and, based on later Hebrew usage and Aramaic cognates, must mean "to compel" (HALOT s.v.; BDB s.v.; cf. Bush, 348). Here the sense is that, since the people were neither compelled to drink nor compelled to abstain, it was an "anything goes" drinking environment (Paton, 142; Moore 1971:8; Fox 2001:274; Bush, 348).

כִּי־כֵן ׀ יִסַּד הַמֶּלֶךְ עַל כָּל־רַב בֵּיתוֹ. *Qatal* 3ms Piel √יסד. Both the כי and the fronted adverb כן trigger inversion to verb-subject order. The function word כי can serve a variety of functions (MNK 40.9; cf. Aejmelaeus); here it gives the basis or cause for the clause that preceded it (MNK 40.9 I.3; WO 38.4a). The Piel verb יסד appears with an על-PP adjunct in Ps 24:2 and Song 5:15, where physical items ("the earth" and "legs," respectively) are founded or laid upon another physical item. Here, however, the context is not physical space but conceptual space: the king has "laid down" or "established" a principle for the chiefs of the palace to uphold. Although יסד typically takes an NP complement, here the complement is the adverb כן, which is then defined by an extraposed appositive infinitive clause לעשות כרצון איש ואיש: "the king had established thus . . . to act according to the desire of each man." The PP על כל־רב ביתו is an adjunct indicating with respect to whom or what the activity of יסד pertains (WO 11.2.13c). The noun בַּיִת (bound, בֵּית) denotes "house," but has a wide variety of connotations from other concrete entities such as "palace" and "temple" to more abstract notions such as "household" or even "dynasty" (see HALOT s.v.; DCH s.v.).

לַעֲשׂוֹת כִּרְצוֹן אִישׁ־וָאִישׁ. Inf constr Qal √עשׂה. The repetitive phrase איש ואיש reflects a convention of using apposition for a distributive meaning, "each man" (see v. 22; WO 12.5). רצון means "favor," "will," or as here, in a nonreligious context, "pleasure, liking" (HALOT s.v.; DCH s.v.; cf. BDB s.v.). The subject of the infinite לעשות is not explicit in the clause, but is assumed from the previous clause, each רב is to act however he wants. The nuance of the verb עשׂה here is "to do" or "to act, behave." The כ-PP is the complement of the bivalent verb and provides the manner of the behavior (on כ for approximations, see WO 11.2.9b and ex. 2); see also 2:4; 3:11; 4:17; 5:8; 9:13.

1:9 גַּם וַשְׁתִּי הַמַּלְכָּה עָשְׂתָה מִשְׁתֵּה נָשִׁים בֵּית
הַמַּלְכוּת אֲשֶׁר לַמֶּלֶךְ אֲחַשְׁוֵרוֹשׁ׃

In what initially feels like a hastily added aside, v. 9 introduces Vashti, one of the central figures of chapter 1, and her banquet for the women. As the next episode clarifies, the introduction of Vashti is hardly inconsequential. This verse thus serves to close the first episode, which focuses on the exorbitant feasting, and transitions to the next episode, which presents the first complication of the story's plot.

גַּם וַשְׁתִּי הַמַּלְכָּה עָשְׂתָה מִשְׁתֵּה נָשִׁים בֵּית הַמַּלְכוּת. *Qatal* 3fs Qal √עשׂה. In vv. 3 and 6 עשׂה has an NP complement משתה and a ל-PP adjunct designating the people for whom the banquet was prepared. In this verse, though, there is no corresponding ל-PP adjunct. Rather, the beneficiaries of the feast are signaled by the clitic host נשים of the NP משתה נשים. The function word גם often marks a constituent for Focus (e.g., "*even Vashti* offered a banquet"), but here it more likely serves as an additive conjunction (MNK 41.4.5) and indicates simply that "Vashti *also* offered a banquet."

וַשְׁתִּ֣י הַמַּלְכָּ֗ה. The name וַשְׁתִּי is possibly of Elamite origin (Bush, 349; HALOT s.v.), or perhaps comes from Persian *vas* ("to desire"; Gehman, 322–23) or *vahista* ("best"; BDB s.v.; Keil, 327; cf. Mayer, 131–32). Note the different word order with ושתי המלכה than with המלך אחשורוש (see comment on 1:2). In the book, the order is as here, ושתי המלכה "Vashti, the queen," four times (1:9, 11, 16, 17) and the opposite, המלכה ושתי "Queen Vashti," twice (1:12, 15). Interestingly, with the proper name "Esther," the order is always אסתר המלכה "Esther, the queen" (5:2, 3, 12; 7:1, 2, 3, 5, 7; 8:1, 7; 9:12, 29, 31). It is possible that the difference in usage, "King/Queen X" (see comment on 1:2) versus "X, the queen" (always for Esther and 4× for Vashti) relates to the identifiability of the referent within the narrative. In the narrative world of the book, there is only one king and he is explicitly introduced in the first verse, making all subsequent references to "the king" unambiguous and the inclusion of the king's name likely a simple clarifying (not defining) appositive strategy or even cultural convention (such as a title) (see comment at 1:2). In contrast, there are clearly multiple queens in the narrative's world and so the NP "the queen" would either need to be followed by a defining Proper Noun, the name of the individual woman, or better, the name used first, followed by the (attributive and clarifying) appositive "the queen," ושתי המלכה, which is the dominant pattern in the book.

מִשְׁתֵּ֣ה. This noun is the bound form of מִשְׁתֶּה. Unlike the common strategy for feminine nouns of replacing the ה of the free forms with a ת ending in the bound forms, masculine nouns built from III-ה roots do not use the ת for the bound form. Instead, only the vowel of the final syllable changes, from the *segol* of the free form to the *ṣere* of the bound form.

בֵּ֖ית הַמַּלְכ֑וּת. The NP (lit. "house of the kingdom"; see comment on מלכות in 1:2) is a locative adjunct to the verb עשתה, though it is not introduced by a preposition, which is the more common pattern (see comment on ימים רבים in v. 4). With the particular noun בית, the expected preposition ב is often missing (see Ruth 1:9), leading some grammarians to suggest that בית in such cases is actually abbreviated writing for בבית (see GKC 118; WO 10.2.2; JM 126h, 133c). Whichever analysis is chosen, the result is the same: the phrase בית המלכות is a verbal adjunct.

אֲשֶׁר לַמֶּלֶךְ אֲחַשְׁוֵרוֹשׁ. Lit., "which was to King Ahashverosh." A copula (see Appendix C) with a ל-PP complement often signals a possessive relationship (WO 11.2.10d). Here the null copula clause inside the relative means "(the house) that belonged to King Ahashverosh." The relative אשר למלך אחשורוש has as its head בית, not המלכות; that is, it is the "house" belonging to Ahashverosh, not the "kingdom," that is in view.

§2: Vashti's Removal (1:10-22)

*10 On the seventh day, when the heart of the king was glad due to wine,
he ordered Mehuman, Biztha, Harbona, Bigtha and Abagtha, Zethar and
Karkas, the seven eunuchs who served before King Ahashverosh, 11 to bring
Vashti, the queen, before the king in a royal turban, to show the peoples and
rulers her beauty, because she was pleasing of appearance. 12 Then Queen
Vashti refused to come at the word of the king, which was (communicated) by
the hand of the eunuchs. So the king was exceedingly angry; his wrath burned
him. 13 Then the king said to the wise men who knew the times (because thus
was the manner of the king in the presence of all who knew law and judgment, 14 the ones closest to him being Karshna, Shetar, Admatha, Tarshish,
Meres, Marsena, and Memukan, the seven princes of Persia and Media who
saw the face of the king, who sat first in the kingdom), 15 "According to law,
what is one to do with Queen Vashti, because she did not do the command of
King Ahashverosh, which was (communicated) by the hand of the eunuchs?"
16 Memukan said before the king and the rulers, "Not against the king alone
did Vashti, the queen, transgress, but against all the rulers and against all the
peoples who are in all the provinces of King Ahashverosh, 17 because the deed
of the Queen will go out unto all women, causing (them) to despise their
husbands with their eyes, when (others) say, "King Ahashverosh said to bring
Vashti, the queen, before him, but she did not come." 18 And this day the
ladies of Persia and Media will say that they heard the matter of the queen to
all the rulers of the king, and contempt and wrath will be more than enough.
19 If it pleases the king, let a royal word go out from him, and let it be written
in the laws of Persia and Media (and it will not pass away!) that Vashti shall
not enter before King Ahashverosh and her royal position the king shall give
to someone like her who is better than her. 20 And let the announcement of the
king, which he will make, be heard in all his kingdom (because it is great).
Then all the women will give honor to their husbands, both great and small."*

[21] The word pleased the king and the rulers, and the king acted according to the word of Memukan. [22] And he sent documents to all the provinces of the king, (sending them) to each province according to its writing, and (sending them) to each people according to its language, so that every man would rule in his house and speak in the language of his people.

1:10 בַּיּוֹם֙ הַשְּׁבִיעִ֔י כְּט֥וֹב לֵב־הַמֶּ֖לֶךְ בַּיָּ֑יִן אָמַ֡ר לִ֠מְהוּמָן
בִּזְּתָ֨א חַרְבוֹנָ֜א בִּגְתָ֤א וַאֲבַגְתָא֙ זֵתַ֣ר וְכַרְכַּ֔ס
שִׁבְעַת֙ הַסָּ֣רִיסִ֔ים הַמְשָׁ֣רְתִ֔ים אֶת־פְּנֵ֖י הַמֶּ֥לֶךְ
אֲחַשְׁוֵרֽוֹשׁ׃

The first episode serves to introduce Ahashverosh, his extravagant banquets, and Vashti. Verses 10-12 move the reader to the next episode and the first plot complication: the king requests that Vashti come and display her beauty (vv. 10-11), but she refuses him (v. 12).

בַּיּוֹם֙ הַשְּׁבִיעִ֔י כְּט֥וֹב לֵב־הַמֶּ֖לֶךְ בַּיָּ֑יִן אָמַ֡ר. Inf constr Qal √טוב and *qatal* 3ms Qal √אמר. The syntactic subject of the clause is null, though the antecedent of the null subject is provided by the המלך in כ-PP that precedes the main verb אמר. The ב-PP and כ-PP are both fronted as scene-setting (temporal) Topics: "in the seventh day" and "when the king's heart was glad with wine." The ordinal השביעי modifies the noun יום adjectivally. Ordinal numerals function as adjectives in contrast to cardinals, which are often in apposition to or bound to the quantified noun (see "Numeral Syntax in Esther" in the Introduction). In the fronted כ-PP, the word טוֹב is an infinitive (though the form טוֹב is ambiguous and may also be taken as the adjective טוֹב, the context suggests the common preposition-infinitive pattern). The subject of the infinitive is לב המלך and the ב-PP is an adjunct indicating the means ("by/with wine") or cause ("because/due to wine") (WO 11.2.5d–e; JM 133c). The same expression occurs elsewhere in the Bible (e.g., 2 Sam 13:28) and is similar to the adjective construction in 5:9, הָמָן ... שָׂמֵחַ וְטוֹב לֵב "Haman ... (went out) happy and good of heart." In the later texts, the collocation of אמר and ל, which denotes "to say to," has the connotation of "to command ל-someone" or "to order ל-someone" (HALOT s.v.; DCH s.v.; BDB s.v.). The ל-PP is an adjunct, as with the normal meaning of אמר; that is, the idiomatic meaning of "command" does not affect the syntax. There are many cases where אמר appears without a PP indicating the addressee (e.g., the infinitive clause באמרם in v. 17); we thus take the verb אמר to be bivalent, requiring a subject and a complement. The complement of אמר is most often direct speech, but may be an infinitive, as here with להביא as here with the complement להביא found in v. 11.

מְהוּמָן בִּזְּתָא חַרְבוֹנָא בִּגְתָא וַאֲבַגְתָא זֵתַר וְכַרְכַּס. In the list of seven names (whose etymology, together with the names in v. 14, has been discussed at length elsewhere; see Paton, 67–69; Gehman, 323–24; Duchesne-Guillemin; Millard, 482–85; Fox 2001:20; Bush, 349), a ו conjunction appears between the last two items in the list (as we would find in English), but also between Bigtha and Abagtha, the fourth and fifth items (cf. the list in v. 14, in which ו never appears). This use of the ו is rare (WO 39.2.1b ex. 3). It is conceivable that Bigtha and Abagtha were considered a pair for some unknown and contextually inaccessible reason, but it may also be that the use of the ו, as a front-edge phrase marker, was simply more variable than we often reconstruct from the dominant extant patterns.

שִׁבְעַת הַסָּרִיסִים. The numeral שבעת is bound to the quantified noun הסריסים (see "Numeral Syntax in Esther" in the Introduction). The noun סריס means either "high official" or "eunuch." The term often refers to a general official (see Gen 37:36 and throughout the Joseph story), but in Esther it is used for specific officials in charge of the king's concubines (2:3, 14, 15; 4:4; etc.). It is likely that these officials would have been emasculated (Bush, 349).

הַמְשָׁרְתִים אֶת־פְּנֵי הַמֶּלֶךְ אֲחַשְׁוֵרוֹשׁ. Participle mp Piel √שרת. The Piel שרת can be monovalent ("to minister") or bivalent with either an NP complement ("to serve, attend X") or, as here, a PP complement, את פני המלך אחשורוש, lit. "with the face of King Ahashverosh." The PP את פני is much less common but similar in meaning to לפני or אל פני. With the verb שרת, the PP את פני is used only here and in 1 Sam 2:18. Otherwise, the PP that שרת takes as its complement is either a simple ל-PP (e.g., 2 Chr 13:10; 22:8) or לפני (e.g., 1 Chr 6:17; 16:37).

1:11 לְהָבִיא אֶת־וַשְׁתִּי הַמַּלְכָּה לִפְנֵי הַמֶּלֶךְ בְּכֶתֶר
מַלְכוּת לְהַרְאוֹת הָעַמִּים וְהַשָּׂרִים אֶת־יָפְיָהּ כִּי־
טוֹבַת מַרְאֶה הִיא׃

Verse 11 continues the clause begun in v. 10, giving the content of the king's command concerning Vashti. She is to appear before him in the royal turban, showing off her beauty for all to see (much like the showing off of the king's riches and greatness found in v. 4).

לְהָבִיא אֶת־וַשְׁתִּי הַמַּלְכָּה לִפְנֵי הַמֶּלֶךְ בְּכֶתֶר מַלְכוּת. Inf constr Hiph √בוא. The verb אמר, in v. 10, takes an indirect speech clause complement, here the infinitive clause beginning with the ל-PP/infinitive clause להביא. An indirect speech complement to אמר is not common, but there is an increase of infinitive indirect speech complements with אמר in LBH (Miller 1996:127–28; see, e.g., 2 Chr 14:3). The verb בוא in the Hiphil is trivalent, with one complement for the person or thing brought (here את ושתי) and the second, locative complement (sometimes an NP, but usually a PP, as here with לפני המלך) for the place to which he/she/it is brought. For ושתי המלכה, see comment on v. 9. In the PP בכתר מלכות, the noun כתר is used in the Hebrew Bible only in Esther (here, 2:17, and 6:8). Though often translated "crown" (BDB s.v.), that term may be misleading: a כתר is more specifically a "turban" worn in the Persian style (HALOT s.v.; DCH s.v.; Keil, 328; Paton, 151; Moore 1971:9; Bush, 350), not a European style "crown" made with precious metals (cf. 6:8, where a כתר is worn by a horse). On the bound relationship between כתר and מלכות, see comment on 1:2.

לְהַרְאוֹת הָעַמִּים וְהַשָּׂרִים אֶת־יָפְיָהּ. Inf constr Hiph √ראה. This ל-PP/infinitive clause is an adjunct of the preceding infinitive להביא and indicates the intended purpose of the action: "to bring Vashti in order to show the people her beauty." As in v. 4, Hiphil ראה is trivalent, "X [first person/agent] causes Y [a second person] to see Z [a third person or thing]," or more smoothly in English, "X shows Z to Y."

כִּי־טוֹבַת מַרְאֶה הִיא. A null copula clause with the 3fs pronoun היא as the subject and the bound phrase טובת מראה as the copular complement. Note that the copular complement is fronted before the subject—this is not the basic order of subject-(copula)-complement. The fronting almost certainly is for Focus, to stress the extent of her beauty. The כי clause could be causal, reporting the reason for the king's action (commanding the eunuchs to bring Vashti; so Paton, 149) or the reason for the people appreciating her beauty. But it may also be complement clause (WO 38.8d; MNK 40.9 II.1) in apposition to the second NP complement of להראות: "to show the peoples and rulers her beauty, i.e., *that* she was pleasing of appearance." The function of the apposition would be to reformulate the second complement and so reinforce and strengthen the assessment of her physical beauty. Though both options are grammatical, we find the causal clause analysis simpler and preferable.

1:12 וַתְּמָאֵ֞ן הַמַּלְכָּ֣ה וַשְׁתִּ֗י לָבוֹא֙ בִּדְבַ֣ר הַמֶּ֔לֶךְ אֲשֶׁ֖ר
בְּיַ֣ד הַסָּרִיסִ֑ים וַיִּקְצֹ֤ף הַמֶּ֙לֶךְ֙ מְאֹ֔ד וַחֲמָת֖וֹ בָּעֲרָ֥ה
בֽוֹ׃

Verse 12 describes an essential event in the narrative, Vashti's refusal of Ahashverosh, without which Esther would not have the opportunity to ascend to the throne and save her people, the Jews.

וַתְּמָאֵ֞ן הַמַּלְכָּ֣ה וַשְׁתִּ֗י לָבוֹא֙ בִּדְבַ֣ר הַמֶּ֔לֶךְ. *Wayyiqtol* 3fs Piel √מאן. At its core, the ו is simply a proclitic left (or front) edge phrase marker (Holmstedt 2013b). When it appears to have a semantic content, the meaning whichever of "and," "or," or "then" that is most appropriate (see Steiner). While an adversative ("but") sense may be felt by the reader, that is an implicature arising from the sequence of events and should not be read back on to the grammatical value of ו. As with many *wayyiqtol* occurrences, "and" or "then" are the most grammatically appropriate translation values. The verb מאן "to refuse" always appears in the Piel; it can be either monovalent or bivalent with an infinitive complement (e.g., in Exodus throughout: מֵאֵן לְשַׁלַּח הָעָם "he (Pharaoh) refused *to send out* the people"). Here it is bivalent, with the ל-PP/infinitive clause לבוא as the complement. For המלכה ושתי ("Queen Vashti"), see comments on vv. 2, 9. The PP בדבר המלך likely modifies the infinitive לבוא, but may also possibly modify the main verb תמאן. If it is the latter, the ב preposition would be adversative (WO 11.2.5d): "she refused ..., *against/contrary to* the word of the king." However, מאן is never modified by a ב-PP elsewhere, which may indicate that the ב-PP be an adjunct to לבוא. Although verbs of motion like בוא often take a ב-PP with a spatial sense (WO 11.2.5b), here the דבר המלך is not a physical entity with spatial dimensions. Instead, the PP בדבר המלך may indicate instrument ("enter *by* the word of the king"; WO 11.2.5d; cf. 3:15) or manner ("enter *in the manner of/according to* the word of the king"; WO 11.2.5e) or, as is most probable, circumstance ("enter *at* the word of the king"; WO 11.2.5d).

אֲשֶׁ֖ר בְּיַ֣ד הַסָּרִיסִ֑ים. This relative clause modifies דבר המלך non-restrictively; it does not define the nature of the דבר but adds something important to the narrative about the דבר. The expression ביד "with the hand of" is often used metaphorically to indicate instrumentality, e.g., something is spoken "through" or "by" somebody (with the verb דִּבֵּר,

see Exod 9:35; Lev 10:11; Num 17:5; Josh 20:2; 1 Kgs 8:53; without an explicit verb but associated with the NP דְּבַר־יהוה, see Mal 1:1; 1 Chr 11:3; 2 Chr 35:6; cf. also instances where דָּבָר is modified by a relative clause including דִּבֵּר בְּיַד, e.g., 1 Kgs 8:56; 2 Kgs 9:36; Jer 37:2; 2 Chr 10:15). Here Ahashverosh's word was communicated to Vashti *through* or *by means of* the eunuchs (Fox 2001:18–19; see also 1:15; 3:13; 8:10). When messages are received second-hand, the specter of miscommunication looms (we think here of Gen 3:3, where the woman's understanding of Yhwh's prohibition in the garden—by necessity received second-hand, since she did not yet exist when it was given—differs from what he actually said to the man in Gen 2:16-17). So, we wonder: did the narrator specify ביד הסריסים in order to set up a darkly humorous context in which Vashti's refusal was based on a miscommunication? Such subtleties (probably signaled in an oral setting by physical hints, such as gestures like winks or nods and changes in speech patterns, such as intonation and speed) seem to characterize Hebrew storytelling (e.g., Gen 2–3; Ruth 3–4).

וַיִּקְצֹ֤ף הַמֶּ֙לֶךְ֙ מְאֹ֔ד. *Wayyiqtol* 3ms Qal √קצף. The verb is monovalent and means "to be angry" (HALOT s.v.; DCH s.v.; BDB s.v.). The item מאד is an adjunct and functions here as a scalar adverb indicating degree (in contrast to its more common use as an item adverb; WO 39.3.1i).

וַחֲמָת֖וֹ בָּעֲרָ֥ה בֽוֹ. *Qatal* 3fs Qal √בער. The expression חמה בערה ב, "wrath burned X," is an idiomatic synonym for קצף and reinforces how angry the king was. The verb בער, "to burn," is more often monovalent, "X burns/is burning," but can also be bivalent, "X burns Y," where a ב-PP marks the constituent effected or destroyed by the burning (HALOT s.v.; DCH s.v.; BDB s.v.). Here the ב-PP marks the referent of the 3ms clitic pronoun (i.e., the king) as the thing being burned. The subject-verb word order of this clause is an example of basic Hebrew word order. Departure from the past narrative *wayyiqtol* is a common technique for presenting simultaneous or parallel events (see also 6:12; 8:14; 9:16). The nonuse of the special narrative verb allows for the basic subject-verb order to emerge. There is no special pragmatic (Topic or Focus) marking on חמתו.

1:13 וַיֹּ֣אמֶר הַמֶּ֔לֶךְ לַחֲכָמִ֖ים יֹדְעֵ֣י הָעִתִּ֑ים כִּי־כֵ֗ן דְּבַ֣ר
הַמֶּ֔לֶךְ לִפְנֵ֕י כָּל־יֹדְעֵ֖י דָּ֥ת וָדִֽין׃

The king responds to Vashti's insulting refusal by conferring with his sages. Midway through the verse, the narrator breaks the flow of the story to describe the process of the king when legal matters were involved.

וַיֹּ֣אמֶר הַמֶּ֔לֶךְ לַחֲכָמִ֖ים יֹדְעֵ֣י הָעִתִּ֑ים. *Wayyiqtol* 3ms Qal √אמר and participle (bound) mp Qal √ידע. There is significant distance between אמר and the direct speech starting in v. 15 because of the extensive parenthesis beginning in this verse; nevertheless, the direct speech starting in v. 15 is the complement of bivalent אמר (contra NRSV's translation of אמר as "to consult"). The mp adjective חכמים is used substantivally, "wise men, advisers" (DCH s.v.) and functions as the complement of the preposition ל. The participle ידעי may be an agentive noun here, in apposition to חכמים: "the king said to the wise men, *the knowers of the times*." However, it is also possible to analyze this as an unmarked relative clause, with the participle the complement of a null copula: "wise men, who (were) knowing the times." Since many relative clauses are unmarked, i.e., lack an introductory אשר, ש, or ה (see Holmstedt 2013a; WO 19.7b), and also since many participles are fundamentally related to adjectives (see Cook 2008), we see the relative clause analysis as the likelier analysis. The same two options also apply to ידעי דת ודין later in this verse and ראי פני המלך in v. 14, the latter of which is parallel to a ה-relative clause, supporting the argument that these are relative clauses. The verb ידע is bivalent and here takes the NP העתים as its (cliticized) complement (on the bound relationship representing the valency of a verb and its complement, see WO 9.5.2, under the "adverbial genitive").

כִּי־כֵ֗ן דְּבַ֣ר הַמֶּ֔לֶךְ לִפְנֵ֕י כָּל־יֹדְעֵ֖י דָּ֥ת וָדִֽין. A null copula clause, with the NP דבר המלך the subject and the adverb כן the fronted copular complement. Although דבר often means "word," it can also connote a "matter," "affair," or "thing" (HALOT s.v.; BDB s.v.); here the sense seems to be very generic, "thing," which in context means "manner" (DCH s.v.). This כי clause intervenes between the verb אמר and its speech complement (v. 15). This is highly unusual word order and the disruptive nature of both the כי clause and v. 14 strongly suggest that both are parenthetical. The phrase כל ידעי דת ודין represents the quantifier כל bound to a null NP that is modified by an unmarked relative clause within which is a null copula and participial complement ידעי,

which itself has a compound NP complement, דת ודין: "all (those) (who) (were) knowing law and judgment." The noun דת is a Persian loanword (Persian *dāta*) meaning "order" or "law" (HALOT s.v.; cf. BDB s.v.), whereas דין is Semitic (Arabic *dīn*, Akkadian *dīnu* and *dēnu*) from the root דין, meaning "legal claim," "judgment," or "quarreling" (HALOT s.v.; cf. BDB s.v.; DCH s.v.). The vocalization of the ו conjunction with a *qameṣ* is used when the conjoined nouns are considered one concept or unit (cf. comment on v. 6)—apparently דת ודין together cover the full range of law, legal behavior, and social order.

1:14 וְהַקָּרֹ֣ב אֵלָ֔יו כַּרְשְׁנָ֤א שֵׁתָר֙ אַדְמָ֣תָא תַרְשִׁ֔ישׁ מֶ֥רֶס
מַרְסְנָ֖א מְמוּכָ֑ן שִׁבְעַ֞ת שָׂרֵ֣י ׀ פָּרַ֣ס וּמָדַ֗י רֹאֵי֙ פְּנֵ֣י
הַמֶּ֔לֶךְ הַיֹּשְׁבִ֥ים רִאשֹׁנָ֖ה בַּמַּלְכֽוּת׃

Continuing the parenthetical pause from the main story line, the narrator names and describes the seven individuals who advise the king on legal matters.

וְהַקָּרֹ֣ב אֵלָ֔יו כַּרְשְׁנָ֤א שֵׁתָר֙ אַדְמָ֣תָא תַרְשִׁ֔ישׁ מֶ֥רֶס מַרְסְנָ֖א מְמוּכָ֑ן. A small clause, with הקרב אליו as the subject and the compound NP list of seven names (on whose etymology, cf. the sources cited in the comment on v. 10) as the complement (so Paton, 152). Small clauses lack their own inflected verb (overt or null; cf. Appendix C). Moreover, they often lack even an uninflected verb to provide lexical content and valency, instead gapping into the position of the uninflected verb a null copy of the verb from a higher clause. In this case, the understood verb is copular, since the preceding, higher clause is copular. The subject הקרב אליו is a complex noun phrase: the adjective קרב functions substantivally, "the close one," and the PP אליו is internal to the NP. NP-internal PPs are restrictive modifiers; thus, the PP here provides a defining piece of information about the referent of קרב: this is not any "close one" but "the one whose close-ness is defined with regard to the king." The compound complement then provides the names to identify these close advisors. Note the lack of ו before the last name of the list (cf. WO 39.2.1b; cf. comment on v. 10).

שִׁבְעַ֞ת שָׂרֵ֣י ׀ פָּרַ֣ס וּמָדַ֗י רֹאֵי֙ פְּנֵ֣י הַמֶּ֔לֶךְ הַיֹּשְׁבִ֥ים רִאשֹׁנָ֖ה בַּמַּלְכֽוּת. Participle mp (bound) Qal √ראה and (free form) Qal √ישב. This long noun phrase is in apposition to the list of seven names, echoing the structure of v. 10 (note also the aural similarities of סריס in v. 10

and שׂר here). The participial clauses, ראי פני המלך and הישבים ראשנה במלכות, are both the copular complement within null copula relative clauses that restrictively modify the head שׂרי פרס ומדי. That is, out of all the many princes, it is these seven that regularly saw the king and so had priority status (cf. Keil, 329). The first relative, with ראי, is unmarked, the second is a ה-relative clause. The bound form of ראי illustrates that the clitic host of a bound participle may also be the complement fulfilling the valency (the verb ראה is bivalent, as is ידע, which is twice bound to its syntactic complement in v. 13).

1:15 כְּדָת֙ מַה־לַּעֲשׂ֔וֹת בַּמַּלְכָּ֖ה וַשְׁתִּ֑י עַ֣ל ׀ אֲשֶׁ֣ר
לֹֽא־עָשְׂתָ֗ה אֶֽת־מַאֲמַר֙ הַמֶּ֣לֶךְ אֲחַשְׁוֵר֔וֹשׁ בְּיַ֖ד
הַסָּרִיסִֽים׃

This verse returns to the main plot after the long parenthesis. The narrator recounts the king's question for his sages: How was he to deal with Vashti's disobedience?

כְּדָת֙ מַה־לַּעֲשׂ֔וֹת בַּמַּלְכָּ֖ה וַשְׁתִּ֑י. A null copula clause and an inf constr Qal √עשׂה. The null copula clause has a null, impersonal (generic) subject and the ל-PP/infinitive clause as the copular complement. The initial PP כדת is an adjunct to the null copula; it has been Topic-fronted in order to establish salient information up front, i.e., that the following discussion must take the law as its context (cf. Holmstedt 2010:9–10; 2009a:126–29). The interrogative מה is also fronted, from the complement position within the embedded infinitive clause. Rather than Topic-fronting, this מה has been fronted for Focus, which is typical with interrogative words, since they introduce an open variable that must be satisfied by the information in the answer. For the sake of comparison, the basic structure of this clause before all constituent movement would be לעשׂות מה במלכה ושתי כדת "(one is) to do what with the queen, Vashti, according to the law."

לַעֲשׂ֔וֹת. The use of an infinitive construct verb with ל in a clause without an overt finite verb has been considered by some to be a "predicative infinitive" (cf. Eskhult 2000:90–91; Kieviet; Kropat, 24–25; Leahy, 142; Qimron 1986:400.02; 1994:3.4.2; JM 123u–x and 124p; WO 36.3.2; 36.2.3f, g). That is, the infinitive takes finite meaning: "what will one do" rather than "what is one to do." However, even in Qumran Hebrew (where the phenomenon is more possible than in LBH) it is unclear whether many infinitives are actually functioning as main, finite verbs or are complements of a null copula, as we analyze the infinitive here. See also 3:14.

בַּמַּלְכָּה וַשְׁתִּי. This is the second instance where Vashti's title uses the same appositional structure as Ahashverosh (see comments on vv. 2, 9 and 12).

עַל ׀ אֲשֶׁר לֹא־עָשְׂתָה אֶת־מַאֲמַר הַמֶּלֶךְ אֲחַשְׁוֵרוֹשׁ בְּיַד הַסָּרִיסִים. *Qatal* 3fs Qal √עשׂה. This על-PP motivates the king's question (on the causal use of על, see WO 11.2.13e). The אשר here does not introduce a relative clause, but nominalizes the following clause as the complement of the preposition על. The PP ביד הסריסים may either be an NP-internal PP—"the by-the-hand-of-the-eunuchs command"—or an unmarked relative clause—"the command (that was) by the hand of the eunuchs"; semantically, the difference between the two syntactic options is negligible since both produce a restrictive modifier that identifies and defines the מאמר being mentioned. Given the parallel in v. 12 (where overt אשר is used), we prefer the relative analysis for the syntax. On the expression ביד, see comment on v. 12. מאמר is a *maqtal* noun (√אמר, "to say") that is used only in Esther (here, 2:20, 9:32) within the Bible, but frequently in rabbinic Hebrew (34 times in the Mishnah). It may reflect the borrowing of Aramaic מֵאמַר (Bergey 1983:100–101; cf. HALOT s.v.).

1:16 וַיֹּאמֶר מְומֻכָן לִפְנֵי הַמֶּלֶךְ וְהַשָּׂרִים לֹא עַל־הַמֶּלֶךְ לְבַדּוֹ עָוְתָה וַשְׁתִּי הַמַּלְכָּה כִּי עַל־כָּל־הַשָּׂרִים וְעַל־כָּל־הָעַמִּים אֲשֶׁר בְּכָל־מְדִינוֹת הַמֶּלֶךְ אֲחַשְׁוֵרוֹשׁ׃

In this verse, the royal advisor, Memukan, suggests that Vashti has not wronged the king only, a trespass of great significance on its own, but she has also wronged every man in the kingdom.

וַיֹּאמֶר מוּמְכָן לִפְנֵי הַמֶּלֶךְ וְהַשָּׂרִים. *Wayyiqtol* 3ms Qal √אמר. The verb אמר is bivalent (see comment on 1.10). Instead of the more common ל-PP to designate the addressee(s), here the לפני-PP may signal a public form of address. The complex preposition לפני (WO 11.3.1a) does not have a single NP complement here, but a compound NP—two NPs conjoined, המלך והשׂרים (WO 11.4.2a). The *Ketiv* (i.e., the letters written in the main body of the MT) reflect the name מוּמְכָן "Mumkan," which differs from vv. 10 and 21 where we find מְמוּכָן "Memukan," which reflects the *Qere* (the marginal consonants and the vowels in text). The *Ketiv* is almost certainly a scribal error, in which the ו was transposed with the second מ.

לֹ֚א עַל־הַמֶּ֣לֶךְ לְבַדּ֔וֹ עָוְתָ֖ה וַשְׁתִּ֣י הַמַּלְכָּ֑ה. *Qatal* 3fs Qal √עוה. The verb עוה ("do wrong; commit iniquity"; DCH s.v.; HALOT s.v.; BDB s.v.) rarely appears in the Qal (only here and Dan 9:5). Related to the noun עָוֹן, "iniquity," the Qal verb is monovalent (as is the Hiphil verb). The adjunct על-PP conveys "disadvantage," indicating the party who is harmed by the iniquity (WO 11.2.13c). The clause as a whole begins the direct speech complement to אמר. The negative לא typically functions on the clausal level and relates to the action or event described by a verb; when it is a clausal adverb, it is adjacent to the verb and applies generally, "X action/event has not occurred." Here the negative לא is distant from the verb, a signal that it is functioning as an item adverb (see WO 39.3.2a) and negates the PP על המלך לבדו; as such, the לא does not negate the verb (leaving the verbal action positively asserted) but excludes the applicability of the action/event to the item negated by לא, "X action/event occurred, excluding Y." Omitting לבדו for the moment, the clause לא על המלך עותה ושתי would mean "Vashti transgressed, but not against the king." The other item adverb, לבדו, which modifies the NP המלך, adds a critical element to the assertion, since it again shifts the scope of the statement, requiring that the set of offended members consists of more than one item, i.e., the king plus unstated others (which are specified in the next clause).

כִּ֤י עַל־כָּל־הַשָּׂרִים֙ וְעַל־כָּל־הָ֣עַמִּ֔ים. The particle כִּי here is adversative "but" (JM 172c; MNK 40.9 II.3; Aejmaleus, 200). The verb עָוְתָה from the preceding clause is elided here: "Vashti, the queen, transgressed not against the king alone but (she transgressed) against all the rulers and all the peoples."

1:17 כִּֽי־יֵצֵ֤א דְבַר־הַמַּלְכָּה֙ עַל־כָּל־הַנָּשִׁ֔ים לְהַבְז֥וֹת
בַּעְלֵיהֶ֖ן בְּעֵינֵיהֶ֑ן בְּאָמְרָ֗ם הַמֶּ֣לֶךְ אֲחַשְׁוֵר֡וֹשׁ אָמַ֞ר
לְהָבִ֨יא אֶת־וַשְׁתִּ֧י הַמַּלְכָּ֛ה לְפָנָ֖יו וְלֹא־בָֽאָה׃

The speech of Memukan, begun in v. 16, continues into v. 17. Memukan asserts that Vashti's wrongdoing will affect all men because the women of the kingdom will emulate Vashti and follow her disobedient example.

כִּֽי־יֵצֵ֤א דְבַר־הַמַּלְכָּה֙ עַל־כָּל־הַנָּשִׁ֔ים. *Yiqtol* 3ms Qal √יצא. This כי clause provides Memukan's motivation for what he asserted in v. 16 (on causal כי, see MNK 40.9 I.3; WO 38.4a). The verb יצא is bivalent, with a locative PP complement indicating either origin or destination (see also 1:19; 4:1, 6; 7:8; 8:15). If the locative origin is both obvious and semantically nonsalient, it may be left null (see 3:15; 5:9; 8:14). Here the locative complement is explicit in the PP על כל הנשים, which indicates the destination or goal of the action. The כי triggers verb-subject order, which obscures the semantics of the *yiqtol* verb—it may be realis ("it will go out") or an irrealis ("it shall/might go out"). If realis, Memukan expresses something he considers a future fact; if irrealis, he expresses a future potential. Given the exaggerated nature of Memukan's predication, we suggest that the verb should be read as realis and so contributes to the humor of Memukan's apocalyptic prediction. The noun דבר does not refer to any "word" of Vashti, since it is not narrowly what she said, but what she did (or, more accurately, did not do); thus, דבר here has the connotation of "deed" (as in, the concrete act of Vashti's disobedience) or "matter" (as in, the event in general).

לְהַבְז֥וֹת בַּעְלֵיהֶ֖ן בְּעֵינֵיהֶ֑ן. Inf constr Hiph √בזה. The Hiphil of בזה occurs only here in the Hebrew Bible. Since the Qal of בזה is bivalent, with either an NP complement (e.g., Gen 25:34) or ל-PP complement (e.g., 2 Sam 6:16), we expect the Hiphil to increase its valency by adding a second complement, i.e., "to cause X to despise Y" (cf. BDB s.v.). But here there is only one obvious complement, בעליהן, and the PP בעיניהן appears best understood as an adjunct of manner (בעיניהן denotes "with their eyes," but connotes "opinion, esteem" [DCH s.v. 2b]; see also 3:6). The trivalency of the verb is probably fulfilled by a null complement referring back to כל הנשים from the higher clause (cf. Paton, 155). The NP בעליהן refers to the women's "masters" or "husbands." The ל-PP/infinitive להבזות clause as a whole is an adjunct to יצא and "explains the circumstances of nature of a preceding action" (WO 36.2.3e, on the "gerundive" ל-infinitive).

בְּאָמְרָ֗ם הַמֶּ֤לֶךְ אֲחַשְׁוֵרוֹשׁ֙ אָמַ֞ר לְהָבִ֨יא אֶת־וַשְׁתִּ֧י הַמַּלְכָּ֛ה לְפָנָ֖יו וְלֹא־בָֽאָה. Inf constr Qal √אמר, *qatal* 3ms Qal √אמר, and *qatal* 3fs Qal √בוא. The ב-PP/infinitive clause is an adjunct to the preceding infinitive, להבזות, and explains the circumstances for the women hearing about Vashti's action, which will provoke the hearers (the women) to despise their husbands. We might expect the women to be the subject of the infinitive, passing the news on to each other and citing it as the excuse for their attitudes toward their husbands. However, if this were the case there would be no reason to shift from the 3fp clitic pronoun, which was just used on the two preceding words, to the 3mp clitic pronoun ם-, which is what occurs on the infinitive אמר. The pronoun shift suggests that the null subject of the infinitive is impersonal, i.e., that it is not the married women who are saying this, but various people who are relaying the report to the women (contra Keil, 330; Paton, 155, 159; and Fox 2001:274). This seems supported by the next verse, which addresses the married women passing the news on to their husbands. The subject-verb order of the main clause in the direct speech, המלך אחשורוש אמר reflects the basic word order of BH (see Holmstedt 2005; 2009; 2011). Not only is there no initial element (e.g., כי, אשר, or a modal verb) to trigger verb-subject order, there is also no discernible pragmatic marking on the subject NP המלך for Topic or Focus. Additionally, typological studies suggest that the environment of direct speech is a more likely context for basic word order examples, since narrative tends to be more syntactically complex (Holmstedt 2005:135–37). The ל-PP/infinitive clause להביא את ושתי המלכה לפניו is the indirect speech complement of the אמר—it is what Ahashverosh ordered to happen (on אמר with the connotation of "order," see comment on v. 10). Note the morphology and word stress of the verb בָּֽאָה. The *qatal* 3fs is morphologically identical to the fs participle, but the two differ in the placement of the word stress: the *qatal* has word stress on the first (penultimate) syllable and the participle has it on the last (ultimate) syllable. The stress distinction between these two forms is one of the few times in BH that stress is phonemic.

1:18 וְהַיּ֨וֹם הַזֶּ֜ה תֹּאמַ֣רְנָה ׀ שָׂר֣וֹת פָּֽרַס־וּמָדַ֗י אֲשֶׁ֤ר
שָֽׁמְעוּ֙ אֶת־דְּבַ֣ר הַמַּלְכָּ֔ה לְכֹ֖ל שָׂרֵ֣י הַמֶּ֑לֶךְ וּכְדַ֖י
בִּזָּי֥וֹן וָקָֽצֶף׃

Memukan's apocalyptic prediction about the effect of Vashti's disobedience continues in v. 18.

וְהַיּ֨וֹם הַזֶּ֜ה תֹּאמַ֣רְנָה ׀ שָׂר֣וֹת פָּֽרַס־וּמָדַ֗י אֲשֶׁ֤ר שָֽׁמְעוּ֙ אֶת־דְּבַ֣ר הַמַּלְכָּ֔ה לְכֹ֖ל שָׂרֵ֣י הַמֶּ֑לֶךְ. *Yiqtol* 3fp Qal √אמר and *qatal* 3mp Qal √שמע. The NP הַיּוֹם הַזֶּה, "this day," is a Topic-fronted scene-setting temporal adjunct. The fronted adjunct triggers verb-subject order, with the verb תאמרנה preceding the subject שׂרות פרס ומדי. The verb is either a realis *yiqtol* "they will say" or an irrealis *yiqtol* "they might/shall say," corresponding to how we understand יֵצֵא in v. 17 (see comment on v. 17). The noun שָׂרוֹת is the plural of שָׂרָה, which means "princess," "noblewoman," or "lady" and is the feminine version of שַׂר. The אשׁר clause is typically taken as a relative clause modifying שָׂרוֹת, i.e., the ladies ... who heard. If so, it is likely a nonrestrictive relative that does not define the women but simply keeps Vashti's deed and its effects front and center. But the relative clause seems redundant, and it leaves the verb אמר without a complement. Most commentators and translators fill in the clause with a null complement referring back to the reported speech of v. 17, "the princesses ... are saying this to all the princes" (Fox 2001:275, emphasis added). Instead, we suggest that the אשׁר clause is the complement of אמר (cf. Gordis, 46; Paton, 156; Clines 1984b:281–82; contra Bush, 351; on אשׁר introducing a speech complement, see Miller 1996:97–98). In this way, the verse makes a new assertion, that the ladies have picked up on the implications of Vashti's disobedience. If so, then there is a tension heightening general-to-specific movement in vv. 17-18, with כל הנשׁים the issue in v. 17 and the more narrow (and more disturbing to the king and his court!) שָׂרוֹת the issue in v. 18. On את־דבר המלכה, see comment on v. 17. The ל-PP at the end of the clause is an adjunct designating כל שׂרי המלך as the speech recipient for the verb אמר (see comment on v. 10 above).

וּכְדַ֖י בִּזָּי֥וֹן וָקָֽצֶף. The word כדי is the combination of the preposition כ and the noun דַּי "sufficiency" (HALOT s.v.; BDB s.v.; DCH s.v.). די is typically bound to a clitic host, with the bound form די, and means "sufficiency of" or "enough of." Here the free form, which is used only here, in Mal 3:10, and in 2 Chr 30:3, indicates that, at least according to the Masoretes, כדי is the copular complement of a null copula clause, with the compound NP בזיון וקצף the subject: "and contempt and wrath (will be) according to sufficiency." In other words, Memukan is saying that there will be "more than enough" contempt toward men as a result of Vashti's actions. The noun בזיון is from the root בזה and is a *qatalān*-pattern noun (JM 88Mb). The noun קצף "anger, wrath" is a *qitl*-pattern segholate noun (cf. with clitic pronoun, קִצְפִּי "my wrath"; see JM 88Ch on the *qitl*-pattern). The vocalization here (קָצֶף), with the *qameṣ* in the first syllable, indicates that the form is "pausal," which may (and here, does) result in a vowel change from the "contextual" form (GKC 29; JM 32; Revell 1980).

1:19 אִם־עַל־הַמֶּ֣לֶךְ ט֗וֹב יֵצֵ֤א דְבַר־מַלְכוּת֙ מִלְּפָנָ֔יו
וְיִכָּתֵ֛ב בְּדָתֵ֥י פָֽרַס־וּמָדַ֖י וְלֹ֣א יַעֲב֑וֹר אֲשֶׁ֨ר לֹֽא־
תָב֜וֹא וַשְׁתִּ֗י לִפְנֵי֙ הַמֶּ֣לֶךְ אֲחַשְׁוֵר֔וֹשׁ וּמַלְכוּתָהּ֙ יִתֵּ֣ן
הַמֶּ֔לֶךְ לִרְעוּתָ֖הּ הַטּוֹבָ֥ה מִמֶּֽנָּה׃

As a solution to the plight that the men of the kingdom now imagine themselves in, Memukan suggests that Vashti be punished. Specifically, she should no longer be allowed to enter before the king (the very thing she refused to do, thus fitting the punishment to the crime); moreover, she should be stripped of her royal position as queen, and her position should be given to someone else.

אִם־עַל־הַמֶּ֣לֶךְ ט֗וֹב. A null copula clause, with a null subject (which cataphorically refers forward to the content of Memukan's proposal), and the adjective טוב as the copular complement. Note that טוב could be parsed as either a ms adjective ("good") or a *qatal* 3ms Qal √טוב. The PP על המלך is an adjunct to the copula and is Focus-fronted. This deferential idiom occurs only in Esther (see also 3:9; 5:4, 8; 7:3; 8:5; 9:13), Chronicles (1 Chr 13:2), and Ezra-Nehemiah (Neh 2:5, 7; cf. Bergey 1983:156). Elsewhere, the more common idiom טוב בעיני־X is used: with אם, see 1 Kgs 21:2; Jer 40:4; 42:6; Zech 11:12; in a nonconditional context with the adjective טוב, see Gen 16:6; 19:8; 20:15; Num 24:1; 36:6; Deut 6:18; Judg 10:15; 19:24; 1 Sam 1:23; 3:18; 11:10; 14:36, 40; 29:6, 9; 2 Sam 3:19; 10:12; 15:26; 19:19, 28, 38, 39; 24:22; 1 Kgs 21:2; 2 Kgs 10:5; 20:3; Isa 38:3; Jer 40:4; Zech 11:12; Mal 2:17; Prov 3:4; Esth 3:11; 8:5, 8; 1 Chr 19:13; 21:23; with the verb יטב, see Gen 34:18; 41:37; 45:16; Lev 10:19, 20; Deut 1:23; Josh 22:30, 33; 1 Sam 18:5; 24:5; 2 Sam 3:36; 18:4; 1 Kgs 3:10; Esth 1:21; 2:4 (2×), 9. Significantly, in the verbal construction there is often the overt subject דבר (see below in v. 21: וייטב הדבר בעיני המלך). Our analysis for this verse follows this basic pattern. The null subject does not function as a dummy or expletive pronoun (like English *there* and *it*) that is used simply to fulfill a requirement for a syntactic subject but has no referential value. Indeed, BH does not use dummy pronouns. Rather, whether דבר or a null subject is used in this idiom, it refers either backwards or forwards to an item in the discourse world, or in many cases, an assertion or proposal (as here, referring forward to the next clause). It is also important to note that replacing בעיני with על appears to be a uniquely LBH phenomenon (cf. Bergey).

יֵצֵא דְבַר־מַלְכוּת מִלְּפָנָיו. *Yiqtol* (irrealis) 3ms √יצא. Following the conditional אם, the irrealis semantics of the main verb apodosis are clear: "if X occurs, then Y shall occur." On the valency of יצא, see comment on v. 17. The form of יצא represents the morphology of I-ו/י prefix verbs, which use the *yaqtil* pattern (JM 41e, 75c; Blau, 221–22): **yayṣiʾ* > **yêṣiʾ* > *yêṣéʾ*. Both the fronted subordinate conditional protasis (אם על המלך טוב) and the irrealis of יצא trigger verb-subject order. On the semantics of the bound relationship in דבר מלכות, see 1:2. The doubly compound preposition מלפניו consists of the preposition מן and the already complex preposition לפני, resulting in "from before" (WO 11.3). Here מלפני indicates the presence of the king as the *origin* of movement, rather than the *destination* that would be signaled by לפני alone.

וְיִכָּתֵב בְּדָתֵי פָרַס־וּמָדַי. *Yiqtol* (irrealis) 3ms Niph √כתב. The Qal of כתב is bivalent, taking an NP subject and an NP complement. The Niphal is the simple passive and so reflects a valency decrease, in which the NP complement of the Qal becomes the subject of the Niphal. The subject is the אשר nominalized clause (see next comment). The ב-PP is an adjunct to כתב, which often has such an adjunct indicating the location or item in which something is written.

וְלֹא יַעֲבוֹר. *Yiqtol* (irrealis) 3ms Qal √עבר. This clause is a parenthesis, signaled by the switch in semantics (Niphal to Qal, positive to negative) and the fact that it interrupts the syntax of the surrounding clause. Qal עבר is often bivalent—when the complement is an NP, the meaning is either "pass by X" or "transgress X" and when the complement is a locative PP, the meaning is "pass by/through/under, etc." (DCH s.v.; HALOT s.v.). But the verb also appears with monovalency, which refers to the subject "passing by" or "passing away" (DCH s.v. Qal 2h). It is the latter meaning that fits this context. While the subject of the monovalent עבר is null, it makes best sense if understood as the proposed law. The parenthesis thus affirms the immutable status of the law. On the use of irrealis *yiqtol* versus irrealis *qatal*, see "Verbal Semantics" in the Introduction.

אֲשֶׁר לֹא־תָבוֹא וַשְׁתִּי לִפְנֵי הַמֶּלֶךְ אֲחַשְׁוֵרוֹשׁ. *Yiqtol* 3fs Qal √בוא. Both the אשר and the negative לא trigger the verb-subject order. The subject of the bivalent motion verb בוא is the NP ושתי and the complement is the locative PP לפני המלך אחשורוש. This אשר clause functions syntactically as the subject of יכתב, and thus provides more specific content for דבר המלכות in the preceding clause. It provides the content of

דבר by specifying what event or action Memukan suggests be made into law—that Vashti would be banned from the royal court. Although the epithet המלכה appears without the PN ושתי in vv. 16 and 18, with no apparent difference from the phrase ושתי המלכה, the use of ושתי *without* the title המלכה here is literarily significant. In vv. 9, 11, 12, 15, 16 and 17 the term המלכה is used with ושתי and in vv. 17 and 18 המלכה is used alone but refers to Vashti. However, beginning in v. 19 ושתי is never again paired with המלכה (cf. 2:1, 4, and 17), signaling that Vashti is being deposed from her royal position (cf. Moore 1971:11; Fox 2001:22).

וּמַלְכוּתָהּ֙ יִתֵּ֣ן הַמֶּ֔לֶךְ לִרְעוּתָ֖הּ הַטּוֹבָ֥ה מִמֶּֽנָּה. *Yiqtol* (jussive semantics) 3ms Qal √נתן. This clause continues the content of Memukan's proposal and, as such, is the second, conjoined half of the compound clause nominalized by the אשר (so also Bush, 351). The NP complement מלכותה is fronted for Topic and signals a shift from Vashti to her status, though it also maintains continuity by virtue of the 3fs clitic pronoun. The fronted Topic NP triggers the verb-subject word order. The verb נתן is trivalent, with an NP complement (indicating the thing given, here מלכותה) and a ל-PP complement (indicating the recipient, here לרעותה הטובה ממנה). The word רעות, "fellow (female), (female) neighbor, (female) companion" (DCH s.v.; cf. HALOT s.v.), does not imply that Vashti's successor had to be her friend or live next to her, or even be someone she knew. Rather, it refers to someone within the same group or of the same social status (Paton, 157). רעות specifies that the chosen woman must be of the appropriate qualities and status to qualify to be a queen, hence our translation "someone like her." A phrase like הטובה ממנָה is typically understood as an attributive adjective, with the ה matching the definite status of the רעות, which is definite due to the clitic pronoun. However, the addition of the comparative PP ממנה, which syntactically relates to טובה, strongly suggests that the more accurate syntactic analysis of this type of construction is ה-relative clause, with a null subject, null copula, and the adjectives as the copula complement: lit. "her-fellow who (she) (is) good more-than-her."

1:20 וְנִשְׁמַע֩ פִּתְגָ֨ם הַמֶּ֤לֶךְ אֲשֶׁר־יַעֲשֶׂה֙ בְּכָל־מַלְכוּת֔וֹ כִּ֥י
רַבָּ֖ה הִ֑יא וְכָל־הַנָּשִׁ֗ים יִתְּנ֤וּ יְקָר֙ לְבַעְלֵיהֶ֔ן לְמִגָּד֖וֹל
וְעַד־קָטָֽן׃

Along with punishing Vashti, Memukan proposes that the news of this punishment be proclaimed throughout the entire kingdom. By making an example of Vashti, Memukan hopes to forestall the imagined empire-wide disobedience of women.

וְנִשְׁמַע פִּתְגָם הַמֶּלֶךְ אֲשֶׁר־יַעֲשֶׂה בְּכָל־מַלְכוּתוֹ. *Qatal* (irrealis) 3ms Niph√שמע. The use of an irrealis verb triggers verb-subject word order. The overt subject is פתגם המלך and the ב-PP בכל מלכותו is a locative adjunct to the verb נשמע. In contrast to v. 19, where the *yiqtol* verbs יִכָּתֵב and יֵצֵא are used with jussive semantics, here an irrealis *qatal* is used. The irrealis *qatal* signals a contingency relationship (continuing the sense of the previous verbs; Cook 2012:250; cf. Bush, 351), whereas neither the irrealis *yiqtol* nor jussive explicitly signals contingency. The noun פתגם ("decision" or "announcement") is borrowed from Persian. It may have entered Hebrew *via* Aramaic (HALOT s.v.; Moore 1971:11). Alternatively, it may reflect the author's conscious use of a Persian word for stylistic reasons, to contribute to the Persian ambiance of the story (see "Externally Motivated Change: Borrowing," "Salient Lexical Features," and the "Conclusion" in the Introduction). The relative clause אשר יעשׂה modifies פתגם and, though it may seem superfluous, it is perhaps intended to affirm that the king himself will issue the report.

כִּי רַבָּה הִיא. This clause is a parenthesis (so also Paton, 158). כי here does not provide temporal or causal information relating to the main verb נשמע, but relates directly to the preceding quantified NP כל מלכותו. That is, the כי clause grounds the inclusion of the word "all" in the preceding phrase—the author says "in *all* his kingdom" instead of "in his kingdom" *because* the kingdom is so large that it must be specified that the whole kingdom is in view here. Or the כי clause may reflect "incidental courtly flattery" (Fox 2001:23; cf. Keil, 332). Within the כי clause, the 3fs pronoun is the overt subject, the copula is null, and the copular complement is the adjective רבה. The word order reflects the Focus-fronting of the complement and signals that Memukan is contrasting his view of the kingdom with other potential views (i.e., it is a normal size, it is small). For similar word order, see טוֹבַת מַרְאֶה הִיא in v. 11.

וְכָל־הַנָּשִׁים יִתְּנוּ יְקָר. *Yiqtol* 3mp Qal √נתן. The verb is masculine, although the subject כל הנשים is feminine (cf. Moore 1971:11). See v. 19 on the valency of נתן. On the meaning of יקר ("honor") see comment on v. 4. The subject-verb order reflects the basic word order of the indicative clause, that is, we interpret here a shift from the jussive modality to the future result that is the goal.

לְמִגָּדוֹל וְעַד־קָטָן. On the expression and the compound preposition, see comment on v. 5. The PP is an NP-internal modifier: it modifies בעליהן not the verb. Rather than indicating some quality of the action of "giving honor," the NP-internal PP delimits the scope of the NP it modifies. In this case, the scope is quite broad, covering husbands from all social classes.

1:21 וַיִּיטַב֙ הַדָּבָ֔ר בְּעֵינֵ֥י הַמֶּ֖לֶךְ וְהַשָּׂרִ֑ים וַיַּ֥עַשׂ הַמֶּ֖לֶךְ כִּדְבַ֥ר מְמוּכָֽן׃

As is the case elsewhere in Esther (2:2-4; 3:8-11), the king is portrayed as taking the first advice offered to him by others (here Memukan), rather than deciding on a plan of action for himself.

וַיִּיטַב֙ הַדָּבָ֔ר בְּעֵינֵ֥י הַמֶּ֖לֶךְ וְהַשָּׂרִ֑ים. *Wayyiqtol* 3ms Qal √יטב. The quote beginning in v. 16 ends at the end of v. 20, returning to the narrator's voice and the narrative past *wayyiqtol* in this verse. On expressions involving something being "good" (either the adjective טוֹב or the verb יטב) "in the eyes of" (בעיני) someone, see comment on v. 19 and 3:6. The expression essentially means "they liked what he said." The noun דבר in this and the next clause has the connotation of "plan, advice."

וַיַּ֥עַשׂ הַמֶּ֖לֶךְ כִּדְבַ֥ר מְמוּכָֽן. *Wayyiqtol* 3ms Qal √עשׂה. Here the verb עשׂה has the meaning "to act, behave" (on the various meanings of עשׂה, see comment on v. 3). On the use of עשׂה with a כ-PP complement, see comment on v. 8. The use of the approximating כ (WO 11.2.9b and ex. 2) signals that what was actually done followed the essential outlines of Memukan's proposal.

1:22 וַיִּשְׁלַ֤ח סְפָרִים֙ אֶל־כָּל־מְדִינ֣וֹת הַמֶּ֔לֶךְ אֶל־מְדִינָ֤ה וּמְדִינָה֙ כִּכְתָבָ֔הּ וְאֶל־עַ֥ם וָעָ֖ם כִּלְשׁוֹנ֑וֹ לִֽהְי֤וֹת כָּל־אִישׁ֙ שֹׂרֵ֣ר בְּבֵית֔וֹ וּמְדַבֵּ֖ר כִּלְשׁ֥וֹן עַמּֽוֹ׃

Chapter 1 closes with the dissemination of documents containing the decree concerning Vashti to the whole kingdom. The decree establishes the authority of men within their households. The problem identified by Memukan—that women everywhere may act up like Vashti—is thus addressed. And yet, significant elements of the story, such as the lack of a queen, remain unresolved and are left for the next episode to address.

וַיִּשְׁלַח סְפָרִים אֶל־כָּל־מְדִינוֹת הַמֶּלֶךְ. *Wayyiqtol* 3ms Qal √שׁלח. The verb שׁלח, when it has the sense of "to send" (rather than "to stretch out"; cf. HALOT s.v.; BDB s.v.; DCH s.v.), is trivalent, with a subject (here null), an NP complement indicating the item sent (here ספרים), and a locative PP complement for the place to which the sending is directed (here אל כל מדינות המלך). A ספר is "something written" (HALOT s.v.), whether a scroll, letter, or just a document in general (as here). It is implied that these are official documents containing the new law and its implementation (i.e., the selection of a new queen). סֵפֶר is a *qitl*-pattern segholate noun (cf. JM 88C a*, h); the original *i* vowel is preserved in, for example, the form of the noun with a 1cs clitic pronoun: סִפְרִי.

אֶל־מְדִינָה וּמְדִינָה כִּכְתָבָהּ וְאֶל־עַם וָעָם כִּלְשׁוֹנוֹ. If these two אל-PPs were alone, they would be appositive to the preceding אל-PP, אל כל מדינות המלך. However, the presence of ככתבה and כלשונו complicate the syntax. Clearly the אל-PPs relate syntactically to the action of sending, but so do the כ-PPs. And yet each כ-PP also relates in some way to only the preceding אל-PP; i.e., ככתבה only relates to אל מדינה ומדינה, and כלשונו only relates to אל עם ועם. For this to happen, we must interpret these two pairs as constituents in two reduced adjunct clauses from which the verb, subject, and first complement are elided. In each אל-PP, the repetition of a noun appositively after itself, e.g., מדינה ומדינה, is a strategy for indicating distribution, diversity, or emphasis (WO 7.2.3); both cases of apposition are used for distribution.

לִהְיוֹת כָּל־אִישׁ שֹׂרֵר בְּבֵיתוֹ וּמְדַבֵּר כִּלְשׁוֹן עַמּוֹ. Inf constr Qal √היה, participle ms Qal √שׂרר and participle ms Piel √דבר. The ל-PP/infinitive clause is an adjunct to main verb וישלח and provides the purpose of the activity. Although it is often the case with ל-PP/infinitives that the subject is null, here it is overt, כל איש. The copular complement consists of the two participles, שׂרר and מדבר, conjoined to create a compound complement. The verb שׂרר, "to rule, reign" (HALOT s.v.; cf. BDB s.v.; DCH s.v.) is related to the nouns שׂר and שׂרה. Although the verbal examples are sparse, it appears that Qal שׂרר can be either monovalent (Isa 32:1) or bivalent. If bivalent, it takes an על-PP complement (Judg 9:22) or ב-PP complement (as here, with בביתו). The Piel דבר is also often bivalent, though the complement is typically an infinitive clause; the PP indicating the addressee is an adjunct. In this clause there is neither an adjunct indicating the speech recipient nor an infinitive complement, indicating that the verb is monovalent. The כ-PP is an adjunct indicating the manner of speaking. Why specify a manner of speaking as part of the purpose of sending the letters? The point may be about authority: if a family resulted from intermarriage, the *man's* language, not the *woman's*, should be spoken by the entire family (Keil, 332; Paton, 161–62; Fox 2001:23; Bush, 352; Levenson, 52; cf. Neh 13:23-24). Thus, the purpose of the sending of the documents is (A) that every man would rule in his house, and (B) that every man would have authority in his house specifically in the matter of which language is spoken.

Episode 2—Esther is Chosen as Queen (2:1-23)

Together with chapter 1, which it mirrors (see introduction to Part I), chapter 2 serves as an introduction to the main story in chapters 3 and following.

§1: Ahashverosh Seeks a Replacement for Vashti (2:1-4)

Chapter 2, beginning after the king's anger has subsided, recounts the way in which the problem of Vashti's removal from queenship is remedied.

[1]After these things, when the wrath of King Ahashverosh abated, he remembered Vashti and what she did and what had been decreed concerning her. [2]And the king's courtiers who attended him said, "Let them seek for the king young ladies, virgins who are good-looking. [3]And let the king appoint overseers in all the provinces of his kingdom. Let them gather every young lady, any virgin that is good looking, to Susa, the citadel, to the harem, into the authority of Hegai, the eunuch of the king, who keeps the women, providing the application of their cosmetics. [4]And let the young lady who will please the king rule instead of Vashti." And the word was pleasing to the king, and he did thus.

2:1 אַחַר֙ הַדְּבָרִ֣ים הָאֵ֔לֶּה כְּשֹׁ֕ךְ חֲמַ֖ת הַמֶּ֣לֶךְ
אֲחַשְׁוֵר֑וֹשׁ זָכַ֤ר אֶת־וַשְׁתִּי֙ וְאֵ֣ת אֲשֶׁר־עָשָׂ֔תָה וְאֵ֥ת
אֲשֶׁר־נִגְזַ֖ר עָלֶֽיהָ׃

After the king calms down, he realizes that his decree has implications for the court that will require action.

אַחַר֙ הַדְּבָרִ֣ים הָאֵ֔לֶּה כְּשֹׁ֕ךְ חֲמַ֖ת הַמֶּ֣לֶךְ אֲחַשְׁוֵר֑וֹשׁ. Inf constr Qal √שׁכך. The temporal אחר-PP (see also 3:1) and the כ-PP/infinitive clause are both fronted adjuncts to the main verb זכר. The fronted adjuncts are scene-setting Topics (Holmstedt 2009:126–29). The verb שׁכך "to subside, lessen" (HALOT s.v.; cf. BDB s.v.) is found only here and in 7:10, Gen 8:1, Num 17:20 (where it is in the Hiphil), and Jer 5:26. Within the infinitive clause, the NP חמת המלך אחשושרוש is the subject of the monovalent verb שׁך.

הַמֶּ֣לֶךְ אֲחַשְׁוֵר֑וֹשׁ. See comment on 1:2.

זָכַ֤ר אֶת־וַשְׁתִּי֙ וְאֵ֣ת אֲשֶׁר־עָשָׂ֔תָה וְאֵ֥ת אֲשֶׁר־נִגְזַ֖ר עָלֶֽיהָ. *Qatal* 3ms Qal √זכר, *qatal* 3fs Qal √עשׂה, and *qatal* 3ms Niph √גזר. The verb זכר is bivalent, requiring a subject (here a null subject) and one NP complement, which is here a compound NP consisting of three conjoined items all introduced by את: the NP ושתי and two null constituents that are each defined by a restrictive אשר relative clause. Note the pausal form עָשָׂתָה (the contextual, nonpausal form is עָשְׂתָה, with a vocal *sheva* in the second syllable). Although pausal forms often occur with disjunctive accents (as here), they do not always, and thus they possibly testify to "patterns of formation of speech units" in earlier than the Masoretic system of accentuation (Revell 1980:176). The Qal of גזר is bivalent and primarily means "to cut (something)" or "to divide (something)," though by extension it connotes an act of deciding or decreeing (BDB s.v.; HALOT s.v.; DCH s.v.). The Niphal, "(something) is cut, divided," reflects a decrease in valency, wherein the complement of the bivalent active Qal becomes the subject of the passive monovalent Niphal (see "Valency" in the Introduction). According to BDB (גזר Qal 6) and Paton (166), the meaning "decree" for גזר is an Aramaism (cf. Jastrow גְּזַר). The collocation גזר על appears only here in the Bible but occurs 11× in the Mishnah (Maʿaś. Š. 5:13; Roš Haš. 2:9; Taʿan. 1:5, 6 [2×]; 2:9; 3:6 [2×]; 4:6; Soṭah 9:14 [2×]); see Bergey 1983:109–10 and Appendix B. The על-PP is an adjunct to the passive verb and either signals the entity about whom the decision concerns (i.e., "what had been decreed *concerning* her") or the entity to whose advantage or disadvantage the action is taken (i.e., "what had been decreed *against* her"; WO 11.2.13c). In the context (i.e., for Ahashverosh's purposes) the difference between these two options is negligible and the result is the same: he lacks a queen.

2:2 וַיֹּאמְרוּ נַעֲרֵי־הַמֶּלֶךְ מְשָׁרְתָיו יְבַקְשׁוּ לַמֶּלֶךְ נְעָרוֹת בְּתוּלוֹת טוֹבוֹת מַרְאֶה׃

The king's courtiers suggest that the king's problem (his lack of a queen) be remedied by a kingdom-wide search. This verse echoes the story of David and Abishag the Shunammite in 1 Kgs 1:1-4, where David's servants suggest יְבַקְשׁוּ ... נַעֲרָה בְתוּלָה ("let them seek a young lady") for the king (cf. Fox 2001:28; Levenson, 54).

וַיֹּאמְרוּ נַעֲרֵי־הַמֶּלֶךְ מְשָׁרְתָיו. *Wayyiqtol* 3mp Qal √אמר and participle mp Piel √שׁרת with 3ms clitic pronoun. The eunuchs of the king appear in 1:10, where they seem to be officials assigned to deal specifically with the king's women. Additionally, the king's highest officials or "cabinet" appear in 1:14. Here in 2:2, the נערים appear—who are they? The uses of נַעַר fall into three general categories: (1) boy; (2) young man; (3) servant (HALOT s.v.; DCH s.v.). Here the third category is more likely in view and the age-related nature of the first two categories irrelevant. The more general designation עֶבֶד appears in 1:3 and 2:18, but here the נערים may refer to a narrower group of servants, the king's courtiers. The participle phrase משרתיו modifies the NP נערי המלך in an unmarked relative clause: "servants ... (who) attended him"; compare the relative participle שׁרת in 1:10.

יְבַקְשׁוּ לַמֶּלֶךְ נְעָרוֹת. *Yiqtol* (jussive semantics) 3mp Piel √בקשׁ. Note the absence of the dagesh in the ק even though its presence is a characteristic of Piel morphology (see comment on ויהי in 1:1). The Piel בקשׁ is a bivalent verb, taking a subject (here null) and an NP complement (here נערות בתולות טובות מראה). The PP למלך is an adjunct indicating the person who benefits from the action (the so-called *dativus commodi*; JM 133d; WO 11.2.10d). This clause is a classic example of a null subject clause in which the null subject is not picking up on a referent identifiable and available in the discourse but rather is unspecified and thus an arbitrary agent (i.e., a generic), similar to English "someone" or generic "them," as in "let them find a beautiful wife for the king" (Paton, 166). This and similar occurrences are often translated as passives, e.g., "let young ladies be sought" (Moore 1971:17; Bush, 357; cf. WO 22.7a; Fox 2001:282), but this poorly reflects the Hebrew grammar and is an accommodation to English literary conventions.

נְעָרוֹת בְּתוּלוֹת טוֹבוֹת מַרְאֶה. The NP בתולות modifies the NP נערות as an appositive that provides an attribute of the נערות—it indicates that these maids must have the quality of virginity (see comments on apposition in 1:6, 10). The NP בתולות is in turn modified by the complex adjectival phrase טֹובֹת מראה, in which the adjective טֹובֹות is bound to the clitic host מראה, "good of appearance." The phrase טובות מראה echoes כי־טובת מראה היא in 1:11 and signals that the search for the new queen centers around the attribute that Vashti possessed and was asked to exhibit publicly: great beauty.

2:3 וְיַפְקֵ֨ד הַמֶּ֣לֶךְ פְּקִידִים֮ בְּכָל־מְדִינ֣וֹת מַלְכוּתוֹ֒
וְיִקְבְּצ֣וּ אֶת־כָּל־נַעֲרָֽה־בְ֠תוּלָה טוֹבַ֨ת מַרְאֶ֜ה אֶל־
שׁוּשַׁ֤ן הַבִּירָה֙ אֶל־בֵּ֣ית הַנָּשִׁ֔ים אֶל־יַ֥ד הֵגֶ֛א סְרִ֥יס
הַמֶּ֖לֶךְ שֹׁמֵ֣ר הַנָּשִׁ֑ים וְנָת֖וֹן תַּמְרוּקֵיהֶֽן׃

The courtier suggests that the search for the new queen extend to all the provinces of the kingdom, with contestants gathered to the king's harem in Susa.

וְיַפְקֵ֨ד הַמֶּ֣לֶךְ פְּקִידִים֮ בְּכָל־מְדִינ֣וֹת מַלְכוּתוֹ֒. Jussive (form and semantics) 3ms Hiph √פקד. Note the "short" *ṣere* /ē/ vowel that characterizes the jussive and *wayyiqtol* forms of the Hiphil, in contrast to the "long" *ḥiriq-yod* /ī/ of the same form of the *yiqtol* (JM 45b, 54a; see also Holmstedt 2000). Modality, whether associated with a jussive or an irrealis *yiqtol* or *qatal*, inverts the basic subject-verb word order to verb-subject. The Qal פקד is notoriously difficult to reduce to a central lexical value (HALOT s.v.; DCH s.v.); contextually פקד appears to mean "visit," "observe," "register," "assign," "punish," "muster," "deposit," and "care"! The verb is mostly bivalent, but can also be trivalent when it means "to visit sins upon somebody" (e.g., Exod 20:5) or "to appoint someone to something" (e.g., Gen 40:4; Num 4:27; Deut 20:9; Jer 49:19 par. 50:44). The semantics of the Hiphil are more consistently trivalent and are limited to the semantic range of "appoint, assign X to Y" with an על-PP complement ("to appoint X over Y") or, as here, a ב-PP complement. The noun פָּקִיד is derived from the same root and means "overseer" (HALOT s.v.; see also DCH s.v.; BDB s.v.). Here it describes those who have been appointed to a temporary position and who are tasked to find eligible נערות in the kingdom.

וְיִקְבְּצ֣וּ אֶת־כָּל־נַעֲרָֽה־בְ֠תוּלָה טוֹבַ֨ת מַרְאֶ֜ה אֶל־שׁוּשַׁ֤ן הַבִּירָה֙. *Yiqtol* (jussive semantics) 3mp Qal √קבץ. The subject of יקבצו is null and is either the unspecified and arbitrary "someone," or is now assumed to be the פקידים appointed in the previous clause. The latter analysis makes better sense to us. The verb קבץ in the Qal is bivalent with a subject and NP complement. The PP אל־שושן הבירה is an adjunct indicating the location or goal of the gathering activity. Though the form of the verb יקבצו is ambiguous—it could be a realis *yiqtol* or a jussive—the fact that it follows the unambiguously jussive יפקד in the preceding clause and both are part of the same speech act strongly suggests that both should be read as jussives. On verbal sequences and semantics, see Cook 2012:312–37 and 319 table 4.5.

נַעֲרָה־בְתוּלָה טוֹבַת מַרְאֶה. On the syntax of this NP, see the similar phrase in v. 2.

אֶל־שׁוּשַׁן הַבִּירָה אֶל־בֵּית הַנָּשִׁים אֶל־יַד הֵגֶא . The first אל-PP is the adjunct to the verb יקבצו and the following two PPs are successively embedded appositives, with אל בית הנשים appositive to אל שׁושן and אל יד הגא appositive to אל בית הנשים. Each appositive serves to specify further the reference of the location identified by the PP it modifies: the location is successively narrowed from the citadel to the harem to the control of a specific administrator. On שׁושן הבירה as "Susa, the citadel," see comment on 1:2.

בֵּית הַנָּשִׁים. This phrase is used only in chapter 2 (vv. 3, 9, 11, 13, 14). It refers either to a physical structure where the king's wives and concubines were housed—i.e., the harem (Bush, 357)—or more generally to the whole institution: the structure, the women, and the administration of it all (see Moore 1971:18). Since the physical structure makes better sense when the phrase is used again in 2:11, we understand it similarly here.

אֶל־יַד הֵגֶא סְרִיס הַמֶּלֶךְ שֹׁמֵר הַנָּשִׁים. A null copula and participle ms Qal √שׁמר. The phrase אל יד is idiomatic for placing someone or something under the authority or control of the person specified (for other metaphorical uses of יד in Esther, see 1:7, 12; 2:21). The name of the eunuch in charge of the women is spelled differently here than elsewhere: here it is הֵגֶא, whereas in vv. 8 (2×) and 15 it is spelled הֵגַי (or הֵגָי in pause). However, it must be the same person, since in v. 8 young ladies (and Esther) are said to be gathered (קבץ) "to Susa, the citadel, to the hand of Hegai" (אל־שושן הבירה אל־יד הגי; cf. Moore 1971:15; Bush, 358; Levenson, 53). The PN הגא is followed by stacked nonrestrictive modifiers, first the appositive NP סריס המלך and then the participial relative clause שֹׁמֵר הַנָּשִׁים. The verb שׁמר means "to keep, watch, preserve, protect" (HALOT s.v.; DCH s.v.; BDB s.v.); here the sense is that Hegai has charge over the women and is responsible for them (Keil, 334). The semantics of the participle שׁמר within the null copula relative clause is progressive; with a specific subject, הגא, and a kind-referring activity, שׁמר, the result is a habitual statement: Hegai keeps the women (on gnomic and habitual statements as generics and their manifestation in BH, see Cook 2005 and "Verbal Semantics" in the Introduction).

וְנָת֖וֹן תַּמְרוּקֵיהֶֽן. Inf abs Qal √נָתוֹן. The verb נתן is often trivalent, "to give X to Y," though appears also to have a bivalent use, "provide X," in which the second, recipient complement is not explicit. An adverbial function, often associated with "intensification," is typically ascribed to the infinitive absolute when used with a finite verb of the same root (WO 35.2.1a); the specific nature of the intensification is open-ended and is contextually determined, e.g., "really, quickly, eventually, harshly." It may be more accurate, however, to associate such infinitives absolute with overt Focus marking on the verb (Galia Hatav, private communication). Another significant use of the infinitive is as a TAM-underspecified verb in an adjunct clause providing attendant circumstances (see WO 35.2.2a–c). In most cases, the infinitive inherits TAM semantics from the preceding finite verb; in this case, the TAM is set by the preceding null copula of the participial relative with שׁמר, "who keeps the women, providing the application of their cosmetics." This use of the infinitive absolute occurs elsewhere in Esther (3:13; 6:9; 9:6, 16 [3×], 17 [2×]). On the place of this feature in a diachronic analysis of the Hebrew of Esther, see Appendix B. The noun תַּמְרוּק is a *taqtul*-pattern noun (JM 88Lu) from the root מרק, "to polish" (DCH s.v.; BDB s.v.). Since the "majority of nouns with ת-preformative are verbal substantives or action nouns" (JM 88Lo), the derived noun תַּמְרוּק means "polishing," which has been taken to connote here either bathing or cosmetics application (cf. HALOT s.v.; DCH s.v.; Moore 1971:18; Bush, 358).

2:4 וְהַֽנַּעֲרָ֗ה אֲשֶׁ֤ר תִּיטַב֙ בְּעֵינֵ֣י הַמֶּ֔לֶךְ תִּמְלֹ֖ךְ תַּ֣חַת
וַשְׁתִּ֑י וַיִּיטַ֧ב הַדָּבָ֛ר בְּעֵינֵ֥י הַמֶּ֖לֶךְ וַיַּ֥עַשׂ כֵּֽן׃

Verse 4 describes the king's approval of the courtier's plan and the subsequent move to enact the plan.

וְהַנַּעֲרָה ... תִּמְלֹךְ תַּחַת וַשְׁתִּי. *Yiqtol* (jussive semantics) 3fs Qal √מלך. Here מלך is monovalent, meaning "to rule" (cf. comment on 1:1) and the תחת-PP is an adjunct. Though the verb is morphologically ambiguous and could be a realis *yiqtol*, it is the third verb in a sequence within the same speech act beginning with the unambiguously jussive יפקד (v. 3). The lengthy subject is fronted for Focus, thereby establishing a membership set including all the young women that the king interviews and contrasting the one woman that pleases the king—*only the one who pleases you* let become queen.

אֲשֶׁר תִּיטַב בְּעֵינֵי הַמֶּלֶךְ. *Yiqtol* 3fs Qal √יטב. The *yiqtol* תיטב defaults to a future temporal frame within relative clauses (see "Verbal Semantics" in the Introduction). On the idiom "to be good in the eyes of" (יטב בעיני), see comments on 1:19, 1:21; see also 3:6 and 5:4.

וַיִּיטַב הַדָּבָר בְּעֵינֵי הַמֶּלֶךְ. *Wayyiqtol* 3ms Qal √יטב. The *wayyiqtol* signals the end of the direct speech and the return to the past tense narrative voice. Whereas in the preceding clause, a "young lady" is said to be "good in the eyes of" (or "pleasing to") the king, here הדבר—i.e., the direct speech of the king's servants immediately preceding this—is pleasing to the king (i.e., "he thought it was a good idea"; cf. Moore 1971:18–19); cf. the parallel in 1:21.

וַיַּעַשׂ כֵּן. *Wayyiqtol* 3ms Qal √עשׂה. Note the "short" form of the *wayyiqtol* for the III-ה verb (see JM 47c). The Qal עשׂה is mostly bivalent and here takes the deictic adverb כן as its complement (see also 6:10; 7:5). The deictic adverb points back to הדבר that pleased him. Note the parallels in this verse with 1:21, both of which show the king's response to advice given to him:

Esther 1:21	כִּדְבַר מְמוּכָן	וַיַּעַשׂ הַמֶּלֶךְ	וַיִּיטַב הַדָּבָר בְּעֵינֵי הַמֶּלֶךְ וְהַשָּׂרִים
Esther 2:4	כֵּן	וַיַּעַשׂ	וַיִּיטַב הַדָּבָר בְּעֵינֵי הַמֶּלֶךְ

The narrator presents the king as a puppet, a character who mostly follows the advice or designs of others.

§2: Esther Wins the King's Favor (2:5-20)

[5]A Jewish man was in Susa the citadel. His name was Mordecai, son of Ya'ir, son of Shimi, son of Qish, a Benjaminite, [6]who was taken into exile from Jerusalem with the exiles who were taken into exile with Jeconiah, the king of Judah, whom Nebuchadnezzar, the king of Babylon, took into exile. [7]And he was foster-fathering Hadassah (she was Esther, the daughter of his

uncle), because she didn't have any parents. The young lady was shapely and good-looking. After the death of her father and her mother, Mordecai took her to himself as a daughter. 8And so it was, when the word of the king and his law were heard, and when many young ladies were gathered to Susa, the citadel, to the authority of Hegai, Esther was taken to the palace of the king, to the authority of Hegai, who kept the women. 9And the young lady was pleasing to him, and she received kindness before him. And he hastened to give her her cosmetics-application and her portions, and to give her the seven ladies who were chosen from the palace of the king. And he transferred her and her ladies to the best of the house of women. 10Esther did not declare her people or her kindred, because Mordecai commanded her that she should not declare (them). 11Every day Mordecai would walk about before the court of the house of women, in order to know how Esther was doing and what would happen with her. 12When the turn of each young lady arrived to come to King Ahashverosh, at the end of her twelve months (spent) according to the law of women (because the days of their cleansings were fulfilled this way: six months were with the oil of myrrh, and six months were with spices and with the cleansings of women), 13at this (time), the young lady would go to the king. All that she asked was given to her to come with her from the house of women to the palace of the king. 14In the evening she would enter and in the morning she would return to the second house of women, to the authority of Sha'ashgaz, the eunuch of the king, who kept the concubines. She would not come again to the king except if the king delighted in her and she was called by name. 15When the turn of Esther, the daughter of Abihail, the uncle of Mordecai (who took [her] to himself as a daughter), arrived to come to the king, she did not seek a thing except what Hegai, the eunuch of the king, who kept the women, would say. And Esther continually received favor in the eyes of all who saw her. 16And Esther was taken to King Ahashverosh, to his royal palace, in the tenth month—it is the month of Tebet—in the seventh year of his kingdom. 17And the king loved Esther more than all the other women, and she received favor and kindness before him more than all the other virgins. And he placed the royal turban on her head and caused her to rule instead of Vashti. 18Then the king prepared a great banquet, the banquet of Esther, for all his rulers and his servants. And he made a provincial rest and he gave a gift according to the power of the king. 19When virgins were gathered a second time, Mordecai was sitting in the gate of the king. 20Esther did not declare her clan or her people, just as Mordecai commanded her, that is, Esther did what Mordecai said, just as she had been in (her) upbringing with him.

2:5 אִ֣ישׁ יְהוּדִ֔י הָיָ֖ה בְּשׁוּשַׁ֣ן הַבִּירָ֑ה וּשְׁמ֣וֹ מָרְדֳּכַ֗י בֶּ֣ן
יָאִ֧יר בֶּן־שִׁמְעִ֛י בֶּן־קִ֖ישׁ אִ֥ישׁ יְמִינִֽי׃

In vv. 5-7, the events of the narrative are paused while we are introduced to the next pair of main characters: Mordecai, a critical supporting character (v. 5) and Esther, the protagonist (v. 7).

אִ֣ישׁ יְהוּדִ֔י הָיָ֖ה בְּשׁוּשַׁ֣ן הַבִּירָ֑ה. *Qatal* 3ms Qal √היה. The lexical copula היה is nearly always bivalent (few cases of the monovalent existential היה occur in the Hebrew Bible and most of them are in Gen 1). Here the subject is the NP איש יהודי and the complement is the PP בשושן הבירה. The avoidance of the *wayyiqtol* by using the *qatal* fulfills a number of narrative functions: it signals a scene change (away from the king's concerns, at least until v. 8) and the introduction of a new character to the narrative (Mordecai). The main narrative progression does not resume until the discourse ויהי in v. 8. The gentilic noun (or, demonym) יהודי is in apposition to איש and qualifies it attributively (see comment on המלך אחשורוש in 1:2), thus, "a man, *being* a Yehudi." Note that English treats gentilics as adjectives, hence the typical translation "a Jewish man." The gentilic noun יהודי "Judean, Jew" (HALOT s.v.) could refer to someone of the kingdom of Judah (2 Kgs 16:6) or, as in this case, someone from the Persian province of Yahud.

וּשְׁמ֣וֹ מָרְדֳּכַ֗י בֶּ֣ן יָאִ֧יר בֶּן־שִׁמְעִ֛י בֶּן־קִ֖ישׁ אִ֥ישׁ יְמִינִֽי. A null copula clause, with the NP שמו as the subject and the PN מרדכי ("Mordecai") as the copular complement. The name מרדכי is the Hebrew rendering of Babylonian *mardukā*, which contains the theophoric element relating to the Babylonian god Marduk (HALOT s.v.; Moore 1971:19; Yamauchi, 106; Fox 2001:30). The phrase בן יאיר בן שמעי בן קיש איש ימיני contains four appositives, with בן יאיר appositional to מרדכי, בן שמעי appositional to יאיר (not בן יאיר), בן קיש appositive to שמעי, and איש ימיני appositive to קיש. Qish may or may not be intended to refer to the father of Saul; regardless, the mention of Qish here serves to evoke Saul and so to connect Haman to Saul and his conflict with Agag (see comments on 3:1, 2). On the appositional syntax of the gentilic ימיני, see comment above on איש יהודי.

2:6 אֲשֶׁ֤ר הָגְלָה֙ מִיר֣וּשָׁלַ֔יִם עִם־הַגֹּלָה֙ אֲשֶׁ֣ר הָגְלְתָ֔ה
עִ֖ם יְכָנְיָ֣ה מֶֽלֶךְ־יְהוּדָ֑ה אֲשֶׁ֣ר הֶגְלָ֔ה נְבוּכַדְנֶאצַּ֖ר
מֶ֥לֶךְ בָּבֶֽל׃

Verse 6 continues to describe the back-story of Mordecai: he was descended from a man deported to Babylon with Jeconiah.

אֲשֶׁר הָגְלָה מִירוּשָׁלַיִם עִם־הַגֹּלָה. *Qatal* 3ms Hoph √גלה. The verb גלה in the Qal means "to uncover" and "to leave," and by a narrow extension "to go into exile"; the Hiphil relates specifically to this last meaning by referring narrowly to the action of deporting, and the Hophal is simply the passive "be deported." The מן and עם-PPs are both adjuncts to the passive Hophal verb. The grammatical crux in this verse involves the identification of the head of the אשר relative clause. All things being equal, the closest viable antecedent is normally the head of a relative clause in Hebrew (Holmstedt 2002:23, 105). However, discourse connections (e.g., anaphora) can and do override the closest antecedent principle. The question here is thus: who went into exile? Was it Mordecai, the noun standing at the front of this long phrase begun in v. 5, or Qish, the closest available and appropriate potential head? For the various arguments for each option, including discussion regarding the identity of Qish (i.e., was this Saul's father or simply Mordecai's great-grandfather who also had that name?), we suggest consulting the standard commentaries. We take the head of the relative clause to be קיש and the tribal designation "Benjaminite" sufficient for the narrative's play on Mordecai's and Haman's descent. The word "Jerusalem" is usually spelled יְרוּשָׁלַםִ, without the י between ל and ם. This instance is one of the few cases where it is spelled with two י, including one just before the ם (also Jer 26:18; 1 Chr 3:5; 2 Chr 25:1; 32:9; JM 16f; cf. WO 7.3d). See also the *Qere-Ketiv* in 4:7. The noun גּוֹלָה (or גֹּלָה as it is spelled here) is derived from the verbal root גלה and refers to the group of people that has been taken into exile: "the deported, exiles," "deportation, exile" (HALOT s.v.), "one who goes into exile," "diaspora" (DCH גלה Qal 2b, c), "exiles, exile" (BDB s.v.).

אֲשֶׁר הָגְלְתָה עִם יְכָנְיָה מֶלֶךְ־יְהוּדָה. *Qatal* 3fs Hoph √גלה. The fs NP גֹּלָה is the clear head of this relative clause, signaled by the gender agreement between the fs NP and the 3fs verb הגלתה. As with the previous occurrence of the Hophal גלה, the verb is monovalent with an עם-PP adjunct.

אֲשֶׁר הֶגְלָה נְבוּכַדְנֶאצַּר מֶלֶךְ בָּבֶל. *Qatal* 3ms Hiph √גלה. Unlike the previous relative, there is some ambiguity concerning the head of this relative clause. Using the principle that "unless context suggests otherwise, a modifier is associated with the closest appropriate antecedent" (see comment on v. 5), we take the nearest NP, יכניה מלך יהודה, to be the relative head. Whereas in the previous two relative clauses, the head was also the subject within the relative, in this case the head functions as the complement of the Hiphil verb within the relative (the nonrelative syntax would be נבוכדנאצר מלך בבל הגלה יכניה מלך יהודה, "Nebuchadnezzar, the king of Babylon, exiled *Jeconiah*"). Note the prefix vowel in the Hiphil הֶגְלָה—although the reasons are not clear, it is common to find *seghol* instead of the paradigmatic *ḥireq* (see JM 54c, 79q). The NP נבוכדנאצר מלך בבל (as well as the syntactically similar יכניה מלך יהודה earlier in this verse) contains an appositive modifier: "Nebuchadnezzar, the king of Babylon." This structure is the same as that used frequently for Vashti in chapter 1 and always for Esther throughout the book (cf. comment on 1:2). Whereas "Vashti, the queen" has the article with "queen," מלך here has no article because it is bound to the proper noun בבל, and therefore inherits its semantic definiteness. Here, the name Nebuchadnezzar is spelled with נ in the second-to-last syllable; in Jeremiah and Ezekiel, the Akkadian pronunciation *Nabû-kudurri-uṣur* is often more accurately reflected by the spelling נְבוּכַדְרֶאצַּר, with ר in the second-to-last syllable. The spelling with נ (either נְבוּכַדְנֶאצַּר or נְבֻכַדְנֶאצַּר) is found in 2 Kings, Jeremiah (8×), Daniel, Chronicles, and Ezra-Nehemiah. The spelling with ר is found in Jeremiah (29×) and Ezekiel.

2:7 וַיְהִ֨י אֹמֵ֜ן אֶת־הֲדַסָּ֗ה הִ֤יא אֶסְתֵּר֙ בַּת־דֹּד֔וֹ כִּ֛י אֵ֥ין לָ֖הּ אָ֣ב וָאֵ֑ם וְהַנַּעֲרָ֤ה יְפַת־תֹּ֙אַר֙ וְטוֹבַ֣ת מַרְאֶ֔ה וּבְמ֤וֹת אָבִ֙יהָ֙ וְאִמָּ֔הּ לְקָחָ֧הּ מָרְדֳּכַ֛י ל֖וֹ לְבַֽת׃

In v. 7 we are finally introduced to the protagonist, Esther. Her backstory includes adoption by her relative Mordecai after the death of her parents, and, of crucial importance to the story, the narrator specifically mentions her beauty.

וַיְהִ֨י אֹמֵ֜ן אֶת־הֲדַסָּה. *Wayyiqtol* 3ms Qal √היה. The participial phrase אמן את הדסה is the complement to the copula היה, with a null subject (contextually identifiable as Mordecai). The verb אמן usually means "to support," but can mean, as it does here, "to foster" (DCH אמן II), i.e., "to act as a foster-father" or "to nurse" (act as a foster-mother) (BDB s.v.), here with the sense of acting as "guardian" (HALOT אמן II; cf. Num 11:12; Isa 49:23; and Ruth 4:16; cf. Moore 1971:20). Later in this verse we read that Mordecai took Esther into his care "as a daughter."

Though it has been suggested that the name הדסה is a Hebrew version of Akkadian *ḫadaššatu* "bride," which is an epithet of the goddess Ishtar (see below on the name אסתר), it is more plausibly derived from the masculine noun הֲדַס "myrtle" (HALOT s.v.; Moore 1971:20; Fox 2001:275; Bush, 363).

הִיא אֶסְתֵּר בַּת־דֹּדוֹ. A null copula clause with subject הִיא and NP complement. As in 1:1 and 3:7, here a pronoun introduces a parenthetical clause. Note that it is the nature of parenthetical clauses to provide information that makes critical connections for the audience; here, the parenthesis clarifies that the הדסה introduced is the very same as אסתר (who is presumably well known to the audience). The attributive appositive בת דדו modifies אסתר: "Esther, the daughter of his uncle." It is syntactically possible to take בת דדו as an appositive to הדסה, but the accentuation and proximity suggests otherwise. The name אסתר may derive either from the Babylonian divine name *Ištar* or from the Persian noun *stāra* "star" (HALOT s.v.; Keil, 336; Moore 1971:20; Fox 2001:30; Bush, 363; Levenson, 58). The noun דוד can mean "beloved" (as in Song of Solomon) or "paternal uncle" (i.e., father's brother) (BDB s.v.; HALOT s.v.). BDB mentions the possibility that this second meaning could be broader, connoting any sort of relative. If דוד means specifically "father's brother," then Esther is Mordecai's cousin (בת־דדו), which is how most commentators have understood the text (Keil, 336; Paton, 170; Moore 1971:26; Fox 2001:30; Bush, 363; Levenson, 58). The probability that Mordecai is Esther's cousin, along with a reading of vv. 5-6 so that it has Mordecai as part of the deportation from Judah, has been used to argue that the book of Esther is not historical, since Esther would then have been entirely too old to seduce King Ahashverosh. But given the syntactic ambiguity of the relative clauses in v. 6, it is possible that Mordecai himself was not part of the deportation but three generations removed from that event. The point is that Mordecai's age cannot be determined. Even within the world of the narrative, he may have been around the same age as Esther, acting as a father figure in spite of his age, or he may have been considerably older than Esther. To inquire into Mordecai's age in order to correlate the book with historical reconstruction is to misidentify the genre (or, at least, misunderstand its conventions) and so impose upon it inappropriate expectations.

כִּי אֵין לָהּ אָב וָאֵם. An אין copula clause with subject אב ואם and ל-PP complement. A copula with ל-PP indicates possession (cf. comment on 1:9). The subordinate כי clause grounds the action or event of the main clause (יהי אמן) by providing the reason why Mordecai was acting as a foster-father to Esther. The אין functions as a negative copula, negating the possessive predication between the subject אב ואם and the complement לה. In copular clauses the expected word order is subject-copula-complement (see "Word Order" in the Introduction). Here, the copula-complement-subject order most likely reflects the Focus-fronting of the predicate (the copula and complement together). The compound subject אב ואם is one conceptual unit, i.e., "parents"; that the two nouns operate as a word pair is indicated by the *qameṣ* (the lengthened *ā*) under the conjunction ו (see comment on בהט ושש in 1:6).

וְהַנַּעֲרָה יְפַת־תֹּאַר וְטוֹבַת מַרְאֶה. A null copula clause with subject הנערה and a compound adjective phrase complement. The etymology of תאר is uncertain (HALOT s.v.); if the noun is derived from תאר, "to change direction" (HALOT s.v.), it may refer to the "outline" or "form" of something (see BDB s.v). The word is always used to describe the "appearance" of something, whether good or bad (HALOT s.v.). טובת מראה, "beautiful of appearance," is how the eligible young women—and Vashti—are described in 1:11, 2:2, and 2:3. The point seems to be that based on her appearance alone (and perhaps the point being made that queens were chosen primarily for their looks), Esther is an ideal candidate. Other women described with this phrase in the Hebrew Bible are Rebecca (Gen 24:16 and 26:7) and Bathsheba (2 Sam 11:3).

וּבְמוֹת אָבִיהָ וְאִמָּהּ לְקָחָהּ מָרְדֳּכַי לוֹ לְבַת. *Qatal* 3ms Qal √לקח with 3fs clitic pronoun. The ב-PP is a Topic-fronted scene-setting (temporal) adjunct. It describes an event that occurred before the action specified by the main verb לקחה: Esther's parents die, and then Mordecai takes her as his daughter (i.e., the two actions do not occur at the same time; see comment on 1:4). Note the compound clitic host, אביה ואמה, for the bound noun מות (the free form is מָוֶת). On the form of the conjunction וּ, see comment on וּמֵאָה in v. 1. The verb לקח is bivalent with an NP complement indicating the thing taken. The NP complement in this clause is represented by the 3fs pronominal clitic, which refers back to Esther. The ב temporal phrase causes inversion to verb-subject order. Note that, since the complement is attached to the verb as a clitic pronoun, it raises with the verb over the subject. Light PPs like לו (i.e., PPs with pronominal clitic complements) often attach themselves syntactically to the verb in the same manner and thus follow the verb and stand between the verb and subject (Holmstedt 2010:63; see, e.g., חפץ בה in 2:14, and צוה לו in 3:2). The PP לו in this clause has not attached itself to the verb, because the clitic pronoun has already done so, effectively blocking the raising of לו. The ל-PP indicates possession (cf. comment on 1:9, and comment above on אין לה), specifically meaning "into his care" or "into his family/household."

לְבַת. According to the Septuagint, Mordecai did not take Esther "as a daughter," but "as a wife" (εἰς γυναῖκα). Because of this (and the evidence of several ancient interpreters), it may be that לקחה מרדכי לו originally lacked לבת and was intended to suggest a marriage (or future betrothed) relationship (cf. Levenson, 58; Fox 2001:275–76). It is more likely, however, that the Septuagint's εἰς γυναῖκα reflect a misreading of בת as ב(י)ת, "house," which in early rabbinic Judaism was a euphemism for "wife" (the same interpretive move was apparently made by the Talmudic tractate B. Meg. 13A; see Fox 2001:276; Paton, 171). Whatever Mordecai's intentions might have been, if Esther had actually been married or formally betrothed, it would likely have removed her from eligibility for the king's search (Moore 1971:20–21). Moreover, according to Bush, the Hebrew phrase לקח ... לבת "to take (someone) as a daughter" is a calque of the Babylonian phrase *ana mārūtim legū* "to take for son/daughter," used to connote legal adoption (364).

2:8 וַיְהִ֗י בְּהִשָּׁמַ֤ע דְּבַר־הַמֶּ֙לֶךְ֙ וְדָת֔וֹ וּֽבְהִקָּבֵ֛ץ נְעָר֥וֹת
רַבּ֛וֹת אֶל־שׁוּשַׁ֥ן הַבִּירָ֖ה אֶל־יַ֣ד הֵגָ֑י וַתִּלָּקַ֤ח אֶסְתֵּר֙
אֶל־בֵּ֣ית הַמֶּ֔לֶךְ אֶל־יַ֥ד הֵגַ֖י שֹׁמֵ֥ר הַנָּשִֽׁים׃

Now that Esther and Mordecai have been introduced, the narrative resumes, recounting that Esther is among the contestants to become the new queen.

וַיְהִי. *Wayyiqtol* 3ms Qal √היה. With this *wayyiqtol* the narrative is resumed (Moore 1971:21). On the nature of the discourse ויהי, see comment on 1:1 (see also 3:4; 5:1, 2).

בְּהִשָּׁמַע דְּבַר־הַמֶּלֶךְ וְדָתוֹ. Inf constr Niph √שמע. The ב-PP/infinitive clause בהשמע דבר המלך ודתו consists of the Niphal passive verb and a compound subject דְּבַר־הַמֶּלֶךְ וְדָתוֹ ("the word of the king and his law"). It is the first of two Topic-fronted temporal scene-setting phrases that are adjuncts to the main verb, ותלקח.

וּבְהִקָּבֵץ נְעָרוֹת רַבּוֹת אֶל־שׁוּשַׁן הַבִּירָה אֶל־יַד הֵגָי. Inf constr Niph √קבץ. A second temporal ב-PP/infinitive clause is conjoined to the first by a ו. Such conjoined temporal clauses may present sequential actions/event or simultaneous actions/events and the only clear determinative is the sense of the passage. Here in v. 8, the action of the second infinitival clause occurs *after* the action of the first infinitival clause (the word of the king first goes out, and then young ladies are gathered). Niphal קבץ is monovalent (the אל-PP is not a complement to the verb, but an adjunct; see comment on v. 3). The NP נערות רבות is the subject of the passive verb. The second אל-PP, אל יד הגי, is in apposition to the first, אל שושן הבירה; see comment on v. 3. This verse restates much of v. 3 (Moore 1971:21), but as a fact of what happened rather than a proposal for what should happen. Young ladies (נערות) are gathered (הקבץ) to Susa the citadel (אל שושַׁן הבירה), specifically, to the authority of Hegai (אל יד הגי), who has charge over the king's women (שמר הנשים). On the expression אל יד הגי, see comment on v. 3.

וַתִּלָּקַח אֶסְתֵּר אֶל־בֵּית הַמֶּלֶךְ אֶל־יַד הֵגַי שֹׁמֵר הַנָּשִׁים. *Wayyiqtol* 3fs Niph √לקח. The *wayyiqtol* initiates the main clause. The fact that two temporal adjunct phrases (the PP/infinitive clauses) precede the *wayyiqtol* provides further evidence that one of the primary functions of the ו is as a phrase edge marker (i.e., it does not start a new main clause here, but marks the edge of the phrase that includes the primary predication). The fronting of the two temporal infinitives (בְּהִשָּׁמַע ... וּבְהִקָּבֵץ ...) has triggered verb-subject order (ותלקח אסתר), as does the very nature of the *wayyiqtol* itself (see Holmstedt 2009; 2011). The two אל-PPs are in apposition; see last paragraph and comment on v. 3. Niphal לקח is monovalent, with a locative/goal PP adjunct (אל יד הגי שמר הנשים). "The house of the king" (בית המלך) here seems to be synonymous with בית הנשים ("the house of women") in v. 3, referring to a house belonging to the king that is for the women's use. Alternatively, בית המלך here may carry its typical meaning, referring more generally to the king's palace (the larger property on which the בית הנשים is located). On the expression שמר הנשים, see comment on v. 3.

2:9 וַתִּיטַב הַנַּעֲרָה בְעֵינָיו וַתִּשָּׂא חֶסֶד לְפָנָיו וַיְבַהֵל
אֶת־תַּמְרוּקֶיהָ וְאֶת־מָנוֹתֶהָ לָתֵת לָהּ וְאֵת שֶׁבַע
הַנְּעָרוֹת הָרְאֻיוֹת לָתֶת־לָהּ מִבֵּית הַמֶּלֶךְ וַיְשַׁנֶּהָ
וְאֶת־נַעֲרוֹתֶיהָ לְטוֹב בֵּית הַנָּשִׁים׃

Esther charms Hegai and wins his favor, which results in preferential treatment for Esther.

וַתִּיטַ֨ב הַנַּעֲרָ֣ה בְעֵינָיו֮. *Wayyiqtol* 3fs Qal √יטב. On the expression יטב בעיני "was pleasing," see comments on 1:19, 1:21, 2:4, and 3:6. It is not immediately clear to whom the 3ms pronominal clitic in בעיניו refers. The larger context, specifically the statement in v. 4 that the king is seeking a pleasing young lady, might suggest to the reader that Esther has already pleased the king in v. 9. This development would occur too early in the narrative, though, and as the reader continues it becomes clear that Hegai is the referent of ו in בעיניו. Interestingly, in the Alpha Text, which testifies to a Hebrew source that may preserve an earlier version of the story (see "The Alpha Text of Esther" in the Introduction), the content from MT's vv. 9-17 is significantly abbreviated, such that Esther is said to go in to the king and impress him immediately after v. 9.

וַתִּשָּׂ֤א חֶ֙סֶד֙ לְפָנָיו֒. *Wayyiqtol* 3fs Qal √נשׂא. With prefix conjugations, the נ of I-נ roots (excepting those with a guttural second root; see JM 72b) is assimilated to the second radical; the resulting long or "doubled" consonant is represented by a *dageš*: **wayyinsāʾ* > *wayyissāʾ*. The verb נשׂא with complement חֵן and/or חֶסֶד is found only in Esther: here (נשׂא חסד לפני), in 2:15 (נשׂא חן בעיני), in 2:17 (נשׂא חן וחסד לפני), and in 5:2 (נשׂא חן בעיני). The idiom נשׂא חסד seems to be synonymous with מצא חן ("to find favor"; HALOT נשׂא Qal 1; BDB נשׂא Qal 3f; DCH נשׂא Qal 8; cf. Keil, 337), which is used often in the Hebrew Bible (e.g., Gen 6:8; Esth 5:8; 7:3; 8:5; see comment on 5:8). Moore suggests that "[נשׂא חן] is more active while [מצא חן] more passive in character" (1971:21; cf. Fox 2001:31; Bush, 364), which makes some contextual sense: נשׂא when the narrator speaks, emphasizing Esther as a heroine, and מצא when Esther speaks to the king, emphasizing her "dependence on the king's good will" (Moore 1971:21).

וַ֠יְבַהֵל אֶת־תַּמְרוּקֶ֨יהָ וְאֶת־מָנוֹתֶ֜הָ לָתֵ֣ת לָ֗הּ. *Wayyiqtol* 3ms Piel √בהל and inf constr Qal √נתן. The verb בהל in the Hebrew Bible typically has to do with "being frightened" (the Niphal passive) or "frightening" (the Piel active). In later biblical texts, the word takes on an additional Aramaic-influenced meaning (related to Arm. בהל in the Pael), "to be hasty" (Jastrow s.v.), i.e., "to hasten" (HALOT s.v.; BDB s.v.; DCH s.v.; cf. Paton, 177; Bergey 1983:111). In the Hebrew Bible, this verb takes an infinitive complement only here and in 6:14 (where it is in the Hiphil; for an extrabiblical example, see 4Q215 fr. 1 col. 3

line 5). The complement is a compound constituent consisting of two infinitive clauses, two separate occurrences of לתת. Notably, in both infinitive clauses the complement NP precedes the infinitive verb (את תמרוקיה ואת מנותה before the first לתת and את שׁבע הנערות הראיות before the second לתת; cf. 3:13). This word order is rare in BH but relatively common in later (including biblical) Aramaic (Keil, 337; Paton, 177; Moore 1971:22; cf. Rosenthal, 185; cf. Dan 2:9 and throughout). The pattern also occurs in the Hebrew documents from Qumran (Carmignac; cf. Qimron 1986 400.05), though this may reflect Aramaic influence. Alternatively, את תמרוקיה ואת מנותה and את שׁבע הנערות הראיות could be taken as a compound complement to finite verb בהל, with the two לתת infinitives as purpose clauses adjunct to בהל. However, in this unlikely scenario the compound complement would be split by an infinitive adjunct and the second occurrence of לתת לה would be redundant. On the meaning of תמרוק, see comment on v. 3.

לָתֵ֣ת לָ֔הּ. Inf constr Qal √נתן. The infinitive of נתן has lost both the first and last letters of its root. The first radical נ is dropped because it does not have a vowel (aphaeresis; JM 72c) and the third radical נ assimilates to the feminine morpheme *-t*, which is added "to reestablish the triliteralism (Barth's law of compensation)" (JM 72d). Long, or geminate, consonants in word-final position shorten (or "degeminate"; JM 18l), which accounts for the lack of the expected *dageš* in the ת to represent the assimilated נ. The derivation of the *i*-class verb is thus: **ntin* > **tin+t* > **titt* > **tit* > *tēt* (lengthening [or lowering] of *i* > *ē* in a stressed syllable). Finally, the vowel of the monosyllabic prepositions when added to a monosyllabic word is often a *qameṣ*, as here: *lā-tēt* לָתֵת. The verb נתן is trivalent, taking an NP complement (את תמרוקיה ואת מנותה) and a ל-PP (לה).

וְאֵת֙ שֶׁ֣בַע הַנְּעָר֔וֹת הָרְאֻי֥וֹת לָֽתֶת־לָ֖הּ מִבֵּ֣ית הַמֶּ֑לֶךְ. Inf constr Qal √נתן. The second infinitive clause complement to בהל has the same order as the first, with the infinitive's complement preceding the nonfinite verb (see comment above). The PP מבית המלך, "from the palace of the king," is a verbal adjunct specifying the location from which the seven ladies were given. It may be tempting to take the PP מבית המלך as a modifier of the NP שׁבע הנערות, "seven from-the-king's-house female attendants," i.e., "seven royal female attendants," but such "NP-internal" modifiers are regularly adjacent to the modified NP; here the distance between the NP and the PP suggests that the PP is more likely an adjunct to לתת that indicates the origin of the thing given. That these נערות came from the בית מלך indicates that they are of high quality (we may infer that the other contestants did not receive such special royal attendants; cf. Paton, 175). On the numeral syntax of שבע הנערות, in which the numeral שבע is bound to the quantified noun הנערות, see "Numeral Syntax in Esther" in the Introduction.

הַנְּעָרוֹת הָרְאֻיוֹת. Passive participle fp Qal √ראה. In the NP הנערות הראיות the plural noun הנערות is modified by a ה relative clause in which the subject is null, the verb is a null copula, and the verbal complement is the Qal passive participle ראיות, lit. "the ladies who (they) (were) chosen." This is the sole occurrence of ראה as a Qal passive participle in the Hebrew Bible, though it is used frequently in the Mishnah and other rabbinic literature (Keil, 337; Paton, 177). The verb in this instance is used in the sense of "seen" > "chosen, selected" (HALOT s.v., DCH s.v.) or "suitable" (BDB s.v.; cf. Bush, 364).

וַיְשַׁנֶּהָ וְאֶת־נַעֲרוֹתֶיהָ לְטוֹב בֵּית הַנָּשִׁים. *Wayyiqtol* 3ms Piel √שנה. Qal שנה can be monovalent or bivalent, meaning "to change" or "to change (something)"; the Piel is the causative of the bivalent Qal and means "(to cause) to change," "to alter," or "to transfer (in)to something" (HALOT s.v.; BDB s.v.; on the Piel *binyan* in general, see comment on 3:1). Note that when the clitic pronoun (here a 3fs complement pronoun) is attached, the ה of the III-ה root falls off (or "apocopates"). The verb takes a compound complement, the 3fs clitic pronoun attached to the verb and the NP את נערותיה. The verb שנה occurs in the Piel only eight times in the Hebrew Bible (1 Sam 21:14; Jer 2:36; 52:33; Ps 34:1; 89:35; Prov 31:5; Job 14:20; Esth 2:9) and the nuance in this verse is not immediately clear. There are at least four plausible analyses. First, שנה could mean "to transfer" (i.e., "to change [place or position]") and the sense of the clause could be that Hegai "transferred Esther and her attendants to the best place in the house of women" (Keil, 337; Paton, 175–78; Moore 1971:9; Fox 2001:30; Bush, 357; HALOT s.v.). Second, שנה could mean that Hegai "transformed" (i.e., "to change [quality or characteristic]") Esther and her attendants into the "best" of the harem, taking לטוב as a second complement PP indicating the new state or quality (WO 11.2.10, exx. 38–45; on superlative adjectives, see 14.5c). A third analysis takes שנה to have the sense of "to mark out, distinguish" (causative of Qal "to differ") as in rabbinic Hebrew (Ehrlich, 112); if so, the ל-PP must modify the verb as a purpose PP with superlative adjective—"he distinguished them as the best of the house of women"—though how Hegai could have agentively "distinguished" them as the "best" is not clear. Finally, the PP לטוב could be taken as a purpose infinitive with an adjunct NP: "he distinguished them so that they did well in the house of the king" (Levenson, 60). This is grammatically feasible, since טֹוב is the appropriate morphological form for the infinitive from the II-ו root; moreover, בית הנשים can function as an adverbial NP or represent the assimilation of the ב preposition to the word בית (see JM 133c). The only weakness of this fourth proposal is the lack of other cases where the Piel שנה takes an infinitival complement; however, with only eight occurrences of the Piel שנה, the lack of another infinitival complement could be coincidence. All things considered, we prefer the first option, although it is difficult to identify determinative features for any of the four.

2:10 לֹא־הִגִּ֣ידָה אֶסְתֵּ֔ר אֶת־עַמָּ֖הּ וְאֶת־מֽוֹלַדְתָּ֑הּ כִּ֧י
מָרְדֳּכַ֛י צִוָּ֥ה עָלֶ֖יהָ אֲשֶׁ֥ר לֹא־תַגִּֽיד׃

Verse 10 takes the reader out of narrative flow to relate a bit more backstory—Esther tells no one that she is Jewish, in accordance with Mordecai's instructions. This point is crucial, since it establishes Esther's anonymity in her dealings with the king and sets up the confrontation with Haman.

לֹא־הִגִּ֣ידָה אֶסְתֵּ֔ר אֶת־עַמָּ֖הּ וְאֶת־מֽוֹלַדְתָּ֑הּ. *Qatal* 3fs Hiph √נגד. The נ of the root has assimilated: **hingīdā* > *higgīdā* (cf. comment on ותשׂא in v. 9). The verb נגד always appears in the Hiphil and means "to declare (something)." It is bivalent—it requires both a subject and an NP complement, though a PP adjunct specifying the addressee is often present. The negation of the verb in this clause triggers inversion to verb-subject order. The word מולדת is a *maqtal*-pattern noun in the feminine. The וֹ vowel is the result of the assimilation and monophthongization (**aw* > **au* > ō) of the initial *a* vowel of the noun pattern and the original ו of the root *ולד. The segholate ending is the result of the consonantal cluster produced by the addition of the feminine ending -t and the subsequent loss of case vowels. Thus, the derivation is **mawlad-t* > **môladt* > *môlédet*. The noun can refer to one's line of descent or place of origin, one's relatives, or one's offspring or descendants (see HALOT s.v.; DCH s.v.). Here it refers to Esther's relatives and so overlaps with עמה "her clan, kin, people" (HALOT s.v.; see DCH עם I 3).

כִּ֧י מָרְדֳּכַ֛י צִוָּ֥ה עָלֶ֖יהָ אֲשֶׁ֥ר לֹֽא־תַגִּֽיד. *Qatal* 3ms Piel √צוה and *yiqtol* (irrealis) 3fs Hiph √נגד. Although כי triggers inversion to verb-subject order, here the Focus-fronting of מרדכי brings the subject back to a higher position than the verb, immediately after the כי. The Focus-fronting signals that it was *Mordecai's* (not Esther's) idea to hide her ethnicity (cf. v. 4) (cf. Moore 1971:22). The verb צוה only occurs in the Piel or Pual. It is typically a trivalent verb, with an enclitic pronoun or NP complement indicating *whom* is commanded and a second complement—an NP, infinitival clause (even a speech clause with לאמר), or a complement clause (introduced, e.g., by אשר)—for *what* is commanded. In some cases, as here, an על or אל-PP is used for the *whom* complement. Thus, in this clause the PP עליה is one complement, and the nominalized clause אשר לא תגיד is the second NP complement: "that she should not declare."

לֹֽא־תַגִּֽיד. *Yiqtol* (irrealis) 3fs Hiph √נגד. Hiphil נגד is bivalent and typically has an overt NP complement. In this clause, the NP complement is null and can be contextually reconstructed from the preceding clause as את עמה ואת מולדתה.

2:11 וּבְכָל־י֣וֹם וָי֔וֹם מָרְדֳּכַי֙ מִתְהַלֵּ֔ךְ לִפְנֵ֖י חֲצַ֣ר בֵּית־
הַנָּשִׁ֑ים לָדַ֙עַת֙ אֶת־שְׁל֣וֹם אֶסְתֵּ֔ר וּמַה־יֵּעָשֶׂ֖ה בָּֽהּ׃

The fact that Mordecai shows up outside the harem each day demonstrates his continued concern for her well-being.

וּבְכָל־י֣וֹם וָי֔וֹם מָרְדֳּכַי֙ מִתְהַלֵּ֔ךְ לִפְנֵ֖י חֲצַ֣ר בֵּית־הַנָּשִׁ֑ים. A null copula clause with its complement the Participle ms Hith √הלך. The Topic-fronting of the temporal adjunct PP בכל יום ויום is a common strategy for setting the scene of the main action or event of the clause. In contrast to the triggered inversion with finite verbs, fronting does not trigger inversion with null copulas. Thus, the word order of this clause—subject, null copula, complement (participle)—reflects the basic order in this clause reflects the basic order for copula (including participle) clauses. In the Hithpael, the verb הלך means "to walk about, go to and fro" and so, by extension, "to live, behave" (HALOT s.v., DCH s.v., BDB s.v.). Here the participle is used for habitual action, and the sense is that Mordecai was typically present at the entrance to the בית הנשים. The לפני-PP adjunct specifies the locale of the "walking about." The phrase כל יום ויום redundantly combines the quantified phrase כל יום "every day" with the semantically similar repetitive apposition יום ויום "day to day, daily." It is doubtful that there is any additional nuance for the overspecified כל יום ויום; rather, it may simply reflect a change in conventions (see Appendix B). On repetitive apposition, see comment on מדינה ומדינה in 1:22. A *qameṣ* is used under ו in יום ויום to indicate that the two nouns are a prosodic unit (see comment on 1:4). Semantically, the PP בכל יום ויום indicates that the action presented by the verb (null copula and participle) is habitual, i.e., it habitually (daily) occurred.

לָדַ֫עַת אֶת־שְׁל֣וֹם אֶסְתֵּ֔ר וּמַה־יֵּעָשֶׂ֖ה בָּֽהּ. Inf constr Qal √ידע and *yiqtol* 3ms Niph √עשׂה. As with I-נ verbs, the infinitive construct in I-ו/י roots reflects the aphaeresis ("taking away") of the initial root consonant and the subsequent addition of the ת. The result is a segholate structure, which in the case of the ידע with its guttural final consonant takes the *a-a* vowel pattern: דַּ֫עַת. On the form of the ל preposition and the reason for the ת suffix, see comment on לָתֵת in v. 9. The infinitival clause is a verbal adjunct specifying the purpose of the action denoted by the participle מִתְהַלֵּךְ: the infinitival clause gives the reason why Mordecai was spending his time at the gate of the house of women. The verb ידע is bivalent: here the subject is null (reconstructable as the subject of the higher clause, מרדכי) and the complement is a compound NP. In the compound complement, the first part is the NP את שׁלום אסתר and the second part a nominalized מה interrogative clause (this is also known as an "indirect question"; WO 18.2c). לדעת שׁלום of someone means to know about their well-being, i.e., "how they are doing" (cf. HALOT שָׁלוֹם; BDB שָׁלוֹם). Mordecai is at the gate because he wants to know how Esther is doing, if she is well, etc.

מַה־יֵּעָשֶׂ֖ה בָּֽהּ. *Yiqtol* 3ms Niph √עשׂה. Syntactically, the interrogative word מה represents both the subject of the passive (and thus monovalent) יעשׂה and the semantic patient. Transforming the clause into a bivalent Qal illustrates the full role of מה: "he (Hegai) did מה with her." In an added semantic twist, though, the verb עשׂה ("to be done" in the Niphal) is used throughout the book of Ecclesiastes as a semantically and syntactically agentless generic expression, "X happens" (see, e.g., Eccl 1:9; Fox 1999:175; Murphy 1992:11). Similarly, it may also mean "happen" here, as well as in 4:1. The PP בָּהּ is an adjunct to the passive verb and specifies more narrowly in what realm (here, to what *entity*) the action applies (WO 11.2.5e).

2:12 וּבְהַגִּ֡יעַ תֹּר֩ נַעֲרָ֨ה וְנַעֲרָ֜ה לָב֣וֹא ׀ אֶל־הַמֶּ֣לֶךְ
אֲחַשְׁוֵר֗וֹשׁ מִקֵּץ֙ הֱי֨וֹת לָ֜הּ כְּדָ֤ת הַנָּשִׁים֙ שְׁנֵ֣ים עָשָׂ֣ר
חֹ֔דֶשׁ כִּ֛י כֵּ֥ן יִמְלְא֖וּ יְמֵ֣י מְרוּקֵיהֶ֑ן שִׁשָּׁ֤ה חֳדָשִׁים֙
בְּשֶׁ֣מֶן הַמֹּ֔ר וְשִׁשָּׁ֤ה חֳדָשִׁים֙ בַּבְּשָׂמִ֔ים וּבְתַמְרוּקֵ֖י
הַנָּשִֽׁים׃

Verse 12 indicates the timing of each woman's visit to the king, as well as the ways in which each woman was beautified in preparation for her visit.

וּבְהַגִּ֡יעַ תֹּר֩ נַעֲרָ֨ה וְנַעֲרָ֜ה לָב֣וֹא ׀ אֶל־הַמֶּ֣לֶךְ אֲחַשְׁוֵר֗וֹשׁ. Inf constr Hiph √נגע, with the first נ of the root assimilated to the ג (see comment on vv. 9 and 10), and Qal inf constr Qal √בוא. The entire ב-PP/infinitive clause of the verse is a temporal adjunct to באה in v. 13. In the larger clause, it is a Topic-fronted scene-setting constituent. The Qal נגע is bivalent and typically means "to touch, strike (someone/thing), reach (something/where)." The Hiphil is either a trivalent causative, "cause (someone) to touch, reach (something/where)" (HALOT s.v.; DCH s.v.) or a bivalent (internal causative), "arrive (somewhere)," in which the patient is assumed and identical to the agent and the only overt complement is locative. Here the subject of הגיע is תר נערה ונערה and the complement is not a locative NP but a movement ל-PP/infinitive clause, לבוא אל המלך אחשורוש: "each girl's turn arrived to enter." On the use of repetitive apposition for distributive meaning in נערה ונערה, see the comment on 1:22.

תֹּר֩. Based largely on context, this noun must mean something like "turn": "when the turn of each young lady came up." The word is only used with this sense in Esther (here and in v. 15), in the Damascus Document (CD 14.11), and the Community Rule (1QS 6.11). The lexica do not explicitly connect this noun to the verbal root תור meaning "to seek out," but instead suggest that it is a primary noun (a basic pan-Semitic word); but the etymology is simply unclear. The context in Esther 2, CD 14, and 1QS reasonably establishes that the semantic range of the word centers around "a turn."

מִקֵּץ֙ הֱי֨וֹת לָ֜הּ כְּדָ֤ת הַנָּשִׁים֙ שְׁנֵ֣ים עָשָׂ֣ר חֹ֔דֶשׁ. Inf constr Qal √היה. The PP מקץ signals the terminus a quo ("the end from which") for the event in the higher clause (see JM 133e); i.e., "at the end of (מקץ) the twelve months" each young lady's time would arrive. The noun קץ,

which is the complement of the preposition מן, is itself the bound head of an infinitival clause clitic host. The subject within the copular infinitive clause is the temporal NP שנים עשׂר חדשׁ, the complement is the PP לה, and the PP כדת הנשׁים is a verbal adjunct: "twelve months existed/passed for her (= each girl) according to the law of women." With copulas, a ל-PP typically indicates possession, which is the case here. In the number phrase שנים עשׂר חדשׁ "twelve months," the noun חדשׁ is in apposition to the preceding numeral (for the options in numeral syntax, see "Numeral Syntax in Esther" in the Introduction). The normal word order with infinitival verbs is verb-subject, which appears both with full NP subjects or clitic subject pronouns. Here the order reflects the tendency for "lighter" constituents to precede "heavier" constituents, barring any other syntactic or pragmatic influences (see 1:5 on HNPS).

כִּ֣י כֵּ֤ן יִמְלְא֖וּ יְמֵ֣י מְרוּקֵיהֶ֑ן. *Yiqtol* 3mp Qal √מלא. Either כי or the Topic-fronted manner adjunct כן trigger the inversion to verb-subject order. Parallel to the narrative flow of chapter 1, chapter 2 is interrupted in the midst of the action with a parenthetical comment introduced by כי כן (see introduction to chap. 1 and comment on Esther 1:13). The NP ימי מרוקיהן is the subject of the monovalent Qal verb ימלאו (on the valency of מלא, see comment on 1:5). This is the only use of מרוקים in the Hebrew Bible (there is also one use in the Dead Sea Scrolls [1Q38], but there is too little context to clarify the meaning of the word). The meaning is the same or similar to תמרוק, which is formed from the same root, מרק "to cleanse." The context here strongly points toward an action noun, "cleansing," rather than a concrete noun referring to an instrument (i.e., something used in the process of cleansing); see comment on v. 3.

שִׁשָּׁ֤ה חֳדָשִׁים֙ בְּשֶׁ֣מֶן הַמֹּ֔ר וְשִׁשָּׁ֤ה חֳדָשִׁים֙ בַּבְּשָׂמִ֔ים וּבְתַמְרוּקֵ֖י הַנָּשִֽׁים. These two null copula clauses give the content of כן "thus" in the preceding clause; i.e., they describe *the way in which* the days of cleansing were fulfilled. Syntactically, both clauses are in apposition to כן. Both null copulas take a ב-PP complement and the subject of each is the temporal phrase specifying the number of months for each type of cleansing activity: "six months (was spent) with oil of myrrh" (contra Fox 2001:35 who sees the ב-PPs as indicating that the women were physically *in* the cleansing materials: "a chemical bath to which the maidens' bodies were subjected"). For the appositional syntax of ששׁה חדשׁים, see comment on 1:1.

2:13 וּבָזֶה֙ הַנַּעֲרָ֔ה בָּאָ֖ה אֶל־הַמֶּ֑לֶךְ אֵת֩ כָּל־אֲשֶׁ֨ר
תֹּאמַ֜ר יִנָּ֤תֵֽן לָהּ֙ לָב֣וֹא עִמָּ֔הּ מִבֵּ֥ית הַנָּשִׁ֖ים עַד־בֵּ֥ית
הַמֶּֽלֶךְ׃

Verse 13 relates that each contestant is allowed to bring things with her to the king, at her request. We are not told what sorts of things might be brought, but this is not the point—rather, the point is to set up the statement in v. 15, where Esther relies on Hegai's advice and takes nothing except what he suggests.

וּבָזֶה֙ הַנַּעֲרָ֔ה בָּאָ֖ה אֶל־הַמֶּ֑לֶךְ אֵת֩ כָּל־אֲשֶׁ֨ר תֹּאמַ֜ר יִנָּ֤תֵֽן לָהּ֙. Participle ms Qal √בוא, *yiqtol* (irrealis) 3fs Qal √אמר and *yiqtol* (irrealis) 3ms Niph √נתן. The adjunct PP בזה recapitulates the temporal clauses (בהגיע ... מקץ ...) of v. 12 (so Paton, 179, 180–81; Moore 1971:23; contra Bush, 365). The fronted temporal phrases are separated from the main clause by the כי כן parenthesis and the בזה is a processing strategy used to signal clearly that the nonparenthetical syntax has been resumed. Syntactically, בזה is in apposition to the entire בהגיע clause in v. 12. The Masoretic accent on the final syllable of באה indicates that they understood this ambiguous morphological form to be a participle (rather than the 3fs *qatal*). The participle is the complement of a null copula, which is the main verb of the entire complex clause. The semantics of the clause are not habitual here (as they are in v. 11), but generic (see "Verbal Semantics"in the Introduction and Cook 2005:118–19, 133; 2012:213–15, 222). Habitual statements require identifiable subjects (such as Mordecai in v. 11), whereas generic statements take generic subjects (such as "each young lady" here). That is, the generic reading of the predication is established by the distributive נערה נערה in v. 12, which is continued in the main clause by the definite הנערה, which in this generic context refers to an instance of the group established by נערה נערה. As a generic statement, the participle expresses something similar to a habitual except without an identifiable subject: "the young lady (whose turn it was) would enter ..." The NP את כל אשר תאמר presents one of the rare examples of a subject of an intransitive or passive verb introduced by the object particle את (WO 10.3.2; see also Andersen 1971; Garr; Müller; and Kroeze). The subject-verb order represents basic BH word order. The generic semantics of the main clause carries through to the subordinate verbs, making both *yiqtol* verbs, תאמר and ינתן, irrealis and generic, "would say" and "would be given."

כָּל־אֲשֶׁר תֹּאמַר. Use of אמר here, lit. "all [of that] which she would say," has the contextually driven nuance of "mention" (HALOT Qal 3), "order" (HALOT Qal 6), or even "desire" (BDB Qal 2). The head of the relative clause is the quantifier כל, which also corresponds by null resumption to the complement role within the relative for the verb תאמר.

יִנָּתֵן לָהּ. The verb is trivalent in the Qal, and so by valency reduction associated with the passive, ינתן here is bivalent, taking as its subject the patient (the thing given = כל אשר תאמר) and its complement the ל-PP (the recipient of the thing given).

לָבוֹא עִמָּהּ מִבֵּית הַנָּשִׁים עַד־בֵּית הַמֶּלֶךְ. Inf constr Qal √בוא. This purpose infinitive modifies the verb ינתן. The null subject is understood from context to be "all that she said," since לבוא is Qal and thus means "to come" (not Hiphil "to bring"). Qal בוא takes one locative/goal complement, here the PP עד בית המלך. The two other PPs are verbal adjuncts, עמה an adjunct of accompaniment and מבית הנשים an adjunct specifying the origin or source.

2:14 בָּעֶרֶב ׀ הִיא בָאָה וּבַבֹּקֶר הִיא שָׁבָה אֶל־בֵּית הַנָּשִׁים שֵׁנִי אֶל־יַד שַׁעַשְׁגַז סְרִיס הַמֶּלֶךְ שֹׁמֵר הַפִּילַגְשִׁים לֹא־תָבוֹא עוֹד אֶל־הַמֶּלֶךְ כִּי אִם־חָפֵץ בָּהּ הַמֶּלֶךְ וְנִקְרְאָה בְשֵׁם׃

After the contestant spent her night with the king, she would not return to the harem, but went instead to a second house, perhaps so that she could not discuss the details of her experiences with those whose turn had not yet come.

בָּעֶרֶב ׀ הִיא בָאָה. Participle fs Qal √בוא (on the morphological ambiguity of the form באה, see comments on 1:17 and 2:13). The participle is the complement to a null copula, with היא as the subject. The pronoun היא refers back to each instance of the נערה נערה, and as such it and the participle are used to continue the genericity of the actions being described—that is, the same pattern occurred for each young woman. The PP בערב is a Topic-fronted temporal adjunct to באה.

וּבַבֹּקֶר הִיא שָׁבָה אֶל־בֵּית הַנָּשִׁים שֵׁנִי אֶל־יַד שַׁעַשְׁגַז סְרִיס הַמֶּלֶךְ שֹׁמֵר הַפִּילַגְשִׁים. Participle fs Qal √שוב, which is the complement to a null copula with the subject היא, and participle ms Qal √שמר.

The PP בבקר is a Topic-fronted temporal adjunct. The Qal of שׁוב takes a locative/goal PP, here אל בית הנשׁים שׁני. The second אל-PP is in apposition (of attribution) to the first אל-PP (similarly, see vv. 3, 8). The NP שׁעשׁגז סריס המלך שׁמר הפילגשׁים recalls the description of Hegai in v. 3 (הגא סריס המלך שׁמר הנשׁים). As there, this NP has a head-appositive-relative structure, with סריס המלך in apposition to שׁעשׁגז and an unmarked relative (containing a null copula and participial phrase complement) modifying שׁעשׁגז (see comment on v. 3). On the expression שׁמר הפילגשׁים, see comment on v. 3.

בֵּ֤ית הַנָּשִׁים֙ שֵׁנִ֔י. The ordinal שׁני appears to modify בית either appositionally or adjectivally (it agrees in everything but definiteness). Moore asserts that שׁני is "grammatically unrelated to the rest of the verse" (1971:23). Fox proposes either to read שׁני as שֵׁנִית, with the ת lost from haplography with א of the following word אל (but this could only occur in paleo-Hebrew script, making it an unlikely solution) or simply to read שׁני as an alternative form of שׁנית. Either way, he takes it as a verbal adjunct, "they returned a second time" (2001:276; so Keil, 338). Similarly, Bush insists we must emend to הַשֵּׁנִי (i.e., so that it agrees with the noun in terms of definiteness) or take one of Fox's two options (Bush, 365; cf. Paton, 181, who also offers these three options). The simplest solution is to recognize that adjectives need not always agree with the noun they modify in terms of definiteness (see Holmstedt 2013a:352), and so the ordinal שׁני modifies בית in the typical adjectival fashion.

לֹא־תָב֥וֹא עוֹד֙ אֶל־הַמֶּ֔לֶךְ. *Yiqtol* 3fs Qal √בוא. The verb is bivalent, with a null subject, a locative אל-PP as the verbal complement, and the adverb עוד as an adjunct. Here the narrator reminds the listener or reader about theme of "entering before the king" (see comment on v. 2 and introduction to chap. 1). This reminder may serve to establish this court rule firmly and so foreshadow the danger Esther puts herself in by going before the king without invitation (Levenson, 62).

כִּ֣י אִם־חָפֵ֥ץ בָּ֛הּ הַמֶּ֖לֶךְ. *Qatal* 3ms Qal √חפץ. The function word כי by itself can be used adversatively, to "restrict the immediately preceding clause" (WO 39.3.5d), i.e., like English "but" or "rather" (cf. MNK 40.9 II.3). When combined with the conditional אם, "if," the result categorizes the following clause as an exceptive (WO 38.6): "but if," "unless," or "except." The compound particle triggers inversion to verb-subject order, and the light PP complement בה attaches to the verb and raises with it ahead of the subject המלך (see comment on v. 7).

וְנִקְרְאָ֥ה בְשֵֽׁם. *Qatal* 3fs Niph √קרא. The Niphal verb נקראה is monovalent, with a null subject (reconstructed as "any of the young women") and the ב-PP as a manner adjunct.

2:15 וּבְהַגִּ֣יעַ תֹּר־אֶסְתֵּ֣ר בַּת־אֲבִיחַ֣יִל דֹּ֣ד מָרְדֳּכַ֡י אֲשֶׁר֩
לָקַֽח־ל֨וֹ לְבַ֜ת לָב֣וֹא אֶל־הַמֶּ֗לֶךְ לֹ֤א בִקְשָׁה֙ דָּבָ֔ר
כִּ֗י אִ֤ם אֶת־אֲשֶׁ֣ר יֹאמַ֛ר הֵגַ֥י סְרִיס־הַמֶּ֖לֶךְ שֹׁמֵ֣ר
הַנָּשִׁ֑ים וַתְּהִ֤י אֶסְתֵּר֙ נֹשֵׂ֣את חֵ֔ן בְּעֵינֵ֖י כָּל־רֹאֶֽיהָ׃

The narrator now addresses Esther's turn to enter before the king. Wisely, Esther takes only what Hegai recommends.

וּבְהַגִּ֣יעַ תֹּר־אֶסְתֵּ֣ר בַּת־אֲבִיחַ֣יִל דֹּ֣ד מָרְדֳּכַ֡י אֲשֶׁר֩ לָקַֽח־ל֨וֹ לְבַ֜ת לָב֣וֹא אֶל־הַמֶּ֗לֶךְ. Inf constr Hiph √נגע, *qatal* 3ms Qal √לקח, and inf constr Qal √בוא. On the form and valency of the infinitive הגיע, and on the noun תר, see comment on v. 12. On the noun דד, see v. 7. This temporal infinitive clause is very similar to the one in v. 12, with Esther as the subject. Esther is modified by the appositive בת אביחיל, within which the PN אביחיל is itself modified by the appositive דד מרדכי, within which the noun מרדכי is modified by a relative clause (for comparison, see Mordecai's genealogy in v. 5).

אֲשֶׁר֩ לָקַֽח־ל֨וֹ לְבַ֜ת. *Qatal* 3ms Qal √לקח. On the phrase לקח לו לבת, see comment on v. 7. In this clause the NP complement לקח for the person/thing taken is syntactically null but can be reconstructed from the context as Esther.

לֹ֤א בִקְשָׁה֙ דָּבָ֔ר. *Qatal* 3fs Piel √בקש. On the valency of Piel בקש, see comment on v. 2. The NP complement דבר has here the meaning "thing," not "word" (see comment on 3:1).

כִּ֗י אִ֤ם אֶת־אֲשֶׁ֣ר יֹאמַ֛ר הֵגַ֥י סְרִיס־הַמֶּ֖לֶךְ שֹׁמֵ֣ר הַנָּשִׁ֑ים. *Yiqtol* 3ms Qal √אמר, null copula, and participle ms √שמר. The כי אם introduces a complex NP-internal adjunct to the bare noun דבר, "a thing except [the thing] that Hegai said ..." (see also 5:12). Within a relative clause, verbs typically default to the basic temporal setting, e.g., a *yiqtol* normally refers to the nonpast. But the larger past time context requires that יֹאמַר within the relative clause must also be set in the past. Why a *yiqtol* is used rather than a *qatal* relates to the imperfective semantics of the *yiqtol*. Two semantic values associated with the *yiqtol* make sense of this choice: (1) past progressive ("what Hegai <u>was telling</u> her"); or

(2) past habitual ("what Hegai would tell her"). The first option would mean Hegai was guiding her choice when her turn came; the second would mean Hegai was apt to give the girls advice and she was taking his. See "Verbal Semantics" in the Introduction.

וַתְּהִ֤י אֶסְתֵּר֙ נֹשֵׂ֣את חֵ֔ן בְּעֵינֵ֖י כָּל־רֹאֶֽיהָ. *Wayyiqtol* 3fs Qal √היה, participle fs √נשׂא, and participle mp √ראה with 3fs clitic pronoun. As with all III-ה verbs, the *wayyiqtol* of היה is shorter than the *yiqtol* (= תִּהְיֶה in the 3fs), indicating the existence of two distinct prefix conjugations in Hebrew. The *wayyiqtol* is always associated with triggered inversion to verb-subject order. In this particular clause the copula היה has a participial complement; it is much more common for the participle to appear without the overt copula (see Miller 1999:9; see also ויהי אמן in v. 7), but in this case the *wayyiqtol* was required by the narrative context. The combination of the *wayyiqtol* copula with the participle results in past progressive semantics: Esther continually impressed people (see Cook 2012:230–33). The expression נשׂא חן means "to receive favor" (cf. comment on v. 9; cf. also v. 17 and 5:2) and the adjunct PP contributes to the idiom by specifying the origin.

2:16 וַתִּלָּקַ֨ח אֶסְתֵּ֜ר אֶל־הַמֶּ֣לֶךְ אֲחַשְׁוֵר֗וֹשׁ אֶל־בֵּ֣ית
מַלְכוּת֔וֹ בַּחֹ֥דֶשׁ הָעֲשִׂירִ֖י הוּא־חֹ֣דֶשׁ טֵבֵ֑ת בִּשְׁנַת־
שֶׁ֖בַע לְמַלְכוּתֽוֹ׃

Verse 16 records the date of this important event, when Esther would win the king's favor and ultimately become the new queen.

וַתִּלָּקַ֨ח אֶסְתֵּ֜ר אֶל־הַמֶּ֣לֶךְ אֲחַשְׁוֵר֗וֹשׁ אֶל־בֵּ֣ית מַלְכוּת֔וֹ. *Wayyiqtol* 3fs Niph √לקח. The *wayyiqtol* triggers inversion to verb-subject order. The first אל-PP is a locative adjunct to the verb, while the second אל-PP is in apposition to the first PP, specifying a locative goal that is more concrete than "to the king." On מלכות, see comment on 1:2.

בַּחֹ֥דֶשׁ הָעֲשִׂירִ֖י הוּא־חֹ֣דֶשׁ טֵבֵ֑ת. This temporal ב-PP is a second adjunct to the verb תלקח. The clarifying parenthesis הוא חדשׁ טבת "it (is) the month of Tebet" is null copula clause with subject הוא and NP complement (see 1:1 and 3:7). The PN טבת is the Hebrew version of Akkadian *ṭebētu*, the Babylonian name of the tenth month (Bush, 366), from the verb *ṭebû* "to sink down" (HALOT s.v.; cf. Paton, 182–83; Moore 1971:24).

בִּשְׁנַת־שֶׁבַע לְמַלְכוּתוֹ. This ב-PP is another temporal adjunct to the verb תלקח. The noun שנת is bound to the numeral (lit. "year of seven"; cf. 1:3; see "Numeral Syntax in Esther" in the Introduction). Whereas in 1:3 the date is given with respect to the king's "reigning" (an infinitive construct; cf. comment on 1:3), here it is given with respect to the king's "kingdom" (a noun). The use of a ל-PP instead of a bound phrase is typical for dating formulas (cf. comment on 1:3). Notably, we only find a noun meaning "kingdom" as complement to ל in later texts (see Dan 1:1; 2:1; 8:1; 1 Chr 26:31; 2 Chr 3:2; 16:1, 12); in earlier texts, when a king's reign is referred to, the king's title or name or an infinitive construct √מלך is the complement of ל. Thus, the change in dating convention may be diachronically significant (cf. Bergey 1983:157–59).

2:17 וַיֶּאֱהַב הַמֶּלֶךְ אֶת־אֶסְתֵּר מִכָּל־הַנָּשִׁים וַתִּשָּׂא־חֵן
וָחֶסֶד לְפָנָיו מִכָּל־הַבְּתוּלֹת וַיָּשֶׂם כֶּתֶר־מַלְכוּת
בְּרֹאשָׁהּ וַיַּמְלִיכֶהָ תַּחַת וַשְׁתִּי׃

Esther's night with the king is successful, and he selects her to become the next queen. One plot complication is resolved, though the issue of Esther's hidden Jewishness lingers.

וַיֶּאֱהַב הַמֶּלֶךְ אֶת־אֶסְתֵּר מִכָּל־הַנָּשִׁים. *Wayyiqtol* 3ms Qal √אהב. The verb אהב in the Qal ("to love") is bivalent, taking an NP complement (את אסתר). To express comparison Hebrew often uses the preposition מן in its comparative function (GKC 133; WO 14.4; JM 141g–h): thus, here יאהב ... את אסתר מכל הנשים means "he loved Esther *more than* all the women." The מן comparative logically implies there were other women whom the king also loved (Fox 2001:37–38; cf. Bush, 366).

וַתִּשָּׂא־חֵן וָחֶסֶד לְפָנָיו מִכָּל־הַבְּתוּלֹת. *Wayyiqtol* 3fs Qal √נשׂא. On the expression נשׂא חן וחסד ("to receive favor and kindness"), see comment on v. 9 (cf. v. 15, v. 17, and 5:2). As with the previous clause, the adjunct מן-PP expresses comparison: "she received favor and kindness ... *more than* all the virgins"; the comparison implies that the NP הבתולות refers to the "other virgins" (i.e., other than Esther, who was herself one of "the virgins").

וַיָּשֶׂם כֶּתֶר־מַלְכוּת בְּרֹאשָׁהּ. *Wayyiqtol* 3ms Qal √שׂים. The verb שׂים in the Qal ("to set," "to place") is always trivalent: here it takes an

NP complement (the thing set or placed; here כתר מלכות) and a locative PP (the place in which it is set or placed; here בראשה). The phrase כתר מלכות recalls the scene in 1:10-12, where the king asks Vashti to come wearing the "turban of the kingdom," but she refuses (Levenson, 62). Esther, the antitype to Vashti, now occupies that role (see introduction to chap. 1). On the meaning of כתר, see comment on 1:11. On מלכות, see comment on 1:2.

וַיַּמְלִיכֶהָ תַּחַת וַשְׁתִּי. *Wayyiqtol* 3ms Hiph √מלך with 3fs clitic pronoun. The Hiphil מלך is the causative of the Qal (see 1:1) and is bivalent ("to cause *someone* to reign"). This clause marks the fulfillment of what was suggested by the king's young servants in v. 4.

2:18 וַיַּעַשׂ הַמֶּלֶךְ מִשְׁתֶּה גָדוֹל לְכָל־שָׂרָיו וַעֲבָדָיו אֵת מִשְׁתֵּה אֶסְתֵּר וַהֲנָחָה לַמְּדִינוֹת עָשָׂה וַיִּתֵּן מַשְׂאֵת כְּיַד הַמֶּלֶךְ׃

Paralleling the first feast thrown by the king in 1:3, Esther is given a feast in honor of her coronation. Whether by convention or as an ad hoc act of largesse, Ahashverosh also grants the entire kingdom a release (perhaps from taxes) and bestows gifts.

וַיַּעַשׂ הַמֶּלֶךְ מִשְׁתֶּה גָדוֹל לְכָל־שָׂרָיו וַעֲבָדָיו אֵת מִשְׁתֵּה אֶסְתֵּר. *Wayyiqtol* 3ms Qal √עשׂה. On the valency and semantics of עשׂה, see 1:3. On the form ויעשׂ, see 1:21. The complement of the bivalent verb is the NP משתה גדול. The masculine adjective גדול matches the gender of משתה, in which the ה is part of the root, not the feminine ending (see comments in 1:3, 9). This clause recalls the first drinking-feast mentioned in 1:3: עשׂה משתה לכל שׂריו ועבדיו (on the structural significance of this, see introduction to chap. 1). The NP את משתה אסתר is in apposition to משתה earlier in this verse: "the king prepared a banquet ..., i.e., the banquet of Esther" (on the types of apposition, see 1:2).

וַהֲנָחָה לַמְּדִינוֹת עָשָׂה. *Qatal* 3ms Qal √עשׂה. The word הנחה, a *hapax legomenon*, is derived from √נוח "to rest"; the morphology is the same of both the Aramaic Haphel infinitive (BDB s.v.; HALOT s.v.) and the Mishnaic abstract noun associated with the Hiphil (Segal 1927:113–14; HALOT s.v.). The context supports the latter analysis, since the word is the complement of the verb עשׂה, which typically takes NP complements rather than infinitival complements. The noun הנחה

"resting" refers either to a holiday, since a day of feasting would possibly be a national holiday, or in light of the next clause (the giving of royal gifts) perhaps a release from taxes (cf. Paton, 184–85). The order complement-adjunct-verb is not basic. Typically when two nonsubject constituents precede the verb, they have both been fronted, either as a Topic-Focus pair or a Focus-Focus pair. The NP הנחה has not been previously introduced and so cannot be a Topic, though it does make good sense as a Focus-fronted constituent, i.e., in a surprising act of generosity "a rest (the king) made." But it is difficult to discern a contextually sensible reason for a second Focus on למדינות—to whom else would the king give a rest? It may be that the ל-PP is not a verbal adjunct indicating the beneficiary of Ahashverosh's act, but is an NP-internal modifier of הנחה. As such, what the king granted was a provincial rest. On NP-internal modifiers, see 1:3, 14.

וַיִּתֵּ֤ן מַשְׂאֵת֙ כְּיַ֣ד הַמֶּֽלֶךְ׃. *Wayyiqtol* 3ms Qal √נתן. The Qal of נתן is usually trivalent (see comment on 1:19; cf. 2:13), requiring a subject, an NP complement, and ל-PP complement. Here there is no overt ל-PP complement; however, given the verb's strongly consistent valency pattern, it is likely that we should understand a null complement reconstructable from the context, perhaps "for his rulers," "for his servants," or "for his provinces" (or all three); see comments on 3:14, 15. The feminine noun משאת comes from the verbal root נשׂא, "to lift," and denotes the act of event of "lifting up," which by extension may connote "tribute, present" (HALOT s.v.). The morphology follows the *maqtil* nominal pattern, with assimilation of the initial נ of the root and the addition of the feminine ת suffix: **manśiʾ+t* > **maśśiʾt* > (?) *maśśʾit* > *maśśʾét*. The noun is singular, though often it is translated as plural "gifts" (no doubt because interpreters understand the unstated recipient of the gift(s) to be plural). On the phrase כיד המלך, see comment on 1:7.

2:19 וּבְהִקָּבֵ֥ץ בְּתוּל֖וֹת שֵׁנִ֑ית וּמָרְדֳּכַ֖י יֹשֵׁ֥ב בְּשַֽׁעַר־
הַמֶּֽלֶךְ׃

Verse 19 mentions a second gathering of virgins. It is not clear whether we are to understand another gathering of women to the king's harem, or a gathering of the initial contestants to a new location, or something else.

וּבְהִקָּבֵץ בְּתוּלוֹת שֵׁנִית וּמָרְדֳּכַי יֹשֵׁב בְּשַׁעַר־הַמֶּלֶךְ. Inf constr Niph √קבץ and participle ms Qal √ישב. The ב-PP/infinitive clause (בהקבץ בתולות שנית) is a fronted temporal adjunct for the main clause, ומרדכי ישב בשער המלך. See 2:8 for a similar fronting construction, where the main verb is a *wayyiqtol*. Whereas the ו between the fronted constituents and the main clause in 2:8 is necessitated by the *wayyiqtol* form, here the ו serves a simple processing function, to demarcate the front edge of the clause and so make the adjunct fronting clear.

וּבְהִקָּבֵץ בְּתוּלוֹת שֵׁנִית. Inf constr Niph √קבץ. On the valency of Niphal קבץ, see comment on v. 8 and on the meaning of בתולות, see comment on v. 2. The ordinal שׁנית is here used adverbially as "a second time." This reference to a second competition *after* Esther was chosen, even though the king seemed greatly satisfied with Esther in vv. 17-18, is difficult to interpret. We could emend the text to שֹׁנוֹת, "various" (Ehrlich, 114; Paton, 192; Moore 1971:29; but cf. Fox 2001:277) or discard it with the Alpha Text (Levenson, 63; but cf. Paton, 187, by the principle of *lectio difficilior*, the Masoretic Text may be taken as earlier; on the Alpha Text, see "The Alpha Text of Esther" in the Introduction). Alternatively, it could be that the second gathering refers to moving the original women to a different location (Fox 2001:38, 277; but cf. Keil, 341, Paton, 186–87, and Bush, 372, esp. on the definiteness of בתולות). Finally, it is possible that the text is here relating a *new* (i.e., a second) gathering of virgins to be the king's concubines (Keil, 341; Paton, 186–87; Bush, 372).

וּמָרְדֳּכַי יֹשֵׁב בְּשַׁעַר־הַמֶּלֶךְ. Participle ms Qal √ישב. On the valency of ישב, see comment on 1:2. It is likely that "sitting in the gate of the king" is idiomatic for "holding a government office" (so Fox 2001:38). There is significant evidence (see Bush, 372–73) for identifying the "gate of the king" as the physical location where the royal court met; by metonymy, this locative reference came to refer to the court itself (this is similar to the English case where the "White House" often refers idiomatically to the executive branch of government). The null copula (which has a default past value due to thc narrative context) and participial complement in the main clause combine to produce a past progressive semantics. The resulting nuance is that *was sitting* in the king's gate *when* this second gathering of virgins occurred.

2:20 אֵ֣ין אֶסְתֵּ֗ר מַגֶּ֤דֶת מֽוֹלַדְתָּהּ֙ וְאֶת־עַמָּ֔הּ כַּאֲשֶׁ֛ר צִוָּ֥ה
עָלֶ֖יהָ מָרְדֳּכָ֑י וְאֶת־מַאֲמַ֤ר מָרְדֳּכַי֙ אֶסְתֵּ֣ר עֹשָׂ֔ה
כַּאֲשֶׁ֛ר הָיְתָ֥ה בְאָמְנָ֖ה אִתּֽוֹ׃

Again, the text tells us that Esther did not reveal her ethnic background to anyone (cf. v. 10). Just as she was obedient to Hegai (and presumably the king, implied by the disobedience of Vashti whom she replaced), Esther is ultimately obedient to Mordecai, who has had her obedience since childhood.

אֵ֣ין אֶסְתֵּ֗ר מַגֶּ֤דֶת מֽוֹלַדְתָּהּ֙ וְאֶת־עַמָּ֔הּ. An אין copula clause, participle fs Hiph √נגד, and *qatal* 3ms Piel √צוה. On the meaning and valency of נגד, see comment on v. 10. Note the assimilation of the נ of the root: **mangid+t* > *maggédet*. The negative copula אין is bound to the clausal subject, אסתר. (A study of the word order of אין and יש clauses is a desideratum in BH grammatical research.) The use of אין with a participle complement is similar to participle phrase with overt copula היה (see comment on ותהי נשׂאת in v. 15 and ויהי אמן in v. 7); the difference between the two constructions is that with אין the copula is inherently negated and temporal frame of reference is inferred from the context (as with null copulas). The participial semantics in this clause appear to signal the durative nature of the activity; i.e., whenever the question arose, Esther never revealed her origins. The syntax and vocabulary of this clause (including the relative) echoes v. 10 (cf. Levenson, 61); in v. 10, Esther does not make it known that she is a Jew in the "house of women," whereas here she withholds her ethnicity while in the king's dwelling. On the meaning of מולדת, see v. 10.

כַּאֲשֶׁ֛ר צִוָּ֥ה עָלֶ֖יהָ מָרְדֳּכָ֑י. *Qatal* 3ms Piel √צוה. On the trivalency and meaning of Piel צוה, see v. 10. The אשר after prepositions often nominalizes the following finite verbal clause so that it might be an acceptable complement for the preposition (Holmstedt forthcoming). However, in this case, צוה is then left with unfilled valency, "Mordecai commanded her [*what?*]." Therefore, the אשר introduces a null head relative clause here, with the content of the null head reconstructed from the context, "(the command) that Mordecai commanded her." Compare the syntax of the similar statement in v. 10, מרדכי צוה עליה אשר לא תגיד, where the אשר clause relays the content of the command: "Mordecai commanded her *that she should not tell*." The null head of the relative also functions by null resumption as the first complement (*what* was commanded) of the verb within the relative clause and the על-PP is the second complement, specifying *whom* was commanded. The presence of the relative אשר triggers inversion to verb-subject order. Note also that the light על-PP raises with the verb above the subject (see comment on v. 7).

וְאֶת־מַאֲמַר מָרְדֳּכַי אֶסְתֵּר עֹשָׂה. Participle fs Qal √עשׂה. The semantics of the participle in this clause are habitual: "Esther was (in the habit of) carrying out Mordecai's command." On the semantic range and valency of עשׂה, see comments on 1:3, 5. Here, עשׂה means "to do" or "to observe" and takes the NP complement את מאמר מרדכי; the connotation of עשׂה מאמר seems to be that Esther "did what Mordecai said." The content of this clause overlaps somewhat with the clause immediately preceding it, and the explanation for this apparent redundancy lies in the word order. The complement of the participle is raised to the front of the main clause for Focus (no inversion occurs because the word order of null copula clauses is not affected by syntactic triggers). The complement is Focus-marked to highlight Esther's past, present, and presumably future modus operandi: she does what Mordecai (above anyone else) says. The contrast inherent to the Focus may foreshadow the tension in chapters 4 and 5, where Esther risks her life by following Mordecai's urging and violates court rules to appear before the king uninvited. The overlap in meaning also suggests that the ו at the front edge of this clause falls under what WO call the "epexegetical" use (33.2.2, 39.2.4). However, it is not that waw carries any such "epexegetical" function; rather, context indicates that the second clause is a clarifying appositive to the previous clause. On מאמר, see 1:15.

כַּאֲשֶׁר הָיְתָה בְאָמְנָה אִתּוֹ. *Qatal* 3fs Qal √היה. The use of היתה here is copular, the null subject represents Esther, the PP באמנה is the copular complement, and the PP אתו is an adjunct. This clause supports the idea that the verse describes Esther's modus operandi: "according to [the manner] that [Esther] was in [her] upbringing with him." In other words, she obeyed him in this matter (not telling anyone about her ethnic identity) just as she had obeyed him throughout the years that he raised her. The word אמנה is a *hapax legomenon*. It is either a noun from the root אמן (Keil, 341) and meaning "care, guardianship" (HALOT אָמְנָה II) or "bringing up, nourishment" (BDB אָמְנָה) with an understood 3fs pronoun, or it is the infinitive construct of אמן with the 3fs clitic pronoun (without the typical *mappiq* to mark the ה as the pronoun) and means "her upbringing" (so G. R. Driver; Moore 1971:30; and Bush, 371; cf. DCH אָמְנָה II; Fox 2001:277). In the latter analysis, the 3fs clitic pronoun must be the verbal complement, "bringing her up," and so the null infinitival subject could only be Mordecai: "in [Mordecai's] bringing her up with him." This is very awkward Hebrew syntax; we consider the first option, that אמנה is a noun, to be more likely.

§3: Mordecai Saves the King (2:21-23)

At this point in the narrative, vv. 21-23 may seem incidental to the plot of the book. However, these verses lay the groundwork for the events of chapter 6. Mordecai's deed later gives reason for the king to exalt Mordecai, thereby setting in motion the complete reversal of Haman's and Mordecai's fortunes.

[21]In those days (Mordecai was sitting in the gate of the king), Bigthan and Teresh, two of the king's eunuchs from the guards of the threshold, became angry and sought to raise a hand against King Ahashverosh. [22]But the matter became known to Mordecai, and he declared (it) to Esther, the queen, and Esther said (it) to the king in the name of Mordecai. [23]The matter was sought out, and it was confirmed, and the two of them were hung on a tree. And it was written in the Book of the Matters of the Days before the king.

2:21 בַּיָּמִ֣ים הָהֵ֔ם וּמָרְדֳּכַ֖י יֹשֵׁ֣ב בְּשַֽׁעַר־הַמֶּ֑לֶךְ קָצַ֡ף
בִּגְתָ֨ן וָתֶ֜רֶשׁ שְׁנֵֽי־סָרִיסֵ֤י הַמֶּ֙לֶךְ֙ מִשֹּׁמְרֵ֣י הַסַּ֔ף
וַיְבַקְשׁוּ֙ לִשְׁלֹ֣חַ יָ֔ד בַּמֶּ֖לֶךְ אֲחַשְׁוֵרֹֽשׁ׃

Verse 21 relates the crime of Bigthan and Teresh, whose plot will be foiled by Mordecai in the following verses.

בַּיָּמִ֣ים הָהֵ֔ם וּמָרְדֳּכַ֖י יֹשֵׁ֣ב בְּשַֽׁעַר־הַמֶּ֑לֶךְ קָצַ֡ף בִּגְתָ֨ן וָתֶ֜רֶשׁ. Participle ms Qal √ישב and *qatal* 3ms Qal √קצף. Most translations and commentaries (Paton, 189; Moore 1971:29; Fox 2001:39; Bush, 371; Levenson, 63) understand one clause here with the main verb קצף, modified by the Topic-fronted temporal ב-PP and a circumstantial participial phrase מרדכי ישב בשער המלך: "In those days, as/while Mordecai was sitting in the gate of the king, Bigthan and Teresh were angry." The triggered verb-subject order of קצף בגתן ותרש confirms that the initial PP בימים ההם belongs to that clause as a temporal adjunct (i.e., its Topic-fronting provides the trigger for the verb-subject inversion). Because the intervening participial clause interrupts the syntax of the main clause it should be classified syntactically as a parenthesis. The notion of a "circumstantial" clause (JM 158a) is not syntactic (there are no formal markers to indicate when some clause is circumstantial); rather, identifying a clause as "circumstantial" reflects a judgment concerning the relationship of two adjacent clauses and, as such, combines various constructions in an ill-conceived categorial menagerie. What many grammarians have identified as a syntactic category is actually a wide variety of syntactic constructions that may only be legitimately grouped together on semantic and discourse levels. In other words, the circumstantial relationship is a semantic judgment that is motivated by a shift in the use of verbs used in the narrative, which is fundamentally a discourse concern. On the grammar of מרדכי ישב בשער המלך, see comment on v. 19.

קָצַ֨ף בִּגְתָ֜ן וָתֶ֗רֶשׁ. On the meaning and valency of קצף, see 1:12. Note the use of the singular verb with the compound subject. Normally a compound subject would appear with a plural verb. The apparent mismatch in agreement, i.e., the use of a singular verb with a plural or compound subject, has been variously explained (see GKC 145, 146; JM 150n–q; and the focused studies in Moreshet; Levi; Revell 1993; Naudé; Doron; and Holmstedt 2009b). Explanations have ranged from syntactic (e.g., verb-subject order allows for "first-conjunct agreement" [Doron; cf. Paton, 192 on this verse], or the compound NP is not the syntactic subject but rather an adjunct to the verb and the syntactic subject is null [Naudé; Holmstedt 2009b]), to discourse-pragmatics (e.g., the verb is singular because the first NP of the compound is more salient in the narrative or simply the primary agent of the action [Revell 1993]). In this particular case, the simplest analysis is that the compound NP is the syntactic subject but that the agreement features are singular since the compound NP is taken as a set or unit—Bigthan and Teresh are a pair whose plural number is resolved as singular to reflect their action as a "unit" (see Holmstedt 2009b:126); cf. v. 23, where the NP "the two of them" takes a plural verb.

בִּגְתָ֨ן וָתֶ֜רֶשׁ שְׁנֵֽי־סָרִיסֵ֤י הַמֶּ֙לֶךְ֙ מִשֹּׁמְרֵ֣י הַסַּ֔ף. Participle mp Qal √שמר. This NP is similar in structure to the NP הגא סריס המלך שמר הנשים in 2:3 and 2:15. Besides the fact that this case has a compound NP, the significant structural difference is the addition of the מן prefix before the participial relative clause. The PP משמרי הסף, with its null head participial relative "[those who] guard the door," modifies either the closer שני סריסי or the further בגתן ותרש. Although modifiers (PPs, relative clauses, adjectives) typically modify the nearest possible NP, since in this case the nearer head is in apposition to the further head and thus both share the same referent, it makes no difference semantically which head is chosen: "Bigthan and Teresh ..., from the guards of the threshold" in this context is functionally no different than "two of the king's eunuchs from the guards of the threshold." In each case the מן-PP designates origin for the item it modifies (WO 11.2.11b), i.e., these two eunuchs came from the threshold guards. Another interesting feature found in this phrase is the form of סריסי, with the *qameṣ* (lengthened /ā/) in a distant open syllable, in contrast to סריס in 2:3, 15. Apparently some forms of the noun reflect the noun pattern *qatīl*, with a short /a/ vowel in the first syllable, which will reduce in a distant open syllable (i.e., in the singular bound and plural forms), while other forms reflect the pattern *qattīl*, in which the short /a/ is not only preserved, but lengthened (to compensate for the /r/ not lengthening); see JM 96Db.

וַיְבַקְשׁוּ֙ לִשְׁלֹ֣חַ יָ֔ד בַּמֶּ֖לֶךְ אֲחַשְׁוֵרֽשׁ. *Wayyiqtol* 3mp Piel √בקש and inf constr Qal √שלח. While Piel בקש often takes an NP complement (c.f., e.g., v. 2), it may also take an infinitive clause complement (BDB s.v.), as here with לשלח יד במלך אחשורש. The idiom שלח יד "to send out a hand" is similar to the English idiom "to lay a hand on" and is a metaphor for violence and harm (HALOT s.v.; BDB s.v.; DCH s.v. 7b, "to raise a hand against someone"). The phrase itself does not necessarily imply killing, though the context may suggest that a death is intended or is the result (Keil, 341 "to slay," Paton, 190 "[to] kill," and Moore 1971:31 and Bush, 371 "to assassinate"). The person against whom the action is directed (i.e., the person who is harmed) is indicated by a ב-PP (or sometimes an אל-PP; HALOT s.v.; BDB s.v.). The verb שלח in this idiom is trivalent, taking a subject (here null), NP complement (here יד), and PP complement designating the recipient of the action (here במלך אחשורש). On other metaphorical uses of יד, see 1:7, 12, and 2:3; on "King Ahashverosh," see 1:2.

2:22 וַיִּוָּדַ֤ע הַדָּבָר֙ לְמָרְדֳּכַ֔י וַיַּגֵּ֖ד לְאֶסְתֵּ֣ר הַמַּלְכָּ֑ה וַתֹּ֧אמֶר אֶסְתֵּ֛ר לַמֶּ֖לֶךְ בְּשֵׁ֥ם מָרְדֳּכָֽי׃

Mordecai uses Esther as a means to warn the king of Bigthan and Teresh's plot against him.

וַיִּוָּדַ֤ע הַדָּבָר֙ לְמָרְדֳּכַ֔י. *Wayyiqtol* 3ms Niph √ידע. Most I-י verbs are originally I-ו, as can be seen here with the return of the consonant ו in many derived *binyanim*. The PP למרדכי is adjunct to the verb indicating the beneficiary of the agent-less action. The subject NP הדבר means "the matter," i.e., Bigthan and Teresh's plot against the king mentioned in the preceding verse (see 1:17). The semantics of the Niphal ידע include an inchoative "phasal aspect" such that ויודע marks the beginning of a new state for the subject הדבר, "it became known (to Mordecai)" (see Cook 2012:25–26; 191–94).

וַיַּגֵּד לְאֶסְתֵּר הַמַּלְכָּה. *Wayyiqtol* 3ms Hiph √נגד. On the valency, meaning, and form of Hiphil נגד, see v. 10; see 1:21 for an explanation of the *ṣere* in the final syllable instead of the *ḥireq-yod* of the Hiphil *yiqtol* paradigm. The complement of Hiphil נגד is null, identifiable from context as the thing (הדבר) made known to Mordecai. The PP לאסתר המלכה is an adjunct to ויגד. On אסתר המלכה, see comment on 1:2.

וַתֹּאמֶר אֶסְתֵּר לַמֶּלֶךְ בְּשֵׁם מָרְדֳּכָי. *Wayyiqtol* 3fs Qal √אמר. There is no overt NP complement to אמר here. Although elsewhere אמר may be monovalent (cf. comment on 1:18), here it is bivalent with a null complement: "Esther said/told [the matter of Bigthan and Teresh] to the king." The PP למלך is an adjunct designating the addressee of the speech. The PP בשם מרדכי, crucial to the intricate plot of the story (see 6:2; also Fox 2001:162), is also adjunct to אמר.

2:23 וַיְבֻקַּשׁ הַדָּבָר֙ וַיִּמָּצֵ֔א וַיִּתָּל֥וּ שְׁנֵיהֶ֖ם עַל־עֵ֑ץ וַיִּכָּתֵ֗ב בְּסֵ֛פֶר דִּבְרֵ֥י הַיָּמִ֖ים לִפְנֵ֥י הַמֶּֽלֶךְ׃

After Mordecai's warning is found to be true, Bigthan and Teresh are executed and displayed in public. Mordecai's good deed is recorded in the royal records—another narrative detail that will play a critical role later in the story.

וַיְבֻקַּשׁ הַדָּבָר֙. *Wayyiqtol* 3ms Pual √בקשׁ. On הדבר in this context, see v. 22. For הדבר to be "sought out" means that what Esther told the king was investigated. The passive Pual בקשׁ is monovalent, having experienced a valency decrease from the active bivalent Piel (on the valency of Piel בקשׁ, see comment on v. 2).

וַיִּמָּצֵ֔א. *Wayyiqtol* 3ms Niph √מצא. The Qal מצא is bivalent, taking a subject NP and an NP complement (the thing found). As the passive form of the root, the Niphal is monovalent—the complement of the Qal is promoted to the subject role in the passive Niphal. The subject is null, but is contextually identifiable as הדבר. The idea of the matter "being found" must mean that it was "found out to exist/be true" or "uncovered."

וַיִּתָּלוּ שְׁנֵיהֶם עַל־עֵץ. *Wayyiqtol* 3mp Niph √תלה. The Qal תלה is bivalent "X hangs Y," where the complement is an NP of the person or thing hung or suspended; the decreased-valency Niphal is monovalent and promotes the complement to the subject role, "Y is hung." The word is often used specifically with the execution of persons by hanging on or attaching to a tree/stake (not "hanging" in the sense that involves a rope around the neck [cf. Bush, 373], but a form of public execution like impalement or crucifixion; cf. Hengel, 22–24 on this method of execution in the ancient Near East; cf. HALOT s.v.; BDB s.v.; DCH s.v.). Although תלה (with the specific sense of execution) often occurs with an על-PP adjunct designating the thing on which someone is hung, the verb also regularly occurs without it (e.g., Gen 40:19, 22; cf. Levenson, 65 on possible intertextuality with the story in Gen 40). The bound numeral and pronominal clitic, שניהם "the two of them," is the subject of the verb and refers to "Bigthan and Teresh." Note the full verb-subject agreement, in contrast to the singular verb used in v. 21; here the two men are not hung as a unit but individually suffer the punishment (similarly, two people cannot "die" as a unit, since their lives are independent).

וַיִּכָּתֵב בְּסֵפֶר דִּבְרֵי הַיָּמִים לִפְנֵי הַמֶּלֶךְ. *Wayyiqtol* 3ms Niph √כתב. On the valency of כתב, see 1:19. The subject is null here; from the context (and given what we read later in 6:2) the null subject is probably to be reconstructed as an account of the whole ordeal, including the fact that Mordecai discovered the plot and alerted the king. ספר here refers to a "writing," from context a collection of documents (see comment on 1:22). The English "book" conveys the size of the "writing," however the ספר is not a book (i.e., codex) in the technical sense. The לפני-PP is adjunct to the verb (see comment on 1:19 on the origins of the preposition לפני).

PART II
Haman and Mordecai in Conflict (3:1–7:10)

Episode 1—The Rise of Haman (3:1-15)

§1: Haman's Rage against Mordecai and the Jews (3:1-7)

Esther 3:1-7 sets the context for the rest of the narrative of Esther, particularly the conflict between Haman and Mordecai. The king decides to advance Haman in his service, and moreover he commands that others do obeisance to him. Mordecai, however, refuses, and the stage is set for the struggle between Mordecai and Haman. Although this particular passage has no exact antithesis later in the book, it is generally mirrored by the downfall of Haman and advancement of Mordecai in chapters 6 and 8, respectively.

[1]After these things King Ahashverosh magnified Haman, son of Hammedatha the Agagite, and promoted him and set his authority over all the rulers who were his peers. [2]And all the servants of the king who were in the gate of the king would bow and prostrate themselves before Haman, because thusly the king commanded concerning him. But Mordecai would not bow and he would not prostrate himself. [3]And the servants of the king who were in the gate of the king said to Mordecai, "Why do you transgress the command of the king?" [4]And so it was, when they said (this) to him day after day, he would not listen to them. And they told (it) to Haman in order to see whether the deeds of Mordecai would last, because he had declared to them that he was a Jew. [5]And Haman saw that Mordecai was not bowing or prostrating himself before him, and Haman was filled with rage. [6]And he despised in his eyes to lay hands on Mordecai alone, for they had declared to him the people of Mordecai. So Haman sought to destroy all the Jews who were in all the kingdom of Ahashverosh, the people of Mordecai. [7]In the first month (it was the month of Nisan), in the twelfth year of King Ahashverosh, one cast a "pur" (that was

the "lot") before Haman day after day and from a month until the twelfth month (it was the month of Adar).

3:1 אַחַ֣ר ׀ הַדְּבָרִ֣ים הָאֵ֗לֶּה גִּדַּל֩ הַמֶּ֨לֶךְ אֲחַשְׁוֵר֜וֹשׁ
אֶת־הָמָ֧ן בֶּֽן־הַמְּדָ֛תָא הָאֲגָגִ֖י וַֽיְנַשְּׂאֵ֑הוּ וַיָּ֙שֶׂם֙ אֶת־
כִּסְא֔וֹ מֵעַ֕ל כָּל־הַשָּׂרִ֖ים אֲשֶׁ֥ר אִתּֽוֹ׃

In v. 1 the narrator indicates that the king elevates Haman within the court, though he does not explain why he does so.

אַחַ֣ר ׀ הַדְּבָרִ֣ים הָאֵ֗לֶּה גִּדַּל֩ הַמֶּ֨לֶךְ אֲחַשְׁוֵר֜וֹשׁ אֶת־הָמָ֧ן בֶּֽן־הַמְּדָ֛תָא הָאֲגָגִ֖י. *Qatal* 3ms Piel √גדל. The PP אחר הדברים האלה occurs frequently at beginning of a new section in the Hebrew Bible (Gen 15:1; 22:1; etc.). It is a Topic-fronted adjunct to the verb גדל. The fronting of the PP results in the inversion to verb-subject order. Piel גדל "to cause to grow," "to bring up," "to magnify" (HALOT s.v.; BDB s.v.; DCH s.v.) is the bivalent version of the monovalent Qal גדל "to grow up," "to become great," "to be great" (HALOT s.v.; BDB s.v.; DCH s.v.). The complement is the NP המן, which is modified by the restrictive appositive בן המדתא. This appositive NP identifies which Haman (among all possible Hamans) is being referred to. The gentilic noun האגגי is also an appositive, though it is unclear whether the head is המן or the closer המדתא, though the choice between the two makes little difference, since the father and son share the same ethnicity. The salient point of including האגגי is that it connects Haman genealogically to Agag, the Amalekite king that Saul defeated and Samuel killed (1 Sam 15). Within the narrative of Esther, mentioning Haman's ancestry serves to reinforce the antagonism that develops between Haman and Mordecai, who is of the line of Saul (or a brother line; see comments on v. 2 and 2:5, 6).

וַֽיְנַשְּׂאֵ֑הוּ. *Wayyiqtol* 3ms Piel √נשא with 3ms clitic pronoun. The Piel נשא overlaps with the Qal in the basic sense of "to raise high," though the Piel alone seems to have the specific nuance of "to promote" that occurs here (see HALOT s.v.; BDB s.v.; DCH s.v.). The subject of the bivalent verb is a null pronoun and refers back to King Ahashverosh and the complement is the 3ms clitic pronoun. In Esther, complements of finite verbs are attached as clitic pronouns seventeen times (2:7, 9, 17; 3:1, 10; 4:5, 7, 10; 5:11 [2×]; 6:9, 11, 13; 7:5, 9; 8:2; 10:2), whereas they are attached to the particle את only twice (9:22, 25; see Bergey 1983:85, esp. n.3; see "Salient Grammatical Features" in the Introduction).

וַיָּ֫שֶׂם֙ אֶת־כִּסְא֔וֹ מֵעַ֕ל כָּל־הַשָּׂרִ֖ים אֲשֶׁ֥ר אִתּֽוֹ. *Wayyiqtol* 3ms Qal √שׂים. The verb שׂים is trivalent, taking a subject and two complements—the thing placed (here כסאו) and the location it is placed (here the מעל-PP). The PP מעל is the combination of מן and על and the semantics of the compound are resolved toward the spatial meaning of על (on compound prepositions, see WO 11.3.3; JM 133j). The NP complement כסאו, "his seat" or "his throne" (HALOT s.v.), is used as a metaphor for authority (BDB s.v.; cf. HALOT s.v. and DCH s.v.).

אֲשֶׁ֥ר אִתּֽוֹ. A null subject, null copula relative clause with the PP אתו as the complement. This relative clause modifies the NP השׂרים, who were not necessarily "with" Haman in a spatial sense, but rather conceptually: they were his peers.

3:2 וְכָל־עַבְדֵ֨י הַמֶּ֜לֶךְ אֲשֶׁר־בְּשַׁ֣עַר הַמֶּ֗לֶךְ כֹּרְעִ֤ים
וּמִֽשְׁתַּחֲוִים֙ לְהָמָ֔ן כִּי־כֵ֖ן צִוָּה־ל֣וֹ הַמֶּ֑לֶךְ וּמָ֨רְדֳּכַ֔י לֹ֥א
יִכְרַ֖ע וְלֹ֥א יִשְׁתַּחֲוֶֽה׃

Verse 2 informs the reader that the king has commanded his servants to do obeisance to Haman. As with the advancement of Haman in v. 1, the reason for the king's command in v. 2 is never given. The conflict between Mordecai and Haman, central to the book of Esther, begins in this verse when Mordecai does not bow to Haman. No clear reason is given for Mordecai's refusal, although the narrator's mention of both Mordecai's tribal affiliation (Benjaminite) and Haman's ancestry (Agagite) suggests that tribal enmity is the intended backdrop (see Fox 2001:42–44 for a good summary and evaluation of the various options).

וְכָל־עַבְדֵ֨י הַמֶּ֜לֶךְ אֲשֶׁר־בְּשַׁ֣עַר הַמֶּ֗לֶךְ כֹּרְעִ֤ים וּמִֽשְׁתַּחֲוִים֙ לְהָמָ֔ן. A null copula clause with a compound participial complement (mp Qal √כרע and Hishtaphel √חוה). Though both כרע and השתחוה are bivalent and require a locative complement, there is but a single PP that may fill both verb's valencies—להמן. There are two syntactic explanations: either the two participles are considered a single valency unit, which allows a single PP to fulfill the valency requirements, or the first verb has a null pronominal complement that cataphorically coreferential with להמן. This linguistic issue has not yet been studied for BH grammar and so we cannot determine which analysis is preferable. Rather than a *wayyiqtol*, the null copula and participle construction is used here to convey habitual actions, "all the servants (except Mordecai) would habitually bow down to Haman." In later BH texts, the participle increasingly displaces the *yiqtol* for generic, i.e., gnomic and habitual, statements (Cook 2012:233; cf. 2005:124). The tense of the habitual activities is determined by context—the null copula participial clause is bounded by the *qatal* and *wayyiqtol* in v. 1 and the *wayyiqtol* in v. 3, all of which have a clear past temporal setting.

כָּל־עַבְדֵ֨י הַמֶּ֜לֶךְ אֲשֶׁר־בְּשַׁ֣עַר הַמֶּ֗לֶךְ. This complex NP is the subject of the null copula participial clause. Within the relative clause modifying כל עבדי המלך is a null copula clause with a null subject and a ב-PP complement. The servants were probably government officials, since the idiom "to sit in the gate of the king" refers to holding a government office (see comment on 2:19).

וּמִֽשְׁתַּחֲוִ֣ים. Participle mp Hishtaphel √חוה. The participle משתחוים is from the root חוה (not שׁחו or שׁחה as in BDB and DCH, respectively; cf. HALOT חוה II). The identification of חוה as the root and the Hishtaphel as the *binyan* is strongly supported by Ugaritic evidence (see WO 21.2.3d; JM 59g, 79t). The *š* infix is common in other Semitic languages as the causative morpheme (parallel to the *h* prefix of the Hiphil in Hebrew) and the *t* infix signals reflexivity, as in the Hithpael; thus the Hishtaphel would prototypically be a causative reflexive, e.g., "to make oneself bow down."

כִּי־כֵ֖ן צִוָּה־ל֣וֹ הַמֶּ֑לֶךְ. *Qatal* 3ms Piel √צוה. This verb appears in both bivalent and trivalent forms (see also 2:10). Here the verb is bivalent, with NP המלך as the overt subject, the deictic adverb כן functioning as the complement (and pointing back to the content of the command—bowing to Haman), and the PP לו as an adjunct indicating not whom was commanded but with regard to whom the command was made, i.e., Haman. The initial כי establishes the clause as causal, giving the reason or cause for the preceding clause (see comment on 1:8). Both כי and the fronted כן trigger word order inversion to verb-subject. Note that the light PP לו raises with the verb over the subject (see comment on 2:7; Holmstedt 2010:63).

וּמָ֨רְדֳּכַ֔י לֹ֥א יִכְרַ֖ע וְלֹ֥א יִֽשְׁתַּחֲוֶֽה. *Yiqtol* (irrealis) 3ms Qal √כרע and Hishtaphel √חוה. Both negation of the verb and irrealis semantics would normally trigger verb-subject order, but מרדכי is here fronted for Focus (he is contrasted with everyone else who would bow to Haman). The contrast signaled by the word order suggests an adversative semantic relationship between these two clauses, with the focused NP מרדכי read with contrastive stress: "but *Mordecai* would not bow." Note, though, that it is the word order and contrast that suggest the adversative relationship; this does not directly concern the grammar of the ו conjunction (see comment on 1:12). The irrealis *yiqtol* יכרע parallels the generic–habitual semantics of the participles in the preceding clause.

3:3 וַ֠יֹּאמְרוּ עַבְדֵ֥י הַמֶּ֛לֶךְ אֲשֶׁר־בְּשַׁ֥עַר הַמֶּ֖לֶךְ לְמָרְדֳּכָ֑י
מַדּ֙וּעַ֙ אַתָּ֣ה עוֹבֵ֔ר אֵ֖ת מִצְוַ֥ת הַמֶּֽלֶךְ׃

In v. 3, the servants of the king question Mordecai about his refusal to bow. The purpose of their question, however, is not clear. Do they want to help Mordecai (using a rhetorical question to suggest that he start bowing), hurt Mordecai (by gleaning harmful information—i.e., that he is a Jew—that they can repeat to Haman; cf. comment on v. 4), or are they merely curious?

וַ֠יֹּאמְרוּ עַבְדֵ֥י הַמֶּ֛לֶךְ אֲשֶׁר־בְּשַׁ֥עַר הַמֶּ֖לֶךְ לְמָרְדֳּכָ֑י. *Wayyiqtol* 3mp Qal √אמר. The subject, עבדי המלך with its restrictive relative clause, is a "heavy" constituent of the type that often moved toward the end of the clause for easier processing (see comment on HNPS in 1:5). Here, though, the other constituents are also relatively heavy—the adjunct PP למרדכי (see comments on 2:7; 3:2) and the direct speech complement. Thus, we see an example of prototypical word order within a triggered verb-subject *wayyiqtol* clause. On the syntax of עבדי המלך אשר בשער המלך, see comment on v. 2.

מַדּ֙וּעַ֙ אַתָּ֣ה עוֹבֵ֔ר אֵ֖ת מִצְוַ֥ת הַמֶּֽלֶךְ. Participle ms Qal √עבר. A null copula clause with a pronominal subject and participle phrase complement. As in v. 2, the participle signals generic-habitual activity. Within the participial domain, the NP את מצות המלך is the complement that fulfills the valency of bivalent Qal עבר. As with the same participial context in v. 2, the null copula–participial clause here establishes its temporal frame from the context, which in this case is the present time setting within the direct speech. In null copula clauses (with or without participles), inversion of the order of subject and verb is not triggered as it is in finite verbal clauses; thus, the initial interrogative מדוע does not affect the order of אתה and עובר (see "Word Order"in the Introduction). The interrogative מדוע is the fusion of מה and the Qal 3ms passive participle ידוע, "what is known" > "why?" (HALOT s.v.; BDB s.v.; JM 102a). The noun מצוה is a *miqtal*-pattern feminine noun from צוה: **miṣway-at* > **miṣwaya* > *miṣwâ* (see JM 88Lf).

3:4 וַיְהִי בְּאָמְרָם אֵלָיו יוֹם וָיוֹם וְלֹא שָׁמַע אֲלֵיהֶם וַיַּגִּידוּ לְהָמָן לִרְאוֹת הֲיַעַמְדוּ דִּבְרֵי מָרְדֳּכַי כִּי־הִגִּיד לָהֶם אֲשֶׁר־הוּא יְהוּדִי׃

Mordecai's fellow servants continue to question him about his lack of obeisance, perhaps urging him to acquiesce. But Mordecai refuses. At some point, the servants informed Haman about Mordecai's lack of bowing—Haman must have made a habit of ignoring those who paid him homage or there would have been no need to alert him to Mordecai's dissent (Fox 2001:45).

וַיְהִי. *Wayyiqtol* 3ms Qal היה. On the nature of the discourse ויהי, see comment on 1:1; see also 2:8, 5:1, 2.

בְּאָמְרָם אֵלָיו יוֹם וָיוֹם וְלֹא שָׁמַע אֲלֵיהֶם. Inf constr Qal √אמר with 3mp clitic pronoun and *qatal* 3ms Qal √שמע. The ב-PP/infinitive clause is a Topic-fronted temporal adjunct to the main verb שמע. An alternative analysis is that both the infinitive אמר and the perfect שמע could be within the domain of the ב preposition and so a compound subordinate clause adjunct to the verb ויגידו. Both analyses are grammatical and there is no good way to determine which is more likely. The 3mp clitic pronoun on אמרם is its subject and, though אמר is normally bivalent with a direct speech complement, the complement is a null pronoun and refers back to the question the other servants asked in v. 3 (we have translated the null pronoun with "this"; contra Bush, 376). The verb is also followed by a PP adjunct indicating the addressee, אליו, and an NP temporal adjunct, יום ויום (on the function of the repetitive apposition, see comment on 1:22). The verb שמע is also bivalent and either requires an NP complement of the thing heard or, as here, an אל or ל-PP complement for the person "listened to" (another pattern is the idiomatic שמע לקול and שמע בקול, which are used in the sense of "obey"). The expression of generic statement is an area of semantic overlap between the *qatal*, *yiqtol*, and participle; therefore, while it may catch our attention that the *qatal* is used here for a habitual statement ("[whenever they asked], Mordecai did not listen to them") rather than the *yiqtol* or participle as in vv. 2-3, this usage falls squarely within the normal function of the BH verbal system (Cook 2005; 2012:250, 270).

בְּאָמְרָם. Inf constr Qal √אמר with 3mp clitic pronoun. The Masoretes indicate by using the *Qere-Ketiv* technique that כאמרם should be read for באמרם, but the difference between the two is negligible. Both prepositions with the infinitive construct establish a temporal subordinate clause. It may be that the two have distinct nuances, as Waltke and O'Connor suggest: "ב denotes in general the temporal proximity of one event to another, כ more specifically the more immediately preceding time" (36.2.2b). If this is correct, then the indeterminate temporal setting indicated by the יום ויום (see 2:11) indicates the *Ketiv* ב is more appropriate than the *Qere* כ.

וַיַּגִּידוּ לְהָמָן. *Wayyiqtol* 3mp Hiph √נגד. The forward assimilation of the root letter, נ, produces a lengthened ("doubled") second root letter: **yangīdū* > *yaggīdū*. This verb is bivalent (see comment on 2:10), though here the NP complement is null: "they made [it] known"; the null complement stands for Mordecai's observed behavior. The PP להמן is an adjunct indicating the recipient of the verbal activity. A second adjunct is the following ל-PP/infinitive clause, which provides the (or a) purpose of their involvement (see below).

לִרְאוֹת הֲיַעַמְדוּ דִּבְרֵי מָרְדֳּכַי. Inf constr Qal √ראה and *yiqtol* 3mp Qal √עמד. The subject of the infinitive is not overt, but the null pronoun can be contextually identified as the עבדי המלך. The complement of bivalent ראה is the embedded interrogative clause, which presents an indirect question (JM 161f): "to see whether the deeds of Mordecai would stand" (< the direct question: "will Mordecai's words/deeds stand?"). עמד דבר is a collocation unique to Esther. It is sometimes argued to be equivalent of קום דבר elsewhere (e.g., Deut 19:15), with the sense of "the word persists," i.e., is valid, legitimate (Fox 2001:277–78; cf. Bush, 379). On whether דבר connotes "word" or "deed" in this clause, see the next comment.

כִּי־הִגִּיד לָהֶם אֲשֶׁר־הוּא יְהוּדִי. *Qatal* 3ms Hiph √נגד and null copula clause with subject הוא and complement יהודי. The אשר nominalizes the null copula clause הוא יהודי so that it may serve as the NP complement of the bivalent הגיד. The כי introduces the clause as the reason or basis for the servants telling Haman about Mordecai. There are two plausible analyses for the role of the כי clause in the discourse and they are tied to the meaning of דברי מרדכי in the higher clause. First, Mordecai's דבר may be a claim implied by the following causal clause, כי הגיד להם אשר הוא יהודי. I.e., the reason that the servants reported

Mordecai was to test his claim that his status as a Jew exempted him from bowing to Haman. Alternatively, Mordecai's דבר may refer to his behavior ("deed") and so the servants' purpose would be "to see whether his deeds/behavior would last." In this second analysis, that Mordecai had told his peers he was a Jew may have encouraged their actions but is not explicitly behind his refusal to bow. The former analysis makes better sense of the כי clause (which feels extraneous in the second analysis) as well as Haman's reaction. If this כי clause implies that Mordecai made a public claim about his exemption due to his Jewishness, then we are given further reason for Haman's response—he realizes that it is not just Mordecai's individual stubbornness that is at issue, but no good Jew would pay him homage by bowing. And so, the narrator deftly makes Mordecai's behavior representative of faithful Jews, in much the same way that Daniel's behavior is presented in the book of Daniel.

וַיַּ֣רְא הָמָ֔ן כִּֽי־אֵ֣ין מָרְדֳּכַ֔י כֹּרֵ֥עַ וּמִֽשְׁתַּחֲוֶ֖ה ל֑וֹ 3:5
וַיִּמָּלֵ֥א הָמָ֖ן חֵמָֽה׃

Perceiving Mordecai's intentional slight against him, Haman is infuriated.

וַיַּ֣רְא הָמָ֔ן כִּֽי־אֵ֣ין מָרְדֳּכַ֔י כֹּרֵ֥עַ וּמִֽשְׁתַּחֲוֶ֖ה ל֑וֹ. *Wayyiqtol* 3ms Qal √ראה, participle ms Qal √כרע and Hishtaphel √חוה. The verb ראה is bivalent; here the subject is the PN המן and the complement is not an NP but the כי nominalized אין copula clause. The *wayyiqtol* of ראה is shortened (וירא), giving evidence that it came from a shorter prefix conjugation. כי nominalizes the אין negative copula clause, which has מרדכי as the subject and the compound participles כרע ומשתחוה as the copular complements. The use of the participles within the כי clausal complement to ראה either presents Mordecai's habitual activity ("he would not bow") or past progressive/durative action ("he was not bowing"). Both fit the semantics of the event and there is no clear way to discern which is more accurate. But the different meaning is very nuanced, so it makes little difference to the interpretation of the narrative. On the root חוה, see comment on v. 2.

וַיִּמָּלֵ֥א הָמָ֖ן חֵמָֽה. *Wayyiqtol* 3ms Niph √מלא. The word חמה "heat" is often used metaphorically for "wrath" or "rage." Niphal מלא typically appears with an NP complement specifying the substance of which the subject becomes full (HALOT s.v.; BDB s.v.; DCH s.v.). Only a few occurrences of Niphal מלא are missing a complement (Exod 7:25 is one example). Thus, we should understand חמה as a complement to Niphal מלא, making this a rare example of a bivalent Niphal. Although the NP המן was an overt subject in the preceding clause, it is again overt in this clause (vs. the use of a null pronoun) in order to clarify which of the two discourse available agents, המן from the preceding main clause or מרדכי from the preceding subordinate clause, has become angry. While it would natural for the listener or reader to assume that the agent of the preceding main clause carried through to this main clause, the overt use of המן removes any possible doubt (see Levinsohn on participant reference in BH narrative).

3:6 וַיִּ֣בֶז בְּעֵינָ֗יו לִשְׁלֹ֤ח יָד֙ בְּמָרְדֳּכַ֣י לְבַדּ֔וֹ כִּֽי־הִגִּ֥ידוּ
ל֖וֹ אֶת־עַ֣ם מָרְדֳּכָ֑י וַיְבַקֵּ֣שׁ הָמָ֗ן לְהַשְׁמִ֧יד אֶת־
כָּל־הַיְּהוּדִ֛ים אֲשֶׁ֛ר בְּכָל־מַלְכ֥וּת אֲחַשְׁוֵר֖וֹשׁ עַ֥ם
מָרְדֳּכָֽי׃

Haman's fury at Mordecai is exceeded only by the extent of his plans for revenge: his anger extends beyond Mordecai to his people, that is, to all those who would dare claim exemption like Mordecai has.

וַיִּ֣בֶז בְּעֵינָ֗יו לִשְׁלֹ֤ח יָד֙ בְּמָרְדֳּכַ֣י לְבַדּ֔וֹ. *Wayyiqtol* 3ms Qal √בזה. The verb בזה "to despise" or "to regard with contempt" (HALOT s.v.; BDB s.v.; DCH s.v.) is normally bivalent, with an NP subject (here a null pronoun that refers back to המן) and an NP complement (e.g., Gen 25:34 וַיִּבֶז עֵשָׂו אֶת־הַבְּכֹרָה), though here the complement is the ל-PP/infinitive clause. The PP בעיניו is an adjunct that specifies the instrument by which the verbal activity occurs, "with his eyes." This expression often connotes "opinion, esteem" (DCH s.v. 2b); see also 1:17. And yet, the meaning of Haman "despising [something] with his eyes," i.e., "despising [something] in his opinion" is elusive. Many either emend the verb to a Niphal (suggested in BHS) or interpret the Qal in this case as functionally equivalent to the Niphal: "he considered it beneath his dignity" (HALOT בזה) or less periphrastically, "it was contemptible in his eyes" (see DCH בזה), where the infinitive clause שלח יד במרדכי must be the syntactic subject. The emendation to Niphal would not involve any consonants, but simply a repointing of Masoretic vowels to וַיִּבָּז. However, it is worth noting that only two other collocations of בזה and בעינים occur in the Hebrew Bible: Ps 15:4, where the Niphal occurs, and in Esth 1:17, with the Hiphil (see comment there). Given the rarity of the collocation, it is quite possible that we simply do not understand the nuance of the idiom and so emendation has little support. We assume the normal semantics and valency of the Qal are in play and admit that the precise nuance of בעיניו eludes us. On the idiom לשלח יד במרדכי, see comment on 2:21.

כִּֽי־הִגִּ֥ידוּ ל֖וֹ אֶת־עַ֣ם מָרְדֳּכָ֑י. *Qatal* 3mp Hiph √נגד. This clause mirrors similar statements in 2:10; in 2:10, however, there is no ל-PP designating the person whom is told something, showing that Hiphil נגד is bivalent and that the ל-PP is a verbal adjunct (cf. comment on v. 4). The plural verb signals that the null pronominal subject does not refer back to the last verbal subject, המן, but further back to the last plural subject, עבדי המלך (v. 3).

וַיְבַקֵּ֣שׁ הָמָ֗ן לְהַשְׁמִ֧יד אֶת־כָּל־הַיְּהוּדִ֛ים. *Wayyiqtol* 3ms Piel √בקשׁ. The narrative verb triggers verb-subject order. The subject is overt due to the switch from the plural subject (identifiable as עבדי המלך) of the preceding clause to the singular המן. The bivalent verb בקשׁ takes an infinitive clause complement (להשמיד, "to destroy ...").

הַיְּהוּדִ֛ים אֲשֶׁ֛ר בְּכָל־מַלְכ֥וּת אֲחַשְׁוֵר֖וֹשׁ עַ֥ם מָרְדֳּכָֽי. Some prefer to change the vocalization of the text to עִם מרדכי "with Mordecai" instead of עַם מרדכי "the people of Mordecai" (BHS; cf. Moore 1971:37). If this revocalization were correct, there would be two possible syntactic interpretations. First, the PP could modify the null copula of the relative clause: "who were in all the kingdom of Ahashverosh *with* Mordecai." Second, the PP could modify the verb of the infinitive clause: "to destroy all the Jews ... *along with* Mordecai." The MT as it is pointed is not difficult, though—עם מרדכי can be understood as an appositive to היהודים. Although separated from היהודים by a relative clause, appositives can be stacked with relative clauses, such that both modify the same head: "the Jews, who were in ..., the people of Mordecai." Thus, there is no need to change the MT vocalization (cf. Keil, 344; Bush, 377; Fox 2001:278).

3:7 בַּחֹ֤דֶשׁ הָֽרִאשׁוֹן֙ הוּא־חֹ֣דֶשׁ נִיסָ֔ן בִּשְׁנַת֙ שְׁתֵּ֣ים
עֶשְׂרֵ֔ה לַמֶּ֖לֶךְ אֲחַשְׁוֵר֑וֹשׁ הִפִּ֣יל פּוּר֩ ה֨וּא הַגּוֹרָ֜ל
לִפְנֵ֣י הָמָ֗ן מִיּ֧וֹם ׀ לְי֛וֹם וּמֵחֹ֛דֶשׁ לְחֹ֖דֶשׁ שְׁנֵים־עָשָׂ֑ר
הוּא־חֹ֥דֶשׁ אֲדָֽר׃

Verse 7 disrupts the narrative flow. It relates the casting of lots before Haman, perhaps to determine the date of the attack against the Jews.

בַּחֹ֤דֶשׁ הָֽרִאשׁוֹן֙ הוּא־חֹ֣דֶשׁ נִיסָ֔ן בִּשְׁנַת֙ שְׁתֵּ֣ים עֶשְׂרֵ֔ה לַמֶּ֖לֶךְ אֲחַשְׁוֵר֑וֹשׁ. There are two Topic-fronted ב-PP temporal phrases modifying the verb הפיל. Multiple Topic-fronted temporal phrases are also found in 1:2, 2:1, and 2:8. The sequence הוא חדש ניסן is a null copula clause between the two ב-PPs; its status as a parenthetical gloss clarifying the referent of החדש הראשון is signaled by the fact that it changes the syntactic pattern (from *qatal* clause to null copula clause) and it interrupts the syntax of the clause surrounding it. There are many such parentheses in Esther, introduced by personal pronouns (see comments on 1:1 and 2:7). The PN ניסן is the Hebrew version of Akkadian *nisannu*, the Babylonian name of the first month (HALOT s.v.; BDB s.v.; cf. Paton, 200; Moore 1971:38). The second temporal PP, בשנת שתים עשׂרה למלך אחשורוש, reflects the convention for dating an occurrence of an event, with the NP-internal ל-PP signalling possession (see comment on 1:3).

הִפִּ֣יל פּוּר֩ ה֨וּא הַגּוֹרָ֜ל לִפְנֵ֣י הָמָ֗ן מִיּ֧וֹם ׀ לְי֛וֹם וּמֵחֹ֛דֶשׁ לְחֹ֖דֶשׁ. *Qatal* 3ms Hiph √נפל. Hiphil נפל means "to throw down" (HALOT s.v.); combining Hiphil נפל with the NP גורל is the expression for casting lots (BDB s.v.; DCH s.v.). The null subject of the verb is generic and impersonal, "one cast lots," and is often transformed in English translation to a passive, "lots were cast" (e.g., Bush, 377). The null copula clause הוא הגורל (subject הוא and complement הגורל) is another explanatory parenthesis (see preceding comment). The PN פור, found only in Esther, is a loanword from Babylonian Akkadian *pūru*, "lot" (HALOT s.v.; cf. Bush, 377). The compound PP מיום ליום is another way of expressing "daily" (cf. BDB יום on the related phrase מִיּוֹם אֶל יוֹם); how this expression differs from יום ויום in 3:4 or בכל יום ויום in 2:11 is unclear. The compound PP מחדש לחדש similarly means "monthly."

בַּחֹ֤דֶשׁ הָֽרִאשׁוֹן֙. The numeral syntax of this phrase, with the ordinal ראשון, differs significantly from cases where cardinal numbers are used with an ordinal sense (e.g., לחדש שנים עשׂר, "until the *twelfth month*"; see "Numeral Syntax in Esther" in the Introduction). As an ordinal, ראשון modifies חדש adjectivally: חדש is unbound (and thus it is able to take the article) and ראשון agrees with it in gender, number, and person. By contrast, in the phrase חדש שנים עשׂר later in the clause, the compound numeral שנים עשׂר is unbound and is either in apposition to חדש, "in the month, twelve," or is the clitic host to the bound noun חדש

(which, as a ms segholate noun, has an ambiguous form that could be either free or bound), "in the month of twelve." The latter is the structure of שׁנת שׁתים עשׂרה, because שׁנת is the bound form of שָׁנָה. In cardinals 11–19 the "digits" numeral precedes the "-teen," as we find in both our examples here (see Hetzron, 169–70).

מִיּ֧וֹם ׀ לְי֛וֹם וּמֵחֹ֛דֶשׁ לְחֹ֥דֶשׁ שְׁנֵים־עָשָׂ֖ר הוּא־חֹ֥דֶשׁ אֲדָֽר. A number of modern interpreters have suggested that v. 7 is redactional and was added to the story at a later point in time, when it was used to legitimize the existence of the festival of Purim (Moore 1971:37–38; Fox 2001:258; Levenson, 70). Indeed, it does appear that the verse underwent some redaction or textual corruption, as evinced specifically in the awkward phrase מיום ליום ומחדשׁ לחדשׁ שׁנים עשׂר (Keil, 345; Paton, 202; Fox 2001:278; Bush, 377, 380). This phrase seems to be a combination of מיום ליום ומחדשׁ לחדשׁ, "day after day and month after month," with מיום ליום מהחדשׁ הראשׁון לחדשׁ שׁנים עשׂר, "day after day, from the first month until the twelfth month." Alternatively, it could be a corruption of מיום ליום ומחדשׁ לחדשׁ ויפל הגורל בארבעה עשׂר לחדשׁ שׁנים עשׂר (following, in part, the Septuagint), with a scribe skipping from the first instance of לחדשׁ to the second (Keil, 345; cf. Tov and Polak). Some commentators reconstruct a different text at this point, utilizing the Alpha Text (cf. Keil, 345; Paton, 202; Moore 1971:38; Fox 2001:278; Bush, 377, 380–81; Levenson, 70; on the Alpha Text, see "The Alpha Text of Esther" in the Introduction). The text as it stands in the Masoretic Text is best understood as "day after day and from a month until the twelfth month"; alternatively, we could understand שׁנים עשׂר as appositional to חדשׁ: "day after day and month after month—the twelfth" (cf. Paton, 202). In the phrase לחדשׁ שׁנים עשׂר, the cardinal number שׁנים עשׂר ("twelve") is used with an ordinal sense ("twelfth") instead of an ordinal, because there are no ordinals above "tenth" (see "The Alpha Text of Esther" in the Introduction).

§2: Haman's Plot (3:8-15)

In the second half of chapter 3, Haman hatches his plan to exact revenge on Mordecai by slaying all the Jews. He makes sure to portray his scheme in such a manner that it seems advantageous to the king. The king, in turn, buys into the plan with seemingly little reflection. Just as vv. 1-7 are mirrored in chapters 6 and 8, Haman's desire to harm all the Jews in vv. 8-15 is mirrored in the end of the book when the Jews slaughter other peoples.

[8]And Haman said to King Ahashverosh, "A certain people is scattered and separate from the (other) peoples throughout the provinces of your kingdom. Their laws differ from (those of) every people-group, and even the laws of the king they do not observe. For the king, to let them alone is not appropriate. [9]If it pleases the king, let 'to-destroy-them!' be written. I will weigh out 10,000 talents of silver into the hands of those who do the work to bring to the treasuries of the king." [10]So the king removed his signet-ring from upon his hand, and he gave it to Haman, son of Hammedatha the Agagite, who was hostile to the Jews. [11]And the king said to Haman, "The silver is given to you, and the people (are given to you), to do with them according to what pleases you." [12]And the scribes of the king were called in the first month, on the thirteenth day in it, and according to all that Haman commanded was written to the satraps of the king and to the governors who were over every province and to the rulers of every people, (being written to) every province according to its writing and (being written to) every people according to its language. It was written in the name of King Ahashverosh, and it was sealed with the signet-ring of the king, [13]letters being sent by the messengers to all the provinces of the king, to exterminate, to slay, and to destroy all the Jews, from young to old, children and women, in one day, on the thirteenth (day) of the twelfth month—it is the month of Adar—and to plunder their spoil. [14]A copy of the writing was to be given as a law in every single province, being revealed to all the people, in order to be ready for that day. [15]The messengers went out hastily by the word of the king, and the law was given in Susa, the citadel, and the king and Haman sat to drink while the city, Susa, was agitated.

3:8 וַיֹּ֤אמֶר הָמָן֙ לַמֶּ֣לֶךְ אֲחַשְׁוֵר֔וֹשׁ יֶשְׁנ֣וֹ עַם־אֶחָ֗ד
מְפֻזָּ֤ר וּמְפֹרָד֙ בֵּ֣ין הָֽעַמִּ֔ים בְּכֹ֖ל מְדִינ֣וֹת מַלְכוּתֶ֑ךָ
וְדָתֵיהֶ֞ם שֹׁנ֣וֹת מִכָּל־עָ֗ם וְאֶת־דָּתֵ֤י הַמֶּ֙לֶךְ֙ אֵינָ֣ם
עֹשִׂ֔ים וְלַמֶּ֥לֶךְ אֵין־שֹׁוֶ֖ה לְהַנִּיחָֽם׃

In v. 8 Haman tactfully brings up the Jewish people and, feigning an advisory role to the king, points out that it is disadvantageous for the king to tolerate them. Of course, Haman really has his own interests in mind, not the king's, a point which will come out in 7:4 when Haman's plans are unravelled.

וַיֹּ֤אמֶר הָמָן֙ לַמֶּ֣לֶךְ אֲחַשְׁוֵר֔וֹשׁ. *Wayyiqtol* 3ms Qal √אמר. The Qal of אמר is bivalent, taking a direct speech complement. The PP למלך

אחשורוש is adjunct, specifying the addressee. On מלך אחשורוש, see comment on 1:2.

יֶשְׁנ֣וֹ עַם־אֶחָ֗ד מְפֻזָּ֤ר וּמְפֹרָד֙ בֵּ֣ין הָֽעַמִּ֔ים בְּכֹ֖ל מְדִינ֣וֹת מַלְכוּתֶ֑ךָ. A copular clause with both the יש and the 3ms clitic pronoun attached to it functioning as the copula (Holmstedt and Jones, 61, n. 18), the NP עם אחד as the subject, and the copular complement the participles (ms Pual √פזר and √פרד). With the elements אין and יש, some prepositions like מן, and some verbs, the 3ms pronominal clitic has the form נו (instead of ו- or הו-; cf. ממנו in 5:9 and איננו in 5:13); it is usually pointed נּוּ-, but with יש it is always pointed נוֹ-, as here (JM 102k; contra Paton, 207). The numeral אחד, "one," can be adjectival ("*a certain* people") or even function like an indefinite article: "a people" (HALOT s.v.; BDB s.v.; DCH s.v.; GKC 125b; WO 15.2.1a, f; Bush, 381). The word עם can be collective, referring to plural people; however here it refers to "people" in the sense of a "people-group" (HALOT s.v.; BDB s.v.).

מְפֻזָּ֤ר וּמְפֹרָד֙ בֵּ֣ין הָֽעַמִּ֔ים בְּכֹ֖ל מְדִינ֣וֹת מַלְכוּתֶ֑ךָ. Participle ms Pual √פזר and √פרד. This verse contains the only Pual instance of פזר and פרד in the Hebrew Bible. The verb פרד is often found with a בין-PP (BDB s.v.), with the meaning "to divide/separate X *from* Y"; the Pual with the בין-PP may have the nuance that this people separated themselves from others, a notion that Haman might have been using to characterize the Jews as recalcitrant, unassimilated, and essentially dangerous to the unity of the kingdom (Bush, 381; also see Moore 1971:39; Fox 2001:48–49; contra RSV "*amongst* the peoples"). The two PPs, בין העמים and בכל מדינות מלכותך, are adjuncts, and clearly located within the lower domain of the participle phrases—but to what precisely are they adjuncts? Both could be sequential adjuncts to the participle מפרד, "divided among the peoples, in all the provinces," or the בין-PP could modify מפרד and the ב-PP could be an NP-internal adjunct to עמים, "divided among [the peoples in all the provinces]." The difference in syntax results in different semantics—if בכל מדינות מלכותך modifies מפרד, it means that the Jews have not assimilated throughout the kingdom; if the PP modifies העמים, it means that the Jews have not assimilated with any people anywhere in the kingdom (though we might expect the quantifier כל before העמים if this were the intention). In discourse terms, the semantic difference is negligible; even so, we consider the first reading, that both PPs modify מפרד to be more likely.

וְדָתֵיהֶ֞ם שֹׁנ֣וֹת מִכָּל־עָ֗ם. A null copula clause with subject דתיהם and participle phrase complement, participle fp Qal √שׁנה (see comment on 2:9 for the range of meanings for שׁנה). On the meaning of דת, see comment on 1:13. The durative semantics of the participle contribute to the generic assertion, that the Jews' "laws are different." Since the subject is identifiable "a certain people," the genericity is resolved as a habitual statement. The מן-PP adjunct provides the point of comparison for what is different about the Jews' laws. Since "laws" are not compared to "people," the מן-PP has a null complement that is modified by כל עם—"their laws differ from (those of) every people-group" (i.e., the ellipsis of the "laws" before כל עם is the only way to make the comparison one of apples to apples, rather than apples to oranges).

וְאֶת־דָּתֵי הַמֶּלֶךְ אֵינָם עֹשִׂים. An אין copula clause with 3mp clitic pronoun and participle mp Qal √עשׂה. The subject of the copula is the clitic pronoun attached to אין, as with ישנו in the first copular clause (cf. WO 37.6a, 39.3.3b). The copular complement is the participle עשׂים, which has durative semantics. Since the referent of the 3mp subject pronoun is identifiable as "a certain people," the resulting generic expression should be understood as habitual—it was not their habit (according to Haman) to follow the king's laws. The verb עשׂה with the complement "laws of the king" has the meaning "to observe" (BDB s.v.) or "to perform" (HALOT s.v.; see comment on 1:3 for the various meanings of עשׂה; see 2:20 for another example of this particular meaning). The phrase דתי המלך is fronted for Focus (see also Moore 1971:39), to isolate the king's laws (as opposed to any other laws, such as this "certain peoples" own laws) as what this people would not follow. The implication is that regardless what their own laws are, at a bare minimum they are obligated to follow royal decrees, which they here accused of not doing. This kind of Focus is often signaled in English by the focus operator "even," as in "*even the king's laws* they don't follow!"

וְלַמֶּלֶךְ אֵין־שֹׁוֶה לְהַנִּיחָם. An אין copula, participle ms Qal √שׁוה, and inf constr Hiph √נוח with 3mp clitic possessive pronoun. The first radical נ is doubled in some II-ו verbs in the Hiphil—as it is in להניחם—possibly by analogy to II-ע verbs in Aramaic (JM 80p; cf. Paton, 207). When Hiphil נוח does not have thc doubled first radical, the meaning is "to cause to rest" (HALOT s.v.; cf. DCH s.v.; BDB s.v.). With the doubled radical, however, the meaning is to "place, set down," "leave behind," or "let alone, allow to remain, leave undisturbed" (DCH s.v.; cf. HALOT s.v.; BDB s.v.; JM 80p). The root שׁוה means to "compare (with)" (DCH s.v.), "agree with, be like, resemble" (BDB s.v.), or "be the same" (HALOT s.v.; DCH s.v.). With a ל-PP it may mean "to be appropriate" (HALOT s.v.; cf. BDB s.v.) or to "be good, be profitable" (DCH s.v.); the only other possible example of this meaning in the Hebrew Bible is כל זה איננו שוה לי in 5:13 (although we argue for a different understanding; see comment on 5:13, and cf. 7:4). Hiphil נוח is bivalent, taking an NP complement, which is manifested as the 3mp clitic pronoun. The subject of the negative אין copula is ל-PP/infinitive clause להניחם; the copular complement is the participle שוה. Within the participle phrase, the complement of שוה is the PP למלך, which has moved from within the participle phrase to the front of the matrix clause for Focus. Although the syntax is complex, the general sense of this clause is clear: Haman's claim is that it is not to the king's benefit to give this people rest.

3:9 אִם־עַל־הַמֶּ֣לֶךְ ט֔וֹב יִכָּתֵ֖ב לְאַבְּדָ֑ם וַעֲשֶׂרֶת֩ אֲלָפִ֨ים
כִּכַּר־כֶּ֜סֶף אֶשְׁקוֹל֙ עַל־יְדֵי֙ עֹשֵׂ֣י הַמְּלָאכָ֔ה לְהָבִ֖יא
אֶל־גִּנְזֵ֥י הַמֶּֽלֶךְ׃

After establishing a negative characterization of the Jews, Haman proposes his plan to rid the kingdom of their presence, sweetening the deal by offering the king a large sum of money. Haman's statement here recalls the advice given to the king in 1:19-21 and 2:2-4. Whereas the advice was given for the king's benefit in chapters 1 and 2, Haman disguises his advice as beneficial to the king, though it is transparent to the audience that he is acting in his own interest.

אִם־עַל־הַמֶּ֣לֶךְ ט֔וֹב יִכָּתֵ֖ב לְאַבְּדָ֑ם. Null copula, *yiqtol* (irrealis) 3ms Niph √כתב, and inf constr Piel √אבד. On the phrase אם על המלך טוב, see comment on 1:19. The subject of monovalent passive יכתב is the ל-PP/infinitive clause לאבדם (see also the last clause in v. 8), yielding the awkward English "let 'to-destroy-them' be written." The language here assumes that for the king "to write" something it effects the desired outcome. The infinitive Piel אבד "to make X perish" or "to destroy" (HALOT s.v.; BDB s.v.) is bivalent and its complement is the attached 3mp clitic pronoun. Both the fronted אם clausal adjunct to the verb יכתב as well as the irrealis semantics of the conditional statement trigger verb-subject order. The אם clause is a Topic-fronted adjunct, which is the common structure of protasis-apodosis relationships in BH—the protasis is fronted to establish the semantic nature (a similar Topic function as scene-setting).

וַעֲשֶׂ֨רֶת אֲלָפִ֜ים כִּכַּר־כֶּ֗סֶף אֶשְׁקוֹל֙ עַל־יְדֵי֙ עֹשֵׂ֣י הַמְּלָאכָ֔ה. *Yiqtol* 1cs Qal √שׁקל and participle mp Qal √עשׂה. The complement of the verb (עשׂרת אלפים ככר כסף) is fronted for Focus (i.e., to drive home the point that he adds this surprising amount, and no less, to encourage the king). The verb שׁקל (related to the noun שֶׁקֶל) means "to weigh out"; when used with money as its complement, the connotation is "to pay" (HALOT s.v.; cf. BDB s.v.; DCH s.v.). The PP על ידי עשׂי המלאכה, "unto the hands of those who do the work," is adjunct to the verb. The irrealis semantics of the *yiqtol* אשׁקול are due to the irrealis "world" established by the conditional, a world in which Haman's offer to pay extra to see the Jews destroyed exists.

עֲשֶׂ֨רֶת אֲלָפִ֜ים כִּכַּר־כֶּ֗סֶף. Lit. "ten of a thousand, talent of silver." The compound numeral עשׂרת אלפים consists of the numeral "ten" bound to "thousand." This compound numeral is the head to the appositive ככר כסף, which is singular because it need not agree with the numeral (cf. JM 142e–j). One wonders if the word ככר is accidental here: a talent (ככר) is equivalent to 3,000 shekels, thus 10,000 talents is 30 million shekels (over 300 tons), a huge amount of silver for anyone to possess (Moore 1971:39; Fox 2001:51–52; Bush, 381–82). Thus "10,000 *shekels* of silver" should perhaps be understood instead, a large amount of money in itself. Alternatively, the excessive amount may be intentional, adding to the sarcasm/comedy of the portrayal of Haman, Ahashverosh, and the Persian court (Bush, 382), or "legendary hyperbole" (Fox 2001:52).

עַל־יְדֵי֙ עֹשֵׂ֣י הַמְּלָאכָ֔ה. Participle mp Qal √עשׂה. That the money is weighed "unto the hands of those who do the work" means that the money goes into their possession (in this case, temporary). On first reading the NP המלאכה might seem to refer to the job of destroying the Jews (אבדם); in other words, the text might seem to say that Haman is offering to pay those who fight and kill the Jews. However, the following purpose clause להביא אל גנזי המלך clarifies that the עשׂי המלאכה are people who will transport the money into the possession of the king's treasuries (Paton, 207; Moore 1971:40; Fox 2001:280; cf. 4:7). Oddly, in v. 11 it is the *king* who is said to give *Haman* the money; it is difficult, therefore, to understand what exactly is happening with this money.

לְהָבִ֖יא אֶל־גִּנְזֵ֥י הַמֶּֽלֶךְ. Inf constr Hiph √בוא. The verb בוא in the Hiphil is trivalent, taking a subject, an NP complement, and locative/goal PP complement. The subject is null, as in most purpose infinitives, but understood to be "those who do the work" (עשי המלאכה). The NP complement is also null, but understood to be the 10,000 talents (עשׂרת אלפים ככר כסף) paid by Haman. The third complement is overt, the PP אל גנזי המלך. The Hebrew word גֶּנֶז only occurs here and in 4:7, though its Aramaic counterpart can be found in Ezra 5:17, 6:1, and 7:20. It means "treasury" (HALOT s.v.; BDB s.v.; DCH s.v.).

3:10 וַיָּסַר הַמֶּלֶךְ אֶת־טַבַּעְתּוֹ מֵעַל יָדוֹ וַיִּתְּנָהּ לְהָמָן בֶּן־
הַמְּדָתָא הָאֲגָגִי צֹרֵר הַיְּהוּדִים׃

Ahashverosh signifies his assent to Haman's plan by giving him his signet ring, with which Haman could issue a decree with the authority of the king (cf. v. 12). The influence of the Joseph story on Esther can be seen in this verse, which echoes Gen 41:42 where the king of Egypt gives his signet ring to Joseph: וַיָּסַר פַּרְעֹה אֶת־טַבַּעְתּוֹ מֵעַל יָדוֹ וַיִּתֵּן אֹתָהּ עַל־יַד יוֹסֵף. In that instance, however, the purpose was to *protect* the Hebrew people, not to *destroy* them (Fox 2001:52).

וַיָּסַר הַמֶּלֶךְ אֶת־טַבַּעְתּוֹ מֵעַל יָדוֹ. *Wayyiqtol* 3ms Hiph √סור. Qal סור means to "turn aside" or "depart" (HALOT s.v.; BDB s.v.; DCH s.v.), often bivalent with a directional PP complement; thus, the causative Hiphil סור is trivalent, meaning "to cause X to turn aside" or "to remove," with an NP complement (here את טבעתו, the thing turning aside) and one directional PP complement (here מעל ידו, denoting the place from which something turns).

וַיִּתְּנָהּ לְהָמָן בֶּן־הַמְּדָתָא הָאֲגָגִי צֹרֵר הַיְּהוּדִים. *Wayyiqtol* 3ms Qal √נתן with 3fs clitic pronoun and participle ms Qal √צרר. The verb נתן is trivalent, taking an NP complement (here the cliticized 3fs pronoun referring back to טבעתו) and a ל-PP complement (here להמן). The NP בן המדתא is appositive to the head המן, while the gentilic האגגי is probably appositive to the head המדתא (i.e., Hammedatha is the Agagite; see comment on v. 1). The unmarked null copula-participial relative צרר היהודים, "(who) (was) showing hostility toward the Jews," must either modify המדתא (with האגגי intervening) or המן (with בן המדתא האגגי intervening). The context of the story indicates that Haman is צרר היהודים, whereas there is no reason to think that Haman's father is. Compare the similar structure in 2:3 and 2:15: הגי סריס המלך שמר הנשים.

3:11 וַיֹּ֨אמֶר הַמֶּ֙לֶךְ֙ לְהָמָ֔ן הַכֶּ֖סֶף נָת֣וּן לָ֑ךְ וְהָעָ֕ם לַעֲשׂ֥וֹת
בּ֖וֹ כַּטּ֥וֹב בְּעֵינֶֽיךָ׃

Having given Haman his signet ring, the king now signifies his assent to Haman's plan verbally, giving him permission to do what he thinks is best.

וַיֹּ֨אמֶר הַמֶּ֙לֶךְ֙ לְהָמָ֔ן. *Wayyiqtol* 3ms Qal √אמר. The Qal אמר takes an NP complement, namely the direct speech immediately following. The ל-PP designating the addressee of the speech is adjunct to the verb.

הַכֶּ֖סֶף נָת֣וּן לָ֑ךְ. Null copula clause and passive participle ms Qal √נתן. The subject of the copular clause is the NP הכסף and the copular complement is the participle phrase. The Qal passive נתן reflects a valency decrease from trivalency to bivalency, and therefore has only one complement, the ל-PP designating the recipient of the thing given. The passive participle is even less event oriented than the active participle (Cook 2012:228, n. 59) and so here references the state or status of the כסף. The temporal setting of the null copula could be present ("is given") if this is intended as a performative statement, future "will be given" if the king's intention is that when needed Haman will get the funds to carry out his little war, or past ("were given" or "has been given") if the transfer has already been effected. Since direct speech has its own deictic center, there is no determinative feature regarding the temporal setting, though we find it more logical that the king is promising the funds and, since royal authority is nearly absolute, the deed is done as he speaks. It is unclear what "the silver" refers to here; the most obvious referent would be the silver mentioned in v. 9, but there Haman is giving, not receiving, the payment. Perhaps the saying is idiomatic for "you have the money" (i.e., "if you can afford your private war, by all means proceed"), or perhaps the king is returning the very money that Haman has just pledged (i.e., "keep the money"; so Fox 2001:52; cf. LXX Τὸ μὲν ἀργύριον ἔχε). For a good discussion of the possibilities, see Moore 1971:40; and Bush, 382).

וְהָעָ֕ם לַעֲשׂ֥וֹת בּ֖וֹ כַּטּ֥וֹב בְּעֵינֶֽיךָ. A null copula and inf constr Qal √עשה. This clause reflects coordinate clause ellipsis, where a constituent identical to the coordinate clauses is represented by a null constituent in the second of the pair (see Miller 2005, 2007 on ellipsis patterns in BH). The null (or "gapped") item here is the copular complement, the passive participle and its adjunct, נתון לך. The PP בו in the purpose infinitive refers back to העם. The PP כטוב בעיניך is the complement to the infinitive עשה, "to behave/act," denoting the manner in which one acts (see comments on 1:3, 8). Within the כ-PP, the complement to the preposition is a null constituent, modified by an unmarked null copula relative clause with the adjectival phrase טוב בעיניך as copular complement: "according to (the manner that is) good in your eyes." On the expression טוב בעיני, see comment on 1:21; 2:4; 2:9.

3:12 וַיִּקָּרְאוּ֩ סֹפְרֵ֨י הַמֶּ֜לֶךְ בַּחֹ֣דֶשׁ הָרִאשׁ֗וֹן בִּשְׁלוֹשָׁ֨ה
עָשָׂ֣ר יוֹם֮ בּוֹ֒ וַיִּכָּתֵ֣ב כְּֽכָל־אֲשֶׁר־צִוָּ֣ה הָמָ֡ן אֶ֣ל
אֲחַשְׁדַּרְפְּנֵֽי־הַ֠מֶּלֶךְ וְאֶל־הַפַּחוֹת֩ אֲשֶׁ֨ר ׀ עַל־מְדִינָ֜ה
וּמְדִינָ֗ה וְאֶל־שָׂרֵ֤י עַם֙ וָעָ֔ם מְדִינָ֤ה וּמְדִינָה֙ כִּכְתָבָ֔הּ
וְעַ֥ם וָעָ֖ם כִּלְשׁוֹנ֑וֹ בְּשֵׁ֨ם הַמֶּ֤לֶךְ אֲחַשְׁוֵרֹשׁ֙ נִכְתָּ֔ב
וְנֶחְתָּ֖ם בְּטַבַּ֥עַת הַמֶּֽלֶךְ׃

The scribes of the king record the new law proposed by Haman; it is sealed with the king's signet ring, giving it his authority, and sent out to all the provinces of the kingdom. The events of 3:12-15, specifically the writing and sending of Haman's plot in the name of the king, are reversed in the events of 8:9-15, where Mordecai's counterplot is sent out in the name of the king (Fox 2001:159–61). The text of 3:12-15 is often echoed nearly verbatim. For further discussion, see below on 8:9-15.

וַיִּקָּרְאוּ֩ סֹפְרֵ֨י הַמֶּ֜לֶךְ בַּחֹ֣דֶשׁ הָרִאשׁ֗וֹן בִּשְׁלוֹשָׁ֨ה עָשָׂ֣ר יוֹם֮ בּוֹ֒. *Wayyiqtol* 3mp Niph √קרא. Niphal קרא is monovalent, taking only a subject (the thing "called," which is the complement of Qal קרא). On the syntax of חדש הראשון, see comment on v. 7. On the digits numeral preceding the teen numeral in שלושה עשר, see comment on v. 7. Whereas in שנת שתים עשרה and חדש שנים עשר of v. 7 the noun is bound to the numeral, in שלושה עשר יום of this verse the numeral precedes the noun. It could be bound to the noun, but is more likely in apposition to the numeral (the form of עשר is the same whether bound or free; see "Numeral Syntax in Esther" in the Introduction). The PP בו modifies the NP יום, with the clitic pronoun complement ו referring to the "first month"; i.e., the scribes are called "on the thirteenth day in it (= the first month)." The use of ב plus a clitic pronoun to refer back to the month given in a dating formula occurs only in Esther in the Hebrew Bible (cf.

8:9; 9:1, 17, 18 [3×], 21), as well as in the Dead Sea Scrolls (e.g., 4Q252 1.4) and MH (Bergey 1984:72; Bush, 377). Typically the PP לחדש is used (e.g., Gen 7:11).

וַיִּכָּתֵב כְּכָל־אֲשֶׁר־צִוָּה הָמָן אֶל אֲחַשְׁדַּרְפְּנֵי־הַמֶּלֶךְ. *Wayyiqtol* 3ms Niph √כתב and *qatal* 3ms Piel √צוה. As a passive Niphal, the verb יכתב has no complement, but what is the subject? The translator of the Septuagint, sensing a difficulty, changed the 3ms passive verb into the 3p aorist active indicative ἔγραψαν "they wrote." For the passive יכתב, the subject is a null pronoun that is modified and defined by the following NP-internal כ-PP, ככל אשר צוה המן, i.e., "(decrees) like all (the decrees) that Haman commanded." The אשר relative clause has a null head that is also modified by the quantifier כל, "all (the decrees) that Haman commanded." Though it is possible for both the main verb כתב and the subordinate verb צוה to take אל-PP adjuncts (see comments on 2:10 and 4:10 for צוה), since the two אל-PPs do not refer to the recipients of the commanding activity but rather to the recipients of the product of the writing activity, they are adjuncts to the main verb יכתב (see also 2 Sam 11:14 and 2 Kgs 10:6). On the semantics of כתב, see comment on 2:23.

אֶל אֲחַשְׁדַּרְפְּנֵי־הַמֶּלֶךְ וְאֶל־הַפַּחוֹת ... וְאֶל־שָׂרֵי עַם וָעָם. Unlike in 2:3, 8, 14, and 16, where several אל-PPs are found in apposition, here the sequence of PPs are not appositional, but conjoined into one compound PP: "It was written ... to the satraps of the king and to the governors ... and to the rulers." On מדינה ומדינה and עם ועם as repetitive apposition for distributives, see comment on 1:22. The word אחשדרפן "governor, satrap" appears only in Esther (here, 8:9, and 9:3), Ezra (8:36) and nine times in the Aramaic of Daniel). It is a loanword from Persian *ḫšatra pāvan*, "protector of the land" (BDB s.v.; HALOT s.v.; Paton, 212; Moore 1971:41).

הַפַּחוֹת אֲשֶׁר | עַל־מְדִינָה וּמְדִינָה. The NP הפחות is modified by a relative with null copula and על-PP complement: "who (they) (were) over every province." The mp פחות (from פֶּחָה "governor") is a loanword meaning from Akkadian *pīḫatu* (short for *bēl pīḫati*, "lord of a district"; CAD *pīḫatu*; cf. HALOT פֶּחָה). Although the word is feminine in form (and Akkadian *pīḫatu* is grammatically feminine), פחה is masculine in Hebrew (see, e.g., agreement with masculine adjectives and verbs in Isa 36:9 and 2 Chr 9:14).

מְדִינָה וּמְדִינָה כִּכְתָבָהּ וְעַם וָעָם כִּלְשׁוֹנוֹ. These two phrases, each of which includes a repetitive apposition and a gapped verb-preposition complex נכתב אל: "(it was written to) each province according to its writing and (it was written to) each people according to its language." Supporting our analysis is the syntax of 1:22, which parallels the syntax here, apart from overt אל prepositions in 1:22 before מדינה ומדינה ככתבה and עם ועם כלשונו. On מדינה ומדינה and עם ועם, see comment on 1:21.

בְּשֵׁם הַמֶּלֶךְ אֲחַשְׁוֵרֹשׁ נִכְתָּב. Null copula clause with null subject and participle phrase complement, participle ms Niph √כתב. The disjunctive accent *ʾatnaḥ* under כלשונו suggests that a new clause begins with בשם (rather than a participial phrase modifying the null subject of the יכתב clause). The adjunct PP בשם המלך is fronted for Focus.

וְנֶחְתָּם בְּטַבַּעַת הַמֶּלֶךְ. Like the previous clause, this clause has a null copula, null subject, and participle phrase complement (ms Niph √חתם); however, in this clause the adjunct PP is not fronted for Focus. Qal חתם, "to seal" (HALOT s.v.; BDB s.v.; DCH s.v.), is bivalent with an NP subject and an NP complement; thus, in the passive Niphal the verb is downgraded to monovalency and requires only a subject (the promoted complement of Qal חתם). As in the יכתב clause earlier in this verse, the null subject can be reconstructed as the decrees that have been written and are now given the official royal seal.

3:13 וְנִשְׁלֹוחַ סְפָרִים בְּיַד הָרָצִים אֶל־כָּל־מְדִינֹות הַמֶּלֶךְ
לְהַשְׁמִיד לַהֲרֹג וּלְאַבֵּד אֶת־כָּל־הַיְּהוּדִים מִנַּעַר
וְעַד־זָקֵן טַף וְנָשִׁים בְּיֹום אֶחָד בִּשְׁלֹושָׁה עָשָׂר
לְחֹדֶשׁ שְׁנֵים־עָשָׂר הוּא־חֹדֶשׁ אֲדָר וּשְׁלָלָם לָבֹוז׃

Verse 13 fills out the details of Haman's law, including a command to destroy *all* the Jews, regardless of age or gender, and the date on which the attack against the Jews was to commence.

וְנִשְׁלֹוחַ סְפָרִים בְּיַד הָרָצִים אֶל־כָּל־מְדִינֹות הַמֶּלֶךְ. Inf abs Niph √שלח and participle mp Qal √רוץ. As in 2:3, an infinitive absolute is used as the verb of a subordinate clause providing circumstantial information relating to the main clause verb. The Qal שלח is often trivalent, requiring a subject and two complements (an NP complement of the thing sent and a PP complement of the goal/recipient). The passive Niphal reflects a valency reduction and so is bivalent, requiring a subject (the thing sent, here the NP ספרים) and a PP complement for the goal/recipient (here אל

כל מדינות המלך). The ב-PP is an adjunct indicating the means or instrument of the שלח activity (see 1:12 on the idiom ביד). The participle רצים is used as a substantive several times in the Hebrew Bible, meaning "[royal] guard," or (in later texts such as Esther) "messengers" (HALOT s.v.; BDB s.v.; DCH s.v.; Moore 1971:41).

לְהַשְׁמִ֡יד לַהֲרֹ֣ג וּלְאַבֵּ֣ד אֶת־כָּל־הַיְּהוּדִ֡ים מִנַּ֣עַר וְעַד־זָקֵ֩ן טַ֨ף וְנָשִׁ֜ים. Inf constr Hiph √שמד, Qal √הרג, and Piel √אבד. These three infinitive clauses are purpose clause adjuncts modifying נשלוח. Though the content of the documents is not explicit, it may be inferred from the purpose they were written and sent (Bush, 377). The root שמד occurs only in the Niphal for "to be exterminated, destroyed" and the Hiphil "to exterminate, destroy" (HALOT s.v.; BDB s.v.; DCH s.v.). All three verbs, השמיד, הרג, and אבד are bivalent. The subjects are null and impersonal, contextually reconstructable as all the non-Jewish people of the kingdom. Though there are three verbs, there is only one NP that could possibly be a complement to any one of the three, את כל היהודים. Two syntactic explanations are available to explain how the valency of all three is fulfilled—(1) either the complement of the first two verbs is a null pronoun, both of which are cataphoric and coreferential with the overt NP complement of the third infinitive, לאבד; or (2) the three verbs form a compound verb and their independent valency requirements are resolved to a requirement of a single complement. The phrase מנער ועד זקן means "from young to old" (see comment on 1:5); this PP modifies the NP היהודים. The collective noun טף (from the verbal root טפף "to mince along" or "to walk carefully") refers to very young children (DCH s.v. and possibly also to elderly people who are unable to walk well (HALOT s.v.). The compound NP טף ונשים is a second, stacked appositive to היהודים, specifying what type of Jews are included among those who would be slain (the type of apposition is inclusion, specifically particularization; Jones 2011:21–22). The point of the complex phrase is that Haman is targeting every single Jew (Moore 1971:41), whether weak or strong including those who have no ability to fight.

בְּי֣וֹם אֶחָ֔ד בִּשְׁלוֹשָׁ֥ה עָשָׂ֛ר לְחֹ֥דֶשׁ שְׁנֵים־עָשָׂ֖ר הוּא־חֹ֣דֶשׁ אֲדָ֑ר. As with the single NP complement for the three bivalent verbs, the two ב-PPs may be adjuncts of the infinitive לאבד only (as the last of the three), or may be understood to provide circumstances related to all three together. The noun "day" is implied in the phrase שלושה עשר לחדש שנים עשר: "the thirteenth [day] of the twelfth month." The parenthetical null copula clause הוא חדש אדר informs the reader of the name of the twelfth month (see comment on v. 7).

וּשְׁלָלָם לָבוֹז. Inf constr Qal √בוז. This infinitive is parallel to the infinitives להשמיד להרג ולאבד and so another purpose adjunct to נשלוח (see above). The complement of the infinitive precedes the infinitive, an order that is rare in BH but more common in texts from Qumran (see comment on 2:9). The inclusion of this ל-PP/infinitive clause established an important characterization element: in 9:10, 15, and 16 the narrator notes that the Jews do not plunder the spoil of their enemies.

3:14 פַּתְשֶׁגֶן הַכְּתָב לְהִנָּתֵן דָּת בְּכָל־מְדִינָה וּמְדִינָה
גָּלוּי לְכָל־הָעַמִּים לִהְיוֹת עֲתִדִים לַיּוֹם הַזֶּה׃

The near redundancy of this verse (the only new information is that there were copies being circulated and that the non-Jewish people should prepare for the event) is intended to slow the narrative and let the enormity of Haman's decree sink in.

פַּתְשֶׁגֶן הַכְּתָב לְהִנָּתֵן דָּת בְּכָל־מְדִינָה וּמְדִינָה. A null copula clause and inf constr Niph √נתן. The subject of the null copula clause is the NP פַּתְשֶׁגֶן and the copular complement is the ל-PP/infinitive clause. The ל-infinitive להנתן used without a governing finite verb is sometimes referred to as the "predicative infinitive" (cf. Bush, 383). Rather than take the infinitive as the main verb, we take it as the complement of a null copula (see comment on 1:15). The noun פתשגן "copy" is a Persian loanword, from *patšagn*, via Aramaic (HALOT s.v.; Moore 1971:42; cf. BDB s.v.; DCH s.v.) used only in Esther (here; 4:8; 8:13) and Ezra (as פַּרְשֶׁגֶן; in Ezra 4:11, 23; 5:6; 7:11; Paton, 212). The noun כתב ("writing"; HALOT s.v.; BDB s.v.; DCH s.v.) is found only in late biblical texts (Ezekiel, Esther, Dan, Ezra-Nehemiah, Chronicles). Since הכתב is definite, it must be known within the discourse world of the narrative (Bekins); although no כתב has been mentioned to this point, the mention of documents (ספרים) in v. 13 and the assertion that something is written (ויכתב and נכתב) in v. 12 provide the contextual background for this known, identifiable discourse entity. The NP דת (see 1:13) is an adjunct to the verb הנתן indicating the manner of the action, that the writing was to be given "as" or "with the authority of" a law. Niphal נתן is bivalent, taking a subject of the thing given and a PP complement for the recipient (cf. comment on 2:13); we must, therefore, understand a null PP complement (cf. v. 15; 2:18), that is, "a copy of the writing was to be given [to all people] as a law." On כל מדינה ומדינה, see comments on 1:22 and 2:11. The PP בכל מדינה ומדינה is a locative/spatial adjunct to the verb להנתן.

גָּל֖וּי לְכָל־הָֽעַמִּ֑ים. Passive participle ms Qal √גלה. The participle phrase is an adjunct to the higher verb הנתן, specifying even further the manner in which the copy was to be given ("being revealed to all the people"). The Qal passive participle of גלה exhibits the original final י consonant of the root, i.e., גלי (cf. JM 79a–c).

לִהְי֥וֹת עֲתִדִ֖ים לַיּ֥וֹם הַזֶּֽה. Inf constr Qal √היה. This ל-PP/infinitive clause is another adjunct to להנתן, providing the purpose of disseminating copies. The complement of the copula להיות is the adjective עתדים (on which, cf. comment on 8:13).

3:15 הָֽרָצִ֞ים יָצְא֤וּ דְחוּפִים֙ בִּדְבַ֣ר הַמֶּ֔לֶךְ וְהַדָּ֥ת נִתְּנָ֖ה בְּשׁוּשַׁ֣ן הַבִּירָ֑ה וְהַמֶּ֤לֶךְ וְהָמָן֙ יָשְׁב֣וּ לִשְׁתּ֔וֹת וְהָעִ֥יר שׁוּשָׁ֖ן נָבֽוֹכָה׃

Verse 15 describes the dissemination of the new law within Susa, which sets up the contrast between Haman's reaction and that of the rest of the city. This characterization of Haman, who calmly ate while all others were disturbed, brings to mind similar surreal contrasts in both the Bible (Jonah versus the sailors during the storm) and nonbiblical literature (e.g., Nero's singing while Rome burned [according to Cassius Dio]).

Note that this is the third verse in a row in which the *wayyiqtol* has been avoided (the last *wayyiqtol* appears in v. 12). While it could be argued that vv. 13-14 are in the narrative background, filling in circumstantial details relating to the verbs ויקראו and ויכתב in v. 12, it is difficult to see the information in v. 15 in any other way than as part of the narrative foreground. We take the departure from the narrative *wayyiqtol* to function here as a narrative structuring device, to signal the closure of a major component of the story.

הָֽרָצִ֞ים יָצְא֤וּ דְחוּפִים֙ בִּדְבַ֣ר הַמֶּ֔לֶךְ. *Qatal* 3mp Qal √יצא and passive participle mp Qal √דחף. The subject is the participle (used substantivally; see v. 13). The PP בדבר המלך could mean "with the word of the king" (i.e., the king's word accompanied the messengers as they went out; JM 133c) or "by the word of the king" (i.e., the word of the king was the instrument effecting the going out of the messengers; JM 133c;

WO 11.2.5d). Given parallels in 1:19 and 21, the latter is preferred. On the variety of senses that דבר can take, see comment on 1:13. The subject-verb word order likely reflects fronting to mark the shift between Topic constituents (here הרצים, in the next clause הדת, etc.). The Qal passive participle דחופים, like גלוי לכל העמים in v. 14, is an adjunct to the verb, describing the manner in which the messengers went out (see comment on v. 14). The verbal root דחף is used only in Esther (here, 6:12, and 8:14) and 2 Chr 26:20. Related to Akkadian *daʾāpu*, "to push, push away," it means "to push away" in the Qal and "to hurry, hasten" in the Niphal (HALOT s.v.; cf. BDB s.v.; DCH s.v.). Thus the action of the messengers is done in a "pushing away" fashion, that is, "hastily."

וְהַדָּת נִתְּנָה בְּשׁוּשַׁן הַבִּירָה. *Qatal* 3fs Niph √נתן. Again the basic subject-verb word order likely reflects Topic-fronting. Even so, the event described is part of the narrative foreground despite the fact that a *wayyiqtol* is not used. As in v. 14, we must understand a null PP complement of Niphal נתן (see v. 14; 2:18): "the law was given [to people] in Susa, the citadel." On the meaning of דת, see comment on 1:13. On שושן הבירה, see comment on 1:2.

וְהַמֶּלֶךְ וְהָמָן יָשְׁבוּ לִשְׁתּוֹת. *Qatal* 3mp Qal √ישב and inf constr Qal √שתה. This third case of subject-verb word order again reflects a Topic switch to the compound subject המלך והמן from those involved in the dissemination of the decree back to the king and Haman. The phrase ישב לשתות may be idiomatic, referring perhaps to the act of social drinking. The verb ישב is typically bivalent and has a locative complement, specifying where the sitting or dwelling occurred. Here, either the complement is null (e.g,. "down" or "in the palace"), or the verb has a monovalent sense, such as "to sit down." In either case, the infinitive לשתות is a purpose adjunct of ישב and so indicates the reason the two sat together.

וְהָעִיר שׁוּשָׁן נָבוֹכָה. *Qatal* 3fs Niph √בוך. The subject העיר שושן is fronted for Focus and contrasted with המלך והמן. The city had just been mentioned two clauses previously and could be taken as a Topic (and thus a switch from המלך והמן), but we sense a contrast between העיר and the previous agent, המלך והמן. An additional implication of the juxtaposition of these two subject-verb clauses is the contemporaneity of the actions or events—*while* the king and Haman drank leisurely, *everyone else in the city* was disturbed. The monovalent verb בוך appears only in the Niphal, and only in Exod 14:3, Joel 1:18, and here (and possibly 4Q412 fragment 1 line 4). Based on the Akkadian cognate *bwk* ("to be disturbed"), the related noun מבוכה ("confusion"), and the current context, it must mean "to be confused" or "to be agitated" (HALOT s.v.; BDB s.v.; DCH s.v.). The internal structure of the NP העיר שושן is appositional, "the city, Susa" (apposition of identification, identifying the city as Susa), not bound, "the city of Susa."

Episode 2—Mordecai's Response (4:1-17)

In episode 2, Mordecai responds to Haman's evil plot and forms a plan of his own to save his people. This episode consists almost entirely of dialogue—mediated by messengers—between Mordecai and Queen Esther, around whom he builds his response to Haman. While Part I (chaps. 1–2) sets the stage for the story of Esther, it is Part II that sets forth the main issues of the storyline of Esther. Within this core of the book, episode 2 presents the primary plot conflict, between Haman and his anger and Mordecai and his people, the Jews. The rest of the story explores this conflict—what does Haman plan? How will Mordecai and Esther respond? Who will prevail, Haman or Mordecai and his heroine Esther?

§1: Mordecai and the Jews Lament Haman's Plot (4:1-3)

[1]And Mordecai found out all that had happened, and Mordecai tore his garments, and put on sackcloth and ash, and went out into the midst of the city, and let out a great and bitter cry. [2]And he came as far as in front of the gate of the king, because there was no entering into the gate of the king in dress of sackcloth. [3]And in every province, (at) the place where the word of the king, that is, his law, arrived, great mourning belonged to the Jews, that is, fasting and weeping and grieving. Sackcloth and ash were being spread out as a bed for many.

4:1 וּמָרְדֳּכַ֗י יָדַע֙ אֶת־כָּל־אֲשֶׁ֣ר נַעֲשָׂ֔ה וַיִּקְרַ֤ע מָרְדֳּכַי֙
אֶת־בְּגָדָ֔יו וַיִּלְבַּ֥שׁ שַׂ֖ק וָאֵ֑פֶר וַיֵּצֵא֙ בְּת֣וֹךְ הָעִ֔יר
וַיִּזְעַ֛ק זְעָקָ֥ה גְדֹלָ֖ה וּמָרָֽה׃

Immediately following the release of Haman's edict (at the end of chap. 3), Mordecai responds in anguish and mourning.

וּמָרְדֳּכַ֗י יָדַע֙ אֶת־כָּל־אֲשֶׁ֣ר נַעֲשָׂ֔ה. *Qatal* 3ms Qal √ידע and Niph √עשׂה. The subject-verb word order continues the subject-verb *qatal* sequence begun in 3:15, marking a second Focus constituent, מרדכי.

The purpose of this case of Focus is to zero in on מרדכי among all those responding to the news of Haman's plan. While the king and Haman drank leisurely, and the city in general was worked up, Mordecai's response is both more severe and more extensive, which both connects this verse to the last episode while at the same transitioning to a new episode that centers on Mordecai. As with the subject-verb clauses in 3:15, the Focus-fronting obscures the basic subject-verb syntax of the language of the book. The overlap would have been disambiguated by both context (the obvious Topic-Focus-Focus pattern of this clause and the previous two) and prosody, i.e., Focus word stress on the Focus-fronted constituent. The verb ידע, typically translated "to know," can have the sense "to hear of, learn" (HALOT s.v.), referring to the moment when knowledge is gained rather than a state of knowing. Qal ידע is bivalent, taking the complement את כל אשר נעשׂה. The relative clause אשר נעשׂה has a null head, which is defined by the following relative clause and quantified by the preceding כל, "all (the things) that had happened" (see 3:12). Niphal עשׂה is monovalent, taking only a subject (the thing that was done or happened); on the meaning "happen," see comment on 2:11.

וַיִּקְרַ֤ע מָרְדֳּכַי֙ אֶת־בְּגָדָ֔יו. *Wayyiqtol* 3ms Qal √קרע. The return to the narrative *wayyiqtol* is accompanied by the expected return to verb-subject order. The verb קרע, "to tear" (often "to rip to pieces as a sign of mourning" as here), is bivalent, taking an NP complement, here את בגדיו. The repetition of the overt subject מרדכי signals a development in the action of the narrative, translated by "so" or "then" (Levinsohn, 6–8): "Mordecai found out about all that was done, *and so* he tore his clothes."

וַיִּלְבַּ֥שׁ שַׂ֖ק וָאֵ֑פֶר. *Wayyiqtol* 3ms Qal √לבשׁ. The expression לבשׁ שׂק ואפר is a common idiom for mourning or humiliation (Paton, 214; Bush, 393; cf. Isa 58:5; Jer 6:26; Jonah 3:6; Dan 9:3). Qal לבשׁ is bivalent, taking the compound NP complement שׂק ואפר as the "clothing" put on. Note the *pataḥ* (a-class) theme vowel; לבשׁ must have originally been or was still considered in some cases to be a stative verb (JM 41f) and so its pattern is that of the יִקְרַב / קָרֵב type, which departs from the *ḥolem* (u-class) theme vowel of the paradigmatic active verb, e.g., יִשְׁמֹר. According to Paton, שׂק is a loanword from Akkadian (215); others speculate that it stems from Egyptian (BDB s.v.); given the presence of cognates in most Semitic languages (HALOT s.v.), it is more probable that this word is simply an early noun, common to Semitic languages.

וַיֵּצֵא֙ בְּת֣וֹךְ הָעִ֔יר. *Wayyiqtol* 3ms Qal √יצא. The PP בתוך העיר, "into the midst of the city," expresses destination and is complement to the bivalent motion verb יצא (see comment on 1.17).

וַיִּזְעַ֛ק זְעָקָ֥ה גְדֹלָ֖ה וּמָרָֽה. *Wayyiqtol* 3ms Qal √זעק. The verb זעק is frequently monovalent, "to cry out"; here, however, it is bivalent with its "cognate accusative" complement (WO 10.2.1f–g), lit. "he cried out a great and bitter cry."

4:2 וַיָּב֕וֹא עַ֖ד לִפְנֵ֣י שַֽׁעַר־הַמֶּ֑לֶךְ כִּ֣י אֵ֥ין לָב֛וֹא אֶל־שַׁ֥עַר
הַמֶּ֖לֶךְ בִּלְב֥וּשׁ שָֽׂק׃

After beginning the (formal) mourning process, Mordecai's next action is to get in position to communicate with Esther by going as near as possible to the palace. He already has in mind that Esther is the key to saving the Jews from Haman. As the following verses show, rather than sending a messenger directly to Esther, Mordecai's mourning clothes illicit a response from Esther.

וַיָּב֕וֹא עַ֖ד לִפְנֵ֣י שַֽׁעַר־הַמֶּ֑לֶךְ. *Wayyiqtol* 3ms Qal √בוא. The compound preposition עד לפני "more accurately [represents] the relation" of the bivalent verb בוא to its PP complement, "the gate of the king" (WO 11.3.3). In other words, Mordecai did not go "as far as" (עד; cf. WO 11.2.12b) the gate of the king or "before" (לפני) the gate, but "as far as the place that is before (or, in front of)" the gate. The implication is that within the king's gate is an area in which it is disallowed to dress inappropriately, so Mordecai went only as close as he could without incurring punishment.

כִּ֣י אֵ֥ין לָב֛וֹא אֶל־שַׁ֥עַר הַמֶּ֖לֶךְ בִּלְב֥וּשׁ שָֽׂק. An אין copula clause with ל-PP/infinitive clause subject (inf constr Qal √בוא). The structure of this clause does not translate directly in English, which uses an expletive "there" construction, as we translate above. The nuance is that "entering into the gate of the king in dress of sackcloth" was not possible (without incurring punishment). Qal בוא is bivalent, taking a subject (here null, as with most ל-PP/infinitive clauses) and PP complement indicating the locative goal, the אל-PP. On the phrase שער המלך, see comment on 2:19. The PP בלבוש שק is an adjunct to the verb and the bound relationship between the cliticized לבוש and the clitic host שק is one where the latter indicates the material of the former (WO 9.5.3d), i.e., Mordecai's לבוש is made of שַׂק. The כִּי signals that this clause provides a reason for the main clause of 4:2. On the use of אין to negate the infinitive, see Appendix B.

4:3 וּבְכָל־מְדִינָה וּמְדִינָה מְקוֹם אֲשֶׁר דְּבַר־הַמֶּלֶךְ וְדָתוֹ מַגִּיעַ אֵבֶל גָּדוֹל לַיְּהוּדִים וְצוֹם וּבְכִי וּמִסְפֵּד שַׂק וָאֵפֶר יֻצַּע לָרַבִּים׃

Mordecai is not the only person to respond to the law inspired by Haman with grief. In this verse, the narrator widens the perspective to the entire kingdom and notes that many Jews mourned when they heard of Haman's plans.

וּבְכָל־מְדִינָה וּמְדִינָה מְקוֹם אֲשֶׁר דְּבַר־הַמֶּלֶךְ וְדָתוֹ מַגִּיעַ. A null copula clause with subject דבר המלך ודתו and participle ms Hiph √נגע complement. This ב-PP as a whole is a Topic-fronted adjunct to the main clause, which is the null copula clause אל גדול ליהודים. Both the quantified phrase כל מדינה and the repetitive apposition in מדינה ומדינה indicate distribution (see comment on 1:22 and 2:11). The word מקום is in apposition to the compound NP מדינה ומדינה and is similarly a locative adjunct, further specifying where in each province the king's דת arrived: "in every province, (at) the place which. ..." Note the bound form of מקום, which is a morphophonological indication that this relative head is defined by the following אשר relative clause (i.e., a restrictive relative). As a bound noun, מקום cannot host the article; yet, the specification provided by the restrictive relative provides the NP מקום with definiteness (similarly, see Gen 1:1; Holmstedt 2008). Within the relative clause, there is a null copula which takes the participle מגיע as its complement. The subject of the null copula is the complex NP דבר המלך ודתו, which is resolved as a singular (thus the singular participle is used; see Holmstedt 2009b, esp. 126, n. 23). Either דבר המלך and דתו constitute a compound NP and so the two elements represent two distinct entities with sufficient referential overlap to be considered a singular concept, or דתו is in apposition to דבר המלך: "the word of the king, i.e., his edict." Both are valid options, though we prefer the latter since דתו as a clarifying appositive makes good sense. The Hiphil נגע is here bivalent "to arrive (somewhere)" (see also 2:12) and the head of the relative, מקום, is covertly resumed within the relative, i.e., "the place that the king's word ... arrived (there)." The subject of the relative clause is the complex NP דבר המלך ודתו. The participle here is situated within the past temporal frame and yet participates with the distributive כל מדינה ומדינה to provide a durative, in-progress semantics for the action—this tragedy was unfolding throughout the kingdom at roughly the same time in each province.

אֵבֶל גָּדוֹל לַיְּהוּדִים וְצוֹם וּבְכִי וּמִסְפֵּד. A null copula clause with subject NP אבל גדול and complement PP ליהודים, expressing possession (cf. comment on 1:9). This clause is the first main clause of the verse, with the ב-PP preceding it a Topic-fronted scene-setting locative adjunct. The three NPs וצום ובכי ומספד are either an extraposed appositive clarifying to אבל גדול, or one-constituent null copula clause consisting of a compound subject (the three NPs) and a gapped copular complement, ליהודים picked up from the previous clause. Since מספד is nearly synonymous with אבל, we consider the appositive analysis to be more likely. As such, the צום ובכי ומספד clarify in somewhat more concrete terms how the Jews experienced a אבל גדול upon hearing the news of the king's edict.

שַׂק וָאֵפֶר יֻצַּע לָרַבִּים. *Yiqtol* 3ms Hoph √יצע. The verb יצע appears in the Hebrew Bible only here and in Isa 14:11; 58:5; and Ps 139:8, always in the Hiphil or Hophal. In the Hophal it means "to be spread out as a bed" (HALOT s.v.; cf. Bush, 390). Since it is passive, it is monovalent and so does not take a complement, making לרבים an adjunct indicating the beneficiary, or, alternatively, the agent ("by many"; so Paton, 215). The *yiqtol* is a realis past imperfective and continues the progressive semantics of the participle מגיע. The compound subject שׂק ואפר is considered a unit and so resolved as a semantic singular for the sake of agreement with the verb יצע.

§2: Mordecai Convinces Esther to Intercede (4:4-17)

[4]And Esther's young ladies came (to her), and her eunuchs, and they related (it) to her, and the queen trembled exceedingly. And she sent garments to clothe Mordecai and to remove his sackcloth from upon him, but he did not accept (them). [5]So Esther called to Hathak, (who was) one of the eunuchs of the king that he stationed before her, and she commanded him concerning Mordecai to learn what this was and what this was about. [6]And Hathak went out to Mordecai, to the city plaza that was before the gate of the king, [7]and Mordecai declared to him all that had happened to him and the amount of the silver which Haman promised to weigh out into the

treasuries of the king in exchange for the Jews, in order to destroy them. [8]And a copy of the writing of the law, which was given in Susa in order to destroy them, he gave him to show Esther, to declare (it) to her and to command her to go in to the king in order to make supplication to him, that is, to request her people from him. [9]So Hathak went and declared to Esther the words of Mordecai. [10]And Esther said to Hathak and she commanded him (to report) to Mordecai: [11]"All the servants of the king and the people of the provinces of the king know that, any man or woman who goes in to the king, in to the inner court, who is not called—one is his law, to kill anyone apart from the one to whom the king holds out the golden scepter and so lives. But I have not been called to go in to the king. It is (another) thirty days." [12]And they declared the words of Esther to Mordecai. [13]And Mordecai said in response to Esther, "Do not yourself plan to escape in the palace of the king, any more than all the (other) Jews, [14]because if you are completely silent at this time, liberation and deliverance will arise for the Jews from another place, but you and the house of your father will perish. Who knows if for a time like this you have achieved royal status? [15]And Esther said in response to Mordecai, [16]"Go. Gather all the Jews who are found in Susa and fast on my behalf. Do not eat and do not drink for three days, night and day. Even I, and my maidservants, will likewise fast. And then I will go in to the king, which is not according to the law. And however I perish, I perish." [17]And Mordecai moved along, and he acted according to all of that which Esther commanded him.

4:4 וַתָּ֩בוֹאינָה נַעֲר֨וֹת אֶסְתֵּ֤ר וְסָרִיסֶ֙יהָ֙ וַיַּגִּ֣ידוּ לָ֔הּ וַתִּתְחַלְחַ֥ל הַמַּלְכָּ֖ה מְאֹ֑ד וַתִּשְׁלַ֨ח בְּגָדִ֜ים לְהַלְבִּ֣ישׁ אֶת־מָרְדֳּכַ֗י וּלְהָסִ֥יר שַׂקּ֛וֹ מֵעָלָ֖יו וְלֹ֥א קִבֵּֽל׃

When Esther hears about Mordecai's mourning, she is frightened and sends nonmourning clothing to Mordecai, either in an attempt to stop Mordecai's public display of grief, or to enable him to enter the king's gate and thus communicate with her (cf. Keil, 350; Paton, 216). As the following verses make clear, Esther is for some reason unaware of Haman's edict, and thus she does not understand Mordecai's actions. Her overture is rebuffed by Mordecai, who intended to make a scene.

וַתָּ֩בוֹאינָה נַעֲר֨וֹת אֶסְתֵּ֤ר וְסָרִיסֶ֙יהָ֙. *Wayyiqtol* 3fp Qal √בוא. *Qere-Ketiv*: וַתָּבוֹאינָה reflects the vocalization of the form without the י linking vowel in the *Qere* (וַתָּבוֹאנָה); the *Ketiv* ותבואינה has the linking vowel (וַתְּבוֹאֶינָה); see JM 80b. The feminine plural features on the verb indicate that the fp NP נערות אסתר is the syntactic subject. But נערות אסתר is conjoined to the mp סריסיה and normally the conjoining of feminine and masculine NPs resolves as masculine (see Holmstedt 2009b). However, it is also often the case the masculine subjects are listed before feminine subjects in a compound. Thus, the position of נערות preceding סריסיה as well as the feminine plural verb signal that, while Esther's entire entourage was aware of the situation and came to report it to her, the primary agents were her handmaids. The verb בוא is typically bivalent and takes a locative complement (whether simply an NP or a PP). However, in rare cases the meaning is clearly not the accomplishment of "entering a place," but rather simply the activity of "coming"; in such cases, the verb may be monovalent (see Ps 71:16, 18). In this clause it is likely that the verb is bivalent, with a null locative complement, "to her/ Esther," which is contextually clarified by the PP לה in the next clause.

וַיַּגִּידוּ לָהּ. *Wayyiqtol* 3mp Hiph √נגד. The plural verb indicates that now the gender features of the compound feminine NP + masculine NP subject have now been resolved as masculine, which is the inclusive gender in Hebrew grammar. Hiphil נגד is bivalent (cf. comment on 2:10), taking a subject and an NP complement of the thing reported or told; a ל-PP adjunct (here לה) often accompanies the verb to indicate the addressee. The complement may be covert if it easily recoverable by contextual reconstruction. Though there might have been some brief ambiguity in what Esther was informed about (the king's edict or Mordecai's behavior), the next two clauses clarify that it is Mordecai's actions that trouble Esther.

וַתִּתְחַלְחַל הַמַּלְכָּה מְאֹד. *Wayyiqtol* 3fs Hithpalpel √חיל. The root חיל (in the Qal, "to writhe, tremble") is found in a variety of less-common *binyanim*, including the Polel, Polal, Hithpolel (Jer 23:19; Ps 37:7; Job 15:20), and Hithpalpel (only here). For the four ת-infix occurrences, it is impossible to determine a distinct meaning, or even a meaning different from that of the Qal, "to writhe in fear."

וַתִּשְׁלַח בְּגָדִים. *Wayyiqtol* 3fs Qal √שלח. Qal שלח is trivalent (see comment on 1:22), taking an NP complement of the thing sent (here בגדים) and a PP complement for where or to whom the sending is aimed (here this second complement is null but contextually recoverable as "to Mordecai"). Note that Esther's immediate response is to address Mordecai's reaction by trying to subvert his protest, though it is quite possible she realize neither his purpose nor the full implications of her action.

לְהַלְבִּישׁ אֶת־מָרְדֳּכַי. Inf constr Hiph √לבשׁ. This purpose infinitive is an adjunct to the verb תשלח. Since Hiphil לבשׁ is the trivalent causative of the bivalent Qal *binyan*, in addition to an NP complement (בגדים syntactically null and assumed from the previous clause) the Hiphil adds a second NP complement for the person who is clothed, e.g. "she clothed Mordecai with clothes." Often one or the other of the NP complements is null and reconstructed from the context. Such is the case in this clause with the first NP complement, בגדים.

וּלְהָסִיר שַׂקּוֹ מֵעָלָיו. Inf constr Hiph √סור. This infinitive is a second adjunct to תשלח and further explains the purpose. Rather than a second action, this should be seen as the simple corollary of the first purpose adjunct: clothing Mordecai assumes the removal of his mourning attire. Specification like this is similar to many cases of parallel stichs in Hebrew poetry, where the second line functionally affirms the first line, either with synonyms or by stating the corollary of the first. The Hiphil סור is trivalent (cf. comment on 3:10), taking a subject (here it is null), an NP complement for the thing removed (here שׂקו), and a PP complement of the locative source (here מעליו).

וְלֹא קִבֵּל. *Qatal* 3ms Piel √קבל. The verb קבל "to accept, receive" used in ancient Hebrew (see the Hiph fp participles in Exod 26:5 and 36:12), but appears to have been displaced by לקח, which is the dominant verb for the semantics "to take, receive." However, קבל reentered the common lexicon in later Hebrew, likely via Aramaic. קבל is thus prominent in later texts of the Hebrew Bible such as Esther and Chronicles as well as in the Dead Sea Scrolls and rabbinic Hebrew. See "Salient Lexical Features" in the Introduction. The verb is bivalent, taking an NP complement (the thing received), here covert but understood to be the garments Esther sent.

4:5 וַתִּקְרָא אֶסְתֵּר לַהֲתָךְ מִסָּרִיסֵי הַמֶּלֶךְ אֲשֶׁר הֶעֱמִיד לְפָנֶיהָ וַתְּצַוֵּהוּ עַל־מָרְדֳּכָי לָדַעַת מַה־זֶּה וְעַל־מַה־זֶּה׃

In this verse, Esther sends a messenger to Mordecai to determine the reason for his mourning.

וַתִּקְרָא אֶסְתֵּר לַהֲתָךְ מִסָּרִיסֵי הַמֶּלֶךְ. *Wayyiqtol* 3fs Qal √קרא. The return to the *wayyiqtol* signals both a return to the narrative progression.

Note that the ל-PP remains behind the subject, with the rest of the predicate, separated from the verb, because it is phonologically heavy, whereas a light PP equivalent like לו would have followed immediately after the verb (see comments on 1:5, 2:7, 14). Qal קרא is bivalent, taking an NP or PP complement for the person called, here the PP להתך.

הֲתָ֞ךְ מִסָּרִיסֵ֤י הַמֶּ֙לֶךְ֙ אֲשֶׁ֣ר הֶעֱמִ֣יד לְפָנֶ֔יהָ. A null copula clause within the unmarked relative clause and a *qatal* 3ms Hiph √עמד. The PP מסריסי המלך is an example of the partitive מן (JM 133e; WO 11.2.11e) and modifies the proper noun התך within the unmarked, null copula relative clause: "Hathak (who) (was) one of the eunuchs of the king." The bound NP סריסי is in turn modified by the אשר relative clause: "the king's eunuchs who he (= the king) stationed before her." Although Qal עמד can be monovalent (see 3:4), it is typically bivalent with a locative complement, "X stands somewhere." The causative Hiphil עמד increases the valency by moving the Qal subject to the complement role and adding a new agentive subject, "X stands/stations Y somewhere." Here the agentive subject is null (but contextually identifiable as the king), the first complement is also null, but clearly identifiable as the head of the relative, סריסי המלך, and the second, locative complement is the PP לפניה.

וַתְּצַוֵּ֖הוּ עַֽל־מָרְדֳּכָ֑י לָדַ֥עַת מַה־זֶּ֖ה וְעַל־מַה־זֶּֽה. *Wayyiqtol* 3fs Piel √צוה with 3ms clitic pronoun and inf constr Qal √ידע. The clitic pronoun is the complement of the verb, the person commanded (here the pronoun refers back to התך, the eunuch). The על-PP is an adjunct indicating the topic of Esther's command, i.e., "concerning Mordecai." The ל-PP/infinitive clause is the second complement of the trivalent verb—the action Esther commanded (on צוה, see comment on 2:10). Within the ל-PP, דעת has the sense of "to learn" (see comment on 4:1); the complement of לדעת is the compound interrogative clause מה זה ועל מה זה.

מַה־זֶּ֖ה וְעַל־מַה־זֶּֽה. These two interrogative clauses contain two null copulas, both with the demonstrative זה as the subject and the interrogative phrases, מה and על מה, as the fronted copular complements (on interrogatives fronted as Focus, see 1:15). In both cases, the deictic זה points to Mordecai's behavior—Esther wants to know what he was doing and why. It is possible that the narrator is characterizing Esther as unaware of the larger situation of the king's anti-Jewish edict due to her relative seclusion in the royal harem.

4:6 וַיֵּצֵא הֲתָךְ אֶל־מָרְדֳּכָי אֶל־רְחוֹב הָעִיר אֲשֶׁר לִפְנֵי
שַׁעַר־הַמֶּלֶךְ׃

Hathak the eunuch, whom Esther sent as a messenger to Mordecai, goes to Mordecai in the city plaza.

וַיֵּצֵא הֲתָךְ אֶל־מָרְדֳּכָי אֶל־רְחוֹב הָעִיר אֲשֶׁר לִפְנֵי שַׁעַר־הַמֶּלֶךְ. *Wayyiqtol* 3ms Qal √**יצא** and a null copula clause within the relative with null subject and ל-PP complement. Like most verbs of motion, Qal **יצא** is bivalent with a locative complement, as with the אל-PP here (see 1.17). The first PP, אל מרדכי, is the verbal adjunct and the second PP, אל רחוב העיר, is in apposition to the first. The null subject of the אשר relative is the same as head of the relative, רחוב העיר. The noun רחוב is related to the verbal root רחב "to be wide" and refers to a broad place of activity, such as a plaza or market square (HALOT s.v.). The אשר relative is likely restrictive and so identifies which רחוב out of numerous possible רחובות Hathak went to. On the phrase שער המלך, see comment on 2:19.

4:7 וַיַּגֶּד־לוֹ מָרְדֳּכַי אֵת כָּל־אֲשֶׁר קָרָהוּ וְאֵת ׀ פָּרָשַׁת
הַכֶּסֶף אֲשֶׁר אָמַר הָמָן לִשְׁקוֹל עַל־גִּנְזֵי הַמֶּלֶךְ
בַּיְּהוּדִיים לְאַבְּדָם׃

In v. 7, Mordecai tells Hathak of Haman's plot to kill the Jews and the money involved.

וַיַּגֶּד־לוֹ מָרְדֳּכַי אֵת כָּל־אֲשֶׁר קָרָהוּ. *Wayyiqtol* 3ms Hiph √נגד and *qatal* 3ms Qal √קרה with 3ms clitic pronoun. On the meaning, valency, and form of Hiphil נגד, see comment on 2:10. The *wayyiqtol* triggers verb-subject order; the light PP לו also moves with the verb and thus precedes the subject (see comments on 2:7 and 2:14). The verbal complement (the thing told) is the compound phrase ... את כל אשר קרהו ואת פרשת הכסף אשר. In the NP כל אשר קרהו, the quantifier כל is followed by a null head relative (see comment on 3:12; 4:1). Qal קרה is bivalent, meaning "to meet or encounter *someone/something*" or "to happen to *someone*" (HALOT s.v.). Thus the 3ms clitic pronoun is the complement. From context, the tense of the relative is past perfect, since Mordecai is presumably relating something that has already occurred *before* the time of narration.

וְאֵ֣ת | פָּרָשַׁ֣ת הַכֶּ֔סֶף. This NP (along with the associated relative clause) is the second half of the compound complement to the verb יגד. The noun פרשה, from the verb פרשׁ "to give a clear decision" or "to make clear/plain" (HALOT פרשׁ; BDB פרשׁ; cf. Num 15:34 and Neh 8:8), means the "exact information" about something, whether the amount of silver in this verse or the details of Mordecai's deeds in 10:2 (cf. Levenson, 78). The noun is used in Esth 4:7 and 10:2, but nowhere else in the Hebrew Bible or Dead Sea Scrolls. It occurs in the Mishnah, but there means "division, section," as in a section of Scripture (Jastrow s.v.).

אֲשֶׁ֤ר אָמַר֙ הָמָ֔ן לִשְׁק֛וֹל עַל־גִּנְזֵ֥י הַמֶּ֖לֶךְ בַּיְּהוּדִ֥יים לְאַבְּדָֽם. *Qatal* 3ms Qal √אמר, inf constr Qal √שׁקל, and inf constr Piel √אבד with 3mp clitic pronoun complement. Note the use of a less common nuance of the verb אמר, "to promise to do X" (DCH s.v. 6). This relative modifies the NP הכסף, though the head is not resumed until a further layer of embedding—there is no role in the אמר clause for הכסף; rather, it is the null complement of the verb שׁקל in אמר complement clause לשׁקול על גנזי המלך. On the meaning and valency of שׁקל, see comment on 3:9. The PPs על גנזי המלך and ביהודיים are adjuncts to שׁקל. On the phrase גנזי המלך, see comment on 3:9. The preposition ב here means "for" or "in exchange for"; the same usage can be found in Hebrew and Ugaritic economic texts, where a certain amount of silver is paid "in exchange for" a commodity (WO 11.2.5d). The *Ketiv* ביהודיים reflects a doubled י in the gentilic noun (pointed בַּיְּהוּדִיִּים), although יהודים is never spelled with the double י in the final syllable outside of Esther in the Hebrew Bible. While this spelling occurs six times (8:1, 7, 13; 9:15, 18), the other spelling יְהוּדִים, which is the *Qere* here, occurs much more frequently (38×). Cf. 2:6, where יְרוּשָׁלַםִ is spelled with fuller orthography as יְרוּשָׁלַיִם. The adjunct infinitive clause לאבדם gives the purpose for Haman's paying of the silver: "to destroy them (= the Jews)."

4:8 וְאֶת־פַּתְשֶׁגֶן כְּתָב־הַדָּת אֲשֶׁר־נִתַּן בְּשׁוּשָׁן
לְהַשְׁמִידָם נָתַן לוֹ לְהַרְאוֹת אֶת־אֶסְתֵּר וּלְהַגִּיד לָהּ
וּלְצַוּוֹת עָלֶיהָ לָבוֹא אֶל־הַמֶּלֶךְ לְהִתְחַנֶּן־לוֹ וּלְבַקֵּשׁ
מִלְּפָנָיו עַל־עַמָּהּ׃

Mordecai provides Hathak with a copy of the new law to give to Esther. Apparently, the essence of Mordecai's plan is to hope that Esther has sufficient influence over the king to save the Jews. It is nothing if not direct and simple, but also naïve, since reversing a דת is beyond even the power of the king (in the world of this story, at least). More interesting than Mordecai's plan is the apparent authority that he continues to hold over Esther, even after her installation as the queen (see also 2:20).

וְאֶת־פַּתְשֶׁגֶן כְּתָב־הַדָּת אֲשֶׁר־נִתַּן בְּשׁוּשָׁן לְהַשְׁמִידָם נָתַן לוֹ. *Qatal* 3ms Niph √נתן and *qatal* 3ms Qal √נתן. The first complement (the extended NP את פתשגן ... להשמידם) of the Qal נתן is Focus-fronted; the PP לו is a second complement to the trivalent verb, denoting the recipient of the thing given. The null subject is understood to be Mordecai from context in v. 7 (where he is the subject). The clitic pronoun in the PP לו refers to Hathak. On the meaning of פתשגן, see comment on 3:14.

אֲשֶׁר־נִתַּן בְּשׁוּשָׁן לְהַשְׁמִידָם. *Qatal* 3ms Niph √נתן and inf constr Hiph √שמד with 3mp clitic pronoun complement. This אשר relative modifies הדת. Niphal נתן is bivalent, taking an NP complement (the valency downgraded subject, which is also the relative head, הדת) and a PP complement for the recipient of the thing given (here null but reconstructable as "to people in general"; cf. comment on 3:14). The infinitive clause להשמידם is a purpose adjunct to the Niphal נתן.

לְהַרְאוֹת אֶת־אֶסְתֵּר. Inf constr Hiph √ראה. This infinitive is adjunct to the verb נָתַן and explains why Mordecai gave a copy of the law to Hathak. The Hiphil ראה is most likely trivalent, with one overt complement (את אסתר) and one null complement ("the thing shown") there is only one overt complement. It is true that mostly bivalent Qal ראה ("to see," "to perceive") can be monovalent (with either the sense of "seeing" or "perceiving"; BDB s.v.; HALOT s.v.) and so the corresponding Hiphil can be bivalent. But the context suggests a trivalent analysis: (A) it is the more common valency of Hiphil ראה; (B) there is something in the near context that could easily be supplied as the second complement, namely את פתשגן כתב הדת; and (C) the very next infinitive להגיד

has a null complement that, from context, must also be coreferential with את פתשגן כתב הדת.

וּלְהַגִּיד לָהּ וּלְצַוּוֹת עָלֶיהָ לָבוֹא אֶל־הַמֶּלֶךְ. Inf constr Hiph √נגד, inf constr Piel √צוה, and inf constr Qal √בוא. The first two infinitives are also purpose adjuncts to נתן. Hiphil נגד is bivalent, taking an NP complement (here null, referring to את פתשגן כתב הדת); the PP לה is adjunct (see comment on 2:10). Piel צוה here takes two complements, the PP עליה designating the recipient of the command, and the third infinitive clause, לבוא אל המלך, which designates the thing commanded (see comments on v. 5 and 2:10).

לְהִתְחַנֶּן־לוֹ. Inf constr Hith √חנן. This ל-PP/infinitive clause is a purpose adjunct to לבוא, for Esther's reason to enter before the king. The Hithpael of חנן (bivalent in the Qal, "to favor someone"; "HALOT חנן I Qal) means "to seek or implore favor" ("BDB חנן I Hith; HALOT חנן I Hith). In the Hebrew Bible, Hithpael חנן always appears with a PP designating the person from whom favor is sought, typically an אל-PP (in Gen 42:21; Deut 3:23; 1 Kgs 8:33, 47; 2 Kgs 1:13; Ps 30:9; 142:2; Job 8:5; 2 Chr 6:37 [par. 1 Kgs 8:47]), but sometimes ל (here [לו] and in 8:3; Hos 12:5; Job 9:15; 19:16) or לפני (in 1 Kgs 8:59; 9:3; 2 Chr 6:24 [par. 1 Kgs 8:33]). It is likely that the PPs in each case are complements to the verb, marking both the object of the supplicating activity and the desired source from which the successful supplication will be granted.

וּלְבַקֵּשׁ מִלְּפָנָיו עַל־עַמָּהּ. Inf constr Piel √בקש. This ל-PP/infinitive clause seems to be a second adjunct clause to לבוא, expressing purpose; if so, it should be understood as an appositive to להתחנן, clarifying what it means that Esther is imploring the king. Piel בקש is typically bivalent with an NP complement (see comment on 2:2). In this clause there is no accessible NP for a verbal complement. Either the complement is null and must be assumed by combining the semantics of the verb and the discourse context, that is, Esther requests [deliverance] for her people (so DCH, בקש על "on behalf of"), or the על-PP is the complement of בקש, as it seems to be in 7:7 (see also Ezra 8:23; Neh 2:4). The compound preposition מלפני with its clitic pronoun complement is an adjunct to בקש indicating the source of the thing Esther is requesting. If it is deliverance that Esther requests, she is asking the king to provide it for her people. If the על-PP is the complement, then Esther's request is for the king to transfer authority over the Jews to her, presumably so that she may save them. We consider both options sensible and have only chosen the latter to provide a translation.

4:9 וַיָּב֖וֹא הֲתָ֑ךְ וַיַּגֵּ֣ד לְאֶסְתֵּ֔ר אֵ֖ת דִּבְרֵ֥י מָרְדֳּכָֽי׃

וַיָּב֖וֹא הֲתָ֑ךְ. *Wayyiqtol* 3ms Qal √בוא. The focus of the verb בוא is the *arrival* of someone or something, whether coming or going, in contrast to הלך or יצא, whose focus is the *departure*. Whereas Hathak "went out" (יצא) from Esther in v. 6, here in v. 9 Hathak comes back (בוא) to Esther. Qal בוא takes a locative PP complement; here it is null, but understood from context to be something like "to Esther."

וַיַּגֵּ֣ד לְאֶסְתֵּ֔ר אֵ֖ת דִּבְרֵ֥י מָרְדֳּכָֽי. *Wayyiqtol* 3ms Hiph √נגד. On the valency and meaning of Hiphil נגד, see comment on 2:10. The PP לאסתר is adjunct to the verb, while את דברי מרדכי is the complement.

4:10 וַתֹּ֤אמֶר אֶסְתֵּר֙ לַהֲתָ֔ךְ וַתְּצַוֵּ֖הוּ אֶֽל־מָרְדֳּכָֽי׃

וַתֹּ֤אמֶר אֶסְתֵּר֙ לַהֲתָ֔ךְ. *Wayyiqtol* 3fs Qal √אמר. The complement of אמר is null, but this null pronoun is cataphoric and so refers forward to the speech v. 11. The PP להתך is an adjunct indicating the recipient of the speaking.

וַתְּצַוֵּ֖הוּ אֶֽל־מָרְדֳּכָֽי. *Wayyiqtol* 3fs Piel √צוה with 3ms clitic pronoun. Piel צוה is normally trivalent (see comment on 2:10), with a complement for *whom* is commanded and an NP or PP-infinitival complement for *what* is commanded. In this verse, the first complement is the clitic pronoun attached to the verb, which refers back to התך. The second complement is null and is likely a messenger idiom ("to order [someone] [to convey a message]"), with an understood "to say" or "to tell" before the speech recipient אל מרדכי (see DCH צוה Piel 20a; so Keil, 351; Bush, 391; cf. Moore 1971:49). See also comments on צוה in 2:10 and 3:12.

4:11 כָּל־עַבְדֵ֨י הַמֶּ֜לֶךְ וְעַם־מְדִינ֣וֹת הַמֶּלֶךְ֮ יֽוֹדְעִים֒ אֲשֶׁ֣ר כָּל־
אִ֣ישׁ וְאִשָּׁ֡ה אֲשֶׁ֣ר יָבֽוֹא־אֶל־הַמֶּלֶךְ֩ אֶל־הֶחָצֵ֨ר הַפְּנִימִ֜ית
אֲשֶׁ֣ר לֹֽא־יִקָּרֵ֗א אַחַ֤ת דָּתוֹ֙ לְהָמִ֔ית לְ֠בַד מֵאֲשֶׁ֨ר יֽוֹשִׁיט־

לֹ֤ו הַמֶּ֙לֶךְ֙ אֶת־שַׁרְבִ֥יט הַזָּהָ֖ב וְחָיָ֑ה וַאֲנִ֗י לֹ֤א נִקְרֵ֙אתִי֙
לָב֣וֹא אֶל־הַמֶּ֔לֶךְ זֶ֖ה שְׁלוֹשִׁ֥ים יֽוֹם׃

Verse 11 contains Esther's response to Mordecai: to approach the king uninvited is a dangerous action, and can be fatal. Implied, but not stated, is Esther's disagreement with (and initial disobedience of) Mordecai's command in v. 8.

כָּל־עַבְדֵ֨י הַמֶּ֜לֶךְ וְעַם־מְדִינ֣וֹת הַמֶּ֗לֶךְ יֹֽדְעִים֙ אֲשֶׁ֣ר. Null copula clause with compound NP כל עבדי המלך ועם מדינות המלך subject and participle mp Qal √ידע complement. The participle predication is generic: "all the servants ... know that ..." The complement of יודעים, the thing known, is a nominalized clause introduced by אשר (see comment on 3:4), אשר כל איש ואשה ... אחת דתו להמית.

כָּל־אִ֣ישׁ וְאִשָּׁ֡ה אֲשֶׁ֣ר יָבֽוֹא־אֶל־הַמֶּלֶךְ֩ אֶל־הֶחָצֵ֨ר הַפְּנִימִ֜ית אֲשֶׁ֣ר לֹֽא־יִקָּרֵ֗א. *Yiqtol* (irrealis) 3ms Qal √בוא and *yiqtol* (irrealis) 3ms Niph √קרא. This NP consists of the head "any man or woman" (כל איש ואשה) modified by two אשר relatives. The long NP is left-dislocated and resumed in the clause proper by the 3ms clitic pronoun in דתו: "Any man or woman who ..., the one law concerning him is to kill ... ." *Yiqtol* בוא has irrealis semantics, since the "man or woman" under consideration is hypothetical, thus "who *might* go." The second אל-PP is specifying apposition to the first אל-PP, אל המלך, which is the locative complement to the verb יבוא. The second relative, אשר לא יקרא, is stacked with the preceding relative (i.e., they both modify the same head), since no constituent within the preceding relative could be said to "not be called." As in the previous relative, the verb יקרא is irrealis because the situation is hypothetical. Niphal קרא is monovalent, taking as its only argument the pivot NP כל איש ואשה.

אַחַ֤ת דָּתוֹ֙ לְהָמִ֔ית. A null copula clause with a fronted copular complement אחת, the subject דתו, and ל-PP/infinitive (inf constr Hiph √מות) purpose clause in apposition to the fronted אחת. This is the main clause within which the preceding left-dislocation is resumed (by the ו in דתו). The copular complement דתו is fronted for Focus, by which Esther drives home the point that visiting the king without an invitation leads to one and only one outcome, being put to death. The verb מות in the Hiphil is bivalent (causative of monovalent Qal "to die"); therefore there is a null complement: "in order to kill [any man]."

לְבַד מֵאֲשֶׁר יוֹשִׁיט־לוֹ הַמֶּלֶךְ אֶת־שַׁרְבִיט הַזָּהָב וְחָיָה. *Yiqtol* (irrealis) 3ms Hiph √ישט and *qatal* (irrealis) 3ms Qal √חיה. This entire phrase is an NP-internal PP modifying the preceding null complement of להמית. Usually meaning "alone" with a clitic pronoun (cf. comment on 1:16), לבד with מן means "besides, apart from" and takes a complement (usually NP) (HALOT s.v.; e.g., Exod 12:37; Josh 17:5; 1 Kgs 5:3). Here the complement is the null head of the relative אשר יושיט לו המלך את שרביט הזהב וחיה. The null head is resumed in the PP לו (cf. Holmstedt 2013a). Until the Mishnah (Šabb. 11:2; Ḥul. 4:3; Tamid 7:3; Makš. 4:4, 6), the verb ישט appears only in Esther (here; 5:2; 8:4) and Ben Sira (4:31; 7:32; 31:14, 18; cf. Bergey 1983:123–24). It is a loanword from Aramaic (Paton, 223; HALOT s.v.), occurring only in the Hiphil *binyan* and meaning "to hold out" (HALOT s.v.; BDB s.v.). The root of the verb was originally ושט* (not ישט), as can be seen in the ו preserved in the *yiqtol* form (cf. comment on 2:22). Hiphil ישט takes at least one complement, the NP את שרביט הזהב. The light PP לו, which could possibly be a second complement (there are too few examples of this verb to tell), raises with verb above subject (the older verb-subject order is preserved in the relative; see "Word Order" in the Introduction). שרביט הזהב is literally "scepter of gold," in which the clitic host indicates the material out of which the bound word is made (WO 9.5.3d, "attributive genitive"). In the Hebrew Bible, the Aramaism שרביט is only found in Esther (here; 5:2 [2×]; 8:4), where it is used instead of שבט (HALOT שרביט; Keil, 352; Paton, 223; Moore 1971:49). שרביט also appears in rabbinic Hebrew (cf. Bergey 1983:50–51), though שבט is still preferred. Words containing this sort of dissimilation from Aramaic (*šabbīt** > *šarbīt*; Bergsträsser, vol. 1:20b) seem to be a feature of later Hebrew, as evidenced in the use of דַּרְמֶשֶׂק for דַּמֶּשֶׂק in Chronicles and the Great Isaiah Scroll.

וְחָיָה. *Qatal* (irrealis) 3ms Qal √חיה. As with the preceding verbs within this hypothetical situation of someone going in to the king unbidden, the verb here is irrealis. This clause belongs, with the preceding clause, inside the relative begun in the phrase לבד מאשר; i.e., the one who forms the exception to the law of death is the one "to whom the king holds out the golden scepter and so lives."

וַאֲנִי לֹא נִקְרֵאתִי לָבוֹא אֶל־הַמֶּלֶךְ. *Qatal* 1cs Niph √קרא and inf constr Qal √בוא. Negation of the verb triggers subject-verb order, after which the pronoun אני is Topic-fronted and thus raised further, ahead of both the negation and the verb. The *qatal* verb communicates perfect action, i.e., a perspective on the action as a whole rather than on a part of the action. The infinitive clause לבוא אל המלך זה שלושים יום is adjunct to נקראתי, expressing purpose. Although the English "called to go" may give the impression that the infinitive is complement to the verb (as in, e.g., "called to preach"), the verb is monovalent as earlier in this verse (יקרא) and in 2:14. בוא takes one locative/goal complement, the PP אל המלך.

זֶ֖ה שְׁלוֹשִׁ֥ים יֽוֹם. A null copula clause with the deictic demonstrative זה as the subject and the number phrase שלושים יום as the copular complement. On the use of the collective singular יום in apposition to a numeral, see comment on 1:1. Contrary to the description of the demonstrative-number pattern זה שלושים יום in most reference works (WO 17.4.1–2; JM 143i), this is not a grammatical pattern for the modification of the number phrase (Holmstedt 2014b); in other words, it is ungrammatical to analyze and translate זה שלושים יום as "these thirty days" (contra, e.g., Bush, 391, n. 11d; Pat-El 2007). Rather, Esther follows her statement that she had not been called to the king with a separate clause that indicates either the time that has passed since her last visit ("it has been thirty days") or the appointed time of her next visit ("it will be [another] thirty days"). Either way, this clause emphasizes Esther's ultimate point that she would be in grave danger if she went to the king now.

4:12 וַיַּגִּ֣ידוּ לְמָרְדֳּכָ֔י אֵ֖ת דִּבְרֵ֥י אֶסְתֵּֽר׃

וַיַּגִּ֣ידוּ לְמָרְדֳּכָ֔י אֵ֖ת דִּבְרֵ֥י אֶסְתֵּֽר. *Wayyiqtol* 3mp Hiph √נגד. On the form and valency of Hiphil נגד, see comment on 2:10. The PP למרדכי is an adjunct to the verb, while the NP את דברי אסתר is the complement. The plural verb here signals that Hathak, who alone had been the intermediary between Esther and Mordecai in vv. 5-11, now disappears from the scene. While an intermediary serves to highlight the spatial and social distance between Mordecai and Esther, at this point we assume that the narrator deemed his presence to have become cumbersome and distracting from the main characters. The result is a return to the unspecified plural agents we first saw in 2:2 (see comment there).

4:13 וַיֹּ֥אמֶר מָרְדֳּכַ֖י לְהָשִׁ֣יב אֶל־אֶסְתֵּ֑ר אַל־תְּדַמִּ֣י
בְנַפְשֵׁ֔ךְ לְהִמָּלֵ֥ט בֵּית־הַמֶּ֖לֶךְ מִכָּל־הַיְּהוּדִֽים׃

His command having been initially refused, Mordecai confronts Esther's self-preserving attitude. Yes, it is dangerous to go before the king, but Mordecai argues that Esther is not immune from the threat simply because she lives in the palace.

וַיֹּ֥אמֶר מָרְדֳּכַ֖י לְהָשִׁ֣יב אֶל־אֶסְתֵּ֑ר. *Wayyiqtol* 3ms Qal √אמר and inf constr Hiph √שׁוב. The *wayyiqtol* triggers verb-subject order. The complement of bivalent אמר is the direct speech after the infinitive clause להשׁיב אל אסתר. The intervening ל-PP/infinitive clause is an adjunct to אמר and provides either the purpose ("to return [an answer] to Esther") or circumstance ("in returning [an answer] to Esther"; WO 36.2.3d, e). The Hiphil שׁוב is often bivalent, but also sometimes trivalent. In either case, the NP for the thing returned is typically present and the locative/goal adjunct of the person or place to which the item is returned may or may not be present (see DCH s.v. Hiphil 4a). In this case, the idiom "to return a message," used in an adverbial role is shortened to the verb and the אל-PP adjunct; the NP complement is null and is easily reconstructed from the context.

אַל־תְּדַמִּ֣י בְנַפְשֵׁ֔ךְ לְהִמָּלֵ֥ט בֵּית־הַמֶּ֖לֶךְ מִכָּל־הַיְּהוּדִֽים. *Yiqtol* (irrealis) 2fs Piel √דמה and inf constr Niph √מלט. Piel דמה here means "to plan" (HALOT s.v.) or "to intend" (BDB s.v.), taking an infinitive clause complement (the event or action planned), here להמלט בית המלך מכל היהודים: "Do not plan ... *to escape*." The verbal adjunct PP בנפשׁך, lit. "in your soul" or "in your self," is used here as a reflexive ("yourself)" and functions similar to בלב in referring to internal speech or thought (cf. Moore 1971:50). The *yiqtol* reveals that the III-ה root דמה was originally דמי.

לְהִמָּלֵ֥ט בֵּית־הַמֶּ֖לֶךְ מִכָּל־הַיְּהוּדִֽים. Inf constr Niph √מלט. Niphal מלט is monovalent, taking only a subject. Infinitives typically continue the subject from the main clause, which is the case here: Esther is the subject of המלט. The PP בבית המלך is an adjunct to the verb and may either be understood as a NP used adverbially or the assimilation of the preposition ב to the word בית (see comment on 1:9). The meaning of the PP מכל היהודים is not entirely clear. It makes no sense for Esther to escape or flee "<u>from</u> the Jews." It is possible that we are to take PP as elliptical for "from <u>the fate of</u> all the Jews," but we can find no good parallel for this in the Bible. The מן preposition may also be used privatively, "without," but how Esther could be saved "without all the Jews" implies an instrumental role of the Jews in Esther's own deliverance, which is quite odd. The likeliest analysis of the מן-PP is comparative, but not in real, quantifiable terms (i.e., deliverance is not quantifiable, so that someone is "more" delivered than another); rather, in rhetorical terms, i.e., "you, Esther, are a Jew and regardless of your position you will not escape any more than all the other Jews."

4:14 כִּ֣י אִם־הַחֲרֵ֣שׁ תַּחֲרִישִׁי֮ בָּעֵ֣ת הַזֹּאת֒ רֶ֣וַח וְהַצָּלָּ֞ה
יַעֲמ֤וֹד לַיְּהוּדִים֙ מִמָּק֣וֹם אַחֵ֔ר וְאַ֥תְּ וּבֵית־אָבִ֖יךְ
תֹּאבֵ֑דוּ וּמִ֣י יוֹדֵ֔עַ אִם־לְעֵ֣ת כָּזֹ֔את הִגַּ֖עַתְּ לַמַּלְכֽוּת׃

Mordecai continues to reason with Esther that the Jews will be delivered whether Esther is the means of deliverance or not. If Esther does not act, however, she and her family may die.

כִּ֣י אִם ... תֹּאבֵ֑דוּ. The first half of the verse is one complex clause, which, as a whole, is a כי motive clause adjunct to תדמי v. 13. Within the כי clause is a conditional adjunct clause introduced by אם followed by the main clause, which begins with רוח. The main clause apodosis is a compound consisting of two clauses, רוח והצלה יעמוד ליהודים ממקום אחר and ואת ובית אביך תאבדו. This first clause puts Esther's choice in larger perspective: if she does not save the Jews, someone will. The second clause, though, drives home the personal consequences: if she does not do something, she and her family will suffer. Within the compound apodosis, the subjects of both clauses are Focus-fronted. In the first, the expected result of Esther's nonaction would be destruction for the Jews, but Mordecai instead asserts that they will still be delivered. In the second clause, the guaranteed deliverance of the Jews *will not* extend to Esther, if she does not act.

אִם־הַחֲרֵ֣שׁ תַּחֲרִישִׁי֮ בָּעֵ֣ת הַזֹּאת֒. Inf abs Hiph and *yiqtol* (irrealis) 2fs Hiph √חרשׁ. Hiphil חרשׁ is monovalent, requiring only a subject. The infinitive absolute החרשׁ is used to mark the corresponding finite verb, תחרישׁי, for Focus. The PP בעת הזאת is a temporal adjunct.

רֶ֣וַח וְהַצָּלָּ֞ה יַעֲמ֤וֹד לַיְּהוּדִים֙ מִמָּק֣וֹם אַחֵ֔ר. *Yiqtol* (irrealis) 3ms Qal √עמד. The irrealis verb (the semantics are set by the conditional context) triggers subject-verb order (as does the protasis clause), however the compound subject (רוח והצלה) is fronted ahead of the verb for Focus. In this case the Focus establishes a contrast between the naturally expected outcome of Esther's nonaction (destruction) and Mordecai's assertion of what will occur regardless (deliverance). The verb עמד seems to have the sense "to stand up" or "to arise" (similar to קום; HALOT s.v.). The verb is monovalent, requiring only a subject; the PPs ליהודים and ממקום אחר are adjunct to the verb. The noun רוח is used only here and in Gen 32:17 (outside the Hebrew Bible, it is used in 1QM 5:17; 4Q491 fr. 1 col. 3.11; 4Q491 fr. 13 line 7; and a few times in Mishnaic Hebrew). It means "space"; here it has a sense of "liberation," i.e., space between a person and something negative (HALOT s.v.). This meaning is found in none of the other instances of רוח. The noun הצלה does not appear in any other ancient Hebrew texts; it comes from the Aramaic infinitive of Hafel נצל, "to deliver" (HALOT s.v.; cf. comment on 2:18 הנחה).

וְאַ֥תְּ וּבֵית־אָבִ֖יךְ תֹּאבֵ֑דוּ. *Yiqtol* (irrealis) 2mp Qal √אבד. This clause forms the second half of the compound apodosis. The irrealis verb (required in the apodosis of a conditional) triggers verb-subject order, but again the subject את ובית אביך is fronted for Focus (I this case, to establish a contrast with the subject of the preceding clause, רוח והצלה). The verb is plural, agreeing in number with the compound subject, which is resolved as masculine (the inclusive gender when the individual constituents are mixed gender; see WO 6.5.3a; cf. JM 149b). Qal אבד is monovalent, requiring only the subject את ובית אביך.

וּמִ֣י יוֹדֵ֔עַ אִם־לְעֵ֣ת כָּזֹ֔את הִגַּ֖עַתְּ לַמַּלְכֽוּת. A null copula clause with subject מי and the copular complement the participle ms Qal √ידע, and *qatal* (irrealis) 2fs Hiph √נגע. The conditional אם clause is the complement for the bivalent ידע. Within the אם clause, the PP לעת כזאת is Topic-fronted, preceding the verb. In עת כזאת the כ-PP NP-internal, i.e., it modifies the noun עת rather than a verb. As in 4:3, Hiphil נגע is bivalent, with a locative complement למלכות (see comment on v. 3; and cf. comment on 2:12). The collocation of הגיע and ל, "arrived at," here as the nuance of attainment or even achievement and the ל refers to a position or status. On מלכות, see comment on 1:2.

4:15 וַתֹּ֥אמֶר אֶסְתֵּ֖ר לְהָשִׁ֥יב אֶֽל־מָרְדֳּכָֽי׃

וַתֹּ֥אמֶר אֶסְתֵּ֖ר לְהָשִׁ֥יב אֶֽל־מָרְדֳּכָֽי. *Wayyiqtol* 3fs Qal √אמר and inf constr Hiph √שוב. The *wayyiqtol* resumes the past tense of the narrative. On the use of להשיב with אמר, see comment on v. 13.

4:16 לֵךְ֩ כְּנ֨וֹס אֶת־כָּל־הַיְּהוּדִ֜ים הַֽנִּמְצְאִ֣ים בְּשׁוּשָׁ֗ן
וְצ֣וּמוּ עָ֠לַי וְאַל־תֹּאכְל֨וּ וְאַל־תִּשְׁתּ֜וּ שְׁלֹ֤שֶׁת יָמִים֙
לַ֣יְלָה וָי֔וֹם גַּם־אֲנִ֥י וְנַעֲרֹתַ֖י אָצ֣וּם כֵּ֑ן וּבְכֵ֞ן אָב֤וֹא
אֶל־הַמֶּ֙לֶךְ֙ אֲשֶׁ֣ר לֹֽא־כַדָּ֔ת וְכַאֲשֶׁ֥ר אָבַ֖דְתִּי אָבָֽדְתִּי׃

Esther relents and implicitly agrees to Mordecai's request.

לֵךְ֩ כְּנ֨וֹס אֶת־כָּל־הַיְּהוּדִ֜ים הַֽנִּמְצְאִ֣ים בְּשׁוּשָׁ֗ן. Impv 2ms Qal √הלך and √כנס, and participle mp Niph √מצא. Qal הלך, "to go," is typically bivalent and takes a locative PP complement; here, though, is an instance of the lesser monovalent usage. הלך takes forms similar to I-ו verbs, thus loosing the first radical ה in the imperative (JM 75g). The verb כנס, used primarily in later texts, means "to gather" in the Qal *binyan* (BDB s.v.; HALOT s.v.). כנס takes one complement, here את כל היהודים, which is modified by the relative clause הנמצאים בשושן.

וְצ֣וּמוּ עָ֠לַי. Impv 2mp Qal √צום. The imperatives switch from singular to plural, since Esther wants "all the Jews" (כל היהודים) whom Mordecai gathered, not just Mordecai, to fast. The preposition על indicates advantage, "on behalf of" (WO 11.2.13c).

וְאַל־תֹּאכְל֨וּ וְאַל־תִּשְׁתּ֜וּ שְׁלֹ֤שֶׁת יָמִים֙ לַ֣יְלָה וָי֔וֹם. *Yiqtol* (jussive semantics) 2mp Qal √אכל and √שתה. Since imperatives cannot be negated, jussive verbs are used with אל. Here the negative commands indicate an urgent or "one-time" prohibition, rather than a permanent prohibition (WO 34.2.1b). The double provision "do not eat and do not drink" fleshes out the command "fast on my behalf." The NP שלשת ימים as well as the compound NP לילה ויום both functional adverbially. In strict syntactic terms, they are adjuncts only to the adjacent verb, תשתו, though by extension it applies to the entire set of instructions.

גַּם־אֲנִ֥י וְנַעֲרֹתַ֖י אָצ֣וּם כֵּ֑ן. *Yiqtol* 1cs Qal √צום. The verb does not agree in number with the subject אני ונערתי ("I and my young women") in order to highlight the greater importance of Esther, as opposed to her young women, in performing the action (contra Moore 1971:51). The particle גם is often an additive conjunction introducing the whole clause ("moreover, I will ..."), but also may overtly mark a constituent for Focus. Here it marks אני for Focus. The presence of the pronoun is typically not necessary with a finite verb, since the agreement features of the verb allow "pro-drop" (see Holmstedt 2013c). However, when the subject is a compound, the pronoun is required to complete the compound NP.

Thus, in this example, the גם is used to make the Focus on אני clear. The adverb כן is an adjunct to the verb.

וּבְכֵ֗ן אָב֤וֹא אֶל־הַמֶּ֙לֶךְ֙ אֲשֶׁ֣ר לֹֽא־כַדָּ֔ת. *Yiqtol* 1cs Qal √בוא and, within the relative, a null copula clause with null subject and כ-PP complement. The (adjunct) PP בכן occurs only twice in the Hebrew Bible (here and in Eccl 8:10), meaning "thereupon" (HALOT כֵּן II 8c; DCH כֵּן I 7c) or "in such circumstances" (BDB כֵּן II 3). It also appears once in Ben Sira and six times in the Dead Sea Scrolls; the Aramaic equivalent (בְּכֵין) is used to translate אָז ("then, thereupon") frequently (BDB כֵּן II 3). The PP אל המלך is the locative complement to the movement verb בוא. The relative clause אשר לא כדת does not modify an NP, as is typical, but rather modifies the event and so is an adjunct to the verb אבוא (for other relatives that modify entire events, see Exod 10:6; Deut 17:3; Josh 4:22-23; 2 Sam 4:10; Jer 7:31; 19:5; 32:35; 48:8; Ps 139:15; 2 Chr 3:1; Holmstedt 2002:68, n. 15). In other words, it is the act of going to the king that is "not according to law."

וְכַאֲשֶׁ֥ר אָבַ֖דְתִּי אָבָֽדְתִּי. *Qatals* 1cs Qal √אבד. In this clause, the PP כאשר אבדתי modifies the main verb אבדתי. In the כ-PP, the אשר nominalizes the following verbal clause, אבדתי, so that it may be taken by the כ as its complement. The result is a simple comparison, though here the nuance seems to be a manner free-choice relative, "however I perish" (for more on free-choice relatives, see comment on 5:3). In other words, Esther can imagine numerous manners of death and has accepted her likely fate on behalf of her people.

4:17 וַיַּעֲבֹ֖ר מָרְדֳּכָ֑י וַיַּ֕עַשׂ כְּכֹ֛ל אֲשֶׁר־צִוְּתָ֥ה עָלָ֖יו אֶסְתֵּֽר׃

Mordecai has commanded Esther several times in the story to do something and she has obeyed; now Esther commands Mordecai, and he obeys, revealing a development in Esther's character at this point. She emerges as a confident queen, a characterization that will continue to grow as the plan unfolds.

וַיַּעֲבֹ֖ר מָרְדֳּכָ֑י. *Wayyiqtol* 3ms Qal √עבר. The *wayyiqtol* resumes the past tense of the narrative. עבר here does not mean "to pass over," nor "to overstep, contravene," but "to go on one's way, move through." The idea is that, having come to the gate to mourn and communicate with Esther, Mordecai now leaves and moves on (both physically, to another location, and psychologically, to undertake his mission; cf. Moore 1971:51). This sense of Qal עבר is monovalent, requiring only the subject מרדכי.

וַיַּ֫עַשׂ כְּכֹל אֲשֶׁר־צִוְּתָה עָלָיו אֶסְתֵּר. *Wayyiqtol* 3ms Qal √עשׂה and *qatal* 3fs Piel √צוה. Qal עשׂה means "to behave/act" here, and takes a complement of manner, the PP ככל אשר צותה עליו אסתר (see comments on 1:3, 8). The quantifier כל, "all," is followed by a null head relative (see comment on 2:20). The PP עליו is the second complement to Piel צוה (see comment on 2:10); the first complement is the null pronoun that resumes the null head of the relative, "all (the words/things/plans)." Verb-subject order occurs because of the relative clause; the light PP עליו follows the verb to a position ahead of the subject (see "Word Order"in the Introduction).

Episode 3—Esther's Plan (5:1-8)

In the first half of chapter 5 (episode 3), Esther enacts the plan proposed by Mordecai in 4:8 and agreed to by Esther in 4:16. She intends to see the king in order to spare her people, although such an act (appearing before the king unrequested) is punishable by death. In 5:4, however, the narrator begins to reveal that Esther's plan is more complicated and subtle than simply asking the king to reverse the edict. Indeed, her plan includes setting a trap for Haman. The multiple invitations for a meal and the deferral of Esther's request for the Jews allows the plot to develop slowly, thus heightening the tension (cf. Moore 1971:56; Levenson, 90).

§1: Esther Invites the King and Haman to a Banquet (5:1-4)

1And so it was, on the third day Esther put on royal dress, and she stood in the inner court of the palace of the king, in front of the palace of the king. And the king was sitting on his royal throne in the royal palace opposite the door of the palace. 2And so it was, when the king saw Esther, the queen, standing in the court, she received favor in his eyes, and the king held out to Esther the golden scepter that was in his hand. And Esther came near, and she touched the head of the scepter. 3And the king said to her, "What is your concern, O Esther, the queen? And whatever is your request, up to half of the kingdom, shall be given to you." 4And Esther said, "If it pleases the king, let the king, and Haman, come today to the banquet that I have prepared for him."

5:1 וַיְהִ֣י ׀ בַּיּ֣וֹם הַשְּׁלִישִׁ֗י וַתִּלְבַּ֤שׁ אֶסְתֵּר֙ מַלְכ֔וּת
וַֽתַּעֲמֹ֞ד בַּחֲצַ֤ר בֵּית־הַמֶּ֙לֶךְ֙ הַפְּנִימִ֔ית נֹ֖כַח בֵּ֣ית
הַמֶּ֑לֶךְ וְהַ֩מֶּלֶךְ֩ יוֹשֵׁ֨ב עַל־כִּסֵּ֤א מַלְכוּתוֹ֙ בְּבֵ֣ית
הַמַּלְכ֔וּת נֹ֖כַח פֶּ֥תַח הַבָּֽיִת׃

Wearing her royal clothes, which was either necessary to enter the court or a strategy to incur favor, Esther approaches the king uninvited. There is tension as the reader wonders whether the king will extend his scepter and thus spare Esther from the death proscribed by the standing law (4:11).

וַיְהִ֣י ׀. *Wayyiqtol* 3ms Qal √היה. On the discourse ויהי, see comment on 1:1.

בַּיּ֣וֹם הַשְּׁלִישִׁ֗י וַתִּלְבַּ֤שׁ אֶסְתֵּר֙ מַלְכ֔וּת. *Wayyiqtol* 3fs Qal √לבשׁ. Qal לבשׁ is bivalent, taking as its complement the thing put on or worn. Since it would be strange for someone to wear a "kingdom" (מלכות) we should understand a null complement here (cf. Fox 2001:67–68), modified by מלכות: "Esther put on (thing[s]) of the kingdom." In other words, Esther wore something royal, whether garments, a robe, or perhaps some sort of accessory. It is not necessary to emend the text to include an explicit complement (cf. Keil, 355; Moore 1971:55); however it is also technically incorrect to say that a complement (like לְבוּשׁ) is not semantically required (contra Bush, 402). מלכות is not definite here, but neither is it in 1:7, 11, 19, and 2:17, all cases where "of the kingdom" indicates a type or category of the cliticized noun that it hosts (see comment on 1:2). The *wayyiqtol* reflects the inversion to verb-subject order. On the Topic-fronted PP before the *wayyiqtol*, see comment on 1:1. On the syntax of יום השלישי, see the similar phrase in 1:10.

וַֽתַּעֲמֹ֞ד בַּחֲצַ֤ר בֵּית־הַמֶּ֙לֶךְ֙ הַפְּנִימִ֔ית נֹ֖כַח בֵּ֣ית הַמֶּ֑לֶךְ. *Wayyiqtol* 3fs Qal √עמד. Qal עמד is bivalent with locative complement (here a ב-PP). The adjective פנימית modifies the head or first word of the compound bound phrase; in other words, it is the חצר, i.e., "inner," not the בית המלך. As a noun נכח means "opposite thing," but it is also used adverbially with a spatial nuance and cliticized to a following NP, resulting in what is essentially a PP, "in front of X" (DCH s.v.; HALOT s.v.; BDB s.v.). The full PP נכח בית המלך is in apposition to the preceding PP בחצר בית המלך הפנימית and so clarifies precisely where Esther stood, not just in the courtyard of the inner palace, but directly in front of the inner palace.

וְהַמֶּ֜לֶךְ יוֹשֵׁ֨ב עַל־כִּסֵּ֤א מַלְכוּתוֹ֙ בְּבֵ֣ית הַמַּלְכ֔וּת נֹ֖כַח פֶּ֥תַח הַבָּֽיִת. A null copula clause with a participle (ms Qal √ישב) as the copular complement. The sequence of *wayyiqtol*s is interrupted in order to present background information, that while Esther was taking her position (and also perhaps while she was dressing), the king was already on his throne. The progressive semantics of the participle are combined with the past setting established by the context (i.e., the preceding *wayyiqtol*) to produce a past progressive action, "was sitting." The clitic hosts מלכותו and המלכות modify the bound words כסא and בית attributively (WO 9.5.3b), i.e., "his royal throne" and "royal palace" (cf. Moore 1971:55). There are three options for the syntactic relationship of the PP בבית המלכות: it could be another adjunct to the verb יושב and so further specify where the king sat; it could be an appositive to על כסא מלכותו, resulting in the same nuance (further specifying where the king sat); and it could be an NP-internal PP modifying כסא (similar to a relative clause), specifying the location of the throne. Similarly, two similar syntactic options exist for נכח פתח הבית it might be a third adjunct to יושב or an appositive to בבית המלכות. There are no criteria for determining which of all these options was intended; thankfully, none of the options result in a significant difference for the textual meaning.

5:2 וַיְהִי֩ כִרְא֨וֹת הַמֶּ֜לֶךְ אֶת־אֶסְתֵּ֣ר הַמַּלְכָּ֗ה עֹמֶ֙דֶת֙
בֶּֽחָצֵ֔ר נָשְׂאָ֥ה חֵ֖ן בְּעֵינָ֑יו וַיּ֨וֹשֶׁט הַמֶּ֜לֶךְ לְאֶסְתֵּ֗ר
אֶת־שַׁרְבִ֤יט הַזָּהָב֙ אֲשֶׁ֣ר בְּיָד֔וֹ וַתִּקְרַ֣ב אֶסְתֵּ֔ר וַתִּגַּ֖ע
בְּרֹ֥אשׁ הַשַּׁרְבִֽיט׃

Esther's life is spared because the king is somehow impressed by her (or simply likes her).

וַיְהִי֩. *Wayyiqtol* 3ms Qal √היה. On the discourse ויהי, see comment on 1:1.

כִּרְא֨וֹת הַמֶּ֜לֶךְ אֶת־אֶסְתֵּ֣ר הַמַּלְכָּ֗ה עֹמֶ֙דֶת֙ בֶּֽחָצֵ֔ר. Inf constr Qal √ראה and participle fs Qal √עמד. The Topic-fronted temporal adjunct כ-PP/infinitive clause modifies the following *qatal* נשאה. The complement of the verb ראות is the small clause consisting of the participial phrase אסתר המלכה עמדת בחצר. I.e., the king did not see just Esther (an NP), but the whole event of "Esther standing in the court" (cf. also 5:13). עמד is bivalent and requires a locative complement (here a ב-PP).

נָשְׂאָה חֵן בְּעֵינָיו. *Qatal* 3fs Qal √נשׂא. On this idiom, see comments on 2:9, 15, 17. Just as Esther previously impressed everyone she encountered in chapter 2, here again she elicits a favorable response from the king. Note that there is no ו connecting the fronted scene-scetting (Topic) PP to the main clause (compare ותלבש in v. 1). While a ו often marks the front phrase edge of the main clause (cf. comment on 2:8), and is obligatory when the verb is the *wayyiqtol*; in the absence of the *wayyiqtol* the ו is optional. Interestingly, Qimron indicates that this use of ו decreased in later ancient Hebrew (1986:400.03).

וַיּוֹשֶׁט הַמֶּלֶךְ לְאֶסְתֵּר אֶת־שַׁרְבִיט הַזָּהָב אֲשֶׁר בְּיָדוֹ. *Wayyiqtol* 3ms Hiph √ישׁט. Hiphil ישׁט takes one NP complement (את שרביט הזהב אשׁר בידו), and possibly a second complement (לאסתר; see comment on 4:11). The אשׁר relative clause may be nonrestrictive (if the שׁרביט הזהב were a unique, identifiable item, which by its nature allows no definition or similar identifying information); but we think it more likely that more than one שׁרביט הזהב is imaginable and so the אשׁר בידו restrictively modifies this שׁרביט by defining it as the one that the king held at that very moment.

וַתִּקְרַב אֶסְתֵּר. *Wayyiqtol* 3fs Qal √קרב. Qal קרב is monovalent, taking only a subject.

וַתִּגַּע בְּרֹאשׁ הַשַּׁרְבִיט. *Wayyiqtol* 3fs Qal √נגע. Qal נגע is bivalent, here with a ב-PP complement (cf. comment on 2:12).

5:3 וַיֹּאמֶר לָהּ הַמֶּלֶךְ מַה־לָּךְ אֶסְתֵּר הַמַּלְכָּה וּמַה־
בַּקָּשָׁתֵךְ עַד־חֲצִי הַמַּלְכוּת וְיִנָּתֵן לָךְ׃

Esther's plan is proving to be wildly successful—the king favors her so much that he offers her what amounts to *carte blanche* to use for her purposes. Thus an exciting plot complication occurs in this verse and leaves the audience on the edge of its collective seat: what will she request?

וַיֹּאמֶר לָהּ הַמֶּלֶךְ. *Wayyiqtol* 3ms Qal √אמר. The *wayyiqtol* verb triggers inversion of subject and verb, and the phonologically light PP לה follows the verb ahead of the subject, resulting in verb-adjunct-subject word order (cf. comment on 2:7). The complement of אמר is the direct speech that follows.

מַה־לָּךְ אֶסְתֵּר הַמַּלְכָּה. A null copular clause, with the interrogative מה as the Focus-fronted subject (see comment on 1:15) and the PP

לך as the copular complement. The question מה לך is literally "what (is) to you" and the nuance of the question depends on the context; see DCH מָה 1i). Here the court context suggests "What is your request?" but since מה בקשתך explicitly occurs in the next clause, a broader nuance is more likely: "what is your concern?" or even "what is your reason (for coming)?" See also Fox (2001:281) and Bush (404) for discussion.

וּמַה־בַּקָּשָׁתֵךְ עַד־חֲצִי הַמַּלְכוּת וְיִנָּתֵן לָךְ. *Yiqtol* (irrealis) 3ms Niph √נתן. The first part of this sequence may be a null copular clause, with the מה a true interrogative, "what is your request?" However, we think it more likely that it is the use of מה as the head of a free-choice relative clause, "whatever is your request … will be given to you" (so also Paton, 235; see Holmstedt [forthcoming] on free-choice relatives in Hebrew). In free-choice relatives, the speaker does not know or does not care what the referent of מה is, which accounts for the indeterminacy and genericity of this kind of relative (similar to "whatever, whomever, whenever, whichever" relatives in English). In this case (and in 5:6, 7:2, and 9:12), the king has no idea, and does not care, what Esther's request will be before he grants it, limiting it to half of his kingdom. Syntactically, the מה is the head of the relative clause, the subject within the relative clause (by null resumption), and the Topic-fronted subject of the bivalent Niphal ינתן. The NP בקשתך is the complement of the null copula clause within the relative and the עד-PP indicates "measure or degree" (WO 11.2.12c). The PP לך is the single complement of the Niphal ינתן, which reflects a valency downgrade due to passivization. On Topic-fronting before a ו marking the phrase edge of the core clause, see comment on 2:8, and the discussions in Moshavi 2010:84–85 and Holmstedt 2014a).

בַּקָּשָׁתֵךְ. Two synonymous words are used in this section to denote a "request, petition, wish." The first, בַּקָּשָׁה, is related to the verb בקש, but comes into Hebrew *via* Aramaic: it is the infinitive form with the feminine ending (HALOT בַּקָּשָׁה). It occurs only in Esther, and once in Ezra (7:6). On synonymous שְׁאֵלָה, see v. 6.

5:4 וַתֹּאמֶר אֶסְתֵּר אִם־עַל־הַמֶּלֶךְ טוֹב יָבוֹא הַמֶּלֶךְ
וְהָמָן הַיּוֹם אֶל־הַמִּשְׁתֶּה אֲשֶׁר־עָשִׂיתִי לוֹ׃

Esther invites the king and Haman to a banquet. The fact that Esther will prepare a משתה recalls the banquets of chapter 1. The use of a banquet allows two character contrasts to be made. On the one hand, Esther's strategic use of a banquet sets her apart from the king's drink-induced folly; on the other hand, Esther's use of a banquet to advance her cause successfully contrasts her with Vashti's political suicide at a banquet. Additionally, there may be an intended role reversal: the king obeys the Esther's request to attend a banquet, in contrast to chapter 1 where Vashti disobey's the king's request (see Fox 2001:69). For the plot development, the invitation of Haman to the banquet sets up the ironic twists of fate that are central to the story's resolution.

וַתֹּ֣אמֶר אֶסְתֵּ֔ר. *Wayyiqtol* 3fs Qal √אמר. The complement of the bivalent verb אמר is the following direct speech quote.

אִם־עַל־הַמֶּ֣לֶךְ ט֑וֹב. A null copula clause with null subject and copular complement טוב. See comment on 1:19. The conditional function word אם signals that the clause is an adjunct to the verb in the main clause, which is יבוא in the following clause.

יָב֨וֹא הַמֶּ֤לֶךְ וְהָמָן֙ הַיּ֔וֹם אֶל־הַמִּשְׁתֶּ֖ה. *Yiqtol* (irrealis) 3ms Qal √בוא. The singular verb appears to have a compound subject (המלך והמן). Either the compound NP המלך והמן is semantically resolved as a unit and thus singular for agreement features (as in 2:21; 4:3), or המלך is the primary agent (Revell 1993; cf. Holmstedt 2009b), signaled by both its position before המן as well as the 3ms agreement features of the verb, and המן is an adjunct that functions similarly to a parenthesis, "Let the king come, and Haman, and. ..." The same pattern—a singular verb with what appears to be a compound (and thus plural) NP subject—is used in vv. 5, 8 and the similar context of 7:1. The אל-PP is the complement of the bivalent motion verb בוא. On the function of היום here, see comment on 1:18.

אֲשֶׁר־עָשִׂ֥יתִי לֽוֹ. *Qatal* 1cs Qal √עשׂה. This relative clause modifies המשתה restrictively. The *qatal* verb defaults to a past time setting when found in a relative clause (see "Verbal Semantics" in the Introduction), suggesting that Esther had already prepared the feast before making her invitation. In 5:8, where Esther invites the king to a second banquet, the *yiqtol* is used in the relative and defaults to the future time setting. This is contextually affirmed by the logic of the sequence of events: the second banquet could not possibly have been prepared at the time of Esther's statement, since the first had not yet ended. Note the preservation of the original third consonant י in the first person singular form (i.e., the root is עשׂי, not עשׂה). On the meaning of עשׂה as "to prepare," see comment on 1:3. The third person pronoun in לו refers to the king and so confirms that the king is the primary invitee in view. In 5:8, in a similar phrase, a third person plural pronoun is used, referring to both the king and Haman, since at that point Haman's participation is moved to the forefront of the developing plot.

§2: Esther Issues a Second Invitation (5:5-8)

[5]And the king said, "Hurry Haman in order to carry out the command of Esther." And the king and Haman came to the banquet that Esther had prepared. [6]And the king said to Esther during the banquet of wine, "Whatever is your petition shall be given to you. And let whatever is your request, up to half of the kingdom, be done." [7]And Esther answered and she said, "(This) is my petition and my request: [8]If I have found favor in the king's eyes, and if it pleases the king to grant my petition and to do my request, let the king and Haman come to the banquet that I will prepare for them. And tomorrow I will act according to the word of the king."

5:5 וַיֹּ֣אמֶר הַמֶּ֔לֶךְ מַהֲרוּ֙ אֶת־הָמָ֔ן לַעֲשׂ֖וֹת אֶת־דְּבַ֣ר
אֶסְתֵּ֑ר וַיָּבֹ֤א הַמֶּ֙לֶךְ֙ וְהָמָ֔ן אֶל־הַמִּשְׁתֶּ֖ה אֲשֶׁר־
עָשְׂתָ֥ה אֶסְתֵּֽר׃

The king's acceptance and subsequent command characterize Haman as an unwitting puppet, which is increasingly what he becomes as Esther's plan unfolds.

וַיֹּ֣אמֶר הַמֶּ֔לֶךְ. *Wayyiqtol* 3ms Qal √אמר. The complement of the bivalent verb אמר is the following direct speech quote.

מַהֲרוּ֙ אֶת־הָמָ֔ן לַעֲשׂ֖וֹת אֶת־דְּבַ֣ר אֶסְתֵּ֑ר. Impv 2mp Piel √מהר and inf constr Qal √עשׂה. The Piel מהר is typically bivalent and here takes the NP את המן as the complement. The ל-PP/infinitive clause is a purpose adjunct to the imperative מהר. On the meanings of עשׂה, see 1:3; on דָּבָר with the connotation "order, command."

וַיָּבֹ֤א הַמֶּ֙לֶךְ֙ וְהָמָ֔ן אֶל־הַמִּשְׁתֶּ֖ה אֲשֶׁר־עָשְׂתָ֥ה אֶסְתֵּֽר. *Wayyiqtol* 3ms Qal √בוא and *qatal* 3fs Qal √עשׂה. On the singular verb with the subject המלך והמן, see comment on v. 4. The Qal בוא is bivalent, taking a locative PP complement (אל המשתה אשר עשׂתה אסתר). The *qatal* within a relative clause defaults to a past time setting (see v. 4; "Verbal Semantics" in the Introduction), but also interacts with the logic and time setting established by the main clause, resulting in a pluperfect sense here ("had prepared").

5:6 וַיֹּאמֶר הַמֶּלֶךְ לְאֶסְתֵּר בְּמִשְׁתֵּה הַיַּיִן מַה־שְּׁאֵלָתֵךְ וְיִנָּתֵן לָךְ וּמַה־בַּקָּשָׁתֵךְ עַד־חֲצִי הַמַּלְכוּת וְתֵעָשׂ׃

The king again offers to Esther to grant any request that she might have, reinforcing the power within Esther's reach. Her deferral, once again, increases the tension—what could her plan of deliverance be?

וַיֹּאמֶר הַמֶּלֶךְ לְאֶסְתֵּר בְּמִשְׁתֵּה הַיַּיִן. *Wayyiqtol* 3ms Qal √אמר. The PP במשתה היין is a temporal adjunct to the verb; the preposition ב may have a temporal nuance, indicating the time at which an action takes place (WO 11.2.5c).

מַה־שְּׁאֵלָתֵךְ. A free-choice relative that is the subject of the verb יִנָּתֵן (see comment on v. 3). The noun שׁאלה is a synonym of בַּקָּשָׁה (see comment on v. 3) and is derived from the verbal root שׁאל, "to ask" (HALOT s.v.). It is a segholate-pattern noun (*_qitl_ > סֵפֶר; JM 88C.h), though the א as the second root letter influences the form (> *_q'il_ > בְּאֵר; JM 88 C.i). Thus the feminine noun שְׁאֵלָה, "request, plea, petition, wish" (DCH s.v.; HALOT s.v.), developed as follows: *_šiʾl-at_ > *_šʾil-at_ > _šəʾelâ_.

וְיִנָּתֵן לָךְ. *Yiqtol* (irrealis) 3ms Niph √נתן. The Niphal reflects the downgrade of the trivalent Qal נתן to bivalency, with a subject (here the מה free-choice relative) and one complement, the ל-PP.

וּמַה־בַּקָּשָׁתֵךְ עַד־חֲצִי הַמַּלְכוּת וְתֵעָשׂ. Jussive (form and semantics) 3fs Niph √עשׂה. For discussion of the syntax, see comment on v. 3. The Niphal jussive of עשׂה is used only in Esther (here; 7:2; 9:12). Since the interrogative-relative מה is indeclinable for gender, the use of the 3fs תעשׂ (as well as 3fs תנתן in 7:2) suggests that, while מה likely defaults to masculine, it may also be influenced by the features of the noun within the relative, as with בקשה here and שׁאלה in 7:2.

5:7 וַתַּעַן אֶסְתֵּר וַתֹּאמַר שְׁאֵלָתִי וּבַקָּשָׁתִי׃

The narrator artfully draws out Esther's second response to the king. This literary artifice increases the tension not just by the content of Esther's request but also by its very form.

וַתַּ֫עַן אֶסְתֵּ֖ר. *Wayyiqtol* 3fs Qal √ענה. As with the jussive verb תעש in v. 6, the verb ותען shows the loss of the third radical ה in the *wayyiqtol* (see comment on 3:5).

וַתֹּאמַ֑ר. *Wayyiqtol* 3fs Qal √אמר. The complement of אמר is the direct speech that follows.

שְׁאֵלָתִ֖י וּבַקָּשָׁתִֽי. A null copula clause. There are at least three acceptable grammatical analyses of this clause. First, Moore (1971:57) and Bush (404–5) suggest that this may be anacoluthon, i.e., an incomplete sentence that Esther decided not to finish, but switched midstream to a new clause (the second invitation in v. 8). Second, the direct speech may be a null copula clause with a null subject that cataphorically refers to the invitation extended in next verse, "(this is) my petition and my request— … ." Finally, this could be a null copula clause with שאלתי ובקשתי as the compound subject and the entirety of the second invitation in v. 8 a nominalized copular complement, "my petition and my request is (that) … ." All three are viable, contextually sensible options and we chose the second for translation simply because it allows a more fluid English rendering. On the nouns שאלה and בקשה, see comments on vv. 6 and 3, respectively.

5:8 אִם־מָצָ֨אתִי חֵ֜ן בְּעֵינֵ֣י הַמֶּ֗לֶךְ וְאִם־עַל־הַמֶּ֙לֶךְ֙ ט֔וֹב
לָתֵת֙ אֶת־שְׁאֵ֣לָתִ֔י וְלַעֲשׂ֖וֹת אֶת־בַּקָּשָׁתִ֑י יָב֧וֹא
הַמֶּ֣לֶךְ וְהָמָ֗ן אֶל־הַמִּשְׁתֶּה֙ אֲשֶׁ֣ר אֶֽעֱשֶׂ֣ה לָהֶ֔ם
וּמָחָ֥ר אֶֽעֱשֶׂ֖ה כִּדְבַ֥ר הַמֶּֽלֶךְ׃

אִם־מָצָ֨אתִי חֵ֜ן בְּעֵינֵ֣י הַמֶּ֗לֶךְ. *Qatal* 1cs Qal √מצא. On the expression "to find favor in the eyes of … ," see comment on נשׂא חסד in 2:9; also see DCH מצא I 8. This and the next, conjoined אם clause are both conditional adjuncts (i.e., a compound conditional protasis) to the main verb יבוא (which is in the conditional apodosis).

וְאִם־עַל־הַמֶּ֙לֶךְ֙ ט֔וֹב לָתֵת֙ אֶת־שְׁאֵ֣לָתִ֔י וְלַעֲשׂ֖וֹת אֶת־בַּקָּשָׁתִ֑י. A null copula clause, inf constr Qal √נתן, and inf constr Qal √עשׂה. In the null copula clause, the subject is a compound consisting of the two coordinated ל-PPs/infinitive clauses. The copular complement is the adjective טוֹב. The light subject follows the heavy complement due to HNPS (see 1:5). On the expression אם על המלך טוב, see comment on 1:19.

יָבוֹא הַמֶּלֶךְ וְהָמָן אֶל־הַמִּשְׁתֶּה אֲשֶׁר אֶעֱשֶׂה לָהֶם. *Yiqtol* (irrealis) 3ms Qal √בוא and *yiqtol* 1cs Qal √עשׂה. On the number agreement of verb and subject here, as well as the argument structure of בוא, see comment on v. 4. Whereas in v. 4, the use of a *qatal* verb in the relative clause implies that Esther has already prepared the banquet, here the use of a *yiqtol* verb (which defaults to a future time setting within a relative clause) indicates that Esther has not yet prepared the second banquet to which she is inviting the king. The shift in recipient of the second banquet she plans in this verse from לו in v. 4 to להם suggests that Esther has now fully drawn Haman into her plan.

וּמָחָר אֶעֱשֶׂה כִּדְבַר הַמֶּלֶךְ. *Yiqtol* 1cs Qal √עשׂה. Note the difference in the meaning of עשׂה in this clause ("to act, do, behave") compared to the previous clause ("to prepare"). The nuance of verbal semantics are clearly the product of both the lexical meaning of the verb and its interaction with the complements and adjuncts it takes; see the discussion of עשׂה in 1:3. The PP כדבר המלך is the complement of עשׂה, indicating the manner in which one behaves (see comment on 1:8). Esther defers her request from the king one more day, heightening the tension, both for the reader as well as for the king (cf. Levenson, 91).

Episode 4—Haman's Plan Implodes (5:9–6:14)

In episode 3 we saw how Esther's plan was cautious and staged: she did not approach the king directly, but used subtler tactics to warm him to her eventual request. In similar fashion, episode 4 represents a second stage of Haman's plan of revenge—whereas his plan to this point had concerned Haman's people, the Jews, in general, now he plots specifically against Mordecai's person.

The episode also sets up the irony to unfold later in the story. Haman recounts his riches to his friends, and they make plans to erect a pole on which to impale or hang Mordecai. Later in Esther, after the tables have been turned, it is Mordecai who will have great riches, and the pole intended for Mordecai will be used to hang Haman.

§1: Haman's Hubris (5:9-14)

9And Haman went out on that day, happily and glad of heart. But when Haman saw Mordecai in the gate of the king and he did not rise and he did not tremble on account of him, Haman was filled with rage against Mordecai. 10And Haman controlled himself, and he came to his house. And he sent (a message) and brought his friends and Zeresh, his wife (to him). [11]*And Haman recounted to them the glory of his riches and the multitude of his children and all (the ways) that the king had magnified him and (the way) that he had exalted him over the rulers and the servants of the king.* [12]*And Haman said, "Indeed, Esther, the queen, did not bring with the king to the banquet which she had prepared anyone except me. And also tomorrow I am invited by her along with the king.* [13]*But all of this—it does not compare for me with every time in which I am seeing Mordecai, the Jew, sitting in the gate of the king."* [14]*And Zeresh, his wife, along with all his friends, said to him, "Let them make a high, fifty cubit tree. And in the morning, say to the king 'Let them hang Mordecai on it.' And come with the king to the banquet happy." And the word pleased Haman, and he made the tree.*

וַיֵּצֵא הָמָן בַּיּוֹם הַהוּא שָׂמֵחַ וְטוֹב לֵב וְכִרְאוֹת 5:9
הָמָן אֶת־מָרְדֳּכַי בְּשַׁעַר הַמֶּלֶךְ וְלֹא־קָם וְלֹא־זָע
מִמֶּנּוּ וַיִּמָּלֵא הָמָן עַל־מָרְדֳּכַי חֵמָה׃

Haman's good mood following the personal banquet with the king and queen is soured by Mordecai's disrespectful behavior, leading him to plot personally a specific revenge against Mordecai.

וַיֵּצֵא הָמָן בַּיּוֹם הַהוּא שָׂמֵחַ וְטוֹב לֵב. *Wayyiqtol* 3ms Qal √יצא. In I-ו/י verbs like יצא, when the initial ו/י of the root follows a vowel, it assimilates to the vowel, leaving the trace of its existence only in the resulting vowel. In this case, the progression occurred as follows: **yayṣiʾ* > **yêṣiʾ* > **yêṣe* (with the final *alef* of the root phonologically quiescent, but written for pragmatic reasons—to distinguish the root) (Holmstedt 2000:148–49; cf. JM 75). The two adjectival phrases שמח and טוב לב are adjuncts to the verb יצא, describing the manner in which Haman "went out." Alternatively, it is possible that the adjective phrases exist within a small clause and technically describe Haman's state of being when he went out: "Haman went out (being) happy and glad of heart." The PP ביום ההוא is a temporal adjunct to the verb יצא (note its position following the verb versus its Topic-fronted position in, e.g., 8:1, 9:11; Gen 15:18).

וְכִרְאוֹת הָמָן אֶת־מָרְדֳּכַי בְּשַׁעַר הַמֶּלֶךְ. Inf constr Qal √ראה. This כ-PP/infinitive clause initiates a temporal adjunct to a main verb ימלא. The two following negated *qatal* clauses lie within the scope of the temporal כ (see also Moore 1971:59; Fox 2001:73; Bush, 409; Levenson, 91;

cf. JM 124q; WO 36.3.2). It is also grammatically acceptable to take the first negated *qatal* ולא קם as the main verb, but it makes little sense that "when Haman saw him, Mordecai didn't stand" (i.e., Mordecai's lack of action was tied to Haman's visual perception). Moreover, the dominant pattern in BH narrative is for the main verb to be a *wayyiqtol.*

וְלֹא־קָם. *Qatal* 3ms Qal √קום. The 3ms *qatal* of קום is identical to the ms participle (cf. בוא in 1:17 and 2:13, and cf. זוע below), though the past time context (see the *wayyiqtol* וימלא) and the negation by לא strongly suggest that this form is a *qatal.* The Qal of קום seems to have two valency entries, one that is monovalent and means simply "to get up" (as here and in 8:4) and one that is bivalent with a locative complement and refers to "standing somewhere" (see, e.g., 7:7).

וְלֹא־זָע מִמֶּנּוּ. *Qatal* 3ms Qal √זוע. In the Hebrew Bible, the word זוע ("to tremble"; HALOT s.v.; cf. BDB s.v.) is only used in Eccl 12:3, here, and possibly in Hab 2:7 (HALOT s.v.). However, it is also used several times in the Dead Sea Scrolls and Ben Sira. As with קום above, the 3ms *qatal* and ms participle are identical in form (cf. בוא in 1:17 and 2:13). Translations and commentaries often understand ממנו here to mean "before him" (RSV; Bush, 411) or "in his presence" (Moore 1971:59; Bush, 409). However, all of the spatial or locative senses of מן deal with source or origin, and none have the sense of location in front of something or someone (WO 11.2.11b). Thus, מן here indicates the cause of the trembling (WO 11.2.11d; Levenson, 91; Fox 2001:73).

וַיִּמָּלֵא הָמָן עַל־מָרְדֳּכַי חֵמָה. *Wayyiqtol* 3ms Niph √מלא. See comment on 3:5, where the same expression occurs. The על-PP has an adversative sense, i.e., "against" (WO 11.2.13c,f).

5:10 וַיִּתְאַפַּק הָמָן וַיָּבוֹא אֶל־בֵּיתוֹ וַיִּשְׁלַח וַיָּבֵא אֶת־
אֹהֲבָיו וְאֶת־זֶרֶשׁ אִשְׁתּוֹ׃

Haman's inner circle provides a therapeutic setting where Haman can air his grievances and boast of his accomplishments. The conclusion of the meeting, where Zeresh and Haman's friends tell Haman to prepare a pole on which to hang Mordecai, sets the scene for the darkly ironic culmination of Haman and Mordecai's conflict.

וַיִּתְאַפַּק הָמָן. *Wayyiqtol* 3ms Hith √אפק. The verb אפק ("to control oneself," HALOT s.v.; cf. BDB s.v.) occurs 7 times in the Hebrew Bible (Gen 43:31; 45:1; 1 Sam 13:12; Isa 42:14; 63:15; 64:11; here), always in the Hithpael. Given its reflexive meaning, it is always monovalent, taking a subject as its only argument. Though the *wayyiqtol* typically presents the next event or action, English narrative conventions would be better satisfied by an adversative "but Haman controlled himself," implying the juxtaposition of inner (his rage) and outer (his control) reactions.

וַיָּבוֹא אֶל־בֵּיתוֹ. *Wayyiqtol* 3ms Qal √בוא. The PP אל ביתו is the locative/goal complement of בוא.

וַיִּשְׁלַח. *Wayyiqtol* 3ms Qal √שׁלח. The bivalent שׁלח is missing an overt complement. Given the context, a null complement should be understood, which satisfies the verbal valency and is easily reconstructed as "a message" (cf. Miller 1996:352–53).

וַיָּבֵא אֶת־אֹהֲבָיו וְאֶת־זֶרֶשׁ אִשְׁתּוֹ. *Wayyiqtol* 3ms Hiph √בוא. Hiphil בוא is trivalent, taking a subject, complement (the one coming), and a second complement indicating the place to which the first complement comes. The second complement here is null but easily understood as "to himself/Haman." The NP אֹהֵב is homophonous with the ms Qal participle; the relationship of the agentive *qotel* noun and the Qal participle remains unclear (WO 37.2; Cook 2008:3, n. 4), though the number of *qotel* forms that appear regularly in nominal roles is relatively small (and includes אהב).

5:11 וַיְסַפֵּר לָהֶם הָמָן אֶת־כְּבוֹד עָשְׁרוֹ וְרֹב בָּנָיו וְאֵת
כָּל־אֲשֶׁר גִּדְּלוֹ הַמֶּלֶךְ וְאֵת אֲשֶׁר נִשְּׂאוֹ עַל־הַשָּׂרִים
וְעַבְדֵי הַמֶּלֶךְ׃

וַיְסַפֵּר לָהֶם הָמָן אֶת־כְּבוֹד עָשְׁרוֹ וְרֹב בָּנָיו. *Wayyiqtol* 3ms Piel √ספר. The phonologically light PP adjunct להם moves with the verb in front of the subject resulting in the typical verb-subject order in clauses with *wayyiqtol* (see comment on לו in 2:7). On bivalent Piel ספר, see comment at 3:1. The complement of ספר is a compound consisting of four constituents: את כבוד ..., רב ..., כל אשר ..., and את אשר ....

וְאֵת כָּל־אֲשֶׁר גִּדְּלוֹ הַמֶּלֶךְ וְאֵת אֲשֶׁר נִשְּׂאוֹ עַל־הַשָּׂרִים וְעַבְדֵי הַמֶּלֶךְ. *Qatal* 3ms Piel √גדל with 3ms clitic pronoun and *qatal* 3ms Piel √נשׂא with 3ms clitic pronoun. On the meaning and valency of Piel גדל and Piel נשׂא, see comment on 3:1. These two NPs make clear reference to Esther 3:1, where the king magnified (גדל), promoted (נשׂא), and established (שׂים) Haman over כל השׂרים. The head of the relative clause

כל אשר גדלו המלך is null, but can be contextually reconstructed "way, manner." This head is not resumed overtly within the relative because it is neither an obligatory argument of the verb גדל nor in an obligatory position (e.g., as a possessive of an NP within the relative): "the way that the king magnified him [in this way]." The same is true of the head of the second relative—it is null and not resumed overtly. In both relatives, the *qatal* verbs default to a past time setting and, in the context of the governing *wayyiqtol*, take a pluperfect sense (cf. "Verbal Semantics" in the Introduction). The על preposition in the last relative clause governs a compound NP complement, השׂרים and עבדי המלך.

5:12 וַיֹּאמֶר֮ הָמָן֒ אַ֣ף לֹא־הֵבִיאָה֩ אֶסְתֵּ֨ר הַמַּלְכָּ֧ה עִם־
הַמֶּ֛לֶךְ אֶל־הַמִּשְׁתֶּ֥ה אֲשֶׁר־עָשָׂ֖תָה כִּ֣י אִם־אוֹתִ֑י
וְגַם־לְמָחָ֛ר אֲנִ֥י קָֽרוּא־לָ֖הּ עִם־הַמֶּֽלֶךְ׃

The high point of Haman's boasting is the fact that he has been invited by the queen to her private banquet for the king. It is thus highly ironic that Esther is using these banquets to counteract Haman's plot against Mordecai.

וַיֹּאמֶר֮ הָמָן֒. *Wayyiqtol* 3ms Qal √אמר. The complement of bivalent אמר is the following direct speech.

אַ֣ף לֹא־הֵבִיאָה֩ אֶסְתֵּ֨ר הַמַּלְכָּ֧ה עִם־הַמֶּ֛לֶךְ אֶל־הַמִּשְׁתֶּ֥ה אֲשֶׁר־עָשָׂ֖תָה כִּ֣י אִם־אוֹתִ֑י. *Qatal* 3fs Hiph √בוא and *qatal* 3fs Qal √עשׂה. Note that the pausal form of the verb is used (עָשָׂתָה instead of nonpausal עָשְׂתָה) though it does not align with one of the typical Masoretic טְעָמִים associated with pausal forms (Revell 1980). In this case, the pausal עשׂתה has a *ṭip̄ḥa*, which is a significant disjunctive accent but still secondary to the *ʾatnaḥ*. The reason for the pausal form at this point is transparent, since it matches the prosody and pragmatics of the speech—the null complement of the verb along with its NP-internal PP "except" modifier, כי אם אותי, is extraposed to the end of the clause for right-edge Focus (Holmstedt 2014a). Haman's excitement that he alone out of all the possible court advisors had been invited to Esther's feast is palpable. The Hiphil בוא takes two complements, one NP complement (the item brought) and a second locative complement for the destination. The locative complement is the אל-PP. The NP complement is the extraposed null item modified by כי אם אותי. The *qatal* verb in the relative defaults to a past time setting and has a simple past value in the context of the present tense deixis of the speech (see comments on vv. 5, 8, and 11).

וְגַם־לְמָחָר אֲנִי קְרוּא־לָהּ עִם־הַמֶּלֶךְ. Participle ms Qal passive √קרא. The PP למחר is essentially synonymous with מָחָר (cf. comment on בכל יום ויום in 2:11); the former is used less often in the Hebrew Bible, only in Exod 8:6, 19; Num 11:18; Josh 7:13; and here (cf. comment on 2:11). In this clause, למחר is Topic-fronted and the גם has its additive function. Note that there is no triggered inversion when the verb is a participle (cf. "Word Order" in the Introduction). Like Niphal קרא, the Qal passive of קרא is monovalent. The PP לה with the Niphal designates the downgraded agentive subject of the Qal (the one calling; cf. GKC 121f; HALOT לְ I 24; BDB לְ 5e). The preposition עם signals accompaniment (WO 11.2.14b), i.e., "along with the king" or "together with the king."

5:13 וְכָל־זֶה אֵינֶנּוּ שֹׁוֶה לִי בְּכָל־עֵת אֲשֶׁר אֲנִי רֹאֶה אֶת־מָרְדֳּכַי הַיְּהוּדִי יוֹשֵׁב בְּשַׁעַר הַמֶּלֶךְ׃

Haman admits how Mordecai's insulting behavior toward him overshadows all the abundance in his life. In so doing, another negative aspect of his character is revealed—he is not only egotistic and vengeful, he is myopic in his inability to see all the good in his life that outweighs the small slight to his ego.

וְכָל־זֶה אֵינֶנּוּ שֹׁוֶה לִי. A copular clause in which the 3ms clitic pronoun attached to the negative אין functions as the copular element (see also 3:8; Holmstedt and Jones, esp. 61–62). The subject is כל זה and the copular complement is the participle (ms Qal √שוה). Whereas in 3:8 שוה was coupled with ל to mean "to be profitable" (cf. comment on 3:8), here the ל-PP is the *lamed* of advantage and the PP is an adjunct to the verb. The complement of שוה is the PP בכל עת (cf. 7:4, where שוה takes a ב-PP complement). The resultant meaning is "*for me* (לי) it does not compare with every time (בכל עת) that I see Mordecai ..." (contra Moore, who views the ב-PP as temporal; 1971:60; cf. WO 11.2.5c).

אֲשֶׁר אֲנִי רֹאֶה אֶת־מָרְדֳּכַי הַיְּהוּדִי יוֹשֵׁב בְּשַׁעַר הַמֶּלֶךְ. Participles ms Qal √ראה and √ישב. The head of this relative clause is עת. The participle ראה takes a participle phrase complement here (מרדכי היהודי יושב בשער המלך), as in v. 2; in other words, the thing Haman sees is "Mordecai ... sitting in the gate of the king." The PP בשער המלך is the locative complement of יושב; cf. comment on 1:2.

5:14 וַתֹּ֩אמֶר֩ ל֨וֹ זֶ֜רֶשׁ אִשְׁתּ֣וֹ וְכָל־אֹהֲבָ֗יו יַֽעֲשׂוּ־עֵץ֮ גָּבֹ֣הַּ
חֲמִשִּׁ֣ים אַמָּה֒ וּבַבֹּ֣קֶר ׀ אֱמֹ֣ר לַמֶּ֗לֶךְ וְיִתְל֤וּ אֶֽת־
מָרְדֳּכַי֙ עָלָ֔יו וּבֹֽא־עִם־הַמֶּ֥לֶךְ אֶל הַמִּשְׁתֶּ֖ה שָׂמֵ֑חַ
וַיִּיטַ֧ב הַדָּבָ֛ר לִפְנֵ֥י הָמָ֖ן וַיַּ֥עַשׂ הָעֵֽץ׃ פ

Zeresh's suggestion to set up a tree to hang Mordecai not only returns Haman to a happy state of mind but also serves as a pivot in the plot development. Identifying the manner of Mordecai's putative demise brings an end to Haman's good fortunes. The rest of episode 4 represents a downward trajectory for Haman, culminating in his end (episode 5).

וַתֹּ֩אמֶר֩ ל֨וֹ זֶ֜רֶשׁ אִשְׁתּ֣וֹ וְכָל־אֹהֲבָ֗יו. *Wayyiqtol* 3fs Qal √אמר. The light PP לו moves with the verb (cf. comment on 2:7) in front of the subject (the subject-verb inversion is triggered by the *wayyiqtol*). On the singular verb תאמר with the ostensibly plural subject זרש אשתי וכל אהביו, see comment on v. 4. On אהביו as an NP "his friends," see comment on v. 10.

יַֽעֲשׂוּ־עֵץ֮ גָּבֹ֣הַּ חֲמִשִּׁ֣ים אַמָּה֒. *Yiqtol* (jussive semantics) 3mp Qal √עשה. The subject of the verb is generic and thus unspecified (see comment on 2:2). The NP עץ is modified by the adjective גבה and then the number phrase חמשים אמה: "a high, fifty cubit tree." The inner structure of חמשים אמה is appositional: "fifty, cubit" (cf. "Numeral Syntax in Esther" in the Introduction).

וּבַבֹּ֣קֶר ׀ אֱמֹ֣ר לַמֶּ֗לֶךְ. Impv ms Qal √אמר. Elsewhere in Esther, imperatives are used by higher-status people toward those of lower-status (Mordecai to Esther, or the king to his subjects; 4:16 [2×]; 5:5; 6:10 [3×]; 7:9; 8:8 [2×]); here, however, Zeresh addresses her husband using an imperative rather than a jussive. Rather than the typical direct speech complement for אמר (see 1:18), here the complement is the next clause, which we should understand as an unmarked indirect speech complement (cf. Miller 1996:120–21).

וְיִתְל֤וּ אֶֽת־מָרְדֳּכַי֙ עָלָ֔יו. *Yiqtol* (jussive semantics) 3mp Qal √תלה. The subject of the verb is left unspecified, since the agent of the verb is generic ("someone"; see comment on 2:2). On the meaning and valency of תלה, as well as the act of hanging or suspending someone on a tree in the ancient world, see comment on 2:23. In a departure from the dominant pattern (see "Word Order" in the Introduction), the phonologically light PP עליו does not immediately follow the verb. This reflects Focus-marking both the verb and the complement, whereas the PP with its clitic pronoun coreferential with the עץ does not carry Focus. The pragmatic effect can be paraphrased as so: "let them HANG MORDECAI on it." Thus, the precise intended function of the tree (hanging) is contrasted with other obvious alternatives for a tree; similarly, the person being hung is contrasted with other known or imaginable alternatives (Mordecai vs. anyone else).

וּבֹא־עִם־הַמֶּלֶךְ אֶל הַמִּשְׁתֶּה שָׂמֵחַ. Impv ms Qal √בוא. The imperative marks the exit from the indirect speech that Haman was instructed to say to the king and resumes the direct speech of Zeresh. On the semantics of the preposition עם, see comment on v. 12. As in v. 9, the adjective שׂמח could be analyzed as either a verbal adjunct indicating manner or a copular complement within a small clause (see discussion at v. 9).

וַיִּיטַב הַדָּבָר לִפְנֵי הָמָן. *Wayyiqtol* 3ms Qal √יטב. Most I-י verbs in Hebrew are originally I-ו (cf. comment on 5:9); יטב, however, is one of only seven verbs that are originally I-י (JM 76), which is reflected in the preservation of the root letter י in the *wayyiqtol* form. On this idiom יטב לפני, see comment on 1:21.

וַיַּעַשׂ הָעֵץ. *Wayyiqtol* 3ms Qal √עשׂה. On the "shorter" form of the *wayyiqtol*, as in the jussive (cf. comment on 5:6), see comment on 3:5.

§2: Mordecai's Fortunes Reversed (6:1-10)

Section 2 (chap. 6) contains the pivotal reversal of Mordecai's fortunes, from inhabiting a low position in the social and political hierarchy and the object of Haman's wrath to elevation to an honored and powerful position than ensures his security. This section also marks the beginning of Haman's demise.

The irony created in vv. 4-10 is especially thick (cf. Levenson, 94–95; Fox 2001:78). Haman and the king's discussion in v. 4 is at cross-purposes—Haman seeking permission to kill Mordecai and the king seeking advice to reward Mordecai. The irony deepens in vv. 6-9, where Haman assumes that he is the object of the king's question about honoring a person who has been of valuable service (cf. Fox 2001:76; Levenson, 95). The culmination of this darkly humorous scene unfolds in vv. 10-12, where he is instructed to honor the very man he had designed to kill. Verse 14 is the denouement of this mini-plot, in which Haman's advisors pronounce his doom and so mark the turning point in the overall plot of the story (Fox 2001:82).

[1]That night, the sleep of the king fled, and he said to bring the Book of the Remembrances, that is, (the Book of) the Matters of the Days, (to him). And they were read before the king. [2]And what was written, that Mordecai told about Bigthan and Teresh, two eunuchs of the king from the guards of the threshold who sought to raise a hand against King Ahashverosh, was found. [3]And the king said, "What has been done as an honor or greatness for Mordecai on account of this?" And the servants of the king who attended him said, "Nothing has been done for him." [4]And the king said, "Who is in the court?" while Haman was entering the outer court of the palace of the king in order to ask the king to hang Mordecai on the tree that he set up for him. [5]And the king's courtiers said to him, "Look—Haman is standing in the court." And the king said, "Let him enter." [6]And Haman came and the king said to him, "What is one to do with the man who the king delights in his honor?" And Haman said to himself, "For whom would the king delight to do honor more than me?" [7]And Haman said to the king, "A man who the king delights in his honor—[8]let them bring royal clothes, which the king has worn, and a horse which the king rides upon and which a royal turban is set upon its head, [9]placing the clothes and the horse in the authority of one of the king's rulers, the nobles, and let them clothe that man, in whose honor the king delights, and let them cause him to ride upon the horse through the square of the city, and let them call out before him, 'Thus will be done for the man who the king delights in his honor.'" [10]And the king said to Haman, "Hurry! Take the clothes and the horse, according to (that) which you said, and do thus for Mordecai the Jew, who is sitting in the gate of the king. Do not neglect a thing from all that you said."

6:1 בַּלַּ֣יְלָה הַה֔וּא נָדְדָ֖ה שְׁנַ֣ת הַמֶּ֑לֶךְ וַיֹּ֗אמֶר לְהָבִ֞יא
אֶת־סֵ֤פֶר הַזִּכְרֹנוֹת֙ דִּבְרֵ֣י הַיָּמִ֔ים וַיִּהְי֥וּ נִקְרָאִ֖ים
לִפְנֵ֥י הַמֶּֽלֶךְ׃

The king, unable to sleep, decides to pass the time by reading. Specifically, he asks for the document referred to at the end of chapter 2, in which Mordecai's report of the assassination attempt was recorded.

בַּלַּ֣יְלָה הַה֔וּא נָדְדָ֖ה שְׁנַ֣ת הַמֶּ֑לֶךְ. *Qatal* 3fs Qal √נדד. The fronted temporal phrase בלילה ההוא triggers verb-subject order. The use of the *qatal* verb rather than a *wayyiqtol* is a common narrative strategy to signal a scene change. In this case, the change is from Haman's house to the king's chambers. The temporal relationship between the two scenes is indicated by the PP בלילה ההוא; that is, whenever the discussion took place in Haman's house, the king's activity took place the night of that same day.

וַיֹּאמֶר לְהָבִיא אֶת־סֵפֶר הַזִּכְרֹנוֹת דִּבְרֵי הַיָּמִים. *Wayyiqtol* 3ms Qal √אמר and inf constr Hiph √בוא. Although fs שֵׁנָה is the subject of the preceding verb נדדה, it is clear from context and the masculine verb ויאמר that the null subject of this clause is the king. The infinitive clause (להביא את ספר ...) is indirect speech and serves as the complement of אמר (see comments on 1:10-11). On the trivalency of להביא, see 1:11. Here the subject is null, as in most ל infinitive clauses, and contextually reconstructible as the people receiving the king's command. The first NP complement (the thing being brought) is את ספר הזכרנות. And the second complement, the locative goal, is null and easily reconstructed as "to him (the king)."

אֶת־סֵפֶר הַזִּכְרֹנוֹת דִּבְרֵי הַיָּמִים. On the meaning of ספר, see comments on 1:22 and 2:23. The noun זכרון is a *qatalān*-pattern noun (cf. JM 88 Mb) (*zakarān* > *zakarōn* > *zakkārōn* > *zikkārōn*) derived from the verb זכר ("to remember"; HALOT זכר I Qal 2), meaning "mention, remembrance" (HALOT s.v.). In this context, when used with ספר, it denotes a commemoration or record of deeds done for the king ("memorial-record"). We assume that the book mentioned is the same as the ספר דברי הימים in 2:23. The appositive relation between ספר הזכר־נות and דברי הימים is thus an "equivalence" apposition ("X, i.e., Y"; see comment on 1:2); we also then assume the understood repetition of ספר before דברי הימים.

וַיִּהְיוּ נִקְרָאִים לִפְנֵי הַמֶּלֶךְ. *Wayyiqtol* 3mp Qal √היה and participle mp Niph √קרא. Here the overt copula ויהיו is used with a participle phrase complement to communicate past habitual time (cf. comment on 1:1): "they were being read" (cf. Fox 2001:75). Qal קרא can have the sense "to recite" or "to read" (HALOT קרא I Qal B), taking a ב-PP complement denoting the thing read (e.g. קרא בספר, "he read the book"). In the Niphal *binyan* (as found here), the complement of the Qal verb (the thing read) becomes the subject (thus there is no ב-PP). The PP לפני המלך is an adjunct of the verb, indicating the location where the materials were read.

6:2 וַיִּמָּצֵ֣א כָת֗וּב אֲשֶׁר֩ הִגִּ֨יד מָרְדֳּכַ֜י עַל־בִּגְתָ֣נָא וָתֶ֗רֶשׁ
שְׁנֵי֙ סָרִיסֵ֣י הַמֶּ֔לֶךְ מִשֹּׁמְרֵ֖י הַסַּ֑ף אֲשֶׁ֤ר בִּקְשׁוּ֙
לִשְׁלֹ֣חַ יָ֔ד בַּמֶּ֖לֶךְ אֲחַשְׁוֵרֽוֹשׁ׃

Mordecai's report of the planned assassination (2:21-23), which had little connection to the main plot when it was related, is now brought back into the picture and its full importance is revealed. The low odds of the timing and connections add to the dark humor and thrill of the story: "By coincidence the king could not sleep that night, by coincidence he whiled away the time listening to a reading of the royal annals, and by coincidence the reader hit upon the mention of Mordecai's discovery of the assassination plot" (Fox 2001:75–76).

וַיִּמָּצֵ֣א כָת֗וּב אֲשֶׁר֩ הִגִּ֨יד מָרְדֳּכַ֜י עַל־בִּגְתָ֣נָא וָתֶ֗רֶשׁ שְׁנֵי֙ סָרִיסֵ֣י הַמֶּ֔לֶךְ מִשֹּׁמְרֵ֖י הַסַּ֑ף. *Wayyiqtol* 3ms Niph √מצא, participle ms Qal passive √כתב, and *qatal* 3ms Hiph √נגד. The subject of the verb is a null head modified by the Qal passive participle כתוב ("[a thing which was] written"). The אשר clause is a nominalized appositive to the null head and so clarifies the substance of what was written (see Moore 1971:62; Fox 2001:75; Bush, 410; Levenson, 93). Within the אשר clause, the bivalency of the Hiphil נגד (see 2:10) is fulfilled by the על-PP ("about/concerning"; WO 11.2.13g) rather than a more typical NP for the complement. As a *qatal* verb within a relative clause, הגיד defaults to a past time setting (see comment on 5:12; "Verbal Semantics" in the Introduction). Note that the spelling of the name Bigthan differs from 2:21 (בִּגְתָן); cf. comment on 2:3 concerning the spelling of the name Hegai. The NP שני סריסי המלך משמרי הסף is in apposition (nonrestrictive) to the compound NP בגתנא ותרש. On the inner syntax of this phrase, see comment on 2:21.

אֲשֶׁ֤ר בִּקְשׁוּ֙ לִשְׁלֹ֣חַ יָ֔ד בַּמֶּ֖לֶךְ אֲחַשְׁוֵרֽוֹשׁ. *Qatal* 3cp Qal √בקש and inf constr Qal √שלח. This אשר clause is a restrictive relative unambiguously identifying which two of the many royal eunuchs were described. Alternatively, the אשר clause could be analyzed as a nominalized clause in apposition to the על-PP and so further specifies what Mordecai reported—about Bigthan and Hegai, i.e., that they conspired to kill the king. On the ל-PP/infinitive clause לשלח יד במלך אחשורוש, see comment on 2:21.

6:3 וַיֹּ֣אמֶר הַמֶּ֔לֶךְ מַה־נַּעֲשָׂ֞ה יְקָ֧ר וּגְדוּלָּ֛ה לְמָרְדֳּכַ֖י עַל־
זֶ֑ה וַ֠יֹּאמְרוּ נַעֲרֵ֤י הַמֶּ֙לֶךְ֙ מְשָׁ֣רְתָ֔יו לֹא־נַעֲשָׂ֥ה עִמּ֖וֹ
דָּבָֽר׃

וַיֹּ֣אמֶר הַמֶּ֔לֶךְ. *Wayyiqtol* 3ms Qal √אמר. The complement of bivalent אמר is the following direct speech.

מַה־נַּעֲשָׂ֞ה יְקָ֧ר וּגְדוּלָּ֛ה לְמָרְדֳּכַ֖י עַל־זֶ֑ה. *Qatal* 3ms Niph √עשה. The interrogative מה is the Focus-fronted (see comment on 1:15) subject of נעשה. The NP יקר וגדולה is an adjunct to the verb specifying or limiting the scope of the ambiguous מה (i.e., the so-called adverbial accusative; WO 10.2.2). In the PP למרדכי, the preposition ל denotes advantage or benefit (cf. WO 11.2.10d). In the PP על זה, the preposition על denotes cause (cf. WO 11.2.13e) and the deictic demonstrative points back to Mordecai's good deed.

וַ֠יֹּאמְרוּ נַעֲרֵ֤י הַמֶּ֙לֶךְ֙ מְשָׁ֣רְתָ֔יו. *Wayyiqtol* 3mp Qal √אמר and participle mp Piel √שרת with 3ms clitic pronoun. The complement of אמר is the direct speech that follows this clause. On the meaning of נער and the syntax of משרתיו, see comment on 2:2.

לֹא־נַעֲשָׂ֥ה עִמּ֖וֹ דָּבָֽר. *Qatal* 3ms Niph √עשה. Since לא negates the verb, and דבר is the subject, this clause is literally, "a thing has not been done with him." The light PP עמו has moved with the verb ahead of the subject, resulting in verb-PP-subject order. The verb raising is triggered by the negation. In the earlier clause in this verse with Niphal עשה, the preposition ל is used to denote the person "for whom" something is done; here the עם is used with the same sense, "to, for" (DCH s.v. 4), though the reasons for the variation is unclear.

6:4 וַיֹּ֥אמֶר הַמֶּ֖לֶךְ מִ֣י בֶחָצֵ֑ר וְהָמָ֣ן בָּ֗א לַחֲצַ֤ר בֵּית־
הַמֶּ֙לֶךְ֙ הַחִ֣יצוֹנָ֔ה לֵאמֹ֣ר לַמֶּ֔לֶךְ לִתְלוֹת֙ אֶֽת־מָרְדֳּכַ֔י
עַל־הָעֵ֖ץ אֲשֶׁר־הֵכִ֥ין לֽוֹ׃

The juxtaposition of the king's question and the arrival of Haman continue the incredible coincidence that the storyteller is using to high effect in this part of the story.

וַיֹּ֫אמֶר הַמֶּ֫לֶךְ מִ֣י בֶחָצֵ֑ר. *Wayyiqtol* 3ms Qal √אמר and null copula clause with a Focus-fronted interrogative (see comment on 1:15) subject מי and complement PP בחצר. The complement of אמר is the direct speech clause מי בחצר.

וְהָמָ֣ן בָּ֗א לַחֲצַ֤ר בֵּית־הַמֶּ֙לֶךְ֙ הַחִ֣יצוֹנָ֔ה. *Qatal* 3ms Qal √בוא. The *qatal* 3ms Qal of בוא is morphologically identical to the ms participle (see also comments on באה in 1:17; 2:13) and the two forms can only be distinguished by contextual clues, though none exist in this particular case. There are thus two possible parsings and three equally plausible semantic readings of the verb in this clause. If בא is a participle, such a clause following a *wayyiqtol* typically indicates simultaneous or at least overlapping actions or events with progressive semantics (the time setting is established contextually); thus, a participial reading would suggest that *just as* the king spoke, Haman was in the act of *entering* the outer court. If בא is a *qatal*, it can be read with simple past semantics, resulting in the simple juxtaposition of the king's speaking and Haman's entrance (i.e., they occurred at the same time); or, *qatal* בא can be read as background information that occurred previous to the king's question and hence pluperfect semantics (i.e., Haman had already entered the outer court when the king asked his question). None of the options lessens the delightful literary artistry. The complement of bivalent בוא is the locative PP לחצר בית המלך החיצונה. Note the designation of the court as "outer" here, versus the "inner" court where no one could go unless summoned by the king (cf. 4:11; 5:1). The adjective חיצון is formed by adding the suffix וֹן (< *-ān*, before the Canaanite shift) to the noun חוּץ "outside (cf. JM 88Me).

לֵאמֹ֣ר לַמֶּ֔לֶךְ לִתְלוֹת֙ אֶֽת־מָרְדֳּכַ֔י עַל־הָעֵ֖ץ. Inf constr Qal √אמר and inf constr Qal √תלה. The item לאמר, which has the form of a ל preposition attached to the Qal infinitive of אמר, is almost always a frozen form serving to introducing direct speech (Miller 1996:199–200). It is not used this way in Esther; however, this sole example in the book is a rare case of לאמר as a purpose ל-PP/infinite clause adjunct to the verb בא. As such, it gives the reason for Haman's appearance in the royal court. The PP למלך is an adjunct to אמר, indicating the addressee, though the normal direct speech complement is missing. Instead, the ל-PP/infinitive clause לתלות is an indirect speech complement (see 1:10-11, 17; 6:1). On תלה על, see comment on 2:23. Note that our translation "ask the king to hang Mordecai" departs from the normal gloss for אמר; this is because "say to the king to hang" is both awkward in English and suggests a bluntness on Haman's part that does not fit the court setting (even Haman has not resorted to telling the king what to do).

אֲשֶׁר־הֵכִין לוֹ. *Qatal* 3ms Hiph √כון. This relative clause modifies העץ. The null subject of the verb is understood from context to be Haman and the clitic pronoun in לו is understood to refer to Mordecai (i.e., *Haman* set up the stake for *Mordecai*). Whereas in 5:14 the tree or stake is said to be "made" (עשׂה), here the tree is "prepared" (Hiphil כון); the sense is of preparing or "making firm" (HALOT s.v. כון Hiph 4) a structure. Hiphil כון is bivalent, taking an NP complement (the thing that is caused to be firm), which is here the null resumption coreferential with the relative head, העץ, "the tree that he prepared [it = the tree] for him."

6:5 וַיֹּאמְרוּ נַעֲרֵי הַמֶּלֶךְ אֵלָיו הִנֵּה הָמָן עֹמֵד בֶּחָצֵר
וַיֹּאמֶר הַמֶּלֶךְ יָבוֹא׃

וַיֹּאמְרוּ נַעֲרֵי הַמֶּלֶךְ אֵלָיו. *Wayyiqtol* 3mp Qal √אמר. The light PP אליו does not immediately follow the verb here, in contrast to what we typically find (see "Word Order" in the Introduction); we can discern no reason for this variation. On the meanings of נַעַר, see comment on 2:2.

הִנֵּה הָמָן עֹמֵד בֶּחָצֵר. Participle ms Qal √עמד. The participle עמד is the complement of a null copula. Within the deixis of the direct speech, the participle conveys present time progressive semantics, "is standing." The PP בחצר is the complement of bivalent Qal עמד (cf. comment on 4:5). הנה is a deictic exclamative by which the speaker directs the addressee's attention to the event, action, or item that is presented immediately after. It is best rendered by the English imperatives, "behold, look!"

וַיֹּאמֶר הַמֶּלֶךְ. *Wayyiqtol* 3ms Qal √אמר. The complement of אמר is the direct speech that follows.

יָבוֹא. *Yiqtol* (jussive semantics) 3ms Qal √בוא. In this II-ו/י, III-א verb, the form of the 3ms jussive and the 3ms *yiqtol* imperfective are identical; however, the context strongly suggests that the verb is a jussive. Qal בוא takes a complement (typically a PP, though sometimes an NP) indicating the locative goal of movement. Here the complement is null, but contextually identifiable as "to me/the king."

6:6 וַיָּבוֹא֮ הָמָן֒ וַיֹּ֤אמֶר לוֹ֙ הַמֶּ֔לֶךְ מַה־לַּעֲשׂ֕וֹת בָּאִ֕ישׁ
אֲשֶׁ֥ר הַמֶּ֖לֶךְ חָפֵ֣ץ בִּיקָר֑וֹ וַיֹּ֤אמֶר הָמָן֙ בְּלִבּ֔וֹ לְמִ֞י
יַחְפֹּ֥ץ הַמֶּ֛לֶךְ לַעֲשׂ֥וֹת יְקָ֖ר יוֹתֵ֥ר מִמֶּֽנִּי׃

Haman's arrogant presumption sets him up for monumental disgrace.

וַיָּבוֹא֮ הָמָן֒. *Wayyiqtol* 3ms Qal √בוא. Qal בוא takes a locative complement indicating the goal of the movement; here that complement is syntactically null but contextually clear as "to him/the king."

וַיֹּ֤אמֶר לוֹ֙ הַמֶּ֔לֶךְ. *Wayyiqtol* 3ms Qal √אמר. The light PP לו (which is an adjunct for אמר indicating the recipient of speech) moves with the verb ahead of the subject. The complement of אמר is the following direct speech.

מַה־לַּעֲשׂ֕וֹת בָּאִ֕ישׁ אֲשֶׁ֥ר הַמֶּ֖לֶךְ חָפֵ֣ץ בִּיקָר֑וֹ. Inf constr Qal √עשׂה and *qatal* 3ms Qal √חפץ. On the syntax and Focus-fronting in מה לעשׂות infinitive construction, see comments on 1:15. The complement of the bivalent עשׂה is the fronted interrogative מה and the ב-PP is an adjunct specifying the scope in which the action occurs (WO 11.2.5e, the "*beth* of specification"). אישׁ is the NP complement of the ב preposition and is itself modified by an אשׁר relative clause. The relative clause is restrictive, defining the type of person to whom the king refers. חפץ is bivalent, with its subject the NP המלך and its sole complement an NP, a ל-PP/infinitive clause (as in the next occurrence of חפץ in this verse), or, as in this clause, a ב-PP. The PP ביקרו not only provides the complement to the verb חפץ, but the 3ms clitic pronoun on יקר ("honor"; HALOT s.v. 2) resumes the head of the relative, אישׁ. Note that the syntax of the clause does not mirror the common, very loose translation, that the king "delights to honor the man" (cf. Moore 1971:64; Fox 2001:75; Bush, 410, 414; Levenson, 94). The word order within relative clauses is typically verb-subject, since אשׁר triggers subject-verb inversion (see "Word Order" in the Introduction). In this clause, the subject-verb order of המלך חפץ has two possible explanations: either המלך is fronted for Topic or Focus (perhaps Focus, indicating that it is the king, and no one else, who desires this thing), or the subject-verb order reflects the beginning of the intrusion of subject-verb order into even subordinate clause syntax (see Holmstedt 2013d).

וַיֹּ֤אמֶר הָמָן֙ בְּלִבּ֔וֹ. *Wayyiqtol* 3ms Qal √אמר. The idiom used here, אמר בלבו, is equivalent to English "to say to oneself," i.e., to think or contemplate internally (cf. Keil, 359; Moore 1971:64). The complement of bivalent Qal אמר is the direct speech clause that follows.

לְמִ֞י יַחְפֹּ֥ץ הַמֶּ֛לֶךְ לַעֲשׂ֥וֹת יְקָ֖ר יוֹתֵ֥ר מִמֶּֽנִּי. *Yiqtol* (irrealis) 3ms Qal √חפץ and inf constr Qal √עשׂה. Unlike the first occurrence of the verb חפץ, this occurrence takes a ל-PP/infinitive clause complement, לעשׂות יקר. The adjunct PP למי indicates the party for whose interest or advantage the action occurs (WO 11.2.10d). The NP יקר is the complement of עשׂות. The phrase יותר ממני is an adjunct not to the closer, embedded verb עשׂות, but to the higher verb יחפץ. The item יותר occurs only here, in 1 Sam 15:15, and seven times in Eccl (2:15; 6:8, 11; 7:11, 16; 12:9, 12), as well as a number of times in the Dead Sea Scrolls, Ben Sira, and the Mishnah. In Eccl 6:8, 11; 7:11; 12:9, יותר functions as a substantive, "advantage," but in all the other biblical occurrences, including here, it functions adverbially, "excessively, too much" (see HALOT s.v.; DCH s.v.). The collocation of יותר and מן is used only here and in Eccl 12:12 and frequently in the Mishnah (Bergey 1984:75–76). With the comparative מן in ממני, the adverb יותר provides the anchor for comparison; that is, just as the adjective עַז provides the quality anchoring the comparison in עַז מִן "stronger than," so יותר anchors the comparison as a simple quantitative comparison relating back to the verbal action, "desire (to honor) more than me."

6:7 וַיֹּ֥אמֶר הָמָ֖ן אֶל־הַמֶּ֑לֶךְ אִ֕ישׁ אֲשֶׁ֥ר הַמֶּ֖לֶךְ חָפֵ֥ץ בִּיקָרֽוֹ׃

Thinking that the king desires to honor him, Haman launches into a description of great and elaborate honors that should be done for the honoree. The clause begun in v. 7 continues through v. 8 into v. 9.

וַיֹּ֥אמֶר הָמָ֖ן אֶל־הַמֶּ֑לֶךְ. *Wayyiqtol* 3ms Qal √אמר. The adjunct אל-PP provides the addressee and the verbal complement is the following direct speech.

אִ֕ישׁ אֲשֶׁ֥ר הַמֶּ֖לֶךְ חָפֵ֥ץ בִּיקָרֽוֹ. *Qatal* 3ms Qal √חפץ. The NP איש, which is modified by a relative clause (see comment on the identical relative in v. 6), is a left-dislocated constituent (sometimes referred to as *casus pendens*). It stands on the edge of the clause and orients the listener to the constituent as the Topic of the subsequent statement. In this particular case, the core clause is very long and complex and the dislocated constituent is not resumed by the more common strategy of a pronoun (independent, such as הוא) or cliticized (such as ו), but by a full copy of the NP—האיש in v. 9 (see comment there; so also Keil, 360). Alternatively, this may be a case of anacoluthon, i.e., interrupted syntax in which the speaker begins one way and finishes differently (cf. Fox 2002:76; Bush, 414–15; Levenson, 96–97).

6:8 יָבִ֙יאוּ֙ לְב֣וּשׁ מַלְכ֔וּת אֲשֶׁ֥ר לָֽבַשׁ־בּ֖וֹ הַמֶּ֑לֶךְ וְס֗וּס אֲשֶׁ֨ר רָכַ֤ב עָלָיו֙ הַמֶּ֔לֶךְ וַאֲשֶׁ֥ר נִתַּ֛ן כֶּ֥תֶר מַלְכ֖וּת בְּרֹאשֽׁוֹ׃

Haman's description of the honor that should be bestowed includes the king's own clothing as well as one of his horses.

יָבִ֙יאוּ֙ לְב֣וּשׁ מַלְכ֔וּת. *Yiqtol* (jussive semantics) 3mp Hiph √בוא. The *yiqtol* imperfective and jussive 3ms form are homophonous; however, the context suggests jussive semantics. The plural verb has an unspecified, generic subject (also הלבישו, הרכיבהו, and קראו in v. 9; cf. comment on 2:2). Hiphil בוא takes two complements, an NP for the item affected and a locative NP or PP. The locative complement is null here, but reconstructible as "to the court" (the clothes are not put on the honored man until v. 9). The NP complement is a compound, consisting of two conjoined, complex NPs: ... לבוש מלכות אשר and ... סוס אשר. The noun לבוש is a *qətūl*-pattern from the root לבש ("to put on," "to clothe"; HALOT לבש). *Qətūl* noun are often collectives (JM 88 Eh); לְבוּשׁ can be singular ("garment") or collective ("clothing" or "clothes"). In the NP לבוש מלכות, the clitic host מלכות indicates the type of category to which the bound word לבוש belongs, "royal clothes" (see comment on 1:2).

אֲשֶׁ֥ר לָֽבַשׁ־בּ֖וֹ הַמֶּ֑לֶךְ. *Qatal* 3ms Qal √לבש. This relative clause modifies לבוש and provides even greater specificity—these are not simply any royal clothes, but clothes that the king has actually worn. As is typical when the verb raises over the subject, the light PP בו attaches to it (note the *maqqef* joining לבש and בו as a single prosodic unit) and so raises with the verb. The verb לבש may be monovalent ("to be clothed"); it is modified by the adjunct PP בו and its subject is המלך. The relative head לבוש is resumed in the clitic pronoun in בו: "clothing which the king is clothed *with it* [= the clothing]." The perfective *qatal* verb is used with simple past semantics (the king wore these clothes at least once) or habitual (the king wears these clothes regularly).

וְס֗וּס אֲשֶׁ֨ר רָכַ֤ב עָלָיו֙ הַמֶּ֔לֶךְ וַאֲשֶׁ֥ר נִתַּ֛ן כֶּ֥תֶר מַלְכ֖וּת בְּרֹאשֽׁוֹ. *Qatal* 3ms Qal √רכב and Niphal √נתן. The NP סוס, which is the second half of the compound complement to the verb of the main clause (בוא), is modified by two relative clauses. In the first relative, the PP עליו is the complement of the bivalent verb רכב and the 3ms clitic pronoun in עליו resumes the relative head סוס. As in the preceding relative clause, the light PP עליו follows the verb before the subject, and the *qatal* verb רכב may signal simple past semantics (the king rode on this horse at least once) or habitual (the king rides on this horse regularly). In the second relative, נתן has the meaning "to set" (HALOT נתן Qal 12). Whereas Qal נתן is trivalent ("to set [NP = something] [PP = somewhere]"), the Niphal reflects a valency downgrade in which the first complement (כתר מלכות) is promoted to the subject. The ב-PP (בראשו) is the locative complement. The head of the relative (סוס) is resumed in the second relative by the 3ms clitic pronoun attached to ראשׁ. Again, the perfective *qatal* verb נתן conveys simple past action (the turban was set on the horse's head at least once) or habitual action (the turban is regularly set on this horse's head, i.e., he is a favorite of the king's). On the meaning of כתר, see comment on 1:11. On כתר מלכות, see comments on 1:2, 11.

6:9 וְנָת֨וֹן הַלְּב֜וּשׁ וְהַסּ֗וּס עַל־יַד־אִ֞ישׁ מִשָּׂרֵ֤י הַמֶּ֙לֶךְ֙
הַֽפַּרְתְּמִ֔ים וְהִלְבִּ֙ישׁוּ֙ אֶת־הָאִ֔ישׁ אֲשֶׁ֥ר הַמֶּ֖לֶךְ חָפֵ֣ץ
בִּיקָר֑וֹ וְהִרְכִּיבֻ֤הוּ עַל־הַסּוּס֙ בִּרְח֣וֹב הָעִ֔יר וְקָרְא֣וּ
לְפָנָ֔יו כָּ֚כָה יֵעָשֶׂ֣ה לָאִ֔ישׁ אֲשֶׁ֥ר הַמֶּ֖לֶךְ חָפֵ֥ץ בִּיקָרֽוֹ׃

Haman finishes by including the public involvement of an unspecified noble, unwittingly establishing the manner of his own public humiliation.

וְנָת֨וֹן הַלְּב֜וּשׁ וְהַסּ֗וּס עַל־יַד־אִ֞ישׁ מִשָּׂרֵ֤י הַמֶּ֙לֶךְ֙ הַֽפַּרְתְּמִ֔ים. Inf abs Qal √נתן. On the use of the infinitive נתון as a subordinate clause verb, see comment on 2:3. Trivalent נתן takes two complements, the compound NP הלבושׁ והסוס (the thing given) and the PP על יד אישׁ (the recipient). On the expression יד אישׁ, see comment on 2:3. הפרתמים is appositional to שׂרי המלך. On the meaning of הפרתמים, cf. comment on 1:3.

וְהִלְבִּ֙ישׁוּ֙ אֶת־הָאִ֔ישׁ אֲשֶׁ֥ר הַמֶּ֖לֶךְ חָפֵ֣ץ בִּיקָר֑וֹ. *Qatal* (irrealis) 3cp Hiph √לבשׁ and *qatal* 3ms Qal √חפץ. The plural verb הלבישׁו has a null subject; as with יביאו, the agent of the verb is generic (see comment on 2:2; cf. Moore 1971:63; Fox 2001:282; Bush, 415–16). The finite verb signals that this clause does not continue the נתון subordinate clause but continues with the next recommendation. Hiphil לבשׁ appears to be trivalent. The first complement (thing put on) is a null pronoun, which anaphorically refers to the clothing previously mentioned. The second complement האישׁ resumes the dislocated NP from v. 7 (see comment there; so also Keil, 360). On האישׁ אשׁר המלך חפץ ביקרו, see comment on 6:6.

וְהִרְכִּיבֻהוּ עַל־הַסּוּס בִּרְחוֹב הָעִיר. *Qatal* (irrealis) 3cp Hiph √רכב with 3ms clitic pronoun. The subject of the plural verb הרכיבהו is left unspecified (cf. comment on 2:2). Hiphil רכב is trivalent, taking an NP complement, which is here anaphorically referred to by the 3ms clitic pronoun attached to the verb, and an על-PP complement. The ב in ברחוב has a spatial sense and the PP is an adjunct to the verb. On the meaning of רחוב, see comment on 4:6.

וְקָרְאוּ לְפָנָיו. *Qatal* (irrealis) 3cp Qal √קרא. The subject of the plural verb קראו is unspecified and generic (cf. comment on 2:2). The complement of קרא is the direct speech of the following clause. The PP לפניו is a locative adjunct.

כָּכָה יֵעָשֶׂה לָאִישׁ אֲשֶׁר הַמֶּלֶךְ חָפֵץ בִּיקָרוֹ. *Yiqtol* 3ms Niph √עשׂה and *qatal* 3ms Qal √חפץ. With the monovalent Niphal יעשׂה, the complement of the bivalent Qal is promoted to the subject role. Thus, the subject is the PP ככה (see comment on 1:8). The adverb כה within the כ-PP is deictic and within the deixis of the direct speech points to everything that the honored man is experiencing when this utterance is proclaimed. On לאישׁ אשׁר המלך חפץ ביקרו, see comment on 6:6.

6:10 וַיֹּאמֶר הַמֶּלֶךְ לְהָמָן מַהֵר קַח אֶת־הַלְּבוּשׁ וְאֶת־
הַסּוּס כַּאֲשֶׁר דִּבַּרְתָּ וַעֲשֵׂה־כֵן לְמָרְדֳּכַי הַיְּהוּדִי
הַיּוֹשֵׁב בְּשַׁעַר הַמֶּלֶךְ אַל־תַּפֵּל דָּבָר מִכֹּל אֲשֶׁר
דִּבַּרְתָּ׃

In this verse we reach the apex of the core plot of Esther, the point at which the king's intended actions are enacted and Haman's are thwarted, and at which the fates of Haman and Mordecai both reverse course.

וַיֹּאמֶר הַמֶּלֶךְ לְהָמָן. *Wayyiqtol* 3ms Qal √אמר. The complement of אמר is the following direct speech.

מַהֵ֠ר. Impv ms Piel √מהר. Piel מהר is typically bivalent, with an NP or PP complement (see 5:5). Here, it could be bivalent, with the valency satisfied by a null complement clause that cataphorically refers to the following finite clause (i.e., semantically it would be similar to the different syntactic construction מהר לקחת, "hurry to take"). This is one of the many grammatical nuances in ancient Hebrew for which we have no criterion for preferring one analysis over the other.

קַ֣ח אֶת־הַלְּב֤וּשׁ וְאֶת־הַסּוּס֙ כַּאֲשֶׁ֣ר דִּבַּ֔רְתָּ. Impv ms Qal √לקח and *qatal* 2ms Piel √דבר. The verb לקח follows the same forms as a I-נ verb, thus loosing the first radical ל in the imperative (JM 72j). The compound NP את הלבוש ואת הסוס is the complement of Qal לקח. The PP כאשר דברת is an adjunct, describing the rule or standard by which Haman should act. Within the PP, the head of the relative is null: "according to [that] which you said [it]."

וַעֲשֵׂה־כֵן֙ לְמָרְדֳּכַ֣י הַיְּהוּדִ֔י הַיּוֹשֵׁ֖ב בְּשַׁ֣עַר הַמֶּ֑לֶךְ. Impv ms Qal √עשה and participle ms Qal √ישב. Imperative verbs (מהר קח עשה) are used instead of irrealis *qatal*s or jussives because of the king's status and position over Haman. עשה is a bivalent verb and here the complement is the deictic adverb כן (see comment on 2:4). The ל-PP indicates the entity that benefits from the action or event ("for"; WO 11.2.10d). היושב בשער המלך is a ה-relative with a null copula clause and participle phrase complement to the null copula. Within the participle phrase, the PP בשער המלך is the locative complement for the bivalent verb ישב.

אַל־תַּפֵּ֣ל דָּבָ֔ר מִכֹּ֖ל אֲשֶׁ֥ר דִּבַּֽרְתָּ. Jussive (form and semantics) 2ms Hiph √נפל and *qatal* 2ms Piel √דבר. A jussive verb is used with the negative אל to indicate an immediate or urgent prohibition (WO 34.2.1b; cf. comment on 4:16). Hiphil נפל is causative and bivalent, meaning "to cause [or allow] X to fall," resulting in a nuance similar to English "to neglect X" (cf. HALOT s.v. hiph 7). The complement of the verb is the NP דבר מכל אשר דברת, which is internally modified by a מן-PP. The relative אשר דברת modifies a null head, "all [of that] which you said [it]."

§3: The Rise of Mordecai (6:11-14)

Following the king's orders, Haman must bring about the various means of honoring and exalting Mordecai. Such an action is clearly understood to be humiliating and devastating to Haman.

[11]And Haman took the clothes and the horse, and he clothed Mordecai, and he caused him to ride through the square of the city. And he called out before him, "Thus will be done for the man in whose honor the king delights." [12]And Mordecai returned to the gate of the king, while Haman hastened to his house, mourning, and covered of head. [13]And Haman recounted to Zeresh, his wife, and to all of his friends, all that had befallen him. And his advisors and Zeresh, his wife, said to him, "If Mordecai, before whom you have begun to fall, is from the seed of the Jews, you will not prevail over him. Indeed, you will surely fall before him!" [14]They were still speaking with him, and the eunuchs of the king arrived. And they hastened to bring Haman to the banquet which Esther had prepared.

6:11 וַיִּקַּח הָמָן אֶת־הַלְּבוּשׁ וְאֶת־הַסּוּס וַיַּלְבֵּשׁ אֶת־
מָרְדֳּכָי וַיַּרְכִּיבֵהוּ בִּרְחוֹב הָעִיר וַיִּקְרָא לְפָנָיו כָּכָה
יֵעָשֶׂה לָאִישׁ אֲשֶׁר הַמֶּלֶךְ חָפֵץ בִּיקָרוֹ׃

In this verse, all of the actions specified by Haman in vv. 8-9 are carried out by Haman but for Mordecai.

וַיִּקַּח הָמָן אֶת־הַלְּבוּשׁ וְאֶת־הַסּוּס. *Wayyiqtol* 3ms Qal √לקח. The verb לקח follows the same forms as a I-נ verb (cf. comment on v. 10; JM 72j); as a result, the first radical ל is assimilated with the second radical ק in the past narrative (*wayyilqaḥ* > *wayyiqqaḥ*). Qal לקח is bivalent and here the NP complement is a compound, את הלבוש and את הסוס.

וַיַּלְבֵּשׁ אֶת־מָרְדֳּכָי. *Wayyiqtol* 3ms Hiph √לבש. Hiphil לבש is trivalent, taking a subject (null, contextually identifiable as Haman) and two complements. The first complement is the one putting something on, מרדכי. The second complement, the thing put on, is null, but understood from context to be לבוש מלכות from v. 8. Note that the English phrase "X clothed Y" incorporates the NP complement into the verb and is thus structurally different from its Hebrew counterpart.

וַיַּרְכִּיבֵהוּ בִּרְחוֹב הָעִיר. *Wayyiqtol* 3ms Hiph √רכב with 3ms clitic pronoun. As with וילבש in the preceding clause, וירכיבהו is missing one complement: Hiphil רכב is trivalent, taking a subject (null, understood to be Haman), a complement denoting the one riding (the 3ms clitic pronoun attached to the verb), and a complement denoting the one being ridden (here null, but contextually identifiable as the horse mentioned in previous verses). The ב-PP is a spatial adjunct.

וַיִּקְרָ֣א לְפָנָ֔יו כָּ֚כָה יֵעָשֶׂ֣ה לָאִ֔ישׁ אֲשֶׁ֥ר הַמֶּ֖לֶךְ חָפֵ֥ץ בִּיקָרֽוֹ. *Wayyiqtol* 3ms Qal √קרא, *yiqtol* 3ms Niph √עשׂה, and *qatal* 3ms Qal √חפץ. See comments on v. 9.

6:12 וַיָּ֥שָׁב מָרְדֳּכַ֖י אֶל־שַׁ֣עַר הַמֶּ֑לֶךְ וְהָמָן֙ נִדְחַ֣ף אֶל־
בֵּית֔וֹ אָבֵ֖ל וַחֲפ֥וּי רֹֽאשׁ׃

When the event is over, the narrator makes Haman's mortification explicit—he hurried home with his head covered in shame.

וַיָּ֥שָׁב מָרְדֳּכַ֖י אֶל־שַׁ֣עַר הַמֶּ֑לֶךְ. *Wayyiqtol* 3ms Qal √שׁוב. The *wayyiqtol* form of שׁוב in the Qal is distinguishable from the *wayyiqtol* form of ישׁב by the vowel of the prefix: שׁוב has *qameṣ*, while ישׁב has *ṣere* (e.g., Gen 4:16 וַיֵּשֶׁב). Qal שׁוב takes one locative complement, denoting the place to which someone "returns"; in this case it is the PP אל שׁער המלך.

וְהָמָן֙ נִדְחַ֣ף אֶל־בֵּית֔וֹ אָבֵ֖ל וַחֲפ֥וּי רֹֽאשׁ. *Qatal* 3ms Niph √דחף and participle ms Qal passive √חפה. There are three plausible pragmatic readings for the subject-verb order in this clause. First, the order could reflect basic subject-verb order (see "Word Order" in the Introduction), and the use of such a clause here carries a discourse implicature of simultaneous action or event—"while" Mordecai went back to his place at the gate, Haman hurried home. Second, the subject המן could be read as fronted to signal a switch in Topic—whereas Mordecai is the agent of the preceding verb, in this clause the Topic switches to Haman. Third, the subject המן might be fronted to contrast Haman with Mordecai. This last option is the least likely, since it is difficult to see how a contrast between Mordecai and Haman would function in the immediate discourse context; rather, it seems to us the juxtaposition between the two characters and their actions is minimal in order to present them as simultaneous (see comments on 1:12; 8:14; 9:16) and maximal in order to signal a Topic switch (marked by the subject-verb order of the second clause) and also possibly a Focus-contrast between the two different actions (if the second verb is focused, it would still result in [nonbasic] subject-verb order since Topics move higher than Foci; see Holmstedt 2011). The Niphal נדחף is monovalent; on the meaning, see comment on 3:15. The phrase אבל וחפוי ראשׁ, an adjective followed by a participial clause, functions syntactically like the phrase שׂמח וטוב לב in 5:9; cf. discussion there.

6:13 וַיְסַפֵּר הָמָן לְזֶרֶשׁ אִשְׁתּוֹ וּלְכָל־אֹהֲבָיו אֵת כָּל־
אֲשֶׁר קָרָהוּ וַיֹּאמְרוּ לוֹ חֲכָמָיו וְזֶרֶשׁ אִשְׁתּוֹ אִם
מִזֶּרַע הַיְּהוּדִים מָרְדֳּכַי אֲשֶׁר הַחִלּוֹתָ לִנְפֹּל לְפָנָיו
לֹא־תוּכַל לוֹ כִּי־נָפוֹל תִּפּוֹל לְפָנָיו׃

Haman relates his troubles to his wife and friends, echoing 5:10-15. There, his confidants gave bold advice on how to crush Mordecai, sharing in Haman's spirit of vengeance. Here, however, they have a decidedly negative tone. It is as if they distance themselves from Haman because they see how his fortunes have turned.

וַיְסַפֵּר הָמָן לְזֶרֶשׁ אִשְׁתּוֹ וּלְכָל־אֹהֲבָיו אֵת כָּל־אֲשֶׁר קָרָהוּ. *Wayyiqtol* 3ms Piel √ספר and *qatal* 3ms Qal √קרה with 3ms clitic pronoun. This clause mirrors 5:11 in content and style, though in 5:11 Haman is gleeful as he recounts his news, whereas here he is in turmoil. On the syntax of this clause, see comment on 5:11.

וַיֹּאמְרוּ לוֹ חֲכָמָיו וְזֶרֶשׁ אִשְׁתּוֹ. *Wayyiqtol* 3mp Qal √אמר. The *wayyiqtol* triggers verb-subject order, and the light PP לו raises with the verb ahead of the subject.

אִם מִזֶּרַע הַיְּהוּדִים מָרְדֳּכַי אֲשֶׁר הַחִלּוֹתָ לִנְפֹּל לְפָנָיו. A null copula clause with subject מרדכי and a PP copular complement, מזרע היהודים. Null copula clauses typically have subject-complement order, even with a conditional particle like אם (see "Word Order" in the Introduction). The fronted complement in this clause has two likely explanations: either the PP is Focus-fronted to contrast היהודים with other potential people groups (who presumably would not bode such ill for Haman) or the complex subject is moved down the clause as a case of HNPS (see discussion at 1:5). Within the אשר relative clause that modifies מרדכי, there is a *qatal* 2ms Hiph √חלל, and inf constr Qal √נפל. The ל-PP/infinitive clause לנפל is the complement of bivalent חלל (see comment on v. 10), and the PP לפניו is the locative complement of bivalent Qal נפל. As a whole, this אם clause is a conditional clause adjunct to the following main verb, תוכל. Some exegetes attempt to explain this conditional away as not a "real" (Bush, 416) or "true" (Fox 2001:79; 282) conditional, since Mordecai's Jewishness was already known to Haman and his household. Such objections ignore the real use of language, though, since conditionals are often used even when the outcome is already known: "If this fellow is Jewish (and we all know that he is!), then you are doomed!" Whether or not the statement in the mouths of Haman's confidants reflects the narrator's perspective (Bush, 417), it is incorrect to say that the structure is not a conditional clause from a grammatical perspective.

לֹא־תוּכַל לוֹ. *Yiqtol* 2ms Qal √יכל. Qal יכל with a ל-PP has the nuance "to prevail over X" (HALOT s.v. 3b); the ל-PP is the complement of the bivalent verb, which more often takes a ל-PP/infinitive clause complement (it is monovalent "to be capable" only in 1 Sam 26:25, Jer 3:5, and Job 31:23). The form of תוכל illustrates how some verbs were originally I-ו but partially changed toward I-י morphology (cf. JM 75). The *binyan* of יוכל is enigmatic. The semantics of "to be able" best fit the Qal; but the morphology only fits the Hofal (< **yuwkal*). JM argues for the Hofal analysis and suggests the following series of semantic shifts: "the original meaning of Hofal, *he will be made capable*, could easily, and may in fact, have weakened to *he will become capable, he will be capable,* becoming finally *he will be able to*, the causative meaning may then have gradually evaporated" (JM 75i).

כִּי־נָפוֹל תִּפּוֹל לְפָנָיו. Inf abs Qal √נפל and *yiqtol* 2ms Qal √נפל. The infinitive נפול is used to mark the finite verb תפול overtly for Focus (cf. comment on 4:14). The particle כי is either an adversative ("you will not prevail, *but* you will fall"; cf. MNK 40.9 II.3; Aejmaleus, 200) or an exclamative, "indeed!" Though both options function well in the context, given the nature of the conditional clause used rhetorically (a condition they know to be the case), we prefer the exclamative use in this case.

6:14 עוֹדָם מְדַבְּרִים עִמּוֹ וְסָרִיסֵי הַמֶּלֶךְ הִגִּיעוּ וַיַּבְהִלוּ לְהָבִיא אֶת־הָמָן אֶל־הַמִּשְׁתֶּה אֲשֶׁר־עָשְׂתָה אֶסְתֵּר׃

The scene ends with the dismayed Haman being rushed off to Esther's final drinking banquet, where Haman's downfall will be completed.

עוֹדָם מְדַבְּרִים עִמּוֹ. A null copula clause with a 3mp clitic pronoun subject and a participle phrase complement (participle mp Piel √דבר). For reasons that are not entirely clear, the 3mp subject clitic pronoun is attracted to עוד, as it is to יש, אין, and הנה (JM 102k). The clitic pronoun is the subject of the clause, while עוד is an adjunct to the (null) copula, and the phrase מדברים עמו is the copular complement. Piel דבר is monovalent and the PP עמו is its adjunct.

וְסָרִיסֵ֤י הַמֶּ֙לֶךְ֙ הִגִּ֔יעוּ. *Qatal* 3cp Hiph √נגע. Hiphil נגע is monovalent (see comment on 2:12). The subject-verb order might reflect no special pragmatic structure (i.e., a "basic" clause), but it is as likely, if not more, that the subject סריסי המלך is a new Topic and so fronted within the phrase structure.

וַיַּבְהִ֙לוּ֙ לְהָבִ֣יא אֶת־הָמָ֔ן אֶל־הַמִּשְׁתֶּ֖ה אֲשֶׁר־עָשְׂתָ֥ה אֶסְתֵּֽר. *Wayyiqtol* 3mp Hiph √בהל, inf constr Hiphil √בוא, and *qatal* 3fs Qal √עשׂה. According to HALOT, Hiphil בהל has a slightly different meaning ("to hurry") than Piel בהל ("to make haste"; cf. comment on 2:9). As with Piel בהל in 2:9, Hiphil בהל takes one complement, a ל-PP/infinitive clause, which specifies what one "hurries" to do. The infinitive הביא takes two complements, the entity being brought, את המן, and the location to which that entity goes, אל המשתה. The relative clause אשר עשׂתה אסתר modifies המשתה. On the time setting of the verb עשׂתה, cf. comment on 5:5. On the meaning of עשׂה as "to prepare," see comment on 1:3.

Episode 5—The End of Haman (7:1-10)

In episode 5 (chap. 7), Esther finally enacts the crucial point of her plan. In her second feast, in the presence of both the king and Haman, she reveals that she and her people are the object of Haman's genocidal plot, and pleads for the king to save her and them. The results are both startling and darkly humorous, with all the emotional and interpersonal chaos of the best melodrama. Whereas episode 4 focuses on a critical change in Mordecai's status, with its implications for Haman's status, episode 5 presents the narrative climax, with a tense confrontation between Esther and Haman in front of the king.

§1: Esther's Banquet (7:1-8)

The account of the second banquet closely mirrors that of the first banquet in chapter 5. The primary difference is that in the first Esther postpones her request, whereas in the second she makes her desires known. This similar narrative structure for both banquets is undoubtedly to envelope the plot-altering event of chapter 6, which Esther could not have predicted, but which critically serves her own tension-increasing strategy of deferring her request over two banquets.

[1]And the king and Haman came to drink with Esther, the queen. [2]And the king said to Esther also on the second day, during the banquet of wine, "Whatever is your petition, O Esther, the queen, shall be given to you. And let whatever is your request, up to half of the kingdom, be done." [3]And Esther, the queen, answered, and said, "If I have found favor in the your eyes, O king, and if it pleases the king, let my life be given to me as my petition, and my people as my request, [4]because I and my people have been sold, in order to exterminate, to kill, and to destroy (us). And if (only) as servants and slave-girls we had been sold, I would have been silent, because (such) distress does not compare with damage to the king." [5]And King Ahashverosh spoke and said to Esther, the queen, "Who is this one? And where is he whose heart filled him to act thus?" [6]And Esther said, "It is a man, an adversary and enemy, Haman, this evil one!" And Haman was terrified of the king and the queen. [7]And the king arose in his wrath from the banquet of wine to the pavilion garden, but Haman remained to request his life from Esther, the queen, because he saw that something bad was determined against him from with the king. [8]And the king returned from the pavilion garden to the house of the wine banquet as Haman was falling on the couch that Esther was on. And the king said, "Even to subdue the queen, with me in the palace?!" The word went out from the mouth of the king and they covered Haman's face.

7:1 וַיָּבֹא הַמֶּלֶךְ וְהָמָן לִשְׁתּוֹת עִם־אֶסְתֵּר הַמַּלְכָּה׃

Esther gives a second banquet for the king and Haman. With this verse, the narrator picks up the story line of Esther and her request of the king, which began in 5:1 with her appearance in the court.

וַיָּבֹא הַמֶּלֶךְ וְהָמָן לִשְׁתּוֹת עִם־אֶסְתֵּר הַמַּלְכָּה. *Wayyiqtol* 3ms Qal √בוא and inf constr Qal √שׁתה. On the singular verb with what appears to be a compound (and thus plural) subject, see the discussions at 2:21; 5:4. The verb בוא is bivalent, typically with a complement indicating the locative goal; here, however, the complement is null and contextually reconstructed as אל משתה (see 5:5, 8). The ל-PP/infinitive clause beginning with לשתות is a purpose adjunct. שתה is typically bivalent, "to drink something," but it can also be a monovalent activity, "to drink," which is the usage here. The PP עם אסתר המלכה is an adjunct to the infinitive.

7:2 וַיֹּאמֶר֩ הַמֶּ֨לֶךְ לְאֶסְתֵּ֜ר גַּ֣ם בַּיּ֤וֹם הַשֵּׁנִי֙ בְּמִשְׁתֵּ֣ה
הַיַּ֔יִן מַה־שְּׁאֵלָתֵ֛ךְ אֶסְתֵּ֥ר הַמַּלְכָּ֖ה וְתִנָּ֣תֵֽן לָ֑ךְ וּמַה־
בַּקָּשָׁתֵ֛ךְ עַד־חֲצִ֥י הַמַּלְכ֖וּת וְתֵעָֽשׂ׃

וַיֹּאמֶר֩ הַמֶּ֨לֶךְ לְאֶסְתֵּ֜ר גַּ֣ם בַּיּ֤וֹם הַשֵּׁנִי֙ בְּמִשְׁתֵּ֣ה הַיַּ֔יִן. *Wayyiqtol* 3ms Qal √אמר. The particle גם is used here as an additive "also" (HALOT s.v. 2; cf. BDB s.v.). That is, the king asks again, in addition to the time he asked at the last banquet (cf. 5:6). The ordinal numeral שני modifies the noun יום adjectivally (see "Numeral Syntax in Esther" in the Introduction). On the sense of the preposition ב in the phrase במשתה היין, see comment on the same phrase in 5:6. The syntax of the PP במשתה היין differs from 5:6, though—here it is appositive to ביום השני and clarifies what "the second day" refers to (it is the second day on which Esther gave her banquet for the king and Haman).

מַה־שְּׁאֵלָתֵ֛ךְ אֶסְתֵּ֥ר הַמַּלְכָּ֖ה וְתִנָּ֣תֵֽן לָ֑ךְ וּמַה־בַּקָּשָׁתֵ֛ךְ עַד־חֲצִ֥י הַמַּלְכ֖וּת וְתֵעָֽשׂ. *Yiqtol* (irrealis) 3fs Niph √נתן and jussive (form and semantics) 3fs Niph √עשׂה. On the syntax of these two clauses, see comment on 5:3. The proper noun אסתר and appositive NP המלכה are together a vocative phrase here. On בקשה and שׁאלה, see comments on 5:3 and 6, respectively.

7:3 וַתַּ֨עַן אֶסְתֵּ֤ר הַמַּלְכָּה֙ וַתֹּאמַ֔ר אִם־מָצָ֨אתִי חֵ֤ן
בְּעֵינֶ֙יךָ֙ הַמֶּ֔לֶךְ וְאִם־עַל־הַמֶּ֖לֶךְ ט֑וֹב תִּנָּֽתֶן־לִ֤י נַפְשִׁי֙
בִּשְׁאֵ֣לָתִ֔י וְעַמִּ֖י בְּבַקָּשָׁתִֽי׃

Esther finally gives voice to her petition—it for no less than her life, and the lives of her people.

וַתַּ֨עַן אֶסְתֵּ֤ר הַמַּלְכָּה֙. *Wayyiqtol* 3fs Qal √ענה. The Qal ענה varies between monovalent and bivalent usage. The common bivalent use frequently has an NP complement of the person answered. The monovalent use is often combined as a verbal hendiadys with אמר, i.e., "x answered and said ...," which occurs here.

וַתֹּאמַ֔ר. *Wayyiqtol* 3fs Qal √אמר. The complement of אמר is the direct speech that follows in the next clause.

אִם־מָצָ֨אתִי חֵ֤ן בְּעֵינֶ֙יךָ֙ הַמֶּ֔לֶךְ. *Qatal* (irrealis) 1cs Qal √מצא. The initial אם marks a subordinate conditional clause, adjunct to the main verb תנתן. On the idiom itself, see comment on 5:8.

וְאִם־עַל־הַמֶּ֖לֶךְ ט֑וֹב. A null copula clause, with a null subject (which cataphorically refers forward to the content of Esther's request), and the adjective טוב as the copular complement. The PP על המלך is an adjunct to the copula and is Focus-fronted as part of the highly deferential idiom. See comment on this same idiom in 1:19. The אם marks this clause as a second (conjoined) conditional clause adjunct to תנתן.

תִּנָּֽתֶן־לִ֤י נַפְשִׁי֙ בִּשְׁאֵ֣לָתִ֔י. *Yiqtol* (jussive semantics) 3fs Niph √נתן. Niphal נתן is bivalent, taking an NP subject (the thing given, here נפשי) and a PP complement (the recipient, here לי). The modality of the jussive has triggered the verb-raising over the subject. Since light PPs attach to the verb and raise with it (see comments on 2:7, 12), both the verb תנתן and the PP complement לי precede the subject here (compare the "heavy" PP in the syntactically similar phrase ותקרא אסתר להתך in 4:5). Concerning the preposition ב in the adjunct PP בשאלתי we agree with many commentators and take the likeliest nuance to be the "*beth* of identity" (*beth essentiæ*; see WO 11.2.5e; also, Moore 1971:68; Bush, 423; Levenson, 99; Fox 2001:81, 83; cf. Paton, 260). Thus, Esther is asking for her life "*as* (her) petition."

וְעַמִּ֖י בְּבַקָּשָׁתִֽי. Rather than viewing תנתן as having a discontinuous compound NP (נפשי ... ועמי) as its subject, it is syntactically simpler to take this as a new clause here with the verb תנתן and the complement לי gapped from the preceding clause: "and (let) my people (be given to me) as my request." On the semantics of ב in the PP בבקשתי, see the comment on בשאלתי above.

7:4 כִּ֤י נִמְכַּ֙רְנוּ֙ אֲנִ֣י וְעַמִּ֔י לְהַשְׁמִ֖יד לַהֲר֣וֹג וּלְאַבֵּ֑ד וְאִלּ֨וּ
לַעֲבָדִ֤ים וְלִשְׁפָחוֹת֙ נִמְכַּ֔רְנוּ הֶחֱרַ֕שְׁתִּי כִּ֣י אֵ֥ין הַצָּ֛ר
שֹׁוֶ֖ה בְּנֵ֥זֶק הַמֶּֽלֶךְ׃

The narrator has Esther use the same words used in the king's edict in 3:13, להשמיד להרוג ולאבד, to confront the king with how her life and the lives of her people are endangered.

כִּ֤י נִמְכַּ֙רְנוּ֙ אֲנִ֣י וְעַמִּ֔י לְהַשְׁמִ֖יד לַהֲר֣וֹג וּלְאַבֵּ֑ד. *Qatal* 1cp Niph √מכר, inf constr Hiph √שמד, Qal √הרג, and Piel √אבד. The Niphal verb נמכרנו is monovalent, with an NP subject, here the compound אני ועמי. The three ל-PP/infinitive clauses provide the purpose for the "selling" of Esther and her people. The infinitives are all active and the null complement, which is easily reconstructed from the context, is 1cp "us," referring to Esther and her people. With these phrases Esther quotes the content of the king's edict in 3:13 (cf. Fox 2001:84; Levenson, 101); however, judging by the question the king asks in 7:5, he does not make the connection that Esther is the victim of his edict (Fox 2001:83). The causal כי indicates that this clause provides the basis for the preceding clauses (cf. MNK 40.9 I.3; WO 38.4a); in other words, the reason Esther wants the king to rescue her and her people is that they need rescuing (otherwise they will be exterminated, slain, and destroyed).

וְאִלּוּ לַעֲבָדִים וְלִשְׁפָחוֹת נִמְכַּרְנוּ הֶחֱרַשְׁתִּי. *Qatal* (irrealis) 1cp Niph √מכר and 1cs Hiph √חרש. The irreal (or counterfactional) conditional אלו (HALOT s.v.) appears to be a combination of two conditional particles, אם and לו (HALOT s.v.). אלו is used only twice in the Hebrew Bible (here and Eccl 6:6; perhaps אִילּוּ in Eccl 4:10 is a third example), though it is the sole irreal conditional in the Mishnah. Using אלו sets up a condition based on an event or action that has not occurred and likely will not occur. Thus, Esther's point is that had they only been sold into slavery, she would not have risked damage to the king's reputation by making this an issue. But the fact is that they were not just sold into slavery—they have been marked for destruction. The compound PP לעבדים ולשפחות is fronted for Focus, thus marking by word order the contrast between the fact (destruction) and the unrealized alternative (slavery). The ל prepositions in this compound PP indicate "purpose" or "goal" (WO 11.2.10d exx. 38, 43–45)—these categories are what Esther and her people could have been sold "as" or "to become." The main clause, or apodosis for the conditional protasis, is a single word, the verb החר שתי. Hiphil חרש means "to be silent" (HALOT s.v.) and appears to be an internal causative of the Qal, which also means "to be deaf" or "to be silent." I.e., Esther would have "silenced herself," which is functionally equivalent to simply "being silent."

כִּי אֵין הַצָּר שֹׁוֶה בְּנֵזֶק הַמֶּלֶךְ. An אין copula clause with subject הצר and a participle (ms Qal √שוה) phrase complement. On the meaning of שוה, see comment on 3:8. Whereas in 3:8 the complement of שוה is a ל-PP, here the complement is a ב-PP, "the distress does not *compare with* the damage of the king." The NP צַר "distress" is homophonous with an adjective meaning "narrow, tight" and another NP meaning "enemy, adversary." All three words have a base with the *pataḥ*, צַר, and a variant with the *qameṣ*, צָר; the intended word can often only be deduced on the basis of which meaning fits the context. The meaning "distress" makes the most sense in this context. The NP נזק, "burden, damage, injury" (HALOT s.v.; DCH s.v.) is attested only here in the Bible, but is common in the Mishnah and later literature. It is a *qitl-* pattern segholate noun (cf. JM 88Ch) derived from the Semitic root נזק "to suffer harm" or "to do harm" (HALOT s.v.), known from Aramaic in both verbal and nominal form (cf., e.g., Dan 6:3; Ezra 4:13, 15; 4QAstronomical Enoch[c] 1 II, 2). In Mishnaic literature, however, נזק is used with frequency (the fourth order of the Mishnah is even titled נזיקין, "damages"). The bound phrase, נזק המלך, "damage of the king," means damage *done to* or *experienced by* the king (see WO 9.5.2 under "adverbial genitive").

7:5 וַיֹּ֙אמֶר֙ הַמֶּ֣לֶךְ אֲחַשְׁוֵר֔וֹשׁ וַיֹּ֖אמֶר לְאֶסְתֵּ֣ר הַמַּלְכָּ֑ה מִ֣י ה֥וּא זֶה֙ וְאֵי־זֶ֣ה ה֔וּא אֲשֶׁר־מְלָא֥וֹ לִבּ֖וֹ לַעֲשׂ֥וֹת כֵּֽן׃

The king appears unable to make the connection between the plot Esther refers to and the edict suggested by Haman in chapter 3. In terms of character development, the narrator depicts an oblivious, if not dense, monarch. From a plot perspective, the king's question heightens the tension and allows Esther to spell out the details and accuse Haman directly.

וַיֹּ֙אמֶר֙ הַמֶּ֣לֶךְ אֲחַשְׁוֵר֔וֹשׁ וַיֹּ֖אמֶר לְאֶסְתֵּ֣ר הַמַּלְכָּ֑ה. *Wayyiqtol* 3ms Qal √אמר, twice. The double use of ויאמר to introduce speech is an uncommon but attested pattern (see, e.g., 1 Kgs 20:28; Miller 1996:6.3.4). In such cases, the first אמר is reduced to monovalency and the second אמר is typically bivalent, with the direct speech as its complement. The PP לאסתר המלכה is an adjunct indicating the speech addressee. This double use of אמר may have a discourse function, perhaps resulting from the climactic tension contained at this point in the plot (it maybe "control the pacing of the verse" [Fox 2001:283] or be a "retarding device of the narrator" [Bush, 428–29]).

מִ֣י ה֥וּא זֶה֙. A copula clause with the 3ms pronoun הוא as the copula, the demonstrative זה the subject, and the Focus-fronted interrogative מי the complement. On הוא used as a pronominal copula, see Holmstedt 2013e; Holmstedt and Jones.

וְאֵי־זֶ֣ה ה֔וּא אֲשֶׁר־מְלָא֥וֹ לִבּ֖וֹ לַעֲשׂ֥וֹת כֵּֽן. A copula clause, with the demonstrative זה as the copula, the interrogative אי the Focus-fronted complement, and the pronoun הוא the subject. On זה as a rare pronominal copula, see Holmstedt and Jones. The relative clause (including *qatal*

3ms Qal √מלא with 3ms clitic pronoun and inf constr Qal √עשה) modifies the pronominal head הוא and resumed it by the 3ms clitic pronoun in the verb מלאו. The relative clause is restrictive and so defines its head. I.e., this is not a simple question of location for a known entity, "where is he?" (in which "he" is known and identifiable to the participants), but a question that seeks the location of a person whose identification is provided by the relative, e.g., "where is the man who has done such a thing?" Note that it is possible to take the relative head הוא as the subject of the verb מלאו and the 3ms clitic pronoun on the verb as a cataphoric reference to לבו (also known as a "proleptic pronoun"; JM 146e), i.e., "he who he has filled it, his heart ..." (so Bush, 423). But this is very awkward and the use of a proleptic pronoun is extremely rare in the Hebrew Bible, though common in Aramaic. We prefer the simpler syntax of the לבו as the subject of מלאו. Qal מלא here is trivalent (cf. 1:5, where Qal מלא is monovalent) and so takes two complements: the first complement (the thing filled) is the 3ms clitic pronoun attached to the verb and the second complement (the thing with which someone is filled) is the ל-PP/infinitive clause לעשות. The infinitive עשות is bivalent and the adverb כן is its complement (see comments on 1:21; 2:4). The idiom "his לב [= mind] filled him in order to do" (מלא with לב and לעשות) must refer to intentions, similar to Eccl 8:11, where "the לב of the sons of men are full to do evil."

7:6 וַתֹּ֣אמֶר־אֶסְתֵּ֔ר אִ֚ישׁ צַ֣ר וְאוֹיֵ֔ב הָמָ֥ן הָרָ֖ע הַזֶּ֑ה וְהָמָ֣ן נִבְעַ֔ת מִלִּפְנֵ֥י הַמֶּ֖לֶךְ וְהַמַּלְכָּֽה׃

וַתֹּ֣אמֶר־אֶסְתֵּ֔ר. *Wayyiqtol* 3fs Qal √אמר. The following direct speech is the complement of bivalent אמר.

אִ֚ישׁ צַ֣ר וְאוֹיֵ֔ב הָמָ֥ן הָרָ֖ע הַזֶּ֑ה. A null copula clause with null subject and an NP complement. The anarthrous איש cannot be the subject of the clause, since that would result in a contextually inappropriate generic statement ("a man is an adversary and enemy"). Similarly, taking המן as the subject and איש צר ואויב, "Haman is an adversary and enemy," results in a clause that makes a predication on an existing subject, המן, rather than an identificational statement, though the context requires the latter. In this light, we must take איש as the complement to the null copula and the subject as a null pronoun that refers back to the זה in the question מי הוא זה in v. 5. Instead of a null pronoun, Esther could have begun with deictic זה, effectively pointing at Haman, but her words indicate that she delays this identification in order to color the guilty party in yet a worse light before naming him. Relating back to the question מי הוא זה, Esther's answer matches the subject זה with the null pronoun subject of her answer and the fills the open variable created by the Focus-fronted interrogative מי (see comment on 1:15) with the complex NP איש צר ואיוב המן הרע הזה. The noun איש is modified by two nouns, צר and איוב (the form of איוב is homophonous with that of a ms Qal participle, but since the verbal root איב is not productive, it it best to take איוב as a noun); the syntax of this modification may either be apposition or relativization. The difference in meaning is minimal in the context, and we find that the abruptness and choppiness that the apposition creates better fits the anger we read into Esther's statement. The compound appositive, צר ואיוב, is followed by another appositive, which finally identifies the culprit by name. Since proper nouns are uniquely referential, the phrase following המן cannot be an adjunct, i.e., "this evil Haman." Rather, it is yet another appositive, by which Esther continues her wrath-filled characterization.

וְהָמָ֣ן נִבְעַ֔ת מִלִּפְנֵ֥י הַמֶּ֖לֶךְ וְהַמַּלְכָּֽה. *Qatal* 3ms Niph √בעת. Since the Topic, המן, is also the subject, subject-verb word order is retained in this clause (see "Word Order" in the Introduction). The verb בעת is used only rarely in the Niphal (here, Dan 8:17, and 1 Chr 21:30); in the Piel it means, "to terrify" or "to frighten" (HALOT s.v.). The three cases of the Niphal (HALOT: "to be gripped by a sudden fear") appear in the presence of some terror that elicits an extreme response. The מלפני PP is an adjunct to the monovalent verb and provides not the location (in the presence of) but the source of Haman's fear (i.e., due to the accusation, he now fears the king and queen themselves).

7:7 וְהַמֶּ֜לֶךְ קָ֤ם בַּחֲמָתוֹ֙ מִמִּשְׁתֵּ֣ה הַיַּ֔יִן אֶל־גִּנַּ֖ת הַבִּיתָ֑ן
וְהָמָ֣ן עָמַ֗ד לְבַקֵּ֤שׁ עַל־נַפְשׁוֹ֙ מֵאֶסְתֵּ֣ר הַמַּלְכָּ֔ה כִּ֣י
רָאָ֔ה כִּֽי־כָלְתָ֥ה אֵלָ֛יו הָרָעָ֖ה מֵאֵ֥ת הַמֶּֽלֶךְ׃

The king's angry departure sets up one of the more humorous scenes in the book, which leads directly to the end of Haman's life. Moreover, in an ironic twist, the narrator provides brief access to Haman's inner thoughts, which motivate him to his next action, the very performance of which (v. 8) enrages the king further.

וְהַמֶּ֫לֶךְ קָ֤ם בַּחֲמָתוֹ֙ מִמִּשְׁתֵּ֣ה הַיַּ֔יִן אֶל־גִּנַּ֖ת הַבִּיתָ֑ן. *Qatal* 3ms Qal √קום. The subject-verb word order continues the same word order from the previous clause, at the end of v. 6. There are multiple options for interpreting the order in this clause. First, it could simply reflect basic, unmarked subject-verb order (see "Word Order"in the Introduction) and for some reason the narrator has stopped using the *wayyiqtol* for basic narrative (the next *wayyiqtol* does not appear until ויאמר in v. 9). Second, the subject הַמֶּלֶךְ could be fronted as a Topic, thus signaling a switch from המן in the previous clause to המלך here. Such fronting typically blocks the use of the *wayyiqtol*, which explains the *qatal* verb. Third, המלך could be fronted for Focus, to contrast Haman, who responds with fear (v. 6) and begging (v. 7, in the next clause), with the king, who responds by exiting the room in anger. If the point was to contrast the king's anger with Haman's begging, only the next clause would require the subject-verb order (see below); this clause could have a *wayyiqtol*, e.g., ויקם המלך. And we see little reason to contrast the king here with the Haman of the previous verse. And so we see either the basic order (for whatever reason the narrator shifts style) or the Topic-fronting explanations to be more likely, with the Topic explanation more in line with expectations for Hebrew narrative. The PP בחמתו is an adjunct to the verb; though קום sometimes takes a ב-PP complement with the meaning "to arise in [some place]" (see comment on 5:9; cf. DCH s.v.; BDB s.v.), חמתו is not a location and the PP makes more sense as a adjunct indicating the manner in which the king rose. The PP ממשתה היין is another adjunct, with מן indicating origin or "movement away from" (WO 11.2.11b). The PP אל גנת הביתן is the locative complement of the bivalent קום. On the phrase ממשתה היין, see comment on 5:6. On גנת הביתן, see comment on 1:5.

וְהָמָ֣ן עָמַ֗ד לְבַקֵּ֤שׁ עַל־נַפְשׁוֹ֙ מֵאֶסְתֵּ֣ר הַמַּלְכָּ֔ה. *Qatal* 3ms Qal √עמד and inf constr Piel √בקש. Unlike the previous subject-verb clause, here we find it quite plausible that the subject-verb order reflects the Focus-fronting of the subject המן, so creating a contrast between the king and Haman and, by extension, their respective actions (for which the basic opposition pair עמד-קום are used). The meaning of עמד here seems to be "to remain" (cf. Bush, 423–24), in contrast to the action of the king, "to rise." Moreover, the bivalent עמד, which typically takes a locative complement, is fulfilled by the ל-PP/infinitive clause beginning with לבקש. Thus, instead of "to stand in [a location]," we have "to remain to [do something]." Within the infinitive clause לבקש על נפשו מאסתר המלכה, the על-PP is the complement of Piel בקש (see comment on 4:8) and the מן-PP is an adjunct indicating the source of the deliverance he seeks.

כִּי רָאָה כִּי־כָלְתָה אֵלָיו הָרָעָה מֵאֵת הַמֶּלֶךְ. *Qatal* 3ms Qal √ראה and *qatal* 3fs Qal √כלה. The first כי introduces a subordinate clause that gives the basis for the main clause (MNK 40.9 I.3; WO 38.4a), while the second כי introduces a nominalized clause (cf. MNK 40.9 II.1; WO 4.4.1b [3]). The verb ראה often takes a concrete NP as its complement, the thing "seen"; here what is seen is not a thing but an event, and so the event is nominalized by the כי to function similarly to an NP complement for ראה (cf. also comment on 3:5).

כָלְתָה אֵלָיו הָרָעָה מֵאֵת הַמֶּלֶךְ. *Qatal* 3fs Qal √כלה. The meaning of כלה here is not "to stop" (HALOT s.v. Qal 1) or "to be finished" (HALOT s.v. Qal 2), but "to be determined" (HALOT s.v. Qal 5). The verb כלה is monovalent, requiring just a subject, the NP הרעה. The PP אליו is an adjunct indicating for whose (dis)advantage the action or event occurs. Note that the light PP אליו has raised with the verb ahead of the subject (the verb raising is triggered by the כי), resulting in verb-adjunct-subject word order. The compound preposition מאת is another verbal adjunct and indicates the source, or in this case, the agent, of the רעה (cf. 1 Sam 20:7, 9, where the compound preposition מעם is used rather than the מאת used here). Alternatively, rather than being a verbal adjunct, מאת המלך may be an NP-internal PP restrictively modifying הרעה; i.e., what has been determined against Haman is the king's punishment. The difference between the two options is syntactically significant, but results in little interpretive difference for the narrative. The NP רעה is often glossed as "evil." Since "evil" does not fit many of the contexts in which the word is used, it is necessary to find a contextually suitable gloss that captures the intended nuance, e.g., "harm" (Bush, 423) or "ruin" (Fox 2001:82). We find the general "something bad" to fit both the specific context as well as the narrator's artistic style of deliberate ambiguity.

7:8 וְהַמֶּ֜לֶךְ שָׁ֨ב מִגִּנַּ֣ת הַבִּיתָ֗ן אֶל־בֵּ֣ית ׀ מִשְׁתֵּ֣ה הַיַּ֔יִן
וְהָמָן֙ נֹפֵ֔ל עַל־הַמִּטָּה֙ אֲשֶׁ֣ר אֶסְתֵּ֣ר עָלֶ֔יהָ וַיֹּ֣אמֶר
הַמֶּ֔לֶךְ הֲ‍ֽגַם לִכְבּ֧וֹשׁ אֶת־הַמַּלְכָּ֛ה עִמִּ֖י בַּבָּ֑יִת הַדָּבָ֗ר
יָצָא֙ מִפִּ֣י הַמֶּ֔לֶךְ וּפְנֵ֥י הָמָ֖ן חָפֽוּ׃

Haman's terrified bumbling compounds his jeopardy—his posture as he beseeched the queen's mercy is mistaken by the king as a physical attack upon his queen.

וְהַמֶּ֜לֶךְ שָׁ֨ב מִגִּנַּ֣ת הַבִּיתָ֗ן אֶל־בֵּ֣ית ׀ מִשְׁתֵּ֣ה הַיַּ֔יִן. *Qatal* 3ms Qal √שׁוב. The subject-verb order and the avoidance of the *wayyiqtol* narrative sequence likely reflects another case of Topic-fronting in order to signal a switch in the Topic, from Haman in the preceding main clause (v. 7) to the king. The verb שׁב is bivalent, taking a subject (המלך) and locative complement (אל בית משתה היין). The PP מגנת הביתן is an adjunct, indicating the origin of the movement (WO 11.2.11b). On משתה היין, see comment on 5:6; on גנת הביתן, see comment on 1:5.

וְהָמָן֙ נֹפֵ֔ל עַל־הַמִּטָּה֙ אֲשֶׁ֣ר אֶסְתֵּ֣ר עָלֶ֔יהָ. A null copula clause with an NP subject, הָמָן, and a participle (ms Qal √נפל) phrase complement. Qal נפל sometimes appears monovalent ("his face fell," Gen 4:5) but is so often associated with a locative PP (e.g., "Abram fell on his face," Gen 17:3) that either it may be bivalent, with an occasionally assumed (null) complement, or it may have both a monovalent and bivalent lexical entry. Here we take the על PP to be a complement indicating the direction or location of Haman falling. The NP מטה ("bed" or "couch") is modified by a restrictive relative—it is not just any couch upon which Haman falls, but the one that holds Esther. Within the relative, the copula is null, the subject is אסתר and the copular complement is the PP עליו, which also resumes the relative head by the 3ms clitic pronoun. The juxtaposition of the two subject-verb (or null copula) clauses often carries an implied discourse value in Hebrew narrative—simultaneity of action or event. Thus, it was at the very moment that the king returned to the room that Haman was falling on the queen's couch (hence our use of the conjunction "as" in our translation).

וַיֹּ֣אמֶר הַמֶּ֔לֶךְ הֲ‍ֽגַם לִכְבּ֧וֹשׁ אֶת־הַמַּלְכָּ֛ה עִמִּ֖י בַּבָּ֑יִת. *Wayyiqtol* 3ms Qal √אמר and inf constr Qal √כבשׁ. The direct speech is the complement of the bivalent אמר, and המלך its subject. Within the speech clause, there is no finite verb. In fact, it does not even look like a complete clause, but a fragment used to reinforce the king's outrage. The גם may be an additive, "and also to ...," or a focus operator, "and even to ... ." Both make good grammatical sense, though in the context of the king's anger, we find the Focus use more likely. It is doubtful that the syntax of this clause presents us with לכבוש as the supposed "predicative infinitive" (contra Bush, 430; see comment on 1:15). The verb כבש means "to subdue" (HALOT s.v.), and in this context clearly indicates that the king interpreted Haman's position as physical or sexual assault (so DCH s.v.). The status of the PP עמי is complicated. Whereas the PP בבית could easily be taken as a simple locative adjunct of כבוש, supplying the "where" for the activity, the same is not true for עמי. It would also be semantically illogical to take עמי as an NP-internal PP modifying the NP המלכה, since "the queen with me" would imply that the king was disambiguating Esther from other queens who were not with him. It must, therefore, be that עמי and בבית function together as a small clause, in which the preposition עם is an adjunct of accompaniment or attendant circumstances (WO 11.2.14) to the verb כבוש and the 1cs clitic pronoun is the subject and the PP בבית the predicate of the copula-less small clause, "with [me (being) in the house]" (similarly, JM 132a; Bush, 424).

הַדָּבָר יָצָא מִפִּי הַמֶּלֶךְ. *Qatal* 3ms Qal √יצא. The subject הדבר refers to an undescribed command relating either to Haman's actions or his punishment, or both. The PP מפי המלך is a complement to the bivalent motion verb יצא and indicates the starting point or origin of the action (WO 11.2.11b; see comment on 1.17). The subject-verb order of the clause reflects yet another Topic-fronting to indicate a switch in Topic, from Haman to the king's command.

וּפְנֵי הָמָן חָפוּ. *Qatal* 3mp Qal √חפה. The verb חפה means "to cover," either covering one's "head in sorrow" or possibly covering a "person to be executed" (HALOT s.v.; Paton, 264; but cf. the critique of Fox 2001:283). The complement of the verb is fronted, both to signal another switch in Topic (our preference) and to avoid any sequentiality (e.g., a *wayyiqtol*), thus using the narrative convention (see comment on the second clause of this verse) of juxtaposing two *qatal* (or *yiqtol*) clauses for simultaneity, or here, near simultaneity. The resulting sense is that the king's command had an immediate effect. The subject of the plural verb חפו is null and cannot be connected to any known, identifiable agents in the discourse; the interpretation of such null subjects is as arbitrary "someone" or the ambiguous "they/them"; such clauses are often translated as passive (see comment on 2:2; WO 4.4.2).

§2: Haman's Death (7:9-10)

This section brings Haman's role in the story to an end, with his demise. But Haman's death does not solve the problem of the impending tragedy for the Jews. And so these two verses represent a mini-resolution, tying off one strand of the story (and bringing the audience some emotional relief as well as a sense of justice having been served) as the narrator brings the audience one step closer to a conclusion.

[9]And Harbona, one of the eunuchs before the king, said, "Moreover, look—the tree that Haman made for Mordecai, who spoke a good word for the king, is standing in the house of Haman, (being) high, fifty cubits." And the king said, "Hang him on it." [10]And they hung Haman on the tree that he had set up for Mordecai. And the wrath of the king abated.

7:9 וַיֹּ֣אמֶר חַ֠רְבוֹנָה אֶחָ֨ד מִן־הַסָּרִיסִ֜ים לִפְנֵ֣י הַמֶּ֗לֶךְ
גַּ֣ם הִנֵּֽה־הָעֵ֣ץ אֲשֶׁר־עָשָׂ֣ה הָמָ֡ן לְמָרְדֳּכַ֞י אֲשֶׁ֧ר
דִּבֶּר־ט֣וֹב עַל־הַמֶּ֗לֶךְ עֹמֵד֙ בְּבֵ֣ית הָמָ֔ן גָּבֹ֖הַּ חֲמִשִּׁ֣ים
אַמָּ֑ה וַיֹּ֥אמֶר הַמֶּ֖לֶךְ תְּלֻ֥הוּ עָלָֽיו׃

This verse and the next clearly echo 5:14, except here it is Haman, not Mordecai, who is to be hung.

וַיֹּ֣אמֶר חַ֠רְבוֹנָה אֶחָ֨ד מִן־הַסָּרִיסִ֜ים לִפְנֵ֣י הַמֶּ֗לֶךְ. *Wayyiqtol* 3ms Qal √אמר. The name חרבונה here is spelled differently from the name חרבונא in 1:10, but this is very possibly the same person (both are eunuchs); cf. the variable spelling of Bigthan in 2:21 and 6:2, and of Hegai in 2:3, 8, and 15. The phrase מן הסריסים לפני המלך is an NP-internal PP modifying the numeral אחד, which stands in apposition to the PN חרבונה. The preposition מן is partitive, "[referring] to part of the noun (or noun equivalent) after the preposition" (WO 11.2.11e).

גַּ֣ם הִנֵּֽה־הָעֵ֣ץ אֲשֶׁר־עָשָׂ֣ה הָמָ֡ן לְמָרְדֳּכַ֞י אֲשֶׁ֧ר דִּבֶּר־ט֣וֹב עַל־הַמֶּ֗לֶךְ עֹמֵד֙ בְּבֵ֣ית הָמָ֔ן גָּבֹ֖הַּ חֲמִשִּׁ֣ים אַמָּ֑ה. A null copula clause with an NP subject (the complex NP העץ ... על המלך) and participle (ms Qal √עמד) phrase complement (עמד בבית המן). Within the relative clauses are *qatal* 3ms Qal √עשׂה and *qatal* 3ms Piel √דבר. The initial גם is additive, implying that what Harbona says should be taken as an additional component of Haman's punishment. The הנה is a deictic exclamative by which Harbona directs his audience's (the king) attention to a story prop left unused since episode 4 (5:14). The participle in the main clause is used to indicate durative action ("it is standing"). Combined with the null copula within the deixis of the speech, the clause has a present time/tense setting. The PP בבית המן is the locative complement of עמד (cf. comment on 5:1). Though in 5:14 the adjective גבה and the numeral phrase חמשים אמה modify the NP העץ, here they are separated from the NP by a significant number of constituents. Rather than an extraposed phrase (why would it have been moved to the end?), the compound modifier גבה חמשים אמה seems better taken as a small clause adjunct to the participle עמד, indicating the manner in which the tree was standing, i.e., "the tree ... is standing, being high and fifty cubits" (see the similar syntax of שמח וטוב לב in 5:9). On the syntax of חמשים אמה, see comment on 5:14 and "Numeral Syntax in Esther" in the Introduction. Within the subject NP, the relative אשר עשה המן למרדכי restrictively modifies העץ and the relative אשר דבר טוב על המלך nonrestrictively modifies מרדכי. The verb עשה is bivalent, taking an NP subject (המן) and NP complement (the relative head העץ). The PP למרדכי is an adjunct to עשה and provides the person or thing for whom it was made (i.e., it is a ל of [dis]advantage; WO 11.2.10d). The Piel דבר is typically bivalent, with a direct or indirect speech complement or with a noun (covert or overt; cf. 6:10) related to speech. Here, then, the simplest analysis is to take the adjective טוב as a substantive, "good word," in reference to Mordecai's report of the plan to assassinate the king (2:21-22). The PP על המלך reflects the use of על in a similar role to the ל of advantage (WO 11.2.13c), so "for the benefit of the king" (Bush, 424).

וַיֹּ֥אמֶר הַמֶּ֖לֶךְ. *Wayyiqtol* 3ms Qal √אמר. The following direct speech is the complement of the bivalent אמר. Note that the Revised Standard Version (and the English Standard Version which follows it) erroneously begins v. 10 at this point. No ancient manuscripts or translations, however, contain such a verse division. The error has been corrected in the New Revised Standard Version.

תְּלֻ֥הוּ עָלָֽיו. Impv mp Qal √תלה. On the valency and meaning of תלה, see comment on 2:23. The PP עליו is a locative adjunct indicating where the hanging was to occur.

7:10 וַיִּתְלוּ֙ אֶת־הָמָ֔ן עַל־הָעֵ֖ץ אֲשֶׁר־הֵכִ֣ין לְמָרְדֳּכָ֑י
וַחֲמַ֥ת הַמֶּ֖לֶךְ שָׁכָֽכָה׃

וַיִּתְלוּ֙ אֶת־הָמָ֔ן עַל־הָעֵ֖ץ אֲשֶׁר־הֵכִ֣ין לְמָרְדֳּכָ֑י. *Wayyiqtol* 3mp Qal √תלה and *qatal* 3ms Hiph √כון. The plural verb has a null, generic subject (cf. comment on 2:2). On the valency and meaning of תלה, see comment on 2:23. On the syntax of the relative, and the meaning and valency of הכין, see comment on 6:4.

וַחֲמַ֥ת הַמֶּ֖לֶךְ שָׁכָֽכָה. *Qatal* 3fs Qal √שכך. This clause clearly recalls 2:1, where the king's wrath abated after the events involving Vashti. שככה means "it subsided" (HALOT s.v.) or "it abated" (BDB s.v.). The subject-verb order either reflects "basic" order (see "Word Order" in the Introduction) or, more likely, the Topic-fronting to indicate a switch to the new Topic, חמת המלך. The subject-verb order is also used here to avoid the temporal sequencing that is often associated with the *wayyiqtol* and so signals a sense of closure to episode 5 as well as the larger Part II of the story.

PART III
The Jews and the Peoples in Conflict (8:1–9:32)

Episode 1—A Plan to Save the Jews (8:1-17)

The plot now moves toward a resolution to the primary problem—how the Jews will survive the kingdom-wide extermination planned by the now-deceased Haman.

§1: The King Empowers Mordecai and Esther (8:1-8)

With the primary adversary defeated, Esther shifts her attention to counteracting his plan, though it proves to be more complicated than she initially hopes.

[1]On that day, King Ahashverosh gave to Esther, the queen, the estate of
Haman, who had been hostile to the Jews. And Mordecai came before the
king, because Esther had declared what he was to her. [2]And the king removed
his signet ring, which he had taken away from Haman, and he gave it to
Mordecai. And Esther appointed Mordecai over the estate of Haman. [3]And
Esther again spoke before the king, and she fell before his feet, and she wept,
and she sought favor toward him to remove the evil of Haman, the Agagite,
and his plan which he had planned against the Jews. [4]And the king held out
the golden scepter to Esther, and Esther rose, and she stood before the king.
[5]And she said, "If it pleases the king, and if I have found favor before him,
and (if) the thing is proper before the king, and (if) I please him, let it be
written to cancel the letters, the plans of Haman, son of Hammedatha the
Agagite, who wrote to destroy the Jews that are in all the provinces of the
king. [6]For how could I watch the ruin that would find my people? And how
could I watch the destruction of my kindred?" [7]And King Ahashverosh said
to Esther, the queen, and to Mordecai, the Jew, "Look—I have given the
estate of Haman to Esther, and they hung him upon the tree because he raised
his hand against the Jews. [8]And you, write concerning the Jews according to

what pleases you, in the name of the king, and seal (it) with the signet ring of the king, because there is no canceling a writing that is written in the name of the king, being sealed with the signet ring of the king."

8:1 בַּיּ֣וֹם הַה֗וּא נָתַ֞ן הַמֶּ֤לֶךְ אֲחַשְׁוֵרוֹשׁ֙ לְאֶסְתֵּ֣ר
הַמַּלְכָּ֔ה אֶת־בֵּ֥ית הָמָ֖ן צֹרֵ֣ר הַיְּהוּדִ֑יים וּמָרְדֳּכַ֗י בָּ֚א
לִפְנֵ֣י הַמֶּ֔לֶךְ כִּֽי־הִגִּ֥ידָה אֶסְתֵּ֖ר מַ֥ה הוּא־לָֽהּ׃

בַּיּ֣וֹם הַה֗וּא נָתַ֞ן הַמֶּ֤לֶךְ אֲחַשְׁוֵרוֹשׁ֙ לְאֶסְתֵּ֣ר הַמַּלְכָּ֔ה אֶת־בֵּ֥ית הָמָ֖ן. *Qatal* 3ms Qal √נתן. The temporal PP ביום ההוא is fronted as a scene-setting Topic (cf. 5:9 where it is not topicalized). The Topic-fronting triggers verb-subject word order. Qal נתן is trivalent, taking a subject (המלך אחשורוש), an NP complement for what is given (את בית המן צרר היהודיים), and a PP complement for the recipient (לאסתר המלכה). The contextual nuance of the NP בית is more than the physical structure(s) belonging to Haman, but his entire "estate" (buildings, possessions, etc.; cf. Moore 1971:77; Fox 2001:90). The use of the *qatal* instead of a *wayyiqtol* (which is also possible even with the fronted PP; see Gen 22:4; Holmstedt 2014a) suggests that the narrator was signaling a shift in scene and avoiding the time sequencing associated with the use of the *wayyiqtol* (see comments on the word order and verbs in vv. 8 and 10).

הָמָ֖ן צֹרֵ֣ר הַיְּהוּדִ֑יים. This is an unmarked relative clause with a null copula and participle (participle ms Qal √צרר) phrase complement (see also 3:10). The relative modifies the noun המן nonrestrictively and so simply serves to keep Haman's status in the forefront of the audience's mind. The participle presents an action or event as durative or progressive and takes it time setting ("tense") from contextual clues. Here, since Haman is now dead, the appropriate time setting is the past-in-the-past (i.e., past perfect), "Haman, who had shown hostility to the Jews." Note that the structure of the English translation "show hostility to" differs from the Hebrew, in which the verb צרר mostly takes an NP complement rather than a PP complement (see Num 25:18 for a rare ל-PP complement). The *Ketiv* הַיְּהוּדִ֑יים has two yods in the ending, while the *Qere* היהודים has the single yod; see comment on 4:7 and "*Qere-Ketiv*" in the Introduction.

וּמָרְדֳּכַ֗י בָּ֚א לִפְנֵ֣י הַמֶּ֔לֶךְ. *Qatal* 3ms Qal √בוא. The PP לפני המלך is the complement of bivalent Qal בוא, denoting the place to which

Mordecai came. That Mordecai "came before the king" (בא לפני המלך) is no small statement, considering the consequences for doing so unbidden. In other words, that he was allowed to come before the king was a great honor bestowed on him. The subject-verb order likely reflects the fronting of the subject for a switch in Topic, from המלך in the preceding main clause to מרדכי here. Additionally, the avoidance of a *wayyiqtol* clause signals that this action did not necessarily follow the previous action or event; rather, the temporal relationship of the king's giving Haman's estate to Esther and Mordecai's appearance is left open-ended—they may have happened in a 1-2 sequence, and a 2-1 sequence, at roughly the same time. See discussion in vv. 8 and 10.

כִּֽי־הִגִּ֣ידָה אֶסְתֵּ֔ר מַ֥ה הוּא־לָֽהּ. *Qatal* 3fs Hiph √נגד and null copula clause with subject הוא and complement מה. This כי clause gives the reason why Mordecai appeared before the king. On the form, meaning, and valency of הגידה, see comment on 2:10. The complement of הגידה is the indirect question מה הוא לה (see WO 18.2c). Within the interrogative clause, the verb is a null copula; the מה is the copular complement, which is fronted for Focus; and the subject is the 3ms pronoun הוא. The PP לה is an adjunct to the null copula, further specifies what the open variable established by מה refers to, i.e., he was *what* with regard to her (see WO 11.2.10d).

8:2 וַיָּ֨סַר הַמֶּ֜לֶךְ אֶת־טַבַּעְתּ֗וֹ אֲשֶׁ֤ר הֶֽעֱבִיר֙ מֵֽהָמָ֔ן וַֽיִּתְּנָ֖הּ לְמָרְדֳּכָ֑י וַתָּ֧שֶׂם אֶסְתֵּ֛ר אֶֽת־מָרְדֳּכַ֖י עַל־בֵּ֥ית הָמָֽן׃

This verse recounts the reversal of the event in 3:10 where the king "removes" his ring and "gives" it to Haman (cf. Fox 2001:90, 159; Levenson, 107).

וַיָּ֨סַר הַמֶּ֜לֶךְ אֶת־טַבַּעְתּ֗וֹ אֲשֶׁ֤ר הֶֽעֱבִיר֙ מֵֽהָמָ֔ן. *Wayyiqtol* 3ms Hiph √סור and *qatal* 3ms Hiph √עבר. Hiphil סור ("to remove" or "to cause something to turn aside from") is trivalent, requiring a subject, an NP complement of the moved item, and a locative (typically PP) complement (cf. comment on 3:10). The subject (המלך) and NP complement (את טבעתו) are clear enough, but the locative complement is null and contextually implied as "from his finger." Hiphil עבר ("to remove, take away") is also trivalent, with a null subject (contextually clear as המלך), a null pronominal complement, which is the null resumption for the relative head טבעתו, and a PP complement, מהמן, indicating the locative source (cf. DCH עבר I Hiph 8; HALOT עבר I Hiph 8).

וַ֠יִּתְּנָ֠הּ לְמָרְדֳּכָ֑י. *Wayyiqtol* 3ms Qal √נתן with 3fs clitic pronoun complement. The second complement of the trivalent Qal נתן is the PP למרדכי, which indicates the recipient.

וַתָּ֧שֶׂם אֶסְתֵּ֛ר אֶֽת־מָרְדֳּכַ֖י עַל־בֵּ֥ית הָמָֽן. *Wayyiqtol* 3fs Qal √שׂים. Note that the verb form within the *wayyiqtol* for שׂים is clearly different than the *yiqtol* imperfective—the form וַתָּשֶׂם is "shorter" in traditional terms or, in phonological terms, exhibits vowel lowering and backing, from a front, high /i/ to a mid, center /ɛ/. The locative complement of trivalent Qal שׂים is על בית המן (cf. 2:17, where the locative complement is a ב-PP). On the meaning of בית here, see comment on v. 1.

8:3 וַתּ֣וֹסֶף אֶסְתֵּ֗ר וַתְּדַבֵּר֙ לִפְנֵ֣י הַמֶּ֔לֶךְ וַתִּפֹּ֖ל לִפְנֵ֣י
רַגְלָ֑יו וַתֵּ֣בְךְּ וַתִּתְחַנֶּן־ל֗וֹ לְהַֽעֲבִיר֙ אֶת־רָעַת֙ הָמָ֣ן
הָאֲגָגִ֔י וְאֵת֙ מַחֲשַׁבְתּ֔וֹ אֲשֶׁ֥ר חָשַׁ֖ב עַל־הַיְּהוּדִֽים׃

In this verse, Esther finally fulfills the request that Mordecai made of her in 4:8, "to seek favor toward him and to request her people from before him."

וַתּ֣וֹסֶף אֶסְתֵּ֗ר וַתְּדַבֵּר֙ לִפְנֵ֣י הַמֶּ֔לֶךְ. *Wayyiqtol* 3fs Hiph √יסף and *wayyiqtol* 3fs Piel √דבר. Hiphil יסף followed by another finite verb has the sense "to do [something] again" (WO 39.3.1b); ותוסף אסתר ותדבר is thus "she added and spoke," but corresponds better to English "she spoke again." Piel דבר is monovalent and here the subject is a null pronoun coreferential with אסתר from the first clause.

וַתִּפֹּ֖ל לִפְנֵ֣י רַגְלָ֑יו. *Wayyiqtol* 3fs Qal √נפל. On the meaning and valency of Qal נפל, see comment on 6:10, 13. The PP לפני רגליו is the locative complement to the verb.

וַתֵּ֣בְךְּ. *Wayyiqtol* 3fs Qal √בכה. In most III-ה verbs, the short form of the *wayyiqtol* (with the final ה dropped) includes an epenthetic *seghol* after the first radical (e.g., Exod 1:20 וַיִּ֫רֶב from √רבה). The verb בכה, however, does not take this helping vowel, and as a result has two *shevas* in a row, the second of which is vocal, *wattēbkə*; cf. JM 79i).

וַתִּתְחַנֶּן־ל֗וֹ לְהַֽעֲבִיר֙ אֶת־רָעַת֙ הָמָ֣ן הָאֲגָגִ֔י וְאֵת֙ מַחֲשַׁבְתּ֔וֹ אֲשֶׁ֥ר חָשַׁ֖ב עַל־הַיְּהוּדִֽים. *Wayyiqtol* 3fs Hith √חנן, inf constr Hiph √עבר, and *qatal* 3ms Qal √חשב. On Hithpael חנן and the use of a ל-PP (here לו) as its complement, see comment on 4:8. This clause clearly recalls Mordecai's command in 4:8 that Esther should "seek favor" from the king (cf. Fox 2001:92). The ל-PP/infinitive clause להעביר is a purpose adjunct to התחתן. The Hiphil of עבר is bivalent here (cf. v. 2 where it is trivalent): the subject is null (contextually reconstructible as the king) and the complement is a compound NP, both parts of which are marked with an את. The noun מַחֲשָׁבָה ("thought, intent, plan"; HALOT s.v.) is a feminine *maqtāl*-pattern noun (cf. JM 88 Le), derived from √חשב. Within the אשר relative clause that modifies מחשבתו, the *qatal* חשב ("to plan"; HALOT s.v. Qal 5) defaults to its prototypical past time frame, though the main clause context pushes it to a narrower nuance, the past-in-the-past, i.e., "which he *had planned*" (see comments on 5:12; 6:2). The preposition על likely has an adversative nuance, "against" (cf. WO 11.2.13c; HALOT חשב Qal 5).

8:4 וַיּ֤וֹשֶׁט הַמֶּ֙לֶךְ֙ לְאֶסְתֵּ֔ר אֵ֖ת שַׁרְבִ֣ט הַזָּהָ֑ב וַתָּ֣קָם
אֶסְתֵּ֔ר וַֽתַּעֲמֹ֖ד לִפְנֵ֥י הַמֶּֽלֶךְ׃

This verse evokes 5:2, where the king spares Esther's life when she presented herself before him unbidden.

וַיּ֤וֹשֶׁט הַמֶּ֙לֶךְ֙ לְאֶסְתֵּ֔ר אֵ֖ת שַׁרְבִ֣ט הַזָּהָ֑ב. *Wayyiqtol* 3ms Hiph √ישט. On the meaning and valency of Hiphil ישט, see comment on 4:11.

וַתָּ֣קָם אֶסְתֵּ֔ר. *Wayyiqtol* 3fs Qal √קום. The *wayyiqtol* form triggers verb-subject word order. On monovalent קום, see comment on 5:9.

וַֽתַּעֲמֹ֖ד לִפְנֵ֥י הַמֶּֽלֶךְ. *Wayyiqtol* 3fs Qal √עמד. On the valency of עמד, see comment on 5:1.

8:5 וַתֹּ֡אמֶר אִם־עַל־הַמֶּ֨לֶךְ טוֹב֜ וְאִם־מָצָ֧אתִי חֵ֣ן לְפָנָ֗יו
וְכָשֵׁ֤ר הַדָּבָר֙ לִפְנֵ֣י הַמֶּ֔לֶךְ וְטוֹבָ֥ה אֲנִ֖י בְּעֵינָ֑יו יִכָּתֵ֞ב
לְהָשִׁ֣יב אֶת־הַסְּפָרִ֗ים מַחֲשֶׁ֜בֶת הָמָ֤ן בֶּֽן־הַמְּדָ֙תָא֙
הָֽאֲגָגִ֔י אֲשֶׁ֣ר כָּתַ֗ב לְאַבֵּד֙ אֶת־הַיְּהוּדִ֔ים אֲשֶׁ֖ר בְּכָל־
מְדִינ֥וֹת הַמֶּֽלֶךְ׃

Verse 5 recounts Esther's request to cancel Haman's edict, issued in chapter 3. From v. 5 to v. 8, there are numerous verbal references to chapter 3. Beginning in v. 9 (to the end of the chapter), the language used is "virtually identical to that used" in 3:12-15 (Bush, 442). This request follows up on her first request in 7:3-4 and presents the simplest resolution to the Jews' dire situation.

וַתֹּאמֶר. *Wayyiqtol* 3fs Qal √אמר. The following direct speech is the complement for bivalent אמר.

אִם־עַל־הַמֶּלֶךְ טוֹב וְאִם־מָצָאתִי חֵן לְפָנָיו. A null copula clause and *qatal* (irrealis) 1cs Qal √מצא. On the expression אם על המלך טוב, see comment on 1:19. On the second אם clause, see the comments on 5:8 and 7:3.

וְכָשֵׁר הַדָּבָר לִפְנֵי הַמֶּלֶךְ. *Qatal* (irrealis) 3ms Qal √כשר. The irrealis perfect is used to continue the previous אם conditional ("if I have found favor before him and *[if]* the thing is proper before the king"). The multiple conditions with which Esther prefaces her request appear at once deferential (cf. Fox 2001:92) and (to us) ingratiating—Esther is perhaps not simply appealing to the king's good will toward her but also making the king seem back in control (whereas in her banquet scheme, he was hardly more than a tool). Qal כשר means "to be proper in someone's view" (see HALOT s.v.). In the Hebrew Bible, Qal כשר occurs here and in Eccl 11:6; it also appears in Ben Sira 13:4, and in the Hiphil in Eccl 10:10, and in a noun form four times in the Dead Sea Scrolls (DCH s.v.; cf. Bush, 437, 444). The subject of the clause, הדבר, is ambiguous in that the content of הדבר is her request, which she has yet to make.

וְטוֹבָה אֲנִי בְּעֵינָיו. Null copula clause with subject אני and adjective complement טובה. Although there is no verb present, this null copula clause continues the conditional statement. Additionally, the copular complement is Focus-fronted, by which Esther's request is made even more deferential and her personal capital is leveraged—"if she *really is pleasing* to the king ..." is on the idiom "good in his eyes," see comments on 1:19, 21; and 3:11.

יִכָּתֵב לְהָשִׁיב אֶת־הַסְּפָרִים מַחֲשֶׁבֶת הָמָן בֶּן־הַמְּדָתָא הָאֲגָגִי. *Yiqtol* (jussive semantics) 3ms Niph √כתב and inf constr Hiph √שׁוב. The subject of the Niphal verb—the thing written—is the extended ל-PP/infinitive clause להשיב, lit. "let to-cancel-the-letters ... be written" (see also 3:9). Hiphil שׁוב means "to cause to return," in this context, "to cancel" or "to revoke" (HALOT s.v. Hiph 6). On the meaning and form of מחשבת, which is here part of an appositive to הספרים, see comment on 8:3. On המן בן המדתא האגגי, see comment on 3:1.

אֲשֶׁר כָּתַב לְאַבֵּד אֶת־הַיְּהוּדִים אֲשֶׁר בְּכָל־מְדִינוֹת הַמֶּלֶךְ. *Qatal* 3ms Qal √כתב and inf constr Piel √אבד. In contexts where there are multiple NPs available as a semantically appropriate head to a relative clause, the general principle in Hebrew is that the nearer antecedent is intended (cf. comment on 2:6). In this clause, both המן ("Haman, who wrote [the letters] ...") and הספרים ("the letters that he [Haman] wrote ...") are appropriate and available as the relative head. If the relative head is המן, then it is resumed by a null pronoun within the relative as the subject of כתב and the complement of כתב is also null and reconstructible as ספרים. Similarly, if ספרים is the relative head, the subject of כתב is null (and reconstructible as המן) and the relative head is resumed by the null pronominal complement of כתב. In either syntactic option, the ל-PP/infinitive clause לאבד is a purpose adjunct indicating the goal of Haman's writing the letters. Both analyses are grammatical and we simply chose המן as the head since it is slightly closer to the אשר.

8:6 כִּי אֵיכָכָה אוּכַל וְרָאִיתִי בָּרָעָה אֲשֶׁר־יִמְצָא אֶת־
עַמִּי וְאֵיכָכָה אוּכַל וְרָאִיתִי בְּאָבְדַן מוֹלַדְתִּי׃

The language of Esther's reason echoes Gen 44:34, where Judah pleads with Joseph to let Benjamin return to their father with Joseph's other brothers (Fox 2001:284; Bush, 437).

כִּי אֵיכָכָה אוּכַל וְרָאִיתִי בָּרָעָה אֲשֶׁר־יִמְצָא אֶת־עַמִּי. *Yiqtol* (irrealis) 1cs Qal √יכל, *qatal* (irrealis) 1cs Qal √ראה, and *yiqtol* (irrealis) 3ms Qal √מצא. The particle איככה, "how?," appears to reflect the combination of either איכה ("how?," itself a combination of אַי and כָּה) and כָּה ("thus," which became כֹּה in BH) or אי ("where," which became אֵי in BH) and כָּכָה ("thus") (HALOT, אֵיכָכָה; cf. Moore 1971:78). On the semantics and *binyan* of יכל, see comment on 6:13. Given that יכל is almost always bivalent (see 6:13), it is likely that the *qatal* clause is an unmarked nominalized complement clause for typically bivalent יכל, i.e., "how could I watch ...?" (see JM 177h; contra DCH s.v. "how can I endure and, i.e., when, I see?"). Note that in this option, the ו simply marks the front edge of the complement clause (see Holmstedt 2013b; 2014a). The context suggests that our irrealis reading of the verbs is the most likely—Esther grounds her request with these two questions, which describe events that have not occurred and that she hopes will not occur. The very fact that she attempts to cancel them out suggests the irrealis semantics. The ב-PP is the complement of the verb ראה; the combination of ראה and ב have the semantic result of "to take a look at" or "to gaze on" (HALOT s.v. 7). The NP רעה is the head of the אשר relative clause in which the verb ימצא connotes "to meet accidentally" (HALOT s.v. 2); English "to find" may have a similar meaning (OED, s.v., I. "to come upon by chance or in the course of events"). On the meaning of רעה, see discussion at 7:7—in the current context, the parallelism with אבדן is instructive. The verb ימצא is masculine, not agreeing with the subject of the relative, the head רעה. One solution is to emend the text to 3fs תמצא (so Moore 1971:78). It may be that the 3ms is a scribal error or even an intentional authorial link related to the similarity of Esther's statement to Gen 44:34 אֶרְאֶה בָרָע אֲשֶׁר יִמְצָא אֶת אָבִי (for arguments in favor of both explanations, see Paton, 27; Moore 1971:78; Fox 2001:284; Bush, 437).

וְאֵיכָכָה אוּכַל֙ וְֽרָאִ֔יתִי בְּאָבְדַ֖ן מוֹלַדְתִּֽי. *Yiqtol* (irrealis) 1cs Qal √יכל and *qatal* (irrealis) 1cs Qal √ראה. See comment above on the syntax of אוכל וראיתי as well as on a ב-PP (באבדן מולדתי) as the complement of ראה. The noun אבדן is a *qutlān*-pattern noun (cf. JM 88 M d) derived from √אבד "to be destroyed" (Qal), "to destroy" (Piel). In the Hebrew Bible, the NP appears only in Esther (here and in 9:5); it does not occur in the Mishnah, but appears three times in the Dead Sea Scrolls (4Q163; 4Q385b; 4Q391) and also in the Talmud (cf. Jastrow s.v.). On the meaning of מולדת, see comment on 2:10.

8:7 וַיֹּ֨אמֶר הַמֶּ֤לֶךְ אֲחַשְׁוֵרֹשׁ֙ לְאֶסְתֵּ֣ר הַמַּלְכָּ֔ה
וּֽלְמָרְדֳּכַ֖י הַיְּהוּדִ֑י הִנֵּ֨ה בֵית־הָמָ֜ן נָתַ֣תִּי לְאֶסְתֵּ֗ר
וְאֹתוֹ֙ תָּל֣וּ עַל־הָעֵ֔ץ עַ֛ל אֲשֶׁר־שָׁלַ֥ח יָד֖וֹ בַּיְּהוּדִֽיים׃

In vv. 7-8 the king responds to Esther's request by both recounting what has already been done on her behalf and allowing Esther and Mordecai to issue a counter-edict. The nature of the counter-edict is not specified in Ahashverosh's generous response, but is narrated in the following section.

וַיֹּ֨אמֶר הַמֶּ֤לֶךְ אֲחַשְׁוֵרֹשׁ֙ לְאֶסְתֵּ֣ר הַמַּלְכָּ֔ה וּֽלְמָרְדֳּכַ֖י הַיְּהוּדִ֑י. *Wayyiqtol* 3ms Qal √אמר. The subsequent direct speech is the complement of bivalent אמר and the two ל-PPs are adjuncts indicating the multiple addressees.

הִנֵּ֨ה בֵית־הָמָ֜ן נָתַ֣תִּי לְאֶסְתֵּ֗ר. *Qatal* 1cs Qal √נתן. On הנה, see comment on 6:5. Besides being topicalized by virtue of the interjection הנה, the NP בית המן ("the estate of Haman") is Topic-fronted. The perfect verb is best translated with a perfect, rather than past tense, English verb ("I have given" instead of "I gave"): the king did not give the estate in the past, but is actually giving the estate in the very statement he is making, i.e., "I hereby have given." On בית המן as "the *estate* of Haman," see comment on 8:1.

וְאֹת֙וֹ תָּל֣וּ עַל־הָעֵ֔ץ. *Qatal* 3mp Qal √תלה. On the meaning and valency of תלה, see comment on 2:23. The subject of the verb is unspecified and generic, lit. "they hung him upon the tree," but meaning "someone hung him upon the tree" (cf. comment on 2:2). The verb complement אתו is Focus-fronted (cf. Moore 1971:79); the clitic pronoun in אתו refers to Haman: "*him* [= Haman] they hung upon the tree."

עַ֥ל אֲשֶׁר־שָׁלַ֖ח יָד֥וֹ בַּיְּהוּדִיִּֽים. *Qatal* 3ms Qal √שלח. The preposition על followed by אשר is often best translated in English as "because"; the combination is not, however, some sort of compound causal particle equivalent to כי. Rather, על communicates cause or basis (WO 11.2.13e) and the complement of על is a nominalized אשר clause. In other words, the clause שלח ידו ביהודיים ("he raised his hand against the Jews"), nominalized by אשר, serves as the complement of על: "on account of he-raised-his-hand-against-the-Jews." The whole על-PP modifies the verb תלו, "they hung." On the phrase שלח ידו, see comment on 2:21. On the *Qere-Ketiv* with ביהודיים, see comment on 4:7.

8:8 וְאַתֶּ֡ם כִּתְבוּ֩ עַל־הַיְּהוּדִ֨ים כַּטּ֤וֹב בְּעֵינֵיכֶם֙ בְּשֵׁ֣ם
הַמֶּ֔לֶךְ וְחִתְמ֖וּ בְּטַבַּ֣עַת הַמֶּ֑לֶךְ כִּֽי־כְתָ֞ב אֲשֶׁר־
נִכְתָּ֣ב בְּשֵׁם־הַמֶּ֗לֶךְ וְנַחְתּ֛וֹם בְּטַבַּ֥עַת הַמֶּ֖לֶךְ אֵ֥ין
לְהָשִֽׁיב׃

וְאַתֶּ֡ם כִּתְבוּ֩ עַל־הַיְּהוּדִ֨ים כַּטּ֤וֹב בְּעֵינֵיכֶם֙ בְּשֵׁ֣ם הַמֶּ֔לֶךְ. Impv mp Qal √כתב. The second person subject of imperatives is typically covert (i.e., a null pronoun) in Hebrew. However, it may be overt when the pronoun is a Topic constituent used to signal a switch in Topic, as in the switch made in the king's speech—from himself in the last verse to his addressees, Esther and Mordecai, in this verse (on the distinction between second person pronouns as subjects of imperatives versus those in vocatives, see Miller 2010). Qal כתב is bivalent (cf. comment on 2:23); here the complement is null and can be contextually reconstructed as "an edict" or "a letter," possibly modified by the PP על היהודים: "Write [*an edict*] concerning the Jews." Alternatively, the null complement may be modified and identified entirely by the PP כטוב בעיניכם, "write [*that* which is] according to what pleases you." On the syntax of כטוב בעיניכם ("according to what pleases you"), see comment on 3:11. The PP בשם המלך ("in the name of the king") is an adjunct to the verb; just as Haman's edict was written in the king's name and sealed with his signet ring in 3:12, here Esther and Mordecai's counter-edict is written in the name of the king and sealed with his signet ring.

וְחִתְמ֖וּ בְּטַבַּ֣עַת הַמֶּ֑לֶךְ. Impv mp Qal √חתם. The verb חתם is bivalent in the Qal (cf. comment on 3:12); here the complement (the thing sealed) is null, but understood to be the thing in the preceding clause that Esther and Mordecai will write. The PP בטבעת המלך is an adjunct to the verb, indicating the instrument with which the verbal action is accomplished (cf. WO 11.2.5d).

כִּֽי־כְתָ֞ב אֲשֶׁר־נִכְתָּ֣ב בְּשֵׁם־הַמֶּ֗לֶךְ. Participle ms Niph √כתב. This כי clause provides the basis for the preceding clause (cf. MNK 40.9 I.3; WO 38.4a)—they must issue a second royal edict rather than simply recalling the first because a royal edict cannot simply be nullified. In v. 3 Esther asked the king to "remove" (Hiphil עבר) Haman's edict, and in v. 5 she asked him to "cancel" (Hiphil שׁוב) Haman's edict. However, in this very verse we read that no edict of the king can be "cancelled" (Hiphil שׁוב) (see Bush, 445; Fox 2001:92; Levenson, 108–9). The head of the אשר relative is the indefinite NP כתב (on the meaning of כְּתָב, cf. comment on 3:14). Within the restrictive relative clause, the head כתב is the subject of a null copula clause with a participle phrase complement. The Niphal participle נִכְתָּב is distinguishable from the Niphal 3ms perfect by the final vowel in the final syllable, a *qameṣ* /ā/ (or ɔ in Tiberian) in the participle versus a *pataḥ* /a/ in the 3ms perfect.

וְנַחְתּ֛וֹם בְּטַבַּ֥עַת הַמֶּ֖לֶךְ. Inf abs Niph √חתם. Although we might expect a participle (נֶחְתָּם) here to continue the preceding relative (cf. 3:12), we instead find an infinitive absolute. This signals that the infinitive clause is both subordinate and also perhaps marks the verb for Focus (see comment on 2:3). The result would both keep the main verb within the relative clause as נכתב ("written … being sealed ...") but puts Focus on נחתום as the critical related step that makes an edict royal and thus noncancelable.

כְּתָ֞ב ... אֵ֥ין לְהָשִֽׁיב. אין copula clause with a ל-PP/infinitive clause subject (inf constr Hiph √שׁוב) and complement NP כתב. Translations typically reflect a change into a passive "be revoked," which ignores the Hebrew syntax and semantics. Rather, the NP כתב can only be the fronted complement of the active, causative bivalent להשיב, since a "writing" cannot "return" something. On the meaning "to cancel" for Hiphil שׁוב, see comment on v. 5. The negative copula with infinitive has an irrealis sense (WO 36.2.3f exx. 40, 42): "to cancel a writing ... is not [allowable, done, possible, etc.]." On the אין ל syntax in Esther, see also comment on 4:2.

§2: The Counter-edict is Issued (8:9-17)

In section 2, the content of the counter-edict is provided, as well as the way it is sent and the response it generates in the kingdom. These elements mirror chapter 3, where Haman issues his edict, and so reflect the undoing of Haman's deed.

[9]*And the scribes of the king were called at that time, in the third month—it is the month of Sivan—on the twenty-third day in it, and according to all that Mordecai commanded was written to the Jews and to the satraps and the governors and the rulers of the provinces which were from India to Cush, 127 provinces, (being written to) every province according to its writing and (being written to) every people-group according to its language, and (being written) to the Jews according to their writing and according to their language.* [10]*He wrote (it) in the name of King Ahashverosh, and he sealed (it) with the signet ring of the king, and he sent documents by the hand of the messengers by horses, riders of the steeds, royal ones, sons of racing mares,* [11]*that the king allowed the Jews who were in every city to assemble and to stand for themselves, to exterminate, to slay, and to destroy any army of a people or a province that are attacking them, (their) children, and (their) women, and to plunder their spoil,* [12]*on one day, in all the provinces of King Ahashverosh, on the thirteenth (day) of the twelfth month—it is the month of Adar.* [13]*A copy of the writing was to be given as an order in every single province, being revealed to all the people, in order for the Jews to be ready for this day to take revenge on their enemies.* [14]*The messengers, riders of the steeds, royal ones, went out hurriedly and hastily with the word of the king, and the law was given in Susa, the citadel.* [15]*And Mordecai went out from*

before the king in royal clothes, violet and white material, and a great crown of gold, and a coat of fine linen and purple. And the city of Susa rejoiced and was merry. [16]And for the Jews was light and joy and jubilation and honor. [17]And in every province and in every city, (every) place at which the word of the king and his law arrived, joy and jubilation, a banquet and a good day, were to the Jews. And many from the peoples of the land were posing as Jews, because the fear of the Jews had fallen upon them.

8:9 וַיִּקָּרְא֣וּ סֹפְרֵֽי־הַמֶּ֣לֶךְ בָּעֵֽת־הַ֠הִיא בַּחֹ֨דֶשׁ
הַשְּׁלִישִׁ֜י הוּא־חֹ֣דֶשׁ סִיוָ֗ן בִּשְׁלוֹשָׁ֣ה וְעֶשְׂרִים֮ בּוֹ֒
וַיִּכָּתֵ֣ב כְּֽכָל־אֲשֶׁר־צִוָּ֣ה מָרְדֳּכַ֣י אֶל־הַיְּהוּדִ֡ים וְאֶ֣ל
הָאֲחַשְׁדַּרְפְּנִֽים־וְהַפַּ֠חוֹת וְשָׂרֵ֨י הַמְּדִינ֜וֹת אֲשֶׁ֣ר ׀
מֵהֹ֣דּוּ וְעַד־כּ֗וּשׁ שֶׁ֣בַע וְעֶשְׂרִ֤ים וּמֵאָה֙ מְדִינָ֔ה
מְדִינָ֤ה וּמְדִינָה֙ כִּכְתָבָ֔הּ וְעַ֥ם וָעָ֖ם כִּלְשֹׁנ֑וֹ וְאֶ֨ל־
הַיְּהוּדִ֔ים כִּכְתָבָ֖ם וְכִלְשׁוֹנָֽם׃

In v. 9 the king's scribes are summoned to write Esther and Mordecai's edict. Verses 9-17 closely parallel 3:12–4:3; for a helpful visual aid showing the relationship between these two passages, see Bush, 442–43 (cf. also Fox 2001:102, 159–61). Verse 9 has essentially the same structure as the first two clauses in 3:12, with a few minor differences. For explanation of the majority of the syntactic structures, see comment on 3:12. For the pertinent differences, see below.

וַיִּקָּרְא֣וּ סֹפְרֵֽי־הַמֶּ֣לֶךְ בָּעֵֽת־הַ֠הִיא בַּחֹ֨דֶשׁ הַשְּׁלִישִׁ֜י הוּא־חֹ֣דֶשׁ סִיוָ֗ן בִּשְׁלוֹשָׁ֣ה וְעֶשְׂרִים֮ בּוֹ֒. *Wayyiqtol* 3mp Niph √קרא. See comment on 3:12. The ordinal numeral שלישי modifies חדש adjectivally (see "Numeral Syntax in Esther" in the Introduction). On the parenthetical clause הוא חדש סיון, see comments on 1:1; 2:7; 3:7. On the PP בשלושה ועשרים בו, see comment on 3:12 and Appendix B.

וַיִּכָּתֵ֣ב כְּֽכָל־אֲשֶׁר־צִוָּ֣ה מָרְדֳּכַ֣י. *Wayyiqtol* 3ms Niph √כתב and *qatal* 3ms Piel √צוה. The main difference with the corresponding clause in 3:12 is that the null subject of ויכתב is understood to be the document in v. 8 that the king suggests Mordecai and Esther write (see comment on ve. 8); compare 3:12, where the null subject anaphorically refers to the ל-PP/infinitive clause לאבדם ("to destroy them") from 3:9. Other slight grammatical differences stem from the change in context: מרדכי

is the subject of צוה (*qatal* 3ms Piel √צוה) in the relative, and היהודים are included as recipients of the document.

הַמְּדִינוֹת אֲשֶׁר | מֵהֹדּוּ וְעַד־כּוּשׁ שֶׁבַע וְעֶשְׂרִים וּמֵאָה מְדִינָה. The אשר relative modifies המדינות. On the phrases מהדו ועד כוש and מאה מדינה, see comment on 1:1.

מְדִינָה וּמְדִינָה כִּכְתָבָהּ וְעַם וָעָם כִּלְשֹׁנוֹ. See comment on 3:12, where we view these two phrases as complements to null אל prepositions that are associated with gapped copies of נכתב.

וְאֶל־הַיְּהוּדִים כִּכְתָבָם וְכִלְשׁוֹנָם. The author specifies that the writing was sent *specifically* to the Jews in *their* writing and language, even though presumably the Jews would be included in the phrase "every people" (עם ועם). The point is to emphasize that this time (unlike with the first edict, where the Jews are the objects), the Jews are engaged as subjects and thus agents of the action commanded in this second edict.

8:10 וַיִּכְתֹּב בְּשֵׁם הַמֶּלֶךְ אֲחַשְׁוֵרֹשׁ וַיַּחְתֹּם בְּטַבַּעַת
הַמֶּלֶךְ וַיִּשְׁלַח סְפָרִים בְּיַד הָרָצִים בַּסּוּסִים רֹכְבֵי
הָרֶכֶשׁ הָאֲחַשְׁתְּרָנִים בְּנֵי הָרַמָּכִים׃

וַיִּכְתֹּב בְּשֵׁם הַמֶּלֶךְ אֲחַשְׁוֵרֹשׁ וַיַּחְתֹּם בְּטַבַּעַת הַמֶּלֶךְ. *Wayyiqtol* 3ms Qal √כתב and *wayyiqtol* 3ms Qal √חתם. Verse 10 uses Qal indicative verbs instead of the null copula clauses with Niphal participle phrase complements found in the parallel 3:12. It is not specified who the subject of the verbs is (and perhaps it is not important for the narrative), but the discourse context suggests Mordecai (cf. Fox 2001:99; contra Bush, 436). If generic subjects were intended, the previous uses suggest that the narrator would more likely have used third person plural verbs (see 2:2; though admittedly we read the 3ms הפיל in 3:7 as generic). The complements of ויכתב and ויחתם are null (cf. 3:12 on the valency of חתם); they are both understood from context to be the "writing" or edict described in the verses preceding. Fox (2001:284) takes the אשר clause of vv. 11-13 as a long, complex nominalized complement clause; but this requires allowing two verbs, ויחתם and וישלח (and also their clauses), to intervene between ויכתב and its complement, which is not grammatically acceptable.

וַיִּשְׁלַח סְפָרִים בְּיַד הָרָצִים בַּסּוּסִים רֹכְבֵי הָרֶכֶשׁ הָאֲחַשְׁתְּרָנִים בְּנֵי הָרַמָּכִים. *Wayyiqtol* 3ms Qal √שלח and Participle mp Qal √רכב.

Instead of using a Niphal infinitive absolute as in 3:13 (cf. comment there), here the narrator used a Qal 3ms *wayyiqtol*. As in the previous clauses, the null subject is understood to be Mordecai (see comment above). On הרצים, see comment on 3:13. The ב-PP is an adjunct to the main verb וישלח, indicating the instrument by which Mordecai sent the documents (WO 11.2.5d). רכבי הרכש ("riders of the steeds" [= "steed riders"]) is in apposition to סוסים, clarifying that the documents were not sent by riderless horses. The NPs האחשתרנים (a Persian word meaning "the royal ones"; HALOT אֲחַשְׁתְּרָן) and בני הרמכים ("sons of racing mares"; cf. HALOT רַמָּכָה) are in apposition to הרכש. Although הרכש is grammatically singular, it has a collective meaning ("steeds"; cf. 1 Kgs 5:8; Mic 1:13; HALOT s.v.; BDB s.v.; Keil, 369; Moore 1971:80); thus, the plural NPs can be appositive to the singular הרכש. In other words, it is the "steeds," not the "riders," that are the "royal ones" and "sons of racing mares."

8:11 אֲשֶׁר֩ נָתַ֨ן הַמֶּ֜לֶךְ לַיְּהוּדִ֣ים ׀ אֲשֶׁ֣ר בְּכָל־עִיר־וָעִ֗יר
לְהִקָּהֵל֮ וְלַעֲמֹ֣ד עַל־נַפְשָׁם֒ לְהַשְׁמִיד֩ וְלַהֲרֹ֨ג וּלְאַבֵּ֜ד
אֶת־כָּל־חֵ֨יל עַ֧ם וּמְדִינָ֛ה הַצָּרִ֥ים אֹתָ֖ם טַ֣ף וְנָשִׁ֑ים
וּשְׁלָלָ֖ם לָבֽוֹז׃

The second half of 3:13 is clearly echoed in this verse, where the tables are turned and the Jews are allowed to להרג, להשמיד, and לאבד those who come against them, including טף ונשים, and to "plunder their spoil" (Moore 1971:41–42, 80–81; Fox 2001:160; Levenson, 110).

אֲשֶׁר֩ נָתַ֨ן הַמֶּ֜לֶךְ לַיְּהוּדִ֣ים ׀ אֲשֶׁ֣ר בְּכָל־עִיר־וָעִ֗יר לְהִקָּהֵל֮ וְלַעֲמֹ֣ד עַל־נַפְשָׁם֒. *Qatal* 3ms Qal √נתן, inf constr Niph √קהל, and inf constr Qal √עמד. Qal נתן with an infinitive clause means "to allow" (HALOT s.v. Qal 8). The verb is still trivalent, as with the meaning "to give," taking the same complements: the thing given (or "allowed") is the compound ל-PP/infinitive clause להקהל ולעמד ("to assemble and to stand ..."), and the recipient of the thing given is ליהודים. The head of the relative clause אשר בכל עיר ועיר is יהודים ("the Jews"). בכל עיר ועיר means "in every city." עיר ועיר on its own means "every city," as does כל עיר; the combination is redundant, still meaning "every city" (cf. comment on 2:11). Niphal קהל (להקהל) is monovalent, meaning "to assemble" (HALOT s.v.) or "to gather." The corresponding bivalent meaning that we would expect to belong to the Qal stem is actually found in the Hiphil, which means "to assemble [a group of people]" or "to summon [a group of people]" (HALOT s.v.); קהל does not occur in the Qal stem. Regarding the infinitive לעמד על נפשם, HALOT lists an idiomatic use of עמד with נפש meaning "to defend one's life" (HALOT עמד Qal 1), however the only examples of this combination are found here and in 9:16. Though this seems to be the meaning of the phrase in context, it is literally "to stand for one's life." The preposition על communicates "advantage" (WO 11.2.13c), thus "the king allowed the Jews ... to stand for the sake of their lives," or with a similar idiom in English, "to stand up for themselves." נפש, "life," is collective here ("lives"; cf. WO 7.2.1d; JM 135b). The entire verse (including, in fact, v. 12) appears to be an אשר relative clause. But this אשר clause stretches the syntax of relativization in Biblical Hebrew (for arguments against taking it as the extraposed complement clause of ויכתב in v. 10, see comment there). The nearest logical relative head is the NP ספרים in the last clause of v. 10 (contra Paton 1908:278; cf. Bush 1996:436). But a relative head must have a syntactic role (i.e., be resumed, overtly or covertly) within the relative clause, and the only role for ספרים to play within this relative is as an instrumental adjunct, i.e., "letters … which [by them] the king allowed the Jews to assemble … ." And yet, it is very consistent that heads resumed in positions that normally reflect a PP are resumed overtly—we expect to see בָּם "by them" or similar in this relative, which reflects how the Noun Phrase Accessibility Hierarchy (NPAH) applies to relative resumption (see Holmstedt 2013a, fc). So, either we have an unusual relative clause in this verse, or we must conjecture the null repetition of ויכתב. We have chosen the former option here, since the NPAH is less an absolute grammatical principle than a general rule of thumb by which language typically operates (whereas we find inserting a copy of ויכתב to be less felicitous).

לְהַשְׁמִיד וְלַהֲרֹג וּלְאַבֵּד. Inf constr Hiph √שמד, Qal √הרג, and Piel √אבד. This phrase comes verbatim from 3:13. These three infinitive clauses are purpose adjuncts to נתן.

אֶת־כָּל־חֵיל עַם וּמְדִינָה הַצָּרִים אֹתָם טַף וְנָשִׁים. Participle mp Qal √צור. The ה-relative phrase הצרים אתם consists of a null copula with participle phrase complement and modifies the quantified NP כל חיל. The verb צור is a by-form of צרר, meaning "to attack, fight" (HALOT צור II; cf. HALOT צרר II) or "to show hostility toward" (DCH s.v.) On טף see comment on 3:13. The compound NP טף ונשים is part of the compound complement to bivalent צור, "any army … that attacks them, children, and woman"; presumably, the reference to טף ונשים is to "*their* (i.e., the attacked Jews') children and women."

וּשְׁלָלָם לָבוֹז. Inf constr Qal √בזז. ושללם לבוז is placed differently here than in 3:13, before the set of PPs beginning ביום אחד ("in one day ..."; in v. 12) instead of after it. The complement of the infinitive precedes the infinitive (see comment on 2:9; cf. 3:13).

8:12 בְּיוֹם אֶחָד בְּכָל־מְדִינוֹת הַמֶּלֶךְ אֲחַשְׁוֵרוֹשׁ בִּשְׁלוֹשָׁה עָשָׂר לְחֹדֶשׁ שְׁנֵים־עָשָׂר הוּא־חֹדֶשׁ אֲדָר׃

Verse 12 comes almost verbatim from 3:13, and consists of three PPs (ביום ... בכל ... בשלושה) all modifying the infinitive לבוז (and, moreover, conceptually modifying all the infinitive clauses in v. 12, that is, "to assemble ... to stand ... to exterminate ... to slay ... to destroy ... to plunder"). See comments on 3:13.

8:13 פַּתְשֶׁגֶן הַכְּתָב לְהִנָּתֵן דָּת בְּכָל־מְדִינָה וּמְדִינָה גָּלוּי לְכָל־הָעַמִּים וְלִהְיוֹת הַיְּהוּדִיִּים עֲתוּדִים לַיּוֹם הַזֶּה לְהִנָּקֵם מֵאֹיְבֵיהֶם׃

A copy of Esther and Mordecai's edict is distributed to every province and people group in the kingdom. This verse comes nearly verbatim from 3:14 (cf. Keil, 369; Levenson, 115). See comment on 3:14 for the features not discussed below as well as 4:7 for the *Qere-Ketiv* of היהודיים.

פַּתְשֶׁגֶן הַכְּתָב לְהִנָּתֵן. Null copula clause with subject פתשגן and ל-PP/infinitive clause complement, inf constr Niph √נתן. See discussion of infinitive without governing finite verb at 1:15.

וְלִהְיוֹת הַיְּהוּדִיִּים. The ו before the ל-PP/infinitive clause is not present in 3:14, nor is the overt subject היהודיים. The role of the subject is obvious—whereas in 3:14 it was all the non-Jews who were supposed to be ready to slaughter the Jews, here it is the Jews, specified as היהודיים, who were supposed to be ready. The ו on the front of the ל-PP/infinitive clause adjunct to הנתן simply marks the front edge of the subordinate clause and is motivated here (vs. its absence in 3:14) by the slightly more complex syntax (e.g., the addition of יהודיים and the addition of a further subordinate ל-PP/infinitive clause).

עֲתִודִים. The *Ketiv* has the adjective עָתוּד (HALOT s.v. עָתוּד), whereas the *Qere* (and the parallel in 3:14) has עָתִיד (HALOT עָתִיד). The difference between the two is negligible (cf. Bush, 438): both mean "ready," and are built off of the verbal root עתד (Piel, "to prepare"; HALOT עתד). However, עָתוּד appears in later Hebrew (here and in 1QM 6:16; 7:5; 10:5; 15:2), whereas עָתִיד is what appears elsewhere in the Hebrew Bible (Deut 32:35; Isa 10:13 [there the *Qere* is עָתוּד]; Job 3:8; 15:24). Note that the parallel verse in Esth 3:14 has עָתִיד, agreeing with the *Qere* here. עָתוּד is a *qatūl*-pattern adjective (JM 88 Ec) (stemming from the passive participle of עתד), עָתִיד is a *qatīl*-pattern adjective (JM 88 Eb) (stemming from the Aramaic passive participle of עתד).

לְהִנָּקֵם מֵאֹיְבֵיהֶם. Inf constr Niph √נקם. The meaning of Niphal נקם is close to Qal נקם and even Piel נקם (cf. HALOT s.v.): the Qal means "to avenge oneself" and is trivalent, taking a subject, an NP complement (oneself), and a second complement (the person or thing upon which revenge is taken), whereas the Niphal is bivalent, taking a subject (the one avenged) and one complement, here in the מן-PP (cf. HALOT s.v. Niph 2).

8:14 הָרָצִים רֹכְבֵי הָרֶכֶשׁ הָאֲחַשְׁתְּרָנִים יָצְאוּ מְבֹהָלִים
וּדְחוּפִים בִּדְבַר הַמֶּלֶךְ וְהַדָּת נִתְּנָה בְּשׁוּשַׁן
הַבִּירָה׃

This verse is repeated nearly verbatim 3:15; see comments there and below for the differences between the two verses.

As in 3:15, the clauses in this verse as well as the next verse exhibit subject-verb word order. We discern multiple reasons for this change in syntax. First, the subject-verb clauses reflect fronting of the subject to indicate shifts in the Topics. Second, the avoidance of the *wayyiqtol* results in two narrative nuances—the implication that the events are functionally simultaneous and a narrative structuring device to signal the closure of this section (see also comments on 1:12; 6:12; 9:16).

הָרָצִים רֹכְבֵי הָרֶכֶשׁ הָאֲחַשְׁתְּרָנִים יָצְאוּ מְבֹהָלִים וּדְחוּפִים בִּדְבַר הַמֶּלֶךְ. Participle mp Pual √בהל. The phrase רכבי הרכש האחשתרנים, which is appositive to הרצים, is not in 3:15; on this phrase, see comment on v. 10. The only other difference between this clause and its parallel in 3:15 is the addition of the participle מבהלים; like דחופים (cf. comment on 3:15), מבהלים is an adjunct to the verb, describing the manner in which the messengers went out (cf. comment on גלוי לכל העמים in 3:14). The meaning of Pual בהל is similar to that of the Piel (cf. comment on 2:9) and even the Hiphil *binyan* (cf. comment on 6:14); HALOT defines only the adjectival use of Pual בהל as "in haste" (HALOT s.v. Pual), i.e., the riders went out in a "hastening" fashion.

8:15 וּמָרְדֳּכַ֞י יָצָ֣א ׀ מִלִּפְנֵ֣י הַמֶּ֗לֶךְ בִּלְב֤וּשׁ מַלְכוּת֙ תְּכֵ֣לֶת
וָח֔וּר וַעֲטֶ֤רֶת זָהָב֙ גְּדוֹלָ֔ה וְתַכְרִ֥יךְ בּ֖וּץ וְאַרְגָּמָ֑ן
וְהָעִ֣יר שׁוּשָׁ֔ן צָהֲלָ֖ה וְשָׂמֵֽחָה׃

Unlike the preceding verses, however, which had some differences but largely paralleled material in chapter 3, v. 15 sharply contrasts with the corresponding text in the second half. In 3:15, the king and Haman sit down to drink, while Susa is thrown into confusion. Here Mordecai goes out exalted, and the city of Susa rejoices—a clear reversal of fortune (cf. Levenson, 116). Also, this verse draws from the description of the king's banquet in 1:6; many of the materials mentioned there are mentioned here as well (Fox 2001:104).

וּמָרְדֳּכַ֞י יָצָ֣א ׀ מִלִּפְנֵ֣י הַמֶּ֗לֶךְ בִּלְב֤וּשׁ מַלְכוּת֙ תְּכֵ֣לֶת וָח֔וּר וַעֲטֶ֤רֶת זָהָב֙ גְּדוֹלָ֔ה וְתַכְרִ֥יךְ בּ֖וּץ וְאַרְגָּמָ֑ן. *Qatal* 3ms Qal √יצא. Qal יצא is bivalent, with a locative complement, a מן-PP expressing origin (here מלפני המלך; on מלפני, cf. comments on 1:17, 19). The PP בלבוש מלכות is also an adjunct to the verb. On לבוש מלכות, see comment on 1:2, 6:8. On the meanings of תכלת and חור, see comment on 1:6. The clitic NP עטרת (free form, עֲטָרָה) is modified by its clitic host זהב, which specifies the material with which the crown was made (cf. WO 9.5.3d), i.e., "a gold crown." The adjective גדולה is a second modifying adjunct to the complex עטרת זהב: "great crown of gold." תכריך is a ת-preformative *taqtīl* noun borrowed from Aramaic (JM 88Lt; cf. Keil, 370; Paton, 281) meaning "coat" or "overgarment" (HALOT s.v.; cf. BDB s.v.). The word occurs only here in the Hebrew Bible, but several times in the Mishnah (Kil. 9:4; Maʿaś. Š. 5:12; Šabb. 23:4; B. Meṣiʿa 1:8; Sanh. 6:5; Kelim 24:12, 16; 26:6). On בוץ and ארגמן, see comment on 1:6. In the NP תכריך בוץ וארגמן, the clitic תכריך is modified by both בוץ and ארגמן (denoting the material with which the תכריך was made; cf. WO 9.5.3d); in other words, the crown is made of fine linen and purple material. The compound NP תכלת וחור ועטרת זהב גדולה ותכריך בוץ וארגמן is appositional to לבוש מלכות; that is, the royal clothes consist of violet, white material, a great crown of gold, and a coat of fine linen and purple.

וְהָעִיר שׁוּשָׁן צָהֲלָה. *Qatal* 3fs Qal √צהל. The verb means "to rejoice" (HALOT s.v.); when used with a horse as its subject, it means "to neigh" (HALOT s.v.), which gives an idea of the vocal nature of Susa's rejoicing. The contrast with העיר שׁושן נבוכה in 3:15 is transparent and suggests that Haman's plot was not widely supported.

וְשָׂמֵחָה. *Qatal* 3fs Qal √שׂמח. The verb שׂמח means "to rejoice" or "to be merry" (HALOT s.v.).

8:16 לַיְּהוּדִים הָיְתָה אוֹרָה וְשִׂמְחָה וְשָׂשֹׂן וִיקָר׃

In this clause, the subject of the copula הָיְתָה (*qatal* 3fs Qal √היה) is the compound NP אוֹרָה וְשִׂמְחָה וְשָׂשֹׂן וִיקָר. The complement of the copula is the PP ליהודים; the preposition ל with the copula is used here to indicate possession (WO 11.2.10d): "the Jews had light and joy and ..." שָׂשׂוֹן, "joy, jubilation" (HALOT s.v.), is a *qatlān*-pattern noun (JM 88Mb) noun from the root שׂושׂ ("to rejoice," HALOT שׂושׂ). On the meaning of יקר, see comment on 1:4. אורה, "light," appears only three times in the Hebrew Bible (here; Isa 26:19; Ps 139:12); it is the Aramaic equivalent of Hebrew אוֹר, "light" (cf. Jastrow אוֹרָה). The fronting of the copular complement PP ליהודים is for Focus—whereas the city may have been happy, the Jews in particular were ecstatic.

8:17 וּבְכָל־מְדִינָה וּמְדִינָה וּבְכָל־עִיר וָעִיר מְקוֹם אֲשֶׁר
דְּבַר־הַמֶּלֶךְ וְדָתוֹ מַגִּיעַ שִׂמְחָה וְשָׂשׂוֹן לַיְּהוּדִים
מִשְׁתֶּה וְיוֹם טוֹב וְרַבִּים מֵעַמֵּי הָאָרֶץ מִתְיַהֲדִים
כִּי־נָפַל פַּחַד־הַיְּהוּדִים עֲלֵיהֶם׃

This verse parallels 4:3, where the Jews outside Susa mourn and weep when they hear Haman's edict. But here the reaction is rejoicing. Moreover, because of the counter-edict, the Jews have now become enviable and intimidating. For the parallel syntactic features, see comments at 4:3.

שִׂמְחָה וְשָׂשׂוֹן לַיְּהוּדִים מִשְׁתֶּה וְיוֹם טוֹב. A null copula with compound NP subject שׂמחה וששׂון (on שׂשׂון, cf. comment on v. 16) and ל-PP complement (ליהודים) communicating possession (WO 11.2.10d).

The two preceding ב-PPs (בכל מדינה ... ובכל עיר ...) are adjuncts to the null copula. The compound NP משתה ויום טוב is in apposition to שׂמחה וששׂון: "joy and jubilation, [in the form of] a drinking banquet and good day, were to the Jews." The use of משתה is probably a reference of some kind to the banquets thrown by the king in chapters 1–2, as well as those given by Esther in chapters 5–7. יום טוב, "a good day," probably indicates something like a "holiday" (cf. HALOT יוֹם I 3).

וְרַבִּ֞ים מֵעַמֵּ֤י הָאָ֙רֶץ֙ מִֽתְיַהֲדִ֔ים. A null copula clause with subject רבים מעמי הארץ and participial (mp Hith √יהד) phrase complement. The verbal root יהד, which is clearly related to the proper noun יְהוּדָה ("Judah") and the gentilic יְהוּדִי ("Jew"), is used nowhere else in any ancient Jewish literature (cf. Paton, 282). From context it must mean "to pose as a Jew" (HALOT יהד) or "to become a Jew" (cf. Moore 1971:81–82; Fox 2001:105–16; Bush, 448; Levenson, 117).

כִּֽי־נָפַ֥ל פַּֽחַד־הַיְּהוּדִ֖ים עֲלֵיהֶֽם. *Qatal* 3ms Qal √נפל. The כי clause provides the reason for the assertion in the main clause (that some were posing as Jews). The verb-subject order reflects inversion triggered by the כי. In the subject NP פחד היהודים, the clitic host היהודים modifies the cliticized NP פחד as the object of the verbal idea (WO 9.5.2b; i.e., it is not that the Jews feared, but that they were feared).

Episode 2—The Jews Prevail (9:1-19)

Several plot complications have now been resolved: Esther and Mordecai have exposed Haman's plot, Haman has been killed, and the king has allowed the Jews to defend themselves against those who would enact Haman's edict. But one tension remains—how the Jews fare on the day decreed for their slaughter. This is addressed and so resolved here in chapter 9. The event is recounted in two sections, (9:1-10) and (9:11-19), the latter occurring one day after the former.

§1: The First Day of Fighting (9:1-10)

1And in the twelfth month—it is the month of Adar—on the thirteenth day in it, when the word of the king and his law arrived to be done, on the day that the enemies of the Jews hoped to rule over them but it being overturned, when the Jews—they!— ruled over their haters, 2the Jews assembled in their cities in all the provinces of King Ahashverosh, in order to raise a hand against those who were seeking their harm. And no man stood before them, because fear of them had fallen upon all the people. 3And all the rulers of the provinces, the satraps, the governors, and those who do the work of the king were supporting the Jews, because the fear of Mordecai had fallen upon them, [4]because Mordecai was great in the palace of the king, and the news of him was traveling through all the provinces because the man, Mordecai, was becoming increasingly great. [5]And the Jews struck all their enemies with a blow of sword, slaughter, and destruction. And they acted according to their desire against those who hated them. [6]And in Susa, the citadel, the Jews killed and destroyed 500 men. [7]And Parshandatha and Dalphon and Aspatha [8]and Poratha and Adalya and Aridatha [9]and Parmashta and Arisai and Aridai and Vayzatha, [10]the ten sons of Haman, son of Hammedatha, enemy of the Jews, they killed. But they did not stretch out their hand to the plunder.

9:1 וּבִשְׁנֵים֩ עָשָׂ֨ר חֹ֜דֶשׁ הוּא־חֹ֣דֶשׁ אֲדָ֗ר בִּשְׁלוֹשָׁ֨ה
עָשָׂ֥ר יוֹם֙ בּ֔וֹ אֲשֶׁ֨ר הִגִּ֧יעַ דְּבַר־הַמֶּ֛לֶךְ וְדָת֖וֹ
לְהֵעָשׂ֑וֹת בַּיּ֗וֹם אֲשֶׁ֨ר שִׂבְּר֜וּ אֹיְבֵ֣י הַיְּהוּדִים֮ לִשְׁל֣וֹט
בָּהֶם֒ וְנַהֲפ֣וֹךְ ה֔וּא אֲשֶׁ֨ר יִשְׁלְט֧וּ הַיְּהוּדִ֛ים הֵ֖מָּה
בְּשֹׂנְאֵיהֶֽם׃

This verse consists of four complex adjunct phrases to the main verb, which is נקהלו of v. 2 (similarly, Keil, 372; contra Bush, 455, who sees the function of the fronting as involving "prominence" and "emphasis"). All the information in v. 1 sets the scene and thus is fronted as one complex Topic. The structure is indeed complex, with multiple appositions, as well as multiple levels of apposition, one parenthesis, and two relative clauses, one of which has an embedded infinitive clause.

וּבִשְׁנֵים֩ עָשָׂ֨ר חֹ֜דֶשׁ הוּא־חֹ֣דֶשׁ אֲדָ֗ר בִּשְׁלוֹשָׁ֨ה עָשָׂ֥ר יוֹם֙ בּ֔וֹ. The numeral syntax in "twelfth month" (שנים עשר חדש) and "thirteenth day" (שלושה עשר יום) is appositive in both cases (cf. "Numeral Syntax in Esther" in the Introduction). On the parenthetical statement (הוא חדש אדר), see comments on 1:1; 2:7; 3:7. The first ב-PP is the initial and primary Topic in the fronted position of the clause. Besides the parenthesis that clarifies the name of the month, the second ב-PP is appositive to the initial ב-PP and specifies the temporal setting further by adding the day.

אֲשֶׁ֨ר הִגִּ֧יעַ דְּבַר־הַמֶּ֛לֶךְ וְדָת֖וֹ לְהֵעָשׂ֑וֹת. *Qatal* 3ms Hiph √נגע and inf constr Niph √עשׂה. This relative is similar in content to the relatives in 4:3 and 8:17, though here the verb is a *qatal* perfective (defaulting within the relative to a past temporal setting). Note that the verb הגיע is singular, suggesting that the compound subject NP דבר ודתו is resolved as a singular unit (cf. comments on 2:21 and 5:4). The head of the relative is null, "Ø that X arrived," for which the context suggests a temporal interpretation, hence the translation as "when" (< "the time that"). The null head and its relative are appositive to the initial ב-PP and further clarify the identication of this special day. Note that in relative clauses with a participle copula (e.g., 8:17 אשר דבר המלך ודתו מגיע) we find subject-participle order, but in relative clauses with finite verbs we find verb-subject order. Hiphil נגע is bivalent (see comment on 2:12). Here the complement is the null resumptive pronoun for the null head, that is, "(the day) that the word and law arrived (then = the day)" (see 8:17 for a similar null resumptive complement with the verb הגיע).

בַּיּוֹם אֲשֶׁר שִׂבְּרוּ אֹיְבֵי הַיְּהוּדִים לִשְׁלוֹט בָּהֶם וְנַהֲפוֹךְ הוּא. *Qatal* 3mp Piel √שׂבר, inf constr Qal √שׁלט, and inf abs Niph √הפך. In the Qal שׂבר means "to test, investigate, inspect," with "expectancy [having] overtones of the moment of proof" (HALOT s.v.). The Piel focuses further on the aspect of "expectancy," meaning "to hope, wait" (HALOT s.v.; BDB s.v.). It is used in later Hebrew texts (Isa 38:18; Pss 104:27; 119:166; 145:15; Ruth 1:13; Neh 2:13, 15), and appears to be borrowed from Aramaic, where the spelling is סבר (cf. Jastrow סְבַר; Dan 7:25; Paton, 284–85). The verb סבר is also used frequently in rabbinic Hebrew (cf. Jastrow סָבַר). Elsewhere, Piel שׂבר mostly takes an אל-PP (Isa 38:18; Pss 104:27; 145:15) or ל-PP (Ps 119:166) complement, though once an עד-PP fulfills its valency (Ruth 1:13). Here, however, the ל-PP/infinitive clause לשלוט fulfills the verb's valency, meaning "to hope *to do something*." שׁלט, another word borrowed from Aramaic (HALOT s.v.; Paton, 285; cf. Dan 2:38-39, 48; 3:27; 5:7, 16; 6:25), means "to gain power over" or "to have power over" and is bivalent with a ב-PP complement (here בהם) denoting the thing subjugated (HALOT s.v.; Keil, 372). The use of the infinitive absolute נהפוך for the second clause within the relative signals that the infinitival clause is both subordinate to the higher verb of the relative, שׂבר, and also perhaps marks the verb for Focus (see comments on 2:3, 8:8). The result would both keep the primary verb within the relative clause as שׂבר ("hoped … but being changed ...") but puts Focus on נהפוך as a salient point the narrator wants to get across—the initial nature of this day was overturned (נהפוך) before it even started. When the verb הפך (Qal "to change, overturn," Niphal "to be changed, overturned") means "to change" it takes a PP adjunct indicating what something is changed *into* (see the ל-PP adjuncts in v. 22). When, as here, it has no PP adjunct, it simply means "overturn" (or passive, "overturned"). The subject הוא refers back to the יום that is the relative head.

אֲשֶׁר יִשְׁלְטוּ הַיְּהוּדִים הֵמָּה בְּשֹׂנְאֵיהֶם. *Yiqtol* 3mp Qal √שׁלט. Like the first אשר relative in this verse, the head of this relative is null (reconstructible as "day," just as in the previous case) and it is resumed by a null pronoun. This is the fourth appositive to the initial ב-PP of the Topic phrase. As noted above, שׁלט takes a ב-PP complement (בשׂנאיהם). The pronoun המה is appositive to the subject היהודים and marks it for *in situ* Focus. It is often translated with an English reflexive pronoun, "the Jews themselves," but this does not convey the force of the Focus clearly enough.

9:2 נִקְהֲלוּ הַיְּהוּדִים בְּעָרֵיהֶם בְּכָל־מְדִינוֹת הַמֶּלֶךְ
אֲחַשְׁוֵרוֹשׁ לִשְׁלֹחַ יָד בִּמְבַקְשֵׁי רָעָתָם וְאִישׁ לֹא־
עָמַד לִפְנֵיהֶם כִּי־נָפַל פַּחְדָּם עַל־כָּל־הָעַמִּים׃

נִקְהֲלוּ הַיְּהוּדִים בְּעָרֵיהֶם בְּכָל־מְדִינוֹת הַמֶּלֶךְ אֲחַשְׁוֵרוֹשׁ. *Qatal* 3mp Niph √קהל. נקהלו is the main verb of the clause begun in v. 1. The fronting of the scene-setting Topic adjunct in v. 1 triggers inversion to verb-subject order (see "Word Order" in the Introduction). Niphal קהל is monovalent, as in 8:11, and the ב-PP following is a locative adjunct. The second ב-PP, בכל מדינות המלך אחשורוש, is appositive to the first, בעריכם, and clarifies that the Jewish gathering occurred kingdom wide. The second PP cannot be an NP-internal adjunct to the noun עריהם, since NP-internal PPs are restrictive and the NP עריהם is already identified by the possessive 3mp clitic pronoun.

לִשְׁלֹחַ יָד בִּמְבַקְשֵׁי רָעָתָם. Inf constr Qal √שׁלח and participle mp Piel √בקשׁ. This ל-PP/infinitive clause is a purpose adjunct to נקהלו. On the expression שׁלח יד, see comment on 2:21. In the complex word במבקשׁי, the ב-preposition has a null NP complement that is modified by a participial relative. The structure of the participial relative is complex and includes a null relative word and a null copula, i.e., "against Ø[the ones] Ø[who] Ø[were] seeking their harm." The participle is cliticized to its complement, the NP clitic host רעתם. The NP רָעָה has a broad range of connotations (see also the discussion at 7:7; HALOT s.v.; DCH s.v.); here the typical "evil" or "misfortune" might work, but "harm" or "injury" seems to capture better the contextual nuance.

וְאִישׁ לֹא־עָמַד לִפְנֵיהֶם. *Qatal* 3ms Qal √עמד. The לא negates the verb not the NP איש, and so English "no man stood before them" may be an acceptable translation but does not reflect the Hebrew structure. The subject-verb order in the presence of the negative לא, which normally triggers inversion to verb-subject, is notable. As with other cases of subject-verb order in Esther, this may reflect the further shift toward strong subject-verb typology that occurs in later Hebrew (see "Word Order" in the Introduction; Holmstedt 2013d). As in 8:11, עמד here seems to have a defensive connotation (cf. HALOT s.v. Qal 1: "with לִפְנֵי to stand firm"; cf. Bush, 461).

כִּי־נָפַל פַּחְדָּם עַל־כָּל־הָעַמִּים. *Qatal* 3ms Qal √נפל. On פחדם, see comment on פחד היהודים in 8:17.

9:3 וְכָל־שָׂרֵי הַמְּדִינוֹת וְהָאֲחַשְׁדַּרְפְּנִים וְהַפַּחוֹת וְעֹשֵׂי
הַמְּלָאכָה אֲשֶׁר לַמֶּלֶךְ מְנַשְּׂאִים אֶת־הַיְּהוּדִים כִּי־
נָפַל פַּחַד־מָרְדֳּכַי עֲלֵיהֶם׃

וְכָל־שָׂרֵי הַמְּדִינוֹת וְהָאֲחַשְׁדַּרְפְּנִים וְהַפַּחוֹת וְעֹשֵׂי הַמְּלָאכָה אֲשֶׁר לַמֶּלֶךְ מְנַשְּׂאִים אֶת־הַיְּהוּדִים. A null copula clause with compound NP subject and participial (mp Piel √נשׂא) phrase complement (מנשׂאים את היהודים). The long compound subject NP consists of four NPs, two of which are complex (i.e., further modified). On אחשדרפנים, see comment on 3:12. On עשׂי המלאכה (participle mp Qal √עשׂה), see comment on 3:9. The relative אשׁר למלך modifies המלאכה and is a more complex structure to indicate possession (the so-called periphrastic genitive, see WO 9.7c). Piel מנשׂאים does not connote physical "carrying" as in the Qal, but has the sense of "supporting" and by extension also "helping" (cf. HALOT s.v. Piel 3; cf. BDB s.v. "support, aid, assist"). Whereas in 3:1 the sense of Piel נשׂא is "to promote," here "to support" is contextually more fitting (contra Levenson, 120; cf. Berlin, 84).

כִּי־נָפַל פַּחַד־מָרְדֳּכַי עֲלֵיהֶם. *Qatal* 3ms Qal √נפל. On פחד מרדכי, see comment on פחד היהודים in 8:17.

9:4 כִּי־גָדוֹל מָרְדֳּכַי בְּבֵית הַמֶּלֶךְ וְשָׁמְעוֹ הוֹלֵךְ בְּכָל־
הַמְּדִינוֹת כִּי־הָאִישׁ מָרְדֳּכַי הוֹלֵךְ וְגָדוֹל׃

כִּי־גָדוֹל מָרְדֳּכַי בְּבֵית הַמֶּלֶךְ. A null copula clause with מרדכי as the NP subject and the adjective גדול as the Focus-fronted complement. This כי clause provides the reason for the assertion in the previous כי clause in v. 3 (cf. comment on 1:8). In other words, it gives the reason why the king's rulers feared Mordecai.

וְשָׁמְעוֹ הוֹלֵךְ בְּכָל־הַמְּדִינוֹת. Participle ms Qal √הלך. The verbal root הלך most often refers to humans "going" or "walking"; however, it is frequently used of inanimate things as well, or even concepts, as here. The *qātil*-pattern noun שֹׁמַע (the first vowel *ā* changed to *ō* as part of the Canaanite shift; the second vowel changed to *a* under influence of ע) is used less frequently than the synonymous *qital*-pattern noun שֵׁמַע (Paton, 285): the former is found here and three other places (Josh 6:27; 9:9; Jer 6:24), while the latter occurs seventeen times in the Hebrew Bible. Both mean "news," "report," or "hearsay" ("rumor") (HALOT שֹׁמַע, שֵׁמַע).

כִּי־הָאִישׁ מָרְדֳּכַי הוֹלֵךְ וְגָדוֹל. A null copula, participle ms Qal √הלך, and inf abs Qal √גדל. This כי clause is a causal adjunct to הולך and thus provides the reason that Mordecai's reputation was spreading—because his stature (presumably in the court) was ever increasing. The participle הולך is the complement of the null copula and provides both progressive aspect as well as the sense of "continuing" or "increasing," which combines with its infinitive complement to produce the verbal complex "becoming increasingly great." Qal גדל, "to be great," "to become great" (HALOT s.v.) is monovalent; compare the bivalent Piel ("to bring up") used in 3:1, 5:11, and 10:2.

9:5 וַיַּכּוּ הַיְּהוּדִים֙ בְּכָל־אֹ֣יְבֵיהֶ֔ם מַכַּת־חֶ֥רֶב וְהֶ֖רֶג וְאַבְדָ֑ן וַיַּעֲשׂ֥וּ בְשֹׂנְאֵיהֶ֖ם כִּרְצוֹנָֽם׃

וַיַּכּוּ הַיְּהוּדִים֙ בְּכָל־אֹ֣יְבֵיהֶ֔ם מַכַּת־חֶ֥רֶב וְהֶ֖רֶג וְאַבְדָ֑ן. *Wayyiqtol* 3mp Hiph √נכה. Note the assimilation of the נ of the root: *wayyankū* > *wayyakkū* (see comment on the assimilation of נ in 2:18). Note also the loss of ה in the *wayyiqtol* form (cf. comment on עשׂה in 2:4). Typically Hiphil נכה ("to strike"; HALOT s.v.) is bivalent with a ב-PP complement indicating the thing struck. However, here there is a second complement, a "cognate accusative" (cf. JM 125q; WO 10.2.1g), מכת חרב והרג ואבדן. The noun מַכָּה is a *maqtal*-pattern from √נכה (< *mankaya), with assimilation of the initial נ and contraction of the original final triphthong to the /-ā/, which was following by a ה *mater lectionis* and likely mistaken for the fs ending, hence both מַכִּים and מַכּוֹת are attested plural forms. The clitic hosts חרב והרג ואבדן specify what *kind* of מַכָּה is in view. On אבדן, see comment on 8:6.

וַיַּעֲשׂוּ בְשֹׂנְאֵיהֶם כִּרְצוֹנָם. *Wayyiqtol* 3mp Qal √עשׂה. The meaning of עשׂה here is not "to do" but "to behave/act," with a כ-PP complement (see comment on 1:8, 21). On the meaning of רצון, see 1:8.

9:6 וּבְשׁוּשַׁ֣ן הַבִּירָ֗ה הָרְג֤וּ הַיְּהוּדִים֙ וְאַבֵּ֔ד חֲמֵ֥שׁ מֵא֖וֹת אִֽישׁ׃

וּבְשׁוּשַׁן הַבִּירָה הָרְגוּ הַיְּהוּדִים. *Qatal* 3mp Qal √הרג. The PP בשושן הבירה is Topic-fronted in order to switch the view from the rest of the kingdom to the results of the fateful day in the capital city. The fronting triggers inversion to verb-subject word order (see "Word Order" in the Introduction). On the appositional structure and on the meaning of בירה, see comment on 1:2. The complement of הרג is the NP חמש מאות איש.

וְאַבֵּד חֲמֵשׁ מֵאוֹת אִישׁ. Inf abs Piel √אבד. The NP following the infinitive is the complement of the bivalent הרג. The infinitive is a subordinate verbal adjunct to the verb הרגו; see the discussion of infinitives absolute in 2:3, 8:8; 9:1. Here it was difficult to translate the Hebrew syntax into similar English; thus our translation reflects two distinct clauses, but this should not be confused with the Hebrew structure. The numeral syntax of חמשׁ מאות איש is appositional (cf. "Numeral Syntax in Esther" in the Introduction).

9:7 וְאֵ֣ת ׀ פַּרְשַׁנְדָּ֗תָא וְאֵ֛ת ׀ דַּלְפ֖וֹן וְאֵ֥ת ׀ אַסְפָּֽתָא׃

A list of names begins in v. 7; when the verse ends we find, in v. 10, that they are the names of Haman's ten sons, and that they were all killed by the Jews.

Most of the names in vv. 7-9 are Persian; our evidence of their meaning comes through Avestan. In our English translation, we have "the Jews slew" in v. 7, but it actually occurs in v. 10. The clause that begins in v. 7 continues until v. 10, where we finally find the verb (הרגו). Everything preceding the verb is part of a compound NP that is the complement to the verb.

Concerning the alignment of the texts in this list of names in the Masoretic Text (vv. 7-9), see the standard commentaries. פרשנדתא means "the searching" one (HALOT s.v.), from Persian (Avestan) *frašna* ("question") *dāta* ("to be given") (Gehman, 327). דלפון is perhaps related to Akkadian *dullupu* ("sleepless") or Arabic *dalūf* ("to have a hooked nose") or *dalifa* ("to have a small nose") (HALOT s.v.).

9:8 וְאֵ֣ת ׀ פּוֹרָ֑תָא וְאֵ֥ת ׀ אֲדַלְיָ֖א וְאֵ֥ת ׀ אֲרִידָֽתָא׃

פורתא is "the generous one" (HALOT s.v.), from Persian (Avestan) *pauru* ("much") *dā* ("to give") (Gehman, 327). אדליא is possibly from Persian (Avestan) *adara* ("the one below") (Gehman, 327).

9:9 וְאֵ֣ת ׀ פַּרְמַ֫שְׁתָּא֩ וְאֵ֣ת ׀ אֲרִיסַ֗י וְאֵ֣ת ׀ אֲרִדַ֛י וְאֵ֥ת
׀ וַיְזָֽתָא׃

פרמשתא is perhaps a combination of Persian (Avestan) *para* ("before") *ma* (a superlative) and *ištha* (another superlative), meaning "the very first" (Gehman, 327–28; cf. HALOT s.v.). אריסי is possibly from Persian (Avestan) *ariya* ("Aryans") and *šay* ("to dwell"), meaning "dwelling among the Aryans" (Gehman, 328). Similarly, ארדי may be from *ariya* and *day* ("to see"), meaning "having the glance of the Aryan" or "looking at the Aryan" (Gehman, 328). ויזתא is from Persian (Avestan) *vaya* ("air, atmosphere") and *zan* ("to bear"; past participle *zāta*), meaning "the son of the atmosphere" (Gehman, 328).

9:10 עֲשֶׂ֨רֶת בְּנֵ֜י הָמָ֧ן בֶּֽן־הַמְּדָ֛תָא צֹרֵ֥ר הַיְּהוּדִ֖ים הָרָ֑גוּ
וּבַּבִּזָּ֕ה לֹ֥א שָׁלְח֖וּ אֶת־יָדָֽם׃

In v. 10 we read that the persons listed in the previous verses are none other than the sons of Haman. The point is that Mordecai's enemy, Haman, has been thoroughly defeated; not only he, but also all of his male heirs have been killed (Fox 2001:110; Bush, 475).

עֲשֶׂ֨רֶת בְּנֵ֜י הָמָ֧ן בֶּֽן־הַמְּדָ֛תָא צֹרֵ֥ר הַיְּהוּדִ֖ים הָרָ֑גוּ. *Qatal* 3mp Qal √הרג. The NP עשׂרת בני המן is in apposition to the compound NP in vv. 7-9. On המן בן המדתא צרר היהודים, see comments on 3:10 and 8:1. The subject of the verb is null, but since the Jews are the only ones doing any killing in the discourse context, the subject should be understood as

היהודים. The verb הרגו is the main verb of the clause begun in v. 7. The long, complex complement is Focus-fronted in order to isolate Haman's sons out of all the non-Jews who were killed.

וּבַבִּזָּה לֹא שָׁלְחוּ אֶת־יָדָם. *Qatal* 3mp Qal √שׁלח. The ב-PP adjunct is Focus-fronted to contrast it with the complement of the preceding clause—whereas the Jews did kill Haman's sons, they did not even touch the spoils of battle. The expression שׁלח יד ב typically has to do with harming some*one* (see comment on 2:21), but here the NP בזה is some*thing*. It makes little sense to speak of *attacking* the spoils of war; rather, the idea here is about *taking* those spoils. Thus, the sense of שׁלח יד ב here is "to lay hands on" (HALOT שׁלח Qal 1 β). This idea that the Jews did not plunder their defeated enemies probably hearkens to 1 Sam 15, where Saul was punished by God for plundering the Amalekites (Moore 1971:87–88; Fox 2001:115; Levenson, 122; Berlin, 85; cf. Bush, 476–77, who dissents); significantly, this is the same conflict that situates the animosity between Mordecai and Haman (cf. comment on 3:1). Because the comment that the Jews did not plunder is repeated again in vv. 15 and 16, it clearly carries significance. Note also that Haman's decree allowed the plunder of the Jews in 3:13, and the counter-edict given in 8:11 gives the Jews permission to plunder their enemies. The word בִּזָּה occurs only in later texts in the Hebrew Bible (here, vv. 15, 16; Dan 11:24, 33; Ezra 9:7; Neh 3:36; 2 Chr 14:13; 25:13; 28:14); note, however, that the related noun בַּז, which has the same meaning, occurs often in earlier texts (cf. Bergey 1983:39).

§2: The Second Day of Fighting (9:11-19)

In section 2 the Jews fight and slay their enemies. Verses 11-13 situate this second scene as an additional day of fighting the day after section 1. The key phrase first found in v. 10—"they did not stretch out their hand to the plunder"—is repeated in vv. 15 and 16, thus emphasizing the theological point (see comment on v. 10).

[11]On that day the number of the ones who were slain in Susa, the citadel, came before the king. [12]And the king said to Esther, the queen, "In Susa, the citadel, the Jews killed and destroyed 500 men and the ten sons of Haman. In the rest of the provinces of the king what have they done? And whatever is your petition shall be given to you. And let whatever is your additional request be done." [13]And Esther said, "If it pleases the king, allow the Jews who are in Susa, even tomorrow, to do according to the law of today. And let them hang the ten sons of Haman on the tree. [14]And the king said for thus to

be done, and a law was given in Susa, and they hung the ten sons of Haman.
[15]*And the Jews who were in Susa gathered also on the fourteenth day of the month of Adar, and they killed in Susa 300 men. But they did not stretch out their hand to the plunder.*
[16]*And the rest of the Jews who were in the provinces of the king gathered, standing for themselves, resting from their enemies, and slaying among their haters 75,000—but they did not stretch out their hand to the plunder—*
[17]*on the thirteenth day of the month of Adar, and so resting on the fourteenth day in it and making it a day of banquet and joy.*
[18]*The Jews who were in Susa gathered on the thirteenth day in it and on the fourteenth day in it, and so they rested on the fifteenth day in it and made it a day of banquet and joy.*
[19]*Therefore, the Jews, the villagers, who dwelled in the cities of the countryside, were making the fourteenth day of the month of Adar (a day of) joy, and (a day of) banquet, and a good day, and (a day of) sending of portions, a man to his neighbor.*

9:11 בַּיּ֣וֹם הַה֗וּא בָּ֣א מִסְפַּ֧ר הַהֲרוּגִ֛ים בְּשׁוּשַׁ֥ן הַבִּירָ֖ה לִפְנֵ֥י הַמֶּֽלֶךְ׃

בַּיּ֣וֹם הַה֗וּא בָּ֣א מִסְפַּ֧ר הַהֲרוּגִ֛ים בְּשׁוּשַׁ֥ן הַבִּירָ֖ה. *Qatal* 3ms Qal √בוא and participle mp Qal Passive √הרג). The initial ב-PP is a fronted scene-setting Topic. The verb בָּא is morphologically ambiguous—both the Qal ms participle and Qal 3ms *qatal* share this same form (see also 6:4). Here, though, the verb-subject order follows the fronted Topic strongly suggesting that the *qatal* verb is intended (the participle does not undergo verb-subject inversion after initial triggers; see "Word Order" in the Introduction). The PP לפני המלך is the locative complement of bivalent בא (cf. comments on 1:11, 19). ההרוגים בשושן הבירה is a ה-relative modifying a null constituent: "(the ones) who were slain in Susa, the citadel." On the meaning of בירה, see comment on 1:2.

9:12 וַיֹּ֨אמֶר הַמֶּ֜לֶךְ לְאֶסְתֵּ֣ר הַמַּלְכָּ֗ה בְּשׁוּשַׁ֣ן הַבִּירָ֡ה הָרְג֩וּ הַיְּהוּדִ֜ים וְאַבֵּ֗ד חֲמֵ֧שׁ מֵא֣וֹת אִישׁ֮ וְאֵת֮ עֲשֶׂ֣רֶת בְּנֵי־הָמָן֒ בִּשְׁאָ֛ר מְדִינ֥וֹת הַמֶּ֖לֶךְ מֶ֣ה עָשׂ֑וּ וּמַה־שְּׁאֵלָתֵ֤ךְ וְיִנָּתֵֽן לָךְ֙ וּמַה־בַּקָּשָׁתֵ֥ךְ ע֖וֹד וְתֵעָֽשׂ׃

Even though it seems that Esther and Mordecai's wishes have been completely fulfilled in the salvation of the Jews and the revenge they take on their enemies, the king asks Esther *again* if she has another request, as in chapters 5 and 7. The continued repetition of the king's offer to Esther to grant anything she wishes, as well as the doubling of the days the Jews killed their enemies, probably serves a literary function, whether comedic (Levinson, 122; Berlin, 85) and/or further characterization of the king (Bush, 475–76; Levinson, 122).

וַיֹּאמֶר הַמֶּלֶךְ לְאֶסְתֵּר הַמַּלְכָּה. *Wayyiqtol* 3ms Qal √אמר. The *wayyiqtol* verb triggers verb-subject order. The ל-PP is an adjunct indicating the addressee and the following direct speech is the complement of bivalent אמר.

בְּשׁוּשַׁן הַבִּירָה הָרְגוּ הַיְּהוּדִים וְאַבֵּד חֲמֵשׁ מֵאוֹת אִישׁ וְאֵת עֲשֶׂרֶת בְּנֵי־הָמָן. For these two clauses, see comment on the same text in 9:6. The only difference here is the addition of the NP את עשרת בני המן, which together with חמש מאות איש makes up the compound NP complement of הרג. On the function of the infinitive אבד, see comment on v. 6. The PP בשושן הבירה is Topic-fronted to set the scene.

בִּשְׁאָר מְדִינוֹת הַמֶּלֶךְ מֶה עָשׂוּ. *Qatal* 3mp Qal √עשה. The PP בשאר מדינות המלך is Topic-fronted to switch the scene to a different location than the previous clause. Alternatively, it is possible that this PP is Focus-fronted and so signals a contrast between the two locations—one in which the king and Esther knew what happened and the other about which king asks his question. Overall this question is awkward, though. Is it rhetorical, and he knows the answer, or does he not know and appeases Esther's perceived disappointment with a second wish? On the association of the מה with a second Focus (see comment on 1:15, and "Word Order" in the Introduction).

וּמַה־שְּׁאֵלָתֵךְ וְיִנָּתֵן לָךְ וּמַה־בַּקָּשָׁתֵךְ עוֹד וְתֵעָשׂ. *Yiqtol* (irrealis) 3ms Niph √נתן and jussive (form and semantics) 3fs Niph √עשה. On the syntax of these two clauses, and on the words בקשה and שאלה, see comments on 5:3 and 6.

9:13 וַתֹּאמֶר אֶסְתֵּר אִם־עַל־הַמֶּלֶךְ טוֹב יִנָּתֵן גַּם־מָחָר
לַיְּהוּדִים אֲשֶׁר בְּשׁוּשָׁן לַעֲשׂוֹת כְּדָת הַיּוֹם וְאֵת
עֲשֶׂרֶת בְּנֵי־הָמָן יִתְלוּ עַל־הָעֵץ׃

Although vv. 7-10 recount the killing of the ten sons of Haman, here Esther requests that the king have them hung, which must refer to the suspending of Haman's sons' already dead bodies (Moore 1971:88; Bush, 467).

וַתֹּאמֶר אֶסְתֵּר. *Wayyiqtol* 3fs Qal √אמר. The complement is the following direct speech.

אִם־עַל־הַמֶּלֶךְ טוֹב. A null copula clause with a null subject and an adjective complement, טוב. On this expression, see comment on 1:19. The clause as a whole is a conditional clause adjunct to the following verb, ינתן.

יִנָּתֵן גַּם־מָחָר לַיְּהוּדִים אֲשֶׁר בְּשׁוּשָׁן לַעֲשׂוֹת כְּדָת הַיּוֹם. *Yiqtol* (jussive semantics) 3ms Niph √נתן and inf constr Qal √עשׂה. The subject of the Niphal verb—the thing given, or "permitted"—is the infinitive clause לעשׂות כדת היום (similarly, see 3:9). The second complement—the recipient of the thing given, which becomes the semantic agent who is "permitted"—is the PP ליהודים. Literally, the syntax is "let to-act-according-to-the-law-of-the-day be given to the Jews," which is resolved in the Hebrew idiom to "allow the Jews to act. ..." The syntactic similarity to 3:9 is likely intentional: just as Haman influenced the king to allow the destruction of the Jews, now Esther influences the king to allow the Jews to destroy other people. On נתן with an infinitive complement, meaning "to allow," see comment on 8:11. On the valency of לעשׂות with a כ-PP, see comment on 1:21. The article in היום, "the day," probably has a deictic force ("this day" = "today"). Since Haman's edict was only for the thirteenth of Adar, the Jews' enemies presumably would not be allowed by law (or prepared, for that matter) to fight on the fourteenth. The Jews are thus given a day of their own to slaughter their enemies (Fox 2001:112; Bush, 476).

וְאֵת עֲשֶׂרֶת בְּנֵי־הָמָן יִתְלוּ עַל־הָעֵץ. *Yiqtol* (jussive semantics) 3mp Qal √תלה. On the use of plural verbs with unspecified, generic subjects, see comment on 2:2. The NP את עשׂרת בני המן is Topic-fronted, to switch back from the Jews in Susa to another of Esther's concerns—the sons of Haman. On the valency of תלה, see comment on 2:23. The ten sons of Haman are not hung on "a" tree (על עץ), i.e., an arbitrary tree; but on "the" tree (על העץ), i.e., the very tree on which Haman was earlier hung in 7:10.

9:14 וַיֹּ֤אמֶר הַמֶּ֙לֶךְ֙ לְהֵעָשֹׂ֣ות כֵּ֔ן וַתִּנָּתֵ֥ן דָּ֖ת בְּשׁוּשָׁ֑ן וְאֵ֛ת
עֲשֶׂ֥רֶת בְּנֵי־הָמָ֖ן תָּלֽוּ׃

וַיֹּאמֶר הַמֶּלֶךְ לְהֵעָשׂוֹת כֵּן. *Wayyiqtol* 3ms Qal √אמר and inf constr Niph √עשׂה. The complement of אמר is the ל-PP/infinitive clause (indirect speech). The subject of the passive infinitive is the adverb כן. On עשׂה and כן, see comment on 2:4.

וַתִּנָּתֵן דָּת בְּשׁוּשָׁן. *Wayyiqtol* 3fs Niph √נתן. The verb נתן, which is trivalent in the Qal is downgraded to bivalency in the passive Niphal (see comment on 2:13). The subject is דת and the single complement is the locative ב-PP.

וְאֵת עֲשֶׂרֶת בְּנֵי־הָמָן תָּלוּ. *Qatal* 3mp Qal √תלה. The complement את עשׂרת בני המן is Topic-fronted (see comment on the same fronted phrase in v. 13). On the valency of תלה, see comment on 2:23.

9:15 וַיִּֽקָּהֲל֞וּ הַיְּהוּדִ֣יים אֲשֶׁר־בְּשׁוּשָׁ֗ן גַּ֠ם בְּי֨וֹם אַרְבָּעָ֥ה
עָשָׂר֙ לְחֹ֣דֶשׁ אֲדָ֔ר וַיַּֽהַרְג֣וּ בְשׁוּשָׁ֔ן שְׁלֹ֥שׁ מֵא֖וֹת
אִ֑ישׁ וּבַבִּזָּ֕ה לֹ֥א שָׁלְח֖וּ אֶת־יָדָֽם׃

In v. 15, the Jews again fight in Susa. In v. 6 they slew 500 men; here they kill an additional 300. Verses 15-16 clearly echo 8:11, containing the king's edict allowing the Jews to defend themselves.

וַיִּקָּהֲלוּ הַיְּהוּדִים אֲשֶׁר־בְּשׁוּשָׁן גַּם בְּיוֹם אַרְבָּעָה עָשָׂר לְחֹדֶשׁ אֲדָר. *Wayyiqtol* 3mp Niph √קהל. On Niphal קהל, see comment on 8:11. On the *Qere-Ketiv* of היהודיים, see comment on 4:7. Regarding the phrase גם ביום ארבעה עשׂר לחדשׁ אדר (and cf. the nearly identical phrase in 9:17, and similar phrases in 3:13 and 8:12), Bergey notes (1983:83) that dating formulae in later Hebrew Bible texts begin with יום, while those in earlier texts do not (e.g., Num 9:11, בַּחֹדֶשׁ הַשֵּׁנִי בְּאַרְבָּעָה עָשָׂר יוֹם). Moreover, in earlier texts יום follows its numeral, whereas in Esther and other later texts it precedes the numeral (83–84). While the latter point is typically true in cases of numerals occurring specifically in dating formulae, Weitzman has argued convincingly against the widely held view that, for numerals in general, earlier texts have the numeral preceding the thing modified and later texts vice versa. On ל-PPs in dating formulas in general, see comment on 1:3.

וַיַּהַרְגוּ בְשׁוּשָׁן שְׁלֹשׁ מֵאוֹת אִישׁ. *Wayyiqtol* 3mp Qal √הרג. Note the singular אִישׁ: with the higher cardinal numerals, the quantified noun is presented as a collective singular (WO 15.2.5a; cf. comment on 1:1).

וּבַבִּזָּה לֹא שָׁלְחוּ אֶת־יָדָם. *Qatal* 3mp Qal √שלח. For this clause, see comment on 9:10.

9:16 וּשְׁאָר הַיְּהוּדִים אֲשֶׁר בִּמְדִינוֹת הַמֶּלֶךְ נִקְהֲלוּ | וְעָמֹד עַל־נַפְשָׁם וְנוֹחַ מֵאֹיְבֵיהֶם וְהָרֹג בְּשֹׂנְאֵיהֶם חֲמִשָּׁה וְשִׁבְעִים אָלֶף וּבַבִּזָּה לֹא שָׁלְחוּ אֶת־יָדָם׃

The Jews who fight outside of Susa are said to have killed 75,000 men. Near context seems to suggest that this fighting occurred on the second day (the fourteenth of Adar), at the same time as the fighting referred to in v. 15. However, we read in the next verse that the fighting outside of Susa occurred only on the first day (the thirteenth of Adar).

וּשְׁאָר הַיְּהוּדִים אֲשֶׁר בִּמְדִינוֹת הַמֶּלֶךְ נִקְהֲלוּ. *Qatal* 3mp Niph √קהל. On Niphal קהל, see comment on 8:11. The switch from the *wayyiqtol* ויקהלו in v. 15 to the *qatal* נקהלו removes the typical implicature of temporal succession associated with *wayyiqtol* (see comments on 1:12; 6:12; 8:14). Thus, the temporal relationship between this verse and v. 15 is open-ended, with content and context suggesting that the events of this verse preceded those of v. 15. The subject-verb word order allowed by the nonuse of the *wayyiqtol* may reflect basic (i.e., pragmatically unmarked) order, or may also reflect additional fronting of the subject to signal a switch of Topic from the Jews in the capital to the Jews outside the capital.

וְעָמֹד עַל־נַפְשָׁם וְנוֹחַ מֵאֹיְבֵיהֶם וְהָרֹג בְּשֹׂנְאֵיהֶם. Inf abs Qal √עמד, √נוח, and √הרג. On the use of the infinitive absolute as a subordinate verb, see comments on 2:3, 8:8, and 9:1. On the meaning of עמד על, see comment on 8:11. The waw on ועמד, ונוח and והרג simply marks the left edge of each subordinate clause (Holmstedt 2013b) and need not be translated.

וְהָרֹג בְּשֹׂנְאֵיהֶם חֲמִשָּׁה וְשִׁבְעִים אָלֶף . Inf abs Qal √הרג. Because Qal הרג takes an NP complement (the person or people slain), here it is the number phrase חמשה ושבעים אלף. The context, as well as specifically the statement in v. 15, implies that the quantity of 75,000 are men (i.e., חמשה ושבעים אלף <u>איש</u>). The adjunct PP בשׂנאיהם indicates the source or domain to which the complement of the verb relates (WO 11.2.5d–e).

וּבַבִּזָּה לֹא שָׁלְחוּ אֶת־יָדָם. *Qatal* 3mp Qal √שׁלח. For this clause, see comment on 9:10. Given the syntax that follows in v. 17, it is best to understand this clause as parenthetical (see comment on v. 17).

9:17 בְּיוֹם־שְׁלֹשָׁה עָשָׂר לְחֹדֶשׁ אֲדָר וְנוֹחַ בְּאַרְבָּעָה
עָשָׂר בּוֹ וְעָשֹׂה אֹתוֹ יוֹם מִשְׁתֶּה וְשִׂמְחָה׃

This verse continues v. 16 and clarifies the order of events related in vv. 15-16.

בְּיוֹם־שְׁלֹשָׁה עָשָׂר לְחֹדֶשׁ אֲדָר. On the structure of this phrase, see comment on 9:15. The placement of the initial ב-PP mirrors v. 15, where another ב-PP (בשׁושׁן) is placed before the complement of the verb. Context informs the reader that the repeated phrase ובבזה לא שׁלחו את ידם (vv. 10, 15, and 16) ought to stand alone as a main clause, as it does in the other cases (see comment on v. 10). Since there is no verb in v. 17 and it makes no sense to read a null copula between any of the constituents, ב-PP and two infinitive clauses should be understood as adjuncts to נקהלו in the main clause v. 16 (similarly Bush, 467). The final clause of v. 16, ובבזה לא שׁלחו את ידם, must be parenthetical. Taking the ב-PP at the beginning of v. 17 as modifying the second-to-last clause in v. 16 provides an appropriate parallel to the statement in v. 15: "the Jews who were Susa gathered also on the fourteenth day of the month of Adar" parallels "the rest of the Jews ... gathered ... on the thirteenth day of the month of Adar." See Bush, 472–74 for additional discussion of the narrative structure of this passage.

וְנוֹחַ בְּאַרְבָּעָה עָשָׂר בּוֹ. Inf abs Qal √נוח. Qal נוח is "to rest"; the connotation here is "repose" (HALOT s.v.; DCH s.v.) or rest "from trouble" (BDB s.v.). On the use of the infinitive absolute as a subordinate verb, see comments on 2:3, 8:8, and 9:1. On the use of בו in dating formulas, see comment on 3:12.

וְעָשֹׂה אֹתוֹ יוֹם מִשְׁתֶּה וְשִׂמְחָה. Inf abs Qal √עשׂה. Similar to שׁנה ל in 2:9, here עשׂה means to "make into" (DCH עשׂה I Qal 2b), that is, to make someone or something into someone or something else. It is trivalent, taking two NP complements; the first (אתו) is the thing changed, the second (יום) is the thing into which it is changed. The naturee of the bound relationship in the phrase יום משׁתה ושׂמחה is such that it describes a day *characterized by* or *consisting of* a banquet (or banquets), and joy (WO 9.5.3, esp. c).

9:18 וְהַיְּהוּדִיים אֲשֶׁר־בְּשׁוּשָׁן נִקְהֲלוּ בִּשְׁלֹשָׁה עָשָׂר בּוֹ וּבְאַרְבָּעָה עָשָׂר בּוֹ וְנוֹחַ בַּחֲמִשָּׁה עָשָׂר בּוֹ וְעָשֹׂה אֹתוֹ יוֹם מִשְׁתֶּה וְשִׂמְחָה׃

Whereas vv. 15 (Jews in Susa) and 16 (Jews outside Susa) parallel each other by describing the activity of the two groups of Jews, including on which days, vv. 17 and 18 are similarly parallel—though in reverse order.

וְהַיְּהוּדִיים אֲשֶׁר־בְּשׁוּשָׁן נִקְהֲלוּ בִּשְׁלֹשָׁה עָשָׂר בּוֹ וּבְאַרְבָּעָה עָשָׂר בּוֹ. *Qatal* 3mp Niph √קהל. On the *Qere-Ketiv* of היהודיים, see comment on 4:7. On Niphal קהל with a ב-PP, see comments on 8:11 and 9:2. On the temporal PPs בשלשה עשר בו and בארבעה עשר בו, see comment on 3:12. The referent of the 3ms clitic pronouns with ב is חדש אדר from v. 17. On the use of the *qatal* and the subject-verb order, see discussion at v. 16.

וְנוֹחַ בַּחֲמִשָּׁה עָשָׂר בּוֹ וְעָשֹׂה אֹתוֹ יוֹם מִשְׁתֶּה וְשִׂמְחָה. Inf abs Qal √נוח and √עשה. See discussion at v. 17.

9:19 עַל־כֵּן הַיְּהוּדִים הַפְּרָוזִים הַיֹּשְׁבִים בְּעָרֵי הַפְּרָזוֹת עֹשִׂים אֵת יוֹם אַרְבָּעָה עָשָׂר לְחֹדֶשׁ אֲדָר שִׂמְחָה וּמִשְׁתֶּה וְיוֹם טוֹב וּמִשְׁלוֹחַ מָנוֹת אִישׁ לְרֵעֵהוּ׃

The victory of the Jews is commemorated by feasting (משתה) and gift giving. The use of משתה recalls the king's and Vashti's banquets given in chapter 1, and Esther's private banquets for the king and Haman, by which she thwarted Haman's plot.

עַל־כֵּן הַיְּהוּדִים הַפְּרָוזִים הַיֹּשְׁבִים בְּעָרֵי הַפְּרָזוֹת עֹשִׂים אֵת יוֹם אַרְבָּעָה עָשָׂר לְחֹדֶשׁ אֲדָר שִׂמְחָה. A null copula clause with subject היהודים הפרוזים and participial (mp Qal √עשה) phrase complement (עשים את יום ... שמחה ומשתה). The NP הפרוזים is appositive to היהודים and is semantically restrictive in that it specifies which Jews in particular are in mind (i.e., those in the rural villages, not in Susa). The difference between the *Ketiv* הפרוזים and *Qere* הַפְּרָזִים is negligible; both refer to people who live in the countryside or a small, unwalled village (cf. HALOT פרז* and פְּרָזִי; DCH פְּרָזִי; BDB פרז and פְּרָזִי). The related word פְּרָזָה (found in the phrase בערי הפרזות) may refer to a "village" or, more probably given the phrasing here, a region in the countryside (cf. DCH פְּרָזָה; HALOT פְּרָזוֹת; BDB פְּרָזָה). All three words are rare: פְּרָזָה occurs here, Ezek 38:11, and Zech 2:8; פְּרָזִי appears only here (as a *Qere*), Deut 3:5, and 1 Sam 6:18; finally, the *Ketiv* הפרוזים (presumably plural of פרוז) occurs only here. The NP היהודים has a second modifier, the ה-relative clause הישבים בערי הפרזות, which includes a null copula clause with a participial (mp Qal √ישב) phrase complement. Whereas in previous uses in Esther the verb ישב had the meaning "to sit," here the context suggests "to dwell" or "to inhabit" (DCH s.v. Qal 6; cf. HALOT s.v. Qal 5; BDB s.v. Qal 3). Qal ישב is bivalent, taking a locative complement, here the PP בערי הפרזות. Qal עשׂה has the sense "to make X into [or function as] Y" (as in vv. 17 and 18 above), and is therefore trivalent. The first complement is את יום ארבעה עשׂר לחדש אדר; the second complement, indicating the new function for the first complement, is a compound NP made up of four NPs: שׂמחה ומשתה ויום ... ומשלוח. In this compound NP the word יום is probably understood as the head of each NP, only overt in one case (יום טוב), but understood in the others (e.g., שׂמחה ומשתה, "(a day of) joy and banquet"; compare 9:17, 18, יום משתה ושׂמחה, and 9:22, ימי משתה ושׂמחה). The sense of יום טוב, "a good day," is probably something like a "holiday" (cf. HALOT יוֹם I 3). The word מִשְׁלוֹח only appears here, in v. 22, and in Isa 11:14. It may be a *miqtāl* noun built off the verbal root שׁלח (JM 88Lf), though since it seems to have both a complement and an adjunct phrase, it should likely be understood as an Aramaized infinitive of שׁלח (JM 49e). The distributive איש לרעהו is a small clause adjunct to מִשְׁלוֹח.

Episode 3—The Jews' Victory Commemorated and Reprised (9:20-32)

Having escaped Haman's edict by defeating their enemies, the Jews are now safe, and the tensions of the plot are resolved for the reader. This penultimate episode contextualizes the entire story and connects it to the Jewish festival of Purim. Regardless whether this was part of the earlier story of Esther (cf. Moore 1971:97; Fox 2001:258), in its present form the connection to Purim is a key aspect of the text (cf. Bush, 486–87).

§1: Mordecai Establishes the Festival (9:20-25)

[20]And Mordecai wrote these words and sent the writings to all the Jews who were in all the provinces of King Ahashverosh, near and far, [21]to enjoin them to be observing the fourteenth day of the month of Adar and the fifteenth day in it, every year, [22]according to the days on which the Jews rested from their enemies and the month that was turned for them from strife to joy and from mourning to a good day; that is, to make them days of feasting and joy and sending of portions, a man to his neighbor, and (sending) gifts to the poor. [23]And the Jews accepted what they had begun to observe and what Mordecai wrote to them, [24]that Haman, the son of Hamedatha, the Agagite, enemy of all the Jews, had planned against the Jews to destroy them and he had cast the Pur—it is the lot—to confuse them and to destroy them, [25]and when it came before the king, he said, "Along with the letter, let his evil plan that he planned against the Jews return upon his own head!" And they hung him and his sons upon the tree.

9:20 וַיִּכְתֹּב מָרְדֳּכַי אֶת־הַדְּבָרִים הָאֵלֶּה וַיִּשְׁלַח סְפָרִים
אֶל־כָּל־הַיְּהוּדִים אֲשֶׁר בְּכָל־מְדִינוֹת הַמֶּלֶךְ
אֲחַשְׁוֵרוֹשׁ הַקְּרוֹבִים וְהָרְחוֹקִים׃

וַיִּכְתֹּב מָרְדֳּכַי אֶת־הַדְּבָרִים הָאֵלֶּה. *Wayyiqtol* 3ms Qal √כתב. Qal כתב is bivalent (see 1:19); here the NP subject is מרדכי and the NP complement is את הדברים.

וַיִּשְׁלַח סְפָרִים אֶל־כָּל־הַיְּהוּדִים. *Wayyiqtol* 3ms Qal √שלח. On the trivalency of שלח, see comment on 1:22. The subject is null, the NP complement is ספרים, and the locative complement is אל כל היהודים.

כָּל־הַיְּהוּדִים אֲשֶׁר בְּכָל־מְדִינוֹת הַמֶּלֶךְ אֲחַשְׁוֵרוֹשׁ הַקְּרוֹבִים וְהָרְחוֹקִים. The two adjectives modify the NP היהודים. Though adjectives typically precede other more complex modifiers (e.g., relative clauses), here the semantics of the modification relationship overrides this preference. Restrictive modifiers, like this אשר clause, preceded non-restrictive modifiers, like these two adjectives. The אשר clause defines the head היהודים such that the Jews to whom Mordecai writes are not just the Jews in Susa or the Jews outside Susa (the two categories so prominently used in the previous episode), but *all* the Jews in the kingdom. The pairing of קרוב and רחוק is a merism, a literary device by which an entity is referred to by two of its parts, often two extremes or poles; e.g., "the heavens and the earth" is often used to refer to the whole of creation. Thus, here קרוב and רחוק confirm the restrictive identification of the אשר relative, that all the Jews at any distance are included (Moore 1971:93).

9:21 לְקַיֵּם֮ עֲלֵיהֶם֒ לִהְי֣וֹת עֹשִׂ֡ים אֵ֠ת י֣וֹם אַרְבָּעָ֤ה עָשָׂר֙
לְחֹ֣דֶשׁ אֲדָ֔ר וְאֵ֛ת יוֹם־חֲמִשָּׁ֥ה עָשָׂ֖ר בּ֑וֹ בְּכָל־שָׁנָ֖ה
וְשָׁנָֽה׃

לְקַיֵּם֮ עֲלֵיהֶם֒ לִהְי֣וֹת עֹשִׂים. Inf constr Piel √קום, Qal √היה, and participle mp Qal √עשׂה. Although קום is a frequently used verbal root, it only occurs 11 times in the Piel in the Hebrew Bible; seven of these are found in Esther 9 (9:21, 27, 29, 31 [3×], 32; cf. also Ezek 13:6; Ps 119:28, 106; Ruth 4:7). In the Mishnah, Piel קום occurs often, with greater frequency than any other *binyan* of קום, suggesting that Esther's frequent use of Piel קום is a feature that became diffuse only in later Hebrew (cf. Bergey 1983:40–41; Bush, 479). The verb seems to be bivalent, with an NP or infinitive clause complement. The contexts suggests the meaning "to enjoin, impose (obligation) upon" (DCH s.v. Piel 2a; cf. BDB s.v. Piel 2c; cf. Bush, 479). The infinitive clause לקים is a purpose adjunct to וישלח of the preceding verse. The על-PP is the complement of קים, indicating who or what is obligated or enjoined, and the second infinitive clause, להיות, is a purpose adjunct, indicating the goal of the obliging. The complement of the copular היה is the following participial clause.

עֹשִׂים אֵ֠ת י֣וֹם אַרְבָּעָ֤ה עָשָׂר֙ לְחֹ֣דֶשׁ אֲדָ֔ר וְאֵ֛ת יוֹם־חֲמִשָּׁ֥ה עָשָׂ֖ר בּ֑וֹ בְּכָל־שָׁנָ֖ה וְשָׁנָה. Participle mp Qal √עשׂה. Qal עשׂה seems to have the sense "to observe" here (cf. Exod 31:16; DCH עשׂה I Qal 1a, esp. the 6th full paragraph on p. 575; HALOT עשׂה I Qal 9;), in contrast to typical uses in Esther ("to prepare," cf. 1:3; or "to behave," cf. 1:21; in general see comment on 1:3). עשׂה is bivalent and so takes an NP complement, here the compound NP את יום ... ואת יום. On יום חמשה עשׂר בו, see comment on 3:12. On the phrase בכל שׁנה ושׁנה, which is an adjunct to עשׂים, see comment on בכל יום ויום in 2:11.

9:22 כַּיָּמִ֗ים אֲשֶׁר־נָ֨חוּ בָהֶ֤ם הַיְּהוּדִים֙ מֵאֹ֣יְבֵיהֶ֔ם
וְהַחֹ֗דֶשׁ אֲשֶׁר֩ נֶהְפַּ֨ךְ לָהֶ֤ם מִיָּגוֹן֙ לְשִׂמְחָ֔ה וּמֵאֵ֖בֶל

לְי֣וֹם ט֑וֹב לַעֲשׂ֣וֹת אוֹתָ֗ם יְמֵי֙ מִשְׁתֶּ֣ה וְשִׂמְחָ֔ה וּמִשְׁלֹ֤חַ מָנוֹת֙ אִ֣ישׁ לְרֵעֵ֔הוּ וּמַתָּנ֖וֹת לָאֶבְיֹנִֽים׃

Verse 22 echoes v. 19 and formalizes the actions from v. 19 (feasting, sending gifts, being joyful) as the new holiday's observances.

כַּיָּמִ֗ים אֲשֶׁר־נָ֨חוּ בָהֶ֤ם הַיְּהוּדִים֙ מֵאֹ֣יְבֵיהֶ֔ם. *Qatal* 3mp Qal √נוח. On the meaning of נוח, see comment on 9:18. The preposition כ has a compound complement consisting of two NPs headed by ימים and החדש, respectively. The entire כ-PP is an adjunct to עשׂים in v. 21.

וְהַחֹ֗דֶשׁ אֲשֶׁר֩ נֶהְפַּ֨ךְ לָהֶ֤ם מִיָּגוֹן֙ לְשִׂמְחָ֔ה וּמֵאֵ֖בֶל לְי֣וֹם ט֑וֹב. *Qatal* 3ms Niph √הפך. This is the second half of the compound complement to כ at the beginning of the verse. הפך (Qal "to change," Niphal "to be changed") sometimes takes a ל-PP indicating what something is changed into (HALOT s.v.); here, the subject החדש (the head of the relative) is changed into joy (לשׂמחה) and into a good day (ליום טוב; on יום טוב, see comment on v. 19); the other ל-PP, להם, is an adjunct to נהפך, indicating advantage or benefit. The מן-PPs are adjuncts that indicate the source or starting point of the change, that is, what החדש was changed *from* (i.e., its state *before* the change into something else).

לַעֲשׂ֣וֹת אוֹתָ֗ם יְמֵי֙ מִשְׁתֶּ֣ה וְשִׂמְחָ֔ה וּמִשְׁלֹ֤חַ מָנוֹת֙ אִ֣ישׁ לְרֵעֵ֔הוּ וּמַתָּנ֖וֹת לָאֶבְיֹנִֽים. Inf constr Qal √עשׂה. This ל-PP/infinitive clause is either a second adjunct to קים in v. 21, or an appositive to the first adjunct of קים, the ל-PP/infinitive clause להיות. Since it clarifies what it means to observe this holiday, we take it as an appositive to להיות. On the meaning and valency of trivalent עשׂה here, see comment on v. 17. The complements of עשׂה are אותם (the thing being changed) and ימי (what אותם are changed into). The clitic ימי is bound to three NPs, משתה ושמחה ומשלוח. On the noun משלוח, see comment on v. 19. The phrase איש לרעהו is a distributive small clause adjunct to משׁ לוח. Reinforcing the verbal parsing of משלוח is the presence of a second complement, מתנות, with a second adjunct, לאביונים. Since the two ל-Pps, לרעהו and לאביונים, are not internal modifiers of the nouns they follow, the existence of both NPs that "complete" the verbal semantics within משלוח as well as adjuncts, each of which goes with a different complement, strongly suggests not only a verbal parsing for משלוח but an ellipsis structure in which משלוח is gapped into the second clause: "sending portions, each [sending] to his neighbor, and (sending) gifts to the poor."

9:23 וְקִבֵּל֙ הַיְּהוּדִ֔ים אֵ֥ת אֲשֶׁר־הֵחֵ֖לּוּ לַעֲשׂ֑וֹת וְאֵ֛ת
אֲשֶׁר־כָּתַ֥ב מָרְדֳּכַ֖י אֲלֵיהֶֽם׃

וְקִבֵּל֙ הַיְּהוּדִ֔ים. *Qatal* 3ms Piel √קבל. The verb-subject word order with a non-irrealis *qatal* verb is unique in the book. If the author was attempting to mimic older Hebrew (as many scholars have suggested), this clause may reflect a mistaken understanding of the earlier Hebrew syntax and/or usage of the irrealis *qatal*. On Piel קבל, see comment on 4:4.

אֵ֥ת אֲשֶׁר־הֵחֵ֖לּוּ לַעֲשׂ֑וֹת. *Qatal* 3cp Hiph √חלל and inf constr Qal √עשה. This NP is the complement of the verb קבל. Since את only marks NPs, its presence indicates that there is a null noun that is the head of the אשר relative, which is necessarily restrictive (as are all relatives that modify a null head). Thus, the content of the null head can be interpreted from the content of the relative along with clues from the content as "custom" or "practice." Hiphil חלל, "to begin" (HALOT s.v. hiph 2), takes an infinitive clause complement ("begin to *do something*"), here לעשות. The relative resumption of the null relative head is embedded further, as the null complement of the bivalent לעשות, "[the custom] that they had begun to observe [it]."

וְאֵ֛ת אֲשֶׁר־כָּתַ֥ב מָרְדֳּכַ֖י אֲלֵיהֶֽם. *Qatal* 3cp Qal √כתב. This null head relative is the second half of the compound complement of קבל— the people accepted two things, the new holiday and what Mordecai wrote about it. On the את אשר, see previous comment. The null head is resumed covertly within the relative, "[the words] that Mordecai had written [them] to them."

9:24 כִּי֩ הָמָ֨ן בֶּֽן־הַמְּדָ֜תָא הָֽאֲגָגִ֗י צֹרֵר֙ כָּל־הַיְּהוּדִ֔ים
חָשַׁ֥ב עַל־הַיְּהוּדִ֖ים לְאַבְּדָ֑ם וְהִפִּ֥ל פּוּר֙ ה֣וּא הַגּוֹרָ֔ל
לְהֻמָּ֖ם וּֽלְאַבְּדָֽם׃

כִּי֩ הָמָ֨ן בֶּֽן־הַמְּדָ֜תָא הָֽאֲגָגִ֗י צֹרֵר֙ כָּל־הַיְּהוּדִ֔ים חָשַׁ֥ב עַל־הַיְּהוּדִ֖ים לְאַבְּדָ֑ם. Participle ms Qal √צרר, *qatal* 3ms Qal √חשב, and inf constr Piel √אבד with 3mp clitic pronoun. Although כי overwhelmingly triggers inversion to verb-subject word order (see "Word Order" in the Introduction), here the subject המן is Topic-fronted, since Haman has not been the Topic of any clause since chapter 7. The complement of חשב is the

ל-PP/infinitive clause לאבדם (cf. HALOT חשב Qal 6). On בן המדתא האגגי צרר כל היהודים, see comment on 3:10. על is adversative with חשב (cf. WO 11.2.13c; HALOT חשב Qal 5). On the valency of Piel אבד, see comment on 3:9. The כי clause as a whole is appositive to the null complement of כתב in v. 23 (and thus also to the null head of that relative clause). That is, what Mordecai wrote, and so what the people accepted, was this retelling of the critical events of the story (see Fox 2001:118–20 for a cogent discussion of the differences between this summary and the previous large narrative, as well an explanation for their reason). Note that the domain of the כי (and thus the summary) extends through v. 25.

וְהִפִּיל פּוּר֙ ה֣וּא הַגּוֹרָ֔ל לְהֻמָּ֖ם וּֽלְאַבְּדָֽם. *Qatal* 3ms Hiph √נפל, and inf constr Qal √המם and Piel √אבד with 3mp clitic pronouns. On the meaning and valency of Hiphil נפל, see comment on 3:7. The verb המם is used only thirteen times in the Hebrew Bible (here; Exod 14:24; 23:27; Deut 2:15; Josh 10:10; Judg 4:15; 1 Sam 7:10; 2 Sam 22:15; Isa 28:28; Jer 51:34; Pss 18:15; 144:6; 2 Chr 15:6); it means "to confuse" (DCH s.v.; cf. HALOT המם I). The two infinitive clauses are adjuncts to הפיל, giving the purpose of the action. On the Akkadian loanword פור and the parenthetical הוא הגורל, see comment on 3:7. This clause continues within the domain of the initial כי as part of the retelling.

9:25 וּבְבֹאָהּ֮ לִפְנֵ֣י הַמֶּלֶךְ֒ אָמַ֣ר עִם־הַסֵּ֔פֶר יָשׁ֞וּב
מַחֲשַׁבְתּ֧וֹ הָרָעָ֛ה אֲשֶׁר־חָשַׁ֥ב עַל־הַיְּהוּדִ֖ים עַל־
רֹאשׁ֑וֹ וְתָל֥וּ אֹת֛וֹ וְאֶת־בָּנָ֖יו עַל־הָעֵֽץ׃

A continuation of the summary of the story that Mordecai "wrote" and which the Jews "accepted."

וּבְבֹאָהּ֮ לִפְנֵ֣י הַמֶּלֶךְ֒ אָמַ֣ר עִם־הַסֵּ֔פֶר. Inf constr Qal √בוא with 3fs clitic pronoun and *qatal* 3ms Qal √אמר. The initial ב-PP/infinitive clause is a Topic-fronted adjunct to the main verb אמר, whose subject is null, but easily identifiable as המלך. The motion verb בוא is bivalent, taking a subject (the 3fs clitic pronoun) and a PP indicating the location to which one goes (לפני המלך). The referent of the 3fs pronominal subject is ambiguous. Esther has not been mentioned for some time and typical narrative conventions would be to invoke her with a proper noun (אסתר) if she were reintroduced as an agent at this point. But if the summary does not reference Esther, it would then entirely omit her role in the event. Moreover, if the subject is not Esther, then what is it? We find it plausible that the pronoun is cataphoric and thus forward looking to the fs NP מחשבה within the direct speech (so Bush, 481–82; Fox 2001:285). The function of the PP עם הספר is another difficulty of the verse. If it goes with אמר, it would be an adjunct, but the semantics are unclear. Perhaps it is instrumental ("*by means of* the letter"), but this is not only awkward—to "say by letter"—but also a questionable use of עם. Another option is to understand the direct speech of the king as beginning with עם הספר (see further comment below).

עִם־הַסֵּפֶר יָשׁוּב מַחֲשַׁבְתּוֹ הָרָעָה אֲשֶׁר־חָשַׁב עַל־הַיְּהוּדִים עַל־רֹאשׁוֹ. *Yiqtol* (irrealis) 3ms Qal √שׁוב and *qatal* 3ms Qal √חשׁב. Understanding עם הספר as part of the direct speech (see comment above), it has its typical sense of accompaniment: "*along with* the letter, let his evil plan ... return" (cf. WO 11.2.14b). In other words, the king wishes that the "letter" should "return" as well as "his evil plan"; compare Fox (2001:285), who understands עם הספר as part of the direct speech, but still gives it an instrumental (and temporal) meaning. The NP הספר is the written edict of Haman referred to in 3:13 and 8:5 (albeit in those cases it is plural ספרים). In other words, the king wishes that both Haman's evil plan and the letter on which it was communicated be "returned upon his head." This expression, שׁוב על, carries the connotation of retribution (cf. DCH שׁוב I Qal 18b, "be paid back"; cf. 1 Ki 2:32); that is, the king wishes for Haman's plot to happen to him, as a sort of fitting punishment.

וְתָלוּ אֹתוֹ וְאֶת־בָּנָיו עַל־הָעֵץ . *Qatal* 3mp Qal √תלה. The plural verb has a null, generic subject (cf. comment on 2:2). On the valency and meaning of תלה, see comment on 2:23.

§2: The Festival and Lots (Purim) (9:26-28)

[26]Therefore, they called these days "Purim," according to the name of the Pur. Therefore, on account of all the words of this letter and what they saw concerning this, and what happened to them, [27]they established (it) and the Jews accepted for themselves and for their seed and for all who were joined to them (and it will not pass away!) to be observing these two days according to their writing and according to their time in every year. [28]And these days are remembered and are observed in every generation, family, province, and city. And these days of Purim will not pass away from among the Jews and the memory of them will not cease from their seed.

9:26 עַל־כֵּ֞ן קָֽרְא֞וּ לַיָּמִ֨ים הָאֵ֤לֶּה פוּרִים֙ עַל־שֵׁ֣ם הַפּ֔וּר
עַל־כֵּ֕ן עַֽל־כָּל־דִּבְרֵ֖י הָאִגֶּ֣רֶת הַזֹּ֑את וּמָֽה־רָא֣וּ עַל־
כָּ֔כָה וּמָ֖ה הִגִּ֥יעַ אֲלֵיהֶֽם׃

After finishing Mordecai's summary, the narrator explains the naming of the holiday.

עַל־כֵּ֞ן קָֽרְא֞וּ לַיָּמִ֨ים הָאֵ֤לֶּה פוּרִים֙ עַל־שֵׁ֣ם הַפּ֔וּר. *Qatal* 3mp Qal √קרא. The combination of Qal קרא with a ל-PP is often used as an idiom for naming (HALOT קרא I Qal 2a; DCH קרא I 11a; BDB קרא I Qal 6e). In the naming idiom, the verb takes two complements—a ל-PP (here לימים האלה) for the item named, and an NP (here פורים) for the name. Since the person or people responsible for naming these days is unimportant, the plural verb has a null, generic subject (cf. comment on 2:2). The על-PP is an adjunct to the main verb that provides the basis or "norm" according to which the days were named (WO 11.2.13e). On the Akkadian loanword פור, see comment on 3:7.

עַל־כֵּ֕ן עַֽל־כָּל־דִּבְרֵ֖י הָאִגֶּ֣רֶת הַזֹּ֑את. The initial PP על כן consists of the preposition על, used with a causal meaning, "on account of X, because X," and its complement, the deictic adverb כן, which refers back to previous items and introduces the effects of those items (see WO 11.3.2a; 39.3.4, esp. exx. 25–26). It may be understood as a Topic-fronted adjunct or it may also be that it has grammaticalized and should be considered a logical adverb, like English "therefore," used clause-initially, like כי. The following על preposition governs a compound complement—the NP כל דברי and two indirect interrogative clauses, מה ראו and מה הגיע. This complex על-PP is a Topic-fronted adjunct to the verb קימו in v. 27. אגרת is an Aramaic loanword found only in Esther, 2 Chronicles, and Nehemiah (Esth 9:26, 29; 2 Chr 30:1, 6; Neh 2:7–9; 6:5, 17, 19; cf. Bergey 1983:148–49; Moore 1971:95).

וּמָֽה־רָא֣וּ עַל־כָּ֔כָה וּמָ֖ה הִגִּ֥יעַ אֲלֵיהֶֽם. *Qatal* 3mp Qal √ראה and 3ms Hiph √נגע. The Hiphil הגיע used as "to befall, happen" occurs only twice, here and in Eccl 8:14 (DCH s.v., Hiph 3). These two interrogative clauses form the second and third parts of the compound complement to על (see comment above). According to Bergey, the phrase על ככה, which occurs in the Hebrew Bible only here, is an idiom that "contrasts diachronically with semantically similar expressions" from earlier Hebrew (1983:165; cf. Bush, 468). The same exact expression is found in a letter found at Wadi Murabba'at (Bergey 1983:165) dating to the Bar Kochba period.

9:27 קִיְּמ֣וּ וְקִבְּלֻ֣ הַיְּהוּדִ֡ים | עֲלֵיהֶ֣ם | וְעַל־זַרְעָ֡ם וְעַ֨ל כָּל־הַנִּלְוִ֤ים עֲלֵיהֶם֙ וְלֹ֣א יַעֲב֔וֹר לִהְי֣וֹת עֹשִׂ֗ים אֵ֣ת שְׁנֵ֤י הַיָּמִים֙ הָאֵ֔לֶּה כִּכְתָבָ֖ם וְכִזְמַנָּ֑ם בְּכָל־שָׁנָ֖ה וְשָׁנָֽה׃

קִיְּמ֣וּ. *Qatal* 3mp Hiph √קים. The clause begun in the middle of v. 26 has its main verb in this first word of v. 27. The sense of Piel קום here is "establish" (DCH s.v. Piel 1b; cf. BDB s.v. Piel 2c); compare v. 21, where the meaning with an על-PP is "impose." The complement of קום is both null and cataphoric and refers to the ל-PP/infinitive clause at the end of the verb which provides the substance of the obligation.

וְקִבְּלֻ֣ הַיְּהוּדִ֡ים | עֲלֵיהֶ֣ם | וְעַל־זַרְעָ֡ם וְעַ֨ל כָּל־הַנִּלְוִ֤ים עֲלֵיהֶם֙. *Qatal* 3ms (*Qere* 3mp) Piel √קבל and participle mp Niph √לוה. The *Ketiv* קבל does not agree in number with the subject, היהודים; the *Qere*, as a result, is plural קִבְּלוּ. The complement of bivalent קבל is the להיות phrase. The verb לוה occurs twelve times, only once in the Qal (Eccl 8:15) but eleven times in the Niphal (here; Gen 29:34; Num 18:2, 4; Isa 14:1; 56:3, 6; Jer 50:5; Zech 2:15; Ps 83:9; Dan 11:34). Niphal לוה means "to join oneself to" and takes an אל-PP, עם-PP, or על-PP (as here) as its complement that indicates the thing being joined to (HALOT לוה I Niph; cf. BDB לָוָה I Niph; DCH לוה II Niph).

וְלֹ֣א יַעֲב֔וֹר. *Yiqtol* 3ms Qal √עבר. The subject of the verb is probably best understood as the obligation that the Jews are accepting, the content of which is only specified in the ל-PP that follows this clause. On the meaning of Qal עבר here, see comment on the same clause in 1:19. The fact that this clause interrupts the syntax of the larger clause, separating the verb קבל from its ל-PP/infinitive clause complement (see next comment), indicates that it is parenthetical, just as it is used in 1:19.

לִהְי֣וֹת עֹשִׂ֗ים אֵ֣ת שְׁנֵ֤י הַיָּמִים֙ הָאֵ֔לֶּה כִּכְתָבָ֖ם וְכִזְמַנָּ֑ם בְּכָל־שָׁנָ֖ה וְשָׁנָֽה. Inf constr Qal √היה and participle mp Qal √עשה. The ל-PP/infinitive clause is a complement clause that fulfills the valency of קבל. This phrase provides the substance of the obligation that the Jews accepted for themselves and their descendants. The complement of the copular היה is the participial phrase. The bivalent עשה has a null subject and the quantified NP שני הימים האלה as its complement and the two כ-PPs as adjuncts. On the meaning of עשׂה in this context, see comment on v. 21. On בכל שנה ושנה, see comment on 2:11.

9:28 וְהַיָּמִים הָאֵלֶּה נִזְכָּרִים וְנַעֲשִׂים בְּכָל־דּוֹר וָדוֹר
מִשְׁפָּחָה וּמִשְׁפָּחָה מְדִינָה וּמְדִינָה וְעִיר וָעִיר וִימֵי
הַפּוּרִים הָאֵלֶּה לֹא יַעַבְרוּ מִתּוֹךְ הַיְּהוּדִים וְזִכְרָם
לֹא־יָסוּף מִזַּרְעָם׃

In v. 28, the narrator continues in his own voice and timeframe. Until "this day" (i.e., the day on which the narrator is actually speaking) the festival of Purim is observed.

וְהַיָּמִים הָאֵלֶּה נִזְכָּרִים וְנַעֲשִׂים בְּכָל־דּוֹר וָדוֹר מִשְׁפָּחָה וּמִשְׁפָּחָה מְדִינָה וּמְדִינָה וְעִיר וָעִיר. A null copula clause with subject הימים and compound participial (mp Niph √זכר and √עשׂה) phrase complement. The extended ב-PP is an adjunct to נעשׂים. The complement כל is bound to four NPs; each of these consists of a repeated noun, giving the sense "every" (e.g., דור ודור, "every generation"), which is redundant with כל (see comment on 2:11). On the sense of Niphal עשׂה (passive of the Qal, "to observe"), see comment on v. 21.

וִימֵי הַפּוּרִים הָאֵלֶּה לֹא יַעַבְרוּ מִתּוֹךְ הַיְּהוּדִים וְזִכְרָם לֹא־יָסוּף מִזַּרְעָם. *Yiqtol* 3mp Qal √עבר and *yiqtol* 3ms Qal √סוף. On Qal עבר as "to pass away, i.e. cease (to exist)" (DCH עבר I Qal 2i), see also above v. 27 and 1:19. Qal סוף, "to come to an end" (HALOT s.v.; DCH s.v.; BDB s.v.), is basically synonymous. The word order in these two clauses is interesting. In the majority of BH narrative, the modality of the negation would have the verb (and negative) raising to a position before the subject, but in both these clauses the subject precedes the negated verb. Either the subjects are Focus-fronted (which does not seem contextually felicitous, since it would imply a contrast with "other days" that are not be observed or remembered) or the syntax reflects the narrator's native "stronger" subject-verb grammar coming through (see Holmstedt 2013d).

§3: Esther and Mordecai Confirm the Festival (9:29-32)

[29]And Esther, the Queen, the daughter of Abihayil, and Mordecai, the Jew, wrote with every authority in order to confirm this second letter of

Purim. [30]*And one sent letters to all the Jews, to 127 provinces, the kingdom of Ahashverosh, that is, words of peace and truth,* [31]*in order to confirm these days of Purim in their times, as Mordecai the Jew and Esther the Queen enjoined them and as they enjoined themselves and their seed concerning customs of fasting and crying out.* [32]*And the command of Esther established these words of Purim and it was written in the book.*

9:29 וַתִּכְתֹּב אֶסְתֵּר הַמַּלְכָּה בַת־אֲבִיחַיִל וּמָרְדֳּכַי
הַיְּהוּדִי אֶת־כָּל־תֹּקֶף לְקַיֵּם אֵת אִגֶּרֶת הַפּוּרִים
הַזֹּאת הַשֵּׁנִית׃

Esther and Mordecai put the full weight of their authority behind the observance of Purim, apparently in a second letter to the Jews.

וַתִּכְתֹּב אֶסְתֵּר הַמַּלְכָּה בַת־אֲבִיחַיִל וּמָרְדֳּכַי אֶת־כָּל־תֹּקֶף. *Wayyiqtol* 3fs Qal √כתב. Note the lack of full agreement between 3fs verb and the compound subject, which would normally be resolved as 3mp (see also 2:21; 4:3; 5:4, 5, 8; and 7:1). However, as we have described previously, the agreement with the first conjunct of the compound subject is best understood as a literary strategy to signal the primary agent (contra Moore 1971:95). Thus, here the narrator presents Esther as the primary force behind the letter, though Mordecai was clearly involved. את is not the object particle but the preposition meaning "with" (WO 11.2.4; contra Bush, 485). The noun תקף only appears here, in 10:2, and in Dan 11:17. It means "might, power, authority" (DCH s.v.; compare HALOT s.v.), roughly synonymous with גְּבוּרָה (the two are used in conjunction in 10:2; cf. Bergey 1983:152; Moore 1971:95–96).

לְקַיֵּם אֵת אִגֶּרֶת הַפּוּרִים הַזֹּאת הַשֵּׁנִית. Inf constr Piel √קום. As in v. 27, the meaning of Piel קום is "to establish," or in better contextual English, "to confirm" (cf. DCH קום Piel 1b, "confirm, ratify, establish"). This purpose infinitive is an adjunct to תכתב. On אגרת, see comment on 9:26; on פור, see comment on 3:7.

9:30 וַיִּשְׁלַח סְפָרִים אֶל־כָּל־הַיְּהוּדִים אֶל־שֶׁבַע וְעֶשְׂרִים
וּמֵאָה מְדִינָה מַלְכוּת אֲחַשְׁוֵרוֹשׁ דִּבְרֵי שָׁלוֹם
וֶאֱמֶת׃

The second letter about Purim from Esther and Mordecai, mentioned in v. 29, is sent out to the Jews of the kingdom.

וַיִּשְׁלַח סְפָרִים אֶל־כָּל־הַיְּהוּדִים אֶל־שֶׁבַע וְעֶשְׂרִים וּמֵאָה מְדִינָה מַלְכוּת אֲחַשְׁוֵרוֹשׁ דִּבְרֵי שָׁלוֹם וֶאֱמֶת. *Wayyiqtol* 3ms Qal √שלח. The subject is both null and generic, that is, some unknown person in charge of sending out official correspondence (see comment on 2:2). The first אל-PP is the second, locative complement of trivalent שלח; that is, the letters were sent to all Jews. The second אל-PP is an adjunct providing the geographic information reinforcing the widespread distribution of the letters. On שבע ועשׂרים ומאה מדינה see comment on 1:1. The NP מלכות אחשורוש is in apposition to the quantified NP preceding it. And, finally, the NP דברי שלום ואמת is an extraposed appositive to ספרים, by which the content of the letters is specified (so also Bush, 485; Fox 2001:286).

9:31 לְקַיֵּם אֶת־יְמֵי הַפֻּרִים הָאֵלֶּה בִּזְמַנֵּיהֶם כַּאֲשֶׁר
קִיַּם עֲלֵיהֶם מָרְדֳּכַי הַיְּהוּדִי וְאֶסְתֵּר הַמַּלְכָּה
וְכַאֲשֶׁר קִיְּמוּ עַל־נַפְשָׁם וְעַל־זַרְעָם דִּבְרֵי הַצֹּמוֹת
וְזַעֲקָתָם׃

לְקַיֵּם אֶת־יְמֵי הַפֻּרִים הָאֵלֶּה בִּזְמַנֵּיהֶם. Inf constr Piel √קום. This ל-PP/infinitive clause is an adjunct to ישלח in 9:30; it gives the purpose for Esther and Mordecai's action of sending letters. On Piel קום, "to establish," see comment on v. 27 (cf. also comment on v. 21). On the Akkadian loanword פור, see comment on 3:7. The 3mp clitic pronoun in בזמניהם ("in their times") refers to ימי הפרים האלה; that is, these "times" are the season in which the days of Purim occur.

כַּאֲשֶׁר קִיַּם עֲלֵיהֶם מָרְדֳּכַי הַיְּהוּדִי וְאֶסְתֵּר הַמַּלְכָּה. *Qatal* 3ms Piel √קום. This כ-PP (and the next one) is an adjunct to the infinitive לקים. The אשר in כאשר nominalizes the following finite verbal clause so that it might be an acceptable complement for the preposition (also see discussion on כאשר in 2:20). This instance of Piel קום does not mean "establish" but "enjoin" or "impose," as in v. 21. Here again Esther and Mordecai are coupled and used with a singular verb (cf. comment on v. 29), but note that Mordecai, not Esther, comes first and is therefore the primary agent.

וְכַאֲשֶׁר קִיְּמוּ עַל־נַפְשָׁם וְעַל־זַרְעָם. *Qatal* 3mp Piel √קום. Here Piel קום has the more common Hebrew meaning "to establish" (see comments above). The complement of קימו is the NP דברי הצמות וזעקתם, though we have inserted "concerning" in the English translation to make it less awkward. The cliticized NP דברי may connote either general "matters" or more specifically "customs" or "practices" (see DCH דָּבָר 3; HALOT דָּבָר 1); we take the latter to be more contextually fitting.

9:32 וּמַאֲמַר אֶסְתֵּר קִיַּם דִּבְרֵי הַפֻּרִים הָאֵלֶּה וְנִכְתָּב בַּסֵּפֶר׃

According to v. 32, Esther's authority helps to establish Purim as a yearly observance.

וּמַאֲמַר אֶסְתֵּר קִיַּם דִּבְרֵי הַפֻּרִים הָאֵלֶּה. *Qatal* 3ms Piel √קום. On מאמר, subject of קים, see comment on 1:15. On the meaning of Piel קום, see comment on 9:27. Note the subject-verb word order, which may reflect the author's stronger subject-verb grammar, or the nonuse of the *wayyiqtol* either to avoid the suggestion of temporal succession or to signal that the narrative unit has ended (see also 8:14).

וְנִכְתָּב בַּסֵּפֶר. A null copula clause with null subject and participial (ms Niph √כתב) phrase complement. On ספר, see comments on 1:22 and 2:23.

PART IV
Epilogue (10:1-3)

Part IV is a short epilogue to the story of Esther, recounting events and information that are external to the story (cf. Bush, 496). The king sets a tax over his kingdom, the author references another work in which events related to Ahashverosh and Mordecai are told, and Mordecai's enduring character and actions—after the story of Esther—are summarized. The epilogue's focus on Mordecai, to the exclusion of Esther, indicates that he is the true hero of the story (Fox 2001:130).

[1]*And King Ahashverosh set a tax over the land and the islands of the sea.* [2]*And every deed of his authority and his might and the full account of the greatness of Mordecai, whom the king exalted—are they not written on the book of the Words of the Days of the Kings of Media and Persia?* [3]*because Mordecai the Jew was second to King Ahashverosh and great to the Jews, and favored by most of his kin, seeking good for his people, and speaking peace to all his seed.*

10:1 וַיָּשֶׂם הַמֶּלֶךְ אֲחַשְׁרֹשׁ מַס עַל־הָאָרֶץ וְאִיֵּי הַיָּם׃

In v. 1 King Ahashverosh places a tax on his entire kingdom. Why the narrator included this is not explained, nor is it immediately clear. In our opinion, Bush offers the likeliest explanation (495), that the reference to Ahashverosh's הארץ ואיי הים (rather than a more generic מלכות), is intended to emphasize the extent of the king's power, which in turn is meant to contextualize the information in vv. 2-3 concerning Mordecai's position.

וַיָּשֶׂם הַמֶּלֶךְ אֲחַשְׁרֹשׁ מַס עַל־הָאָרֶץ וְאִיֵּי הַיָּם. *Wayyiqtol* 3ms Qal √שׂים. On the valency of שׂים, here with complements מס and על הארץ ואיי הים, see comment on 2:17. The *Ketiv* אחשרש is noticeably shorter than the typical spelling אחשורוש; although in four other cases in Esther (2:21; 3:12; 8:7, 10) the second ו (a *mater lectionis* indicating a long *ō*) is not included, here the first ו, which has consonantal value, is dropped. This leads to the awkward vocalization in the copy-text where both a *sheva* and a *ṣere* appear under the first שׁ. The *Qere*, indicated by this vocalization and indicated in the margin, is the typical spelling. מס typically indicates "forced labor" (HALOT s.v.; DCH מַס I 1). It seems improbable, however, that the king would impose forced labor on most of his subjects (i.e., over his kingdom generally; cf. Fox 2001:129); therefore, the word seems to refer to something less harsh, probably a "tax" (DCH מַס I 2) or "forced payment" (Moore 1971:98). This is the sense carried by מַס in rabbinic Hebrew (Fox 2001:129; cf. Jastrow מַס II).

10:2 וְכָל־מַעֲשֵׂה תָקְפּוֹ וּגְבוּרָתוֹ וּפָרָשַׁת גְּדֻלַּת מָרְדֳּכַי
אֲשֶׁר גִּדְּלוֹ הַמֶּלֶךְ הֲלוֹא־הֵם כְּתוּבִים עַל־סֵפֶר
דִּבְרֵי הַיָּמִים לְמַלְכֵי מָדַי וּפָרָס׃

As in 9:28, the narrator's own timeframe and point of reference comes through in v. 2.

וְכָל־מַעֲשֵׂה תָקְפּוֹ וּגְבוּרָתוֹ וּפָרָשַׁת גְּדֻלַּת מָרְדֳּכַי אֲשֶׁר גִּדְּלוֹ הַמֶּלֶךְ. *Qatal* 3ms Piel √גדל with 3ms clitic pronoun. These two complex NPs are left-dislocated and resumed within the clause proper (which begins with הלוא) by the 3mp pronoun הם. On תקף, see comment on 9:29. On פרשה, see comment on 4:7.

הֲלוֹא־הֵם כְּתוּבִים עַל־סֵפֶר דִּבְרֵי הַיָּמִים לְמַלְכֵי מָדַי וּפָרָס. A null copula with subject הם and participial (mp Qal passive √כתב) phrase complement. The על-PP is an adjunct to the passive כתובים and indicates where the deeds were written down. The PP למלכי מדי ופרס is an NP-internal modifier to ימים.

10:3 כִּי ׀ מָרְדֳּכַי הַיְּהוּדִי מִשְׁנֶה לַמֶּלֶךְ אֲחַשְׁוֵרוֹשׁ וְגָדוֹל
לַיְּהוּדִים וְרָצוּי לְרֹב אֶחָיו דֹּרֵשׁ טוֹב לְעַמּוֹ וְדֹבֵר
שָׁלוֹם לְכָל־זַרְעוֹ׃

The book of Esther ends by describing Mordecai and his enduring legacy as a leader in the Jewish community.

כִּ֣י ׀ מָרְדֳּכַ֣י הַיְּהוּדִ֗י מִשְׁנֶה֙ לַמֶּ֣לֶךְ אֲחַשְׁוֵר֔וֹשׁ. A null copula clause with subject מרדכי and adjective complement משנה. The gentilic היהודי is in apposition to the proper noun מרדכי. If Mordecai were not a known entity within the discourse and his name were common, the appositive gentilic could be restrictive, identifying *which* Mordecai was in mind. However, in this context Mordecai's identity is well established and the appositive is nonrestrictive. Its presence likely serves to remind the audience that it was not simply another courtier who was a hero, but a Jewish one. The whole כי clause, which is compound and encompasses this as well as the following four clauses, grounds the outstanding assertion that a full account of Mordecai's actions were preserved in Persian royal archives—it was because of Mordecai's greatness.

וְגָדוֹל֙ לַיְּהוּדִ֔ים. A null copula clause with null subject (understood as מרדכי from context) and adjectival complement גדול. The ל-PP is an adjunct that specifies the most pertinent beneficiaries of Mordecai's greatness.

וְרָצ֖וּי לְרֹ֣ב אֶחָ֑יו. A null copula clause with participial (ms Qal passive √רצה) phrase complement. Qal רצה means "to take pleasure in" (HALOT s.v. I Qal 1; cf. DCH s.v. I Qal 1). The passive indicates someone in whom pleasure is taken, or in other words, who is favored or favorable to others (cf. HALOT s.v. I Niph; DCH s.v. I Niph). The ל-PP is an adjunct indicating the agent of the passive verb (WO 11.2.10g).

דֹּרֵ֥שׁ טוֹב֙ לְעַמּ֔וֹ. A null copula clause with participial (ms Qal √דרש) phrase complement. The complement of Qal דרש, the thing "sought," is the NP טוב. The PP לעמו is an adjunct to דרש that communicates the beneficiary of the action (cf. WO 11.2.10d).

וְדֹבֵ֥ר שָׁל֖וֹם לְכָל־זַרְעֽוֹ. A null copula clause with participial (ms Qal √דבר) phrase complement. Of 1,144 instances of the verb דבר in the Hebrew Bible, only forty are in the Qal *binyan* (thirty-nine of these are participles; one, in Ps 51:6, is an infinitive). The difference between Qal and Piel דבר is negligible (cf. HALOT דבר II Qal); both mean "to speak." Qal or Piel דבר is often bivalent and with שלום as its complement it may reflect an idiom for effecting peace and wholeness by speech (שלום; see Jer 9:7; Zech 9:10; Pss 35:20; 85:9). Or it may be that דבר should be taken as monovalent (cf. 1:22) and שלום should be understood as NP adjunct used for manner "he spoke peaceably" (cf. 7:9 דבר טוב, "he spoke well").

APPENDIX A
Numeral Syntax in Esther

Order within Compound Numerals

		Order
1:1	שֶׁ֣בַע וְעֶשְׂרִ֔ים וּמֵאָ֖ה	1s-10s-100s
1:4	שְׁמוֹנִ֥ים וּמְאַ֖ת	10s-100s
2:12	שְׁנֵ֣ים עָשָׂ֣ר חֹ֔דֶשׁ	1s-teen
3:7	שְׁתֵּ֣ים עֶשְׂרֵ֔ה	1s-teen
3:7	שְׁנֵים־עָשָׂ֖ר	1s-teen
3:12	בִּשְׁלוֹשָׁ֨ה עָשָׂ֜ר	1s-teen
3:13	בִּשְׁלוֹשָׁ֥ה עָשָׂ֛ר	1s-teen
3:13	שְׁנֵים־עָשָׂ֖ר	1s-teen
8:9	בִּשְׁלוֹשָׁ֨ה וְעֶשְׂרִ֜ים	1s-10s
8:9	שֶׁ֣בַע וְעֶשְׂרִ֣ים וּמֵאָ֔ה	1s-10s-100s
8:12	בִּשְׁלוֹשָׁ֥ה עָשָׂ֛ר	1s-teen
8:12	שְׁנֵים־עָשָׂ֖ר	1s-teen
9:1	בִּשְׁנֵים֩ עָשָׂ֨ר	1s-teen
9:1	בִּשְׁלוֹשָׁ֨ה עָשָׂ֥ר י֜וֹם	1s-teen
9:15	אַרְבָּעָ֤ה עָשָׂר֙	1s-teen
9:16	חֲמִשָּׁ֤ה וְשִׁבְעִים֙	1s-10s
9:17	שְׁלֹשָׁ֥ה עָשָׂ֖ר	1s-teen
9:17	בְּאַרְבָּעָ֤ה עָשָׂר֙	1s-teen
9:18	בִּשְׁלֹשָׁ֥ה עָשָׂ֛ר	1s-teen

***Order within Compound Numerals** (cont.)*

		Order
9:18	בְּאַרְבָּעָה עָשָׂר	1s-teen
9:18	בַּחֲמִשָּׁה עָשָׂר	1s-teen
9:19	אַרְבָּעָה עָשָׂר	1s-teen
9:21	אַרְבָּעָה עָשָׂר	1s-teen
9:21	חֲמִשָּׁה עָשָׂר	1s-teen
9:30	שֶׁבַע וְעֶשְׂרִים וּמֵאָה	1s-10s-100s

Syntax of Ordinal Numeral and Modified Noun

		Order	Structure
1:10	בַּיּוֹם הַשְּׁבִיעִי	noun – number	adjectival
2:14	בֵּית הַנָּשִׁים שֵׁנִי	noun – number	adjectival
2:16	בַּחֹדֶשׁ הָעֲשִׂירִי	noun – number	adjectival
2:19	שֵׁנִית	N/A	(adverbial use)
3:7	בַּחֹדֶשׁ הָרִאשׁוֹן	noun – number	adjectival
3:12	בַּחֹדֶשׁ הָרִאשׁוֹן	noun – number	adjectival
5:1	בַּיּוֹם הַשְּׁלִישִׁי	noun – number	adjectival
7:2	בַּיּוֹם הַשֵּׁנִי	noun – number	adjectival
8:9	בַּחֹדֶשׁ הַשְּׁלִישִׁי	noun – number	adjectival
9:29	אִגֶּרֶת הַפּוּרִים הַזֹּאת הַשֵּׁנִית	noun – number	adjectival

Syntax of Cardinal Numeral and Modified Noun

** = the vowel pointing is our only indication of whether the word is bound or free*

		Order	Structure	Ordinal Use or אחד
1:1	שֶׁבַע וְעֶשְׂרִים וּמֵאָה מְדִינָה	number – noun	apposition	
1:3	בִּשְׁנַת שָׁלוֹשׁ	noun – number	bound	✓
1:4	שְׁמוֹנִים וּמְאַת יוֹם	number – noun	bound	
1:5	שִׁבְעַת יָמִים	number – noun	bound	
1:10	שִׁבְעַת הַסָּרִיסִים	number – noun	bound	
1:14	שִׁבְעַת שָׂרֵי	number – noun	bound	
2:9	שֶׁבַע הַנְּעָרוֹת	number – noun	apposition*	
2:12	שְׁנֵים עָשָׂר חֹדֶשׁ	number – noun	(formally ambiguous)	
2:12	שִׁשָּׁה חֳדָשִׁים	number – noun	apposition	
2:12	שִׁשָּׁה חֳדָשִׁים	number – noun	apposition	
2:16	בִּשְׁנַת־שֶׁבַע	noun – number	bound	✓
2:21	שְׁנֵי־סָרִיסֵי	number – noun	bound	
2:23	שְׁנֵיהֶם	number – noun	bound	
3:7	בִּשְׁנַת שְׁתֵּים עֶשְׂרֵה	noun – number	bound	✓
3:7	לְחֹדֶשׁ שְׁנֵים־עָשָׂר	noun – number	(formally ambiguous)	✓
3:8	עַם־אֶחָד	noun – number	bound*	✓
3:9	עֲשֶׂרֶת אֲלָפִים כִּכַּר־כֶּסֶף	number – noun	apposition	
3:12	בִּשְׁלוֹשָׁה עָשָׂר יוֹם	number – noun	(formally ambiguous)	✓
3:13	בְּיוֹם אֶחָד	noun – number	(formally ambiguous)	✓
3:13	בִּשְׁלוֹשָׁה עָשָׂר	(null noun)	(null noun)	✓
3:13	לְחֹדֶשׁ שְׁנֵים־עָשָׂר	noun – number	(formally ambiguous)	✓
4:11	אַחַת דָּתוֹ	number – noun	(formally ambiguous)	
4:11	שְׁלוֹשִׁים יוֹם	number – noun	(formally ambiguous)	

***Syntax of Cardinal Numeral and Modified Noun** (cont.)*

		Order	Structure	Ordinal Use or אחד
4:16	שְׁלֹשֶׁת יָמִים	number – noun	bound	
5:14	חֲמִשִּׁים אַמָּה	number – noun	(formally ambiguous)	
6:2	שְׁנֵי סָרִיסֵי	number – noun	bound	
7:9	אֶחָד מִן־הַסָּרִיסִים	number – noun	number with NP internal PP	
7:9	חֲמִשִּׁים אַמָּה	number – noun	(formally ambiguous)	
8:9	בִּשְׁלוֹשָׁה וְעֶשְׂרִים	(null noun)	(null noun)	✓
8:9	שֶׁבַע וְעֶשְׂרִים וּמֵאָה מְדִינָה	number – noun	apposition	
8:12	בְּיוֹם אֶחָד	noun – number	(formally ambiguous)	✓
8:12	בִּשְׁלוֹשָׁה עָשָׂר	(null noun)	(null noun)	✓
8:12	לְחֹדֶשׁ שְׁנֵים־עָשָׂר	noun – number	(formally ambiguous)	✓
9:1	בִּשְׁנֵים עָשָׂר חֹדֶשׁ	number – noun	(formally ambiguous)	✓
9:1	בִּשְׁלוֹשָׁה עָשָׂר יוֹם	number – noun	(formally ambiguous)	✓
9:6	חֲמֵשׁ מֵאוֹת אִישׁ	number – noun	(formally ambiguous)	
9:10	עֲשֶׂרֶת בְּנֵי	number – noun	bound	
9:12	חֲמֵשׁ מֵאוֹת אִישׁ	number – noun	(formally ambiguous)	
9:12	עֲשֶׂרֶת בְּנֵי	number – noun	bound	
9:13	עֲשֶׂרֶת בְּנֵי	number – noun	bound	
9:14	עֲשֶׂרֶת בְּנֵי	number – noun	bound	
9:15	בְּיוֹם אַרְבָּעָה עָשָׂר	noun – number	(formally ambiguous)	✓
9:15	שְׁלֹשׁ מֵאוֹת אִישׁ	number – noun	(formally ambiguous)	
9:16	חֲמִשָּׁה וְשִׁבְעִים אָלֶף	(null noun)	(null noun)	

		Order	Structure	Ordinal Use or אחד
9:17	בְּיוֹם־שְׁלֹשָׁה עָשָׂר	noun – number	(formally ambiguous)	✓
9:17	בְּאַרְבָּעָה עָשָׂר	(null noun)	(null noun)	✓
9:18	בִּשְׁלֹשָׁה עָשָׂר	(null noun)	(null noun)	✓
9:18	בְּאַרְבָּעָה עָשָׂר	(null noun)	(null noun)	✓
9:18	בַּחֲמִשָּׁה עָשָׂר	(null noun)	(null noun)	✓
9:19	יוֹם אַרְבָּעָה עָשָׂר	noun – number	(formally ambiguous)	✓
9:21	יוֹם אַרְבָּעָה עָשָׂר	noun – number	(formally ambiguous)	✓
9:21	יוֹם־חֲמִשָּׁה עָשָׂר	noun – number	(formally ambiguous)	✓
9:27	שְׁנֵי הַיָּמִים	number – noun	bound	
9:30	שֶׁבַע וְעֶשְׂרִים וּמֵאָה מְדִינָה	number – noun	apposition	

APPENDIX B
Bergey's Features for Diachronic Analysis

The chart below derives from Bergey 1983. It combines the list of features that Bergey discusses in his thesis, enumerated on pp. 27–28 (grammatical features) and 90–91 (lexical features), with his summary charts on 178–80 and 183–84. Bergey argues that these 22 grammatical and 36 lexical features characterize LBH and that "the book of Esther's place in the linguistic milieu of postexilic BH prose appears to be closer to the latter part of the postexilic literary spectrum than to the earlier" (1983:185).

In our own analysis of the data Bergey used, we concluded that a considerable number of the features lacked enough occurrences ("tokens" in statistical analysis) even to consider for characterizing either Esther's language or any other book. These features are grayed out in the chart below. The remaining, nongrayed features exhibit more potential for statistically significant diachronic variation. However, each feature must be examined independently and using all the ancient Hebrew data available (not just the texts and corpora listed in the chart), along the lines of our preliminary analysis of the four features we examined in "Dating Esther Linguistically" in the Introduction.

	Esth	Earlier Feature	Jer	Ezek	Dan	Ezra	Neh	Chr	DSS	MH
Morphology										
G1	שְׁתִיָּה	שְׁתוֹת, שָׁתֹה								x
G2	מַלְכוּת	מַמְלָכָה	x		x	x	x	x	x	x
G3	חָיָה	חַי		x			x		CD	
G4	אִלּוּ	לוּ								x
G5	בִּזָּה	בַּז			x	x	x	x		
G6	קִיַּם	הֵקִים		x						x
Orthography										
G7	יְרוּשָׁלַיִם	יְרוּשָׁלַם	x					x	x	x
G8	כָּתַב/צִוָּה עַל	כָּתַב/צִוָּה אֶל	x			x		x	x	x
Phonology										
G9	שַׁרְבִיט	שֵׁבֶט								x
Syntax										
G10	infinitive + ב/כ (w/o וַיְהִי/וְהָיָה)	וַיְהִי/וְהָיָה ב/כ + infinitive		x	x	x	x	x	x	
G11	זָהָב וָכֶסֶף	כֶּסֶף וְזָהָב	x	x	x	x		x	x	
G12	אֶסְתֵּר/וַשְׁתִּי הַמַּלְכָּה	הַמַּלְכָּה אֶסְתֵּר/וַשְׁתִּי	x		x	x	x	x	x	x
G13	אֲשֶׁר "that"	כִּי "that"		x	x	x	x	x		שׁ

	Esth	Earlier Feature	Jer	Ezek	Dan	Ezra	Neh	Chr	DSS	MH
G14	אִישׁ הָיָה ... וּשְׁמוֹ	וַיְהִי אִישׁ ... וּשְׁמוֹ								x
G15	כָל־יוֹם וָיוֹם	יוֹם יוֹם						x	x	x
G16	הוּא יְהוּדִי	יְהוּדִי הוּא							x	x
G17	בּוֹ (referential)	לְחֹדֶשׁ								x
G18	אֵין + infinitive	לְבִלְתִּי + infinitive				x		x	x לא	לא
G19	-יוֹתֵר מִ	-מִ								x
G20	גָּבֹהַּ חֲמִשִּׁים אַמָּה	חֲמִשִּׁים אַמָּה גָבֹהַּ	x	x				x	x	x
G21	בְּיוֹם X לְחֹדֶשׁ Y	Y לְחֹדֶשׁ יוֹם X			x	x	x	x	x	
G22	אֵת + suffix decline) in usage(	אֵת + suffix			x	x	x	x	x	x
Lexemes										
L1	יְקָר	כָּבוֹד								
L2	בּוּץ	שֵׁשׁ		x				x		x
L3	רִצְפָּה	מַרְצֶפֶת, קַרְקַע		x				x		x
L4	כֶּתֶר	עֲטָרָה, נֵזֶר								x
L5	מַאֲמַר	דָּבָר, מִצְוָה								x
L6	פִּתְגָם	דָּבָר, מִצְוָה							x	
L7	כְּתָב	מִכְתָּב, סֵפֶר		x	x	x	x	x		x
L8	לָשׁוֹן	שָׂפָה	x	x	x		x		x	x

	Esth	Earlier Feature	Jer	Ezek	Dan	Ezra	Neh	Chr	DSS	MH
L9	גזר (עַל)	צוה (עַל)								x
L10	בהל	חפז, מהר						x		x
L11	שׁנה	חלף	x						x	x
L12	שׁנה מִ-	אַחֵר							BnSr	x
L13	דָּת	מִשְׁפָּט, חֹק ,תּוֹרָה				x				x
L14	זעק/זְעָקָה	צעק/צְעָקָה	x	x			x	x	x	
L15	ישׁט	נטה ,שׁלח							BnSr	x
L16	עמד	קום		x	x	x	x	x	x	x
L17	כנס	אסף ,קבץ		x			x	x	x	x
L18	בְּכֵן	אָז							x	
L19	בַּקָּשָׁה	שְׁאֵלָה				x			x	x
L20	זוע	חרד							x	x
L21	נִבְעַת	ירא ,פחד			x			x	x	x
L22	תַּכְרִיךְ	אַדֶּרֶת etc.								x
L23	שׁלט	משׁל					x		x	x
L24	שְׁאָר	יֶתֶר				x	x	x	x	x
L25	קבל	לקח				x		x	x	x
L26	אִגֶּרֶת	סֵפֶר					x	x		x
L27	זְמָן	מוֹעֵד					x		BnSr	x
L28	תֹּקֶף	חָזְקָה			x					x

	Esth	Earlier Feature	Jer	Ezek	Dan	Ezra	Neh	Chr	DSS	MH
Expressions										
L29	עָשָׂה כִּרְצוֹן				x	x	x		x	x
L30	טוֹב + עַל						x	x		
L31	בִּשְׁנַת X לְמַלְכוּת Y		x		x			x		
L32	וַיִּיטַב (הַדָּבָר) לִפְנֵי						x		x	
L33	כָּשֵׁר הַדָּבָר לִפְנֵי								BnSr	x
L34	יוֹם טוֹב									x
L35	עַל־כָּכָה								x	לכך
L36	קִיֵּם עַל נֶפֶשׁ								x	

APPENDIX C
Glossary of Linguistic Concepts

Like all technical fields, linguistics thrives on specialized terminology. Unfortunately, the terminology often results in some opacity, if not confusion, for biblical and textual studies students and scholars who have not been trained in linguistics. And yet, it is often not desirable to avoid all technical terminology: doing so would not only result in unwieldy verbosity but remove studies like this from their explicit grounding in a linguistic theory and/or specific linguistic studies. To facilitate the nonlinguist's reading of this volume, we provide here a short list of linguistic terms used throughout the introduction and verse-by-verse comments. For convenience and to point the reader to perhaps the single most useful linguistics volume for the nonlinguist, we have based as many definitions as possible on David Crystal's *A Dictionary of Linguistics and Phonetics* (6th ed. Oxford: Blackwell, 2008), with the number in brackets after the entry representing the page number from Crystal.

Adjectival (*see* adjective)

Adjective [11]. "A term used in the grammatical classification of words to refer to the main set of items which specify the attributes of nouns."

Adjunct [12]. "[An] optional or secondary element in a construction: an adjunct may be removed without the structural identity of the rest of the construction being affected."

Adverb(ial) [14]. "A term used in the grammatical classification of words to refer to a heterogeneous group of items whose most frequent function is to specify the mode of action of the verb. ... Syntactically, one can relate adverbs to such questions as *how*, *where*, *when* and *why*, and classify them accordingly, as adverbs of 'manner,' 'place,' 'time,' etc."

Adversative [15]. "In grammar and semantics, a form or construction which expresses an antithetical circumstance. Adversative meaning can be expressed in several grammatical ways (as 'adversatives'), such as through a conjunction (*but*), adverbial (*however, nevertheless, yet, in spite of that, on the other hand*), or preposition (*despite, except, apart from, notwithstanding*)."

Agreement [18]. "A traditional term used in grammatical theory and description to refer to a formal relationship between elements, whereby a form of one word requires a corresponding form of another (i.e., the forms agree)."

Anacoluthon [24]. "A traditional rhetorical term, sometimes encountered in linguistic studies of conversational speech. It refers to a syntactic break in the expected grammatical sequence within a sentence, as when a sentence begins with one construction and remains unfinished, e.g., *The man came and—are you listening?* 'Anacolutha' have come to be especially noticed in linguistic studies as an area of performance features which a grammar of a language would aim to exclude."

Anaphora (also anaphoric pronoun, long-distance anaphora) [25]. "[T]he process or result of a linguistic [item (e.g., pronoun)] deriving its interpretation from some previously expressed unit or meaning (the antecedent). Anaphoric reference is one way of marking the identity between what is being expressed and what has already been expressed. In such a sentence as *He did that there*" each word has an anaphoric reference [... and is thus] anaphorically related to a corresponding [referent] in the preceding context." Anaphora operates within clause boundaries and across clause boundaries, although the greater the distance between the anaphor and its antecedent, the greater potential there is for other constituents that also agree with the anaphor to intervene and create difficulty for interpretation.

Aphaeresis [29]. "A term used in comparative philology, and sometimes in modern phonology, to refer to the deletion of an initial sound in a word; often contrasted with syncope and apocope (*see* Apocopation)."

Apocopation [30]. "A term used in comparative philology, and sometimes in modern phonology, to refer to the deletion of the final element in a word; often contrasts with aphaeresis and syncope."

Apposition(al) [31]. "A traditional term retained in some models of grammatical description for a sequence of units which are constituents at the same grammatical level, and which have an identity or similarity of reference."

Appositive. The second (or third, fourth, etc.) item in an appositional structure.

Appositive Head. The first item in an appositional structure.

Appositive of Attribution. An appositive that describes the head. ("X, being Y")

Appositive of Equivalence. An appositive that is equated with the head. ("X, i.e./namely Y")

Appositive of Inclusion. ("X, e.g./esp. Y")

Nonrestrictive Appositive. An appositive that does not define or limit the head.

Restrictive Appositive. An appositive that defines or limits the head.

Stacked Appositives. An appositive that modifies a head that is already modified by a preceding appositive.

Aspect (*see* Tense-Aspect-Mood)

Asseverative כי. The use of כי to reinforce an affirmation (see JM 164b, although we take it to be a stronger reinforcement than described there). Translatable by English "certainly, indeed."

Assimilation [39]. "A general term in phonetics which refers to the influence exercised by one sound segment upon the articulation of another, so that the sounds become more alike, or identical."

Bound (construction). A morpheme is bound if it "cannot occur on its own as a separate word" [59]. The so-called "construct state" of nouns involves a variant form of the noun that is bound to the following noun (bound construction).

Bivalent (*see* Valency).

Casus Pendens (*see* Dislocation).

Clause [78]. "[A] unit of grammatical organization smaller than the sentence but larger than phrases, words, or morphemes."

Comparative clause. A clause in which two entities are compared (e.g., Prov 22:1, מִכֶּסֶף וּמִזָּהָב חֵן טוֹב, "favor is better than silver and than gold").

Conditional clause [99]. "[A clause] whose semantic role is the expression of hypotheses or conditions."

Nominalized clause. A subordinate clause, typically introduced by כי or אשר, which functions syntactically in the main clause as an NP would. Nominalized clauses can thus function as the subject of the main clause or as a complement of the verb.

Null copula clause (*see* Copula)

Purpose clause. A clause expressing the reason for which an action was taken.

Reduced (*see* Small Clause)

Relative clause. A subordinate clause that modifies a Noun phrase.

Head. The relative head, or pivot, is the word modified by the relative clause.

Headless Relative. A relative clause whose head is null (covert).

Nonrestrictive Relative. A relative clause that does not define or limit the modified Noun phrase.

Restrictive Relative. A relative clause that defines or limits the modified Noun phrase.

Unmarked Relative. A relative clause that is not introduced by a relative pronoun.

Result clause [415]. "[A] clause ... whose meaning expresses the notion of consequence or effect."

Small clause [440]. "[A] clause that contains neither a finite verb nor an infinitival *to*."

Subordinate clause. A clause (of any kind) that is subordinated (see Subordination) within a larger clause.

Temporal clause. A subordinate clause indicating when the events of the main clause occur.

Clitic [80]. "A term used in grammar to refer to a form which resembles a word, but which cannot stand on its own as a normal utterance, being phonologically dependent upon a neighboring word (its host) in a construction."

Complement [92]. "A term used in the analysis of grammatical function, to refer to a major constituent of sentence or clause structure, traditionally associated with 'completing' the action specified by the verb. In its broadest sense, complement therefore is a very general notion, subsuming all obligatory features of the predicate other than the verb, e.g. objects (e.g. *She kicked **the ball***) and adverbials (e.g. *She was **in the garden***)." This notion of *obligatory completion* extends to PPs and NPs as well, so that these phrases also can require complements (e.g., *to **the bank***).

Concessive [98]. "In grammar, referring to a word or construction which expresses the meaning of 'concession.' The point expressed in the main clause continues to be valid despite the point being made in the subordinate clause (the concessive clause). In English, the most widely used markers of concession are *although* and *though*."

Conjunction [101]. "[An] item or a process whose primary function is to connect words or other constructions."

Constituent [104]. "[A] linguistic unit which is a functional component of a larger construction."

Construct (*see* Bound [construction])

Copula (verbal, nonverbal, null) [116]. "[A] linking verb, i.e., a verb which has little independent meaning, and whose main function is to relate other elements of clause structure, especially subject and complement." In Hebrew, the verbal copula is היה. The verbal copula is omitted more often than not in favor of a null copula (i.e., a phonologically unexpressed copula) that defaults to the tense-aspect of the discourse context. Null copula clauses are variously referred to as "nominal clauses" or "verbless clauses." A nonverbal copula is an overt constituent (i.e., not a null item, but an overt item such as a pronoun) that is used to link the two components of a copular clause. See Pustet 2003; also see Doron 1986, Rothstein 1995, Kummerow 2011, and Holmstedt and Jones 2014 for further discussion of the copula in Hebrew.

Covert (*see* Null)

Deixis/deictic [133]. The process of (and as an adjective, the words used in) "[referring] directly to the personal, temporal or locational characteristics of the situation within which an utterance takes place, whose meaning is thus relative to that situation"; e.g., the first and second person pronouns אֲנִי, אֲנַחְנוּ, אַתָּה, אַתְּ, אַתֶּם, and אַתֶּן are deictic, as are the demonstrative זֹאת, זֶה, and אֵלֶּה, and also nonpronominal words such as הִנֵּה and עַתָּה. Within a discourse, deixis is relativized and thus concerns "backwards or forwards" reference (anaphora and cataphora), for example, English "that, the following, the former." See Diessel 1999 for a typological discussion of demonstratives and deixis.

Demonstrative [135]. "[A] class of items whose function is to point to an entity in the situation or elsewhere in a sentence." The Hebrew items זֶה, זֹאת, and אֵלֶּה (and when used to modify nouns, הוּא, הִיא, הֵם, and הֵן) "have their reference fixed by gestures, speaker knowledge, or other means. Depending on their grammatical role, they are often called 'demonstrative determiners'" (בַּיּוֹם הַהוּא "on that day") "or 'demonstrative pronouns'" (מַה זֹּאת עָשִׂית "what is this you have done?"). "Demonstratives fall within the general class of deictic expressions, and are sometimes contrasted with 'pure indexicals.'" See Diessel 1999 for a typological discussion of demonstratives.

Dislocation (Left and Right) [273], s.v. left dislocation; 418, s.v. right dislocation]. "[A] type of sentence in which one of the constituents appears in initial (left) [or final (right)] position and its canonical position is filled by a pronoun or a full lexical noun phrase with the same reference, e.g. *John, I like him/the old chap*" or "*I know that woman/her, Julie.*" See Gross 1987, Naudé; Holmstedt 2012, 2014a.

Exclamative [177]. "Traditionally, an exclamation refers to any emotional utterance, usually lacking the grammatical structure of a full sentence, and marked by strong intonation, e.g. *Gosh! Good grief!*" The most common exclamative in Hebrew is the deictic הִנֵּה, though the exclamative use of כִּי also occurs (this is sometimes referred to as the "asseverative" כי).

Extraposition (extraposed) [182]. "A term used in grammatical analysis to refer to the process or result of moving (or extraposing) an element from its normal position to a position at or near the end of the sentence."

Focus (fronting) [192–93]. "A term used by some linguists in a two-part analysis of sentences which distinguishes between the information assumed by speakers, and that which is at the centre (or 'focus') of their communicative interest; 'focus' in this sense is opposed to presupposition. (The contrast between given and new information makes an analogous distinction.) E.g., in the sentence *It was **Mary** who came to tea, Mary* is the focus (as the intonation contour helps to signal). Taking such factors into account is an important aspect of inter-sentence relationships: it would not be possible to have the above sentence as the answer to the question *What did Mary do?* but only to *Who came to tea?*" In Hebrew, constituents are typically fronted (*see* Fronting) to indicate Focus.

Fronting [201]. "[Any] transformation which transposes a constituent from the middle or end of a string to initial position. E.g., the rule of '*Wh*-fronting' places a *Wh*-phrase (e.g. *where, which books*) in initial position, transposing it from the underlying noninitial position (cf. *John walked there → John walked where → where did John walk*)."

Gapping [166]. Gapping occurs when "[an unambiguously specifiable] part of the structure has been omitted, which is recoverable from a scrutiny of the context."

Genitive. A term properly used to describe a particular *case*, borrowed in the study of Hebrew (particularly in WO's description) to describe various way in which a noun can be modified along the lines of English *of*.

Gnomic. A term used to describe a clause, or a verb within a clause, that communicates a general truth or maxim.

Grammaticalization [218, s.v. grammar]. The process whereby a word with semantic content is used to express grammatical functions. "An example of grammaticalization (grammaticization) is the use of the English motion verb *go*, as in *She is going to London*, which has become a marker of tense in *It's going to rain*." A case of grammaticalization in Hebrew concerns the word אֲשֶׁר, which seems have been a noun "step, place" in prebiblical Hebrew (based on Semitic evidence) but has grammaticalized into a function introducing nominal (relative, complement) clauses. See Holmstedt 2007 for a discussion of אשר and grammaticalization.

Interrogative [251]. "A term used in the grammatical classification of sentence types, and usually seen in contrast to declarative. It refers to verb forms or sentence/clause types typically used in the expression of questions, e.g. the inverted order of *is he coming?* or the use of an interrogative word (or simply 'interrogative'), often subclassified as interrogative adjectives (e.g. *which*), adverbs (e.g. *why*) and pronouns (e.g. *who*)."

Inversion [254]. "A term used in grammatical analysis to refer to the process or result of syntactic change in which a specific sequence of constituents is seen as the reverse of another."

Linguistic Typology [499, s.v. typological linguistics]. "A branch of linguistics which studies the structural similarities between languages, regardless of their history, as part of an attempt to establish a satisfactory classification, or typology, of languages. Typological comparison is thus distinguished from the historical comparison of languages—the province of comparative philology and historical linguistics—and its groupings may not coincide with those set up by the historical method. For example, in respect of the paucity of inflectional endings, English is closer to Chinese than it is to Latin."

Mood (*see* Tense-Aspect-Mood)

Monophthongization [311]. "[A] change in vowel quality from a diphthong[, a vowel which changes in quality during a syllable,] to a monophthong[, a vowel where there is no detectable change in quality during a syllable]."

Monovalent (*see* Valency)

Nominal Clause (*see* Copula)

Noun Phrase (NP) [367, 333]. "A single element of structure [consisting] minimally of the noun"; NPs may consist of a single noun (e.g., דָּבָר, "thing") or may contain additional constituents that modify the noun (e.g., הַדָּבָר הַקָּשֶׁה אֲשֶׁר אֶעֱשֶׂה מָחָר, "the difficult thing that I am going to do tomorrow").

Null copula (*see* Copula)

Null (covert) [335]. "An application in generative grammar of the mathematical use of this term, with the general meaning of empty or zero, as in 'null subject' (a phonologically empty constituent, PRO) or 'null element'"; in other words, a constituent that exists but is not phonologically overt (verbalized).

Null (covert) Complement. A phrase used to refer to a constituent that must exist, given the argument structure of a verb or noun phrase, but is not phonologically overt. Null complements may or may not be reconstructable from context.

Null (covert) Subject. A phrase used to refer to a subject that must exist, given the argument structure of a verb, but is not phonologically overt. Null subjects may or may not be reconstructable from context.

Null (covert) Verb. A verb that is not phonologically overt (*see* Gapping).

Overt (*see* Null)

Partitive. A preposition used to "[refer] to part of the noun (or noun equivalent) after the preposition" (WO 11.2.11e) (e.g., אֶחָד מִן־הַסָּרִיסִים, "one of the eunuchs").

Pivot (*see* Clause, Relative Clause, Head)

Predicate. [381]. "[A] major constituent of sentence structure ... containing all obligatory constituents other than the subject," within a "two-part analysis" of clauses (*see* Subject).

Prepositional Phrase (PP) [383]. "[The] set of items which typically precede noun phrases (often single nouns or pronouns), to form a single constituent of structure." "[Prepositions] can combine with not only an NP but also a PP (e.g. *since before breakfast*) [or] a clause (e.g. *since they finished their breakfast*)."

Pronoun [391–92]. "A term ... referring to the closed set of items that can be used to substitute [syntactically] for a noun phrase." Pronouns are often divided into classes, such as personal, demonstrative, interrogative, reflexive, indefinite, and relative. Additionally, anaphor and deixis differences indicate that first and second person pronouns must be distinguished from third person pronouns. Such a divide is clear in Hebrew, where the third person subject pronouns הוּא, הִיא, הֵם, and הֵן are also used as distal demonstratives and, as argued above, nonverbal copulas. See Bhat 2004 on pronouns in general and Holmstedt 2013g for a discussion of pronouns in Phoenician that is directly applicable to BH.

Proper Noun (PN) [392]. "[T]he name of an individual person, place, etc."

Relative Clause (*see* Clause)

Resumptive (resumption) [415]. "[An] element or structure which repeats or in some way recapitulates the meaning of a prior element." In Hebrew, resumption occurs especially in relative clauses, where pronouns are the typical resumptive element, e.g., הָאָרֶץ אֲשֶׁר עָבַרְנוּ בָהּ (Num 13:32, "the land that they explored *it*").

Small Clause (*see* Clause)

Spirantization (lenition) [274]. "[A] weakening in the overall strength of a sound[.] Typically, [spirantization] involves the change from a stop to a fricative, a fricative to an approximant, a voiceless sound to a voiced sound, or a sound being reduced (lenite) to zero." In BH, spirantization occurs with the consonants ב, ג, ד, כ, פ, and ת (see JM §19).

Subject [461]. "[A] major constituent of sentence or clause structure, traditionally associated with the 'doer' of an action, as in ***The cat*** *bit the dog*. [Many] approaches make a twofold distinction in sentence analysis between subject and predicate" (*see* Predicate).

Subordination [462]. "A term used in grammatical analysis to refer to the process or result of linking linguistic units so that they have different syntactic status, one being dependent upon the other, and usually a constituent of the other."

Substantive [463]. A term referring to "items which function as nouns, though lacking some of the formal characteristics of that class (cf. the 'substantival function' of adjectives, *in the poor*, *the rich*, etc.)."

Tense (*see* Tense-Aspect-Mood)

Tense-Aspect-Mood (TAM). A bundle of features present in verbs.

Aspect [38]. "A category used in the grammatical description of verbs (along with tense and mood), referring primarily to the way the grammar marks the duration or type of temporal activity denoted by the verb."

Mood [312]. "Mood (modality, or mode) refers to a set of syntactic and semantic contrasts signaled by alternative paradigms of the verb, e.g. indicative (the unmarked form), subjunctive, imperative. Semantically, a wide range of meanings is involved, especially attitudes on the part of the speaker towards the factual content of the utterance, e.g. uncertainty, definiteness, vagueness, possibility."

Tense [479]. "A category used in the grammatical description of verbs (along with aspect and mood), referring primarily to the way the grammar marks the time at which the action denoted by the verb took place."

Topic (fronting) [48]. "[T]he entity (person, thing, etc.) about which something is said, whereas the further statement made about this entity is the comment." In Hebrew, constituents are fronted (see Fronting) to indicate Topic.

Trivalent (*see* Valency)

Valency [507]. "The number and type of bonds which syntactic elements may form with each other"; in particular in this book, the number of arguments necessary to complete a verb phrase.

Avalent. The valency of a verb requiring no arguments [subject and complements].

Monovalent. The valency of a verb requiring one argument.

Bivalent. The valency of a verb requiring two arguments.

Trivalent. The valency of a verb requiring three arguments.

Verb Phrase (VP). The phrase of which the verb is the head, that is, the predicate of a verbal clause. (*see* Predicate)

Verbless Clause (*see* Copula)

BIBLIOGRAPHY

Abraham, Kathleen. 2011. "The Reconstruction of Jewish Communities in the Persian Empire: The Āl-Yahūdu Clay Tablets." Pages 261–64 in *Light and Shadows—The Catalog—The Story of Iran and the Jews*, edited by Hagai Segev, and Asaf Schor. Tel Aviv: Beit Hatfutsot.

Aejmelaeus, Anneli. 1986. "Function and Interpretation of KY in Biblical Hebrew." *Journal of Biblical Literature* 105 (2): 193–209.

Andersen, Francis I. 1971. "Passive and Ergative in Hebrew." Pages 1–15 in *Near Eastern Studies in Honor of William Foxwell Albright*, edited by H. Goedicke. Baltimore: The Johns Hopkins Press.

Andersen, Francis I., and A. Dean Forbes. 1983. "Prose Particle Counts of the Hebrew Bible." Pages 165–83 in *The Word of the Lord Shall Go Forth: Essays in Honor of David Noel Freedman in Celebration of His Sixtieth Birthday*, edited by Carol Meyers, and M. O'Connor. Winona Lake, Ind.: Eisenbrauns.

Bailey, Charles-James N. 1973. *Variation and Linguistic Theory*. Arlington, Va.: Center for Applied Linguistics.

Bauer, H. and P. Leander. 1922. *Historische Grammatik der hebräischen Sprache des Alten Testamentes*. Halle: Max Niemeyer.

Beaulieu, Paul-Alain. 2011. "Yahwistic Names in Light of Late Babylonian Onomastics." Pages 245–66 in *Judah and the Judeans in the Achaemenid Period: Negotiating Identity in an International Context*, edited by Oded Lipschits, Gary N. Knoppers, and Manfred Oeming. Winona Lake, Ind.: Eisenbrauns.

Bekins, Peter J. 2013. "Non-Prototypical Uses of the Definite Article in Biblical Hebrew." *Journal of Semitic Studies* 58 (2): 225–40.

Bendavid, Aba. 1967. *The Language of the Bible and the Language of the Mishna*. 2 vols. Corrected and revised ed. Tel Aviv: Devir. (Hebrew)

Bergey, Ronald L. 1983. "The Book of Esther—Its Place in the Linguistic Milieu of Post-Exilic Biblical Hebrew Prose: A Study of Late Biblical Hebrew." Ph.D. diss., Dropsie College.

———. 1984. "Late Linguistic Features in Esther." *Jewish Quarterly Review* 75 (1): 66–78.

Berlin, Adele. 2001. *Esther*. The JPS Bible Commentary. Philadelphia: The Jewish Publication Society.

Bhat, D.N.S. 2004. *Pronouns*. Oxford: Oxford University Press.

Blau, Joshua. 2010. *Phonology and Morphology of Biblical Hebrew*. Linguistic Studies in Ancient West Semitic 2. Winona Lake, Ind.: Eisenbrauns.

Bergsträsser, G. 1918. *Hebräische Grammatik*. 2 vols. Leipzig: F. C. W. Vogel.

Bickerman, Elias. 1967. *Four Strange Books of the Bible*. New York: Schocken.

Bordreuil, P., and D. Pardee. 2009. *A Manual of Ugaritic*. Linguistic Studies in Ancient West Semitic 3. Winona Lake, Ind.: Eisenbrauns.

Brosius, Maria. 2006. *The Persians: An Introduction*. New York: Routledge.

Brown, Francis, S. R. Driver, and C. A. Briggs. 1979. *The New Brown-Driver-Briggs Hebrew-English Lexicon*. Peabody, Mass.: Hendrickson. [= BDB]

Bush, Frederic W. 1996. *Ruth, Esther*. Word Biblical Commentary 9. Dallas, Tex.: Word Books.

Buth, Randall. 1999. "Word Order in the Verbless Clause: A Generative-Functional Approach." Pages 79–108 in *The Verbless Clause in Biblical Hebrew: Linguistic Approaches*, edited by Cynthia L. Miller. Linguistics Studies in Ancient West Semitic 1. Winona Lake, Ind.: Eisenbrauns.

Bybee, Joan L. 2002. "Main Clauses are Innovative, Subordinate Clauses are Conservative: Consequences for the Nature of Constructions." Pages 1–18 in *Complex Sentences in Grammar and Discourse: Essays in Honor of Sandra A. Thompson*, edited by Joan L. Bybee, and Michael Noonan. Amsterdam: John Benjamins.

Campbell, Lyle. 2004. *Historical Linguistics: An Introduction*. 2nd ed. Edinburgh: Edinburgh University Press.

Carmignac, Jean. 1966. "Un aramaisme biblique et qumranien: l'infinitif place après son complément d'objet." *Revue de Qumran* 20 (5): 503–20.

Carnie, Andrew. 2006. *Syntax: A Generative Introduction*. 2nd ed. Malden, Mass.: Blackwell.

———. 2008. *Constituent Structure*. Oxford Surveys in Syntax and Morphology 5. Oxford: Oxford University Press.

Clines, David J. A. 1984a. *The Esther Scroll: The Story of the Story*. Journal for the Study of the Old Testament Supplement Series 30. Sheffield: JSOT Press.

———. 1984b. *Ezra, Nehemiah, Esther*. The New Century Bible Commentary. Grand Rapids: Eerdmans.

———. 1993–2012. *The Dictionary of Classical Hebrew*. 8 vols. Sheffield: Sheffield Academic. [= DCH]

Cook, John A. 2004. "The Semantics of Verbal Pragmatics: Clarifying the Roles of *Wayyiqtol* and *Weqatal* in Biblical Hebrew Prose." *Journal of Semitic Studies* 49: 247–73.

———. 2005. "Genericity, Tense, and Verbal Patterns in the Sentence Literature of Proverbs." Pages 117–33 in *Seeking Out the Wisdom of the Ancients: Essays Offered to Honor Michael V. Fox on the Occasion of His Sixty-Fifth Birthday*, edited by Ronald L. Troxel, Kelvin G. Friebel, and Dennis R. Magary. Winona Lake, Ind.: Eisenbrauns.

———. 2006. "The Finite Verbal Forms in Biblical Hebrew Do Express Aspect." *Journal of the Ancient Near Eastern Society* 30: 21–35.

———. 2008. "The Hebrew Participle and Stative in Typological Perspective." *Journal of Northwest Semitic Languages* 34 (1): 1–19.

———. 2012. *Time and the Biblical Hebrew Verb: The Expression of Tense, Aspect, and Modality in Biblical Hebrew*. Linguistic Studies in Ancient West Semitic 7. Winona Lake, Ind.: Eisenbrauns.

———. 2013. "The Verb in Qohelet." Pages 309–42 in *The Words of the Wise Are Like Goads: Engaging Qohelet in the 21st Century*, edited by Mark J. Boda, Tremper Longman, III, and Cristian G. Rata. Winona Lake, Ind.: Eisenbrauns.

Creason, Stuart. 1991. "Discourse Constraints on Null Complements in Biblical Hebrew." *University of Chicago Working Papers in Linguistics* 7: 18–47.

Crystal, David. 1970. "New Perspectives for Language Study: I Stylistics." *English Language Teaching* 24: 99–106.

———. 1987. "Style: The Varieties of English." Pages 199–222 in *The English Language*, edited by W. F. Bolton, and David Crystal. London: Penguin.

———. 2008. *A Dictionary of Linguistics and Phonetics*. 6th ed. Oxford: Blackwell.

Davidson, A. B. 1901. *Introductory Hebrew Grammar: Hebrew Syntax*. Edinburgh: T&T Clark.

Diessel, Holger. 1999. *Demonstratives: Form, Function, and Grammaticalization*. Typological Studies in Language 42. Amsterdam: John Benjamins.

Doron, E. 1986. "The Pronominal 'Copula' as Agreement Clitic." Pages 313–65 in *The Syntax of Pronominal Clitics*, edited by Hagit Borer. New York: Academic.

———. 2000. "VSO and Left-Conjunct Agreement: Biblical Hebrew vs. Modern Hebrew." Pages 75–95 in *The Syntax of Verb-Initial Languages*, edited by Andrew Carnie and Eithne Guilfoyle. Oxford: Oxford University Press.

Dresher, Bezalel Elan. 1994. "The Prosodic Basis of the Tiberian Hebrew System of Accents." *Language* 70 (1): 1–52.

———. 2012. "Methodological Issues in the Dating of Linguistic Forms: Considerations from the Perspective of Contemporary Linguistic Theory." Pages 19–38 in *Diachrony in Biblical Hebrew*, edited by Cynthia L. Miller-Naudé and Ziony Zevit. Winona Lake, Ind.: Eisenbrauns.

Driver, Godfrey R. 1954. "Problems and Solutions." *Vetus Testamentum* 4: 225–45.

Driver, Samuel R. 1892. *A Treatise on the Use of the Tenses in Hebrew and Some Other Syntactical Questions*. Reprint, with introductory essay by W. Randall Garr. 3rd ed. Grand Rapids: Eerdmans.

Duchesne-Guillemin, Jacques. 1953. "Les noms des eunuques d'Assuérus." *Muséon* 66: 105–8.

Ehrlich, A. B. 1914. *Randglossen zur hebräischen Bibel textkritisches, sprachliches, und sachliches*, VII. Leipzig: Hinrichs.

Eskhult, Mats. 2000. "Verbal Syntax in Late Biblical Hebrew." Pages 84–93 in *Diggers at the Well*, edited by T. Muraoka and J. F. Elwolde. Leiden: Brill.

———. Forthcoming. "The Literary Style and Linguistic Stage of Ruth as Compared to Esther." In *Discourse, Dialogue, and Debate in the Bible: Essays in Honour of Frank Polak*, edited by Athalyah Brenner-Idan, Sheffield: Sheffield Phoenix.

Ewald, Heinrich. 1891. *Syntax of the Hebrew Language of the Old Testament*. Translated by James Kennedy. Edinburgh: T&T Clark.

Fassberg, Steven E. 2008. "The Infinitive Absolute as Finite Verb and Standard Literary Hebrew of the Second Temple Period." Pages 47–60 in *Conservatism and Innovation in the Hebrew Language of the Hellenistic Period*, edited by J. Joosten and J. S. Rey. Leiden: Brill.

Forbes, A. Dean. 2012. "The Diachrony Debate: Perspectives from Pattern Recognition and Meta-Analysis." *Hebrew Studies* 53: 7–42.

———. 2014. "On Dating Biblical Hebrew Texts: Constraints and Options." Paper presented at the Conference of the International Syriac Language Project. July 2, St. Petersburg.

Forbes, A. Dean, and Francis I. Andersen. 2012. "Dwelling on Spelling." Pages 127–46 in *Diachrony in Biblical Hebrew*, edited by Cynthia L. Miller-Naudé and Ziony Zevit. Winona Lake, Ind.: Eisenbrauns.

Fox, Michael V. 1991. *The Redaction of the Books of Esther: On Reading Composite Texts*. The Society of Biblical Literature Monograph Series 40. Atlanta: Scholars Press.

———. 2001. *Character and Ideology in the Book of Esther*. Grand Rapids: Eerdmans. [1st ed. 1991]

Garr, W. Randall. 1991. "Affectedness, Aspect, and Biblical Hebrew *'et*." *Zeitschrift für Althebraistik* 4: 119–34.

Gehman, Henry S. 1924. "Notes on the Persian Words in the Book of Esther." *Journal of Biblical Literature* 43: 321–28.

Gibson, J. C. L. 1994. *Davidson's Introductory Hebrew Grammar: Syntax*. Edinburgh: T&T Clark.

Givón, Talmy. 1991. "The Evolution of Dependent Clause Morpho-syntax in Biblical Hebrew." Pages 257–310 in *Approaches to Grammaticalization*, edited by E. C. Traugott and B. Heine. Amsterdam: John Benjamins.

Gordis, Robert. 1976. "Studies in the Esther Narrative." *Journal of Biblical Literature* 95 (1): 43–58.

Gordon, Elizabeth, and Mark Williams. 1998. "Raids on the Articulate: Code-Switching, Style-Shifting and Post-Colonial Writing." *The Journal of Commonwealth Literature* 33 (2): 75–96.

Greenstein, Edward L. 2003. "The Language of Job and Its Poetic Function." *Journal of Biblical Literature* 122 (4): 651–66.

Gross, Walter. 1987. *Die Pendenskonstruktion im Biblischen Hebräisch*. Studien zum althebräischen Satz I. Arbeiten zu Text und Sprache im Alten Testament 27. St. Ottilien: EOS.

Hale, Mark. 2007. *Historical Linguistics: Theory and Method*. Blackwell Textbooks in Linguistics 21. Malden, Mass.: Blackwell.

Harris, Alice C., and Lyle Campbell. 1995. *Historical Syntax in Cross-Linguistic Perspective*. Cambridge Studies in Linguistics 74. Cambridge: Cambridge University Press.

Haupt, Paul. 1908. "Critical Notes on Esther." *The American Journal of Semitic Languages and Literatures* 24 (2): 97–186.

Hengel, Martin. 1977. *Crucifixion*. Translated by John Bowden. Philadelphia: Fortress.

Hetzron, Robert. 1977. "Innovations in the Semitic Numeral System." *Journal of Semitic Studies* 22 (2): 167–201.

Holmstedt, Robert D. 2000. "The Phonology of Classical Hebrew: A Linguistic Study of Long Vowels and Syllable Structure." *Zeitschrift für Althebraistik* 13 (2): 145–56.

———. 2002. "The Relative Clause in Biblical Hebrew: A Linguistic Analysis." Ph.D. diss., University of Wisconsin-Madison.

———. 2005. "Word Order in the Book of Proverbs." Pages 135–54 in *Seeking Out the Wisdom of the Ancients: Essays Offered to Honor Michael V. Fox on the Occasion of His Sixty-Fifth Birthday*, edited by Ronald L. Troxel, Kelvin G. Friebel, and Dennis R. Magary. Winona Lake, Ind.: Eisenbrauns.

———. 2007. "The Etymologies of Hebrew *ʾăšer* and *šeC-*." *Journal of Near Eastern Studies* 66 (3): 177-91.

———. 2008. "The Restrictive Syntax of Genesis i I." *Vetus Testamentum* 58: 56–67.

———. 2009a. "Word Order and Information Structure in Ruth and Jonah: A Generative-Typological Analysis." *Journal of Semitic Studies* 54 (1): 111–39.

———. 2009b. "So-Called 'First-Conjunct Agreement' in Biblical Hebrew." Pages 105–29 in *Afroasiatic Studies in Memory of Robert Hetzron: Proceedings of the 35th Annual Meeting of the North American Conference on Afroasiatic Linguistics* (NACAL 35), edited by Charles Häberl. Newcastle on Tyne: Cambridge Scholars.

———. 2009c. "אֲנִי וְלִבִּי: The Syntactic Encoding of the Collaborative Nature of Qohelet's Experiment." *Journal of Hebrew Scriptures* 9 (29): 1–26.

———. 2010. *Ruth: A Handbook on the Hebrew Text*. Baylor Handbook on the Hebrew Bible. Waco, Tex.: Baylor University Press.

———. 2011. "The Typological Classifications of the Hebrew of Genesis: Subject-Verb or Verb-Subject?" *The Journal of Hebrew Scriptures* 11 (14): 1–39.

———. 2012. "Historical Linguistics and Biblical Hebrew." Pages 97–124 in *Diachrony in Biblical Hebrew*, edited by Cynthia L. Miller-Naudé and Ziony Zevit. Winona Lake, Ind.: Eisenbrauns.

———. 2013a. "Relative Clause: Biblical Hebrew." Pages 350–57 in *Encyclopedia of Hebrew Language and Linguistics*, Vol. 3: *P–Z*, edited by Geoffrey Khan. Leiden: Brill.

———. 2013b. "Hypotaxis." Pages 220–22 in *Encyclopedia of Hebrew Language and Linguistics*, Vol. 2: *G–O*, edited by Geoffrey Khan. Leiden: Brill.

———. 2013c. "Pro-drop." Pages 265–67 in *Encyclopedia of Hebrew Language and Linguistics*, Vol. 3: *P–Z*, edited by Geoffrey Khan. Leiden: Brill.

———. 2013d. "Investigating the Possible Verb-Subject to Subject-Verb Shift in Ancient Hebrew: Methodological First Steps." *Kleine Untersuchungen zur Sprache des Alten Testaments und seiner Umwelt* 15: 3–31.

———. 2013e. "The Nexus between Text Criticism and Linguistics: A Case Study from Leviticus." *Journal of Biblical Literature* 132 (3): 473–94.

———. 2013f. The Grammar of שׁ and אשר in Qohelet. Pages 283–307 in *The Words of the Wise Are Like Goads: Engaging Qohelet in the 21st Century*, edited by Mark J. Boda, Tremper Longman, III, and Cristian G. Rata. Winona Lake, Ind.: Eisenbrauns.

———. 2013g. "The Syntax and Pragmatics of Subject Pronouns in Phoenician." Pages 84–110 in *Linguistic Studies in Phoenician Grammar: In Memory of J. Brian Peckham*, edited by Robert D. Holmstedt and Aaron Schade. Winona Lake, Ind.: Eisenbrauns.

———. 2014a. "Constituents at the Edge in Biblical Hebrew." *Kleine Untersuchungen zur Sprache des Alten Testaments und seiner Umwelt* 17: 1–50.

———. 2014b. "Analyzing זֶה Grammar and Reading זֶה Texts of Ps 68:9 and Judg 5:5." *Journal of Hebrew Scriptures* 14 (8):1-26.

———. Forthcoming. *The Relative Clause in Biblical Hebrew.* Linguistic Studies in Ancient West Semitic. Winona Lake, Ind.: Eisenbrauns.

Holmstedt, Robert D., and Andrew R. Jones. 2014. "The Pronoun in Tripartite Verbless Clauses in Biblical Hebrew: Resumption for Left-Dislocation or Pronominal Copula?" *Journal of Semitic Studies* 59 (1): 53–89.

Huesman, John. 1956. "Finite Uses of the Infinitive Absolute." *Biblica* 37: 271–95.

Hurvitz, Avi. 1995. "Continuity and Innovation in Biblical Hebrew—The Case of 'Semantic Change' in Post-Exilic Writings." *Abr-Nahrain Supplement* 4: 1–10.

———. 2000. "The Recent Debate on Late Biblical Hebrew: Solid Data, Experts' Opinions, and Inconclusive Evidence." *Hebrew Studies* 47: 191–210.

Jastrow, Marcus. 1903. *A Dictionary of the Targumim, the Talmud Balbi and Yerushalmi, and the Midrashic Literature.* New York: G. P. Putnam's Sons. [= Jastrow]

Jobes, Karen H. 1996. *The Alpha-Text of Esther: Its Character and Relationship to the Masoretic Text.* Atlanta: Scholars Press.

———. 1999. *Esther*. The NIV Application Commentary 4. Grand Rapids: Zondervan.

Jones, Andrew R. 2011. "Apposition in Biblical Hebrew." Unpublished manuscript.

———. 2012. "Word Order in Daniel 8–12: Differentiation From Imperial Aramaic." Paper read at the Annual Meeting of the Society of Biblical Literature, Chicago, November 20.

Joosten, Jan. 1998. "The Functions of the Semitic D Stem: Biblical Hebrew Materials for a Comparative-Historical Approach." *Orientalia* 67 (2): 202–30.

———. 2002. "Do the Finite Verbal Forms in Biblical Hebrew Express Aspect?" *Journal of the Ancient Near Eastern Society* 29: 49–70.

Joüon, Paul. 1947. *Grammaire de l'Hébreu Biblique*. Rome: Pontifical Biblical Institute.

Joüon, Paul, and Takamitsu Muraoka. 2006. *A Grammar of Biblical Hebrew*. 2nd ed. Rome: Pontifical Biblical Institute. [= JM]

Kautzsch, Emil. 1910. *Gesenius' Hebrew Grammar*. Translated by A. E. Cowley. 2nd Eng. ed. Oxford: Clarendon. [= GKC]

Keil, C. F. 1873. *The Books of Ezra, Nehemiah, and Esther*. Translated by Sophia Taylor. Edinburgh: T&T Clark.

Kieviet, P. J. 1997. "The Infinitive Construct in Late Biblical Hebrew: An Investigation into the Synoptic Parts of Chronicles." *Dutch Studies on Near Eastern Languages and Cultures* 3: 45–73.

Koehler, Ludwig, Walter Baumgartner, and Johann J. Stamm, eds. 2001. *The Hebrew and Aramaic Lexicon of the Old Testament*. Translated and edited under the supervision of M. E. J. Richardson. Leiden: Brill. [= HALOT]

Kroch, Anthony. 1989. "Reflexes of Grammar in Patterns of Language Change." *Language Variation and Change* 1: 199–244.

———. 2001. "Syntactic Change." Pages 699–729 in *The Handbook of Contemporary Syntactic Theory*, edited by Mark Baltin and Chris Collins. Malden, Mass.: Blackwell.

Kroeze, Jan H. 1997. "Alternatives for the Accusative in Biblical Hebrew." Pages 11–25 in *Studien zur hebraischen Grammatik*, edited by A. Wagner. Freiburg: Vendenhoeck & Ruprecht.

Kropat, Arno. 1909. *Die Syntax des Autors der Chronik verglichen mit der seiner Quellen: Ein Beitrag zur historischen Syntax des Hebräischen*. Gießen: Alfred Töpelman.

Kummerow, David. 2011. "Functional-typological and Constructional Linguistic Studies on Tiberian Hebrew: Anaphora, Deixis, and the Verbal System." Th.D. thesis, The Australian College of Theology, Sydney.

Lambdin, Thomas O. 1953. "Egyptian Loan Words in the Old Testament." *Journal of the American Oriental Society* 73 (3): 145–55.

Leahy, T. 1960. "Studies in the Syntax of 1QS." *Biblica* 41: 135–57.

Levenson, Jon D. 1997. *Esther*: A Commentary. Old Testament Library. Louisville, Ky.: Westminster John Knox.

Levi, Yaakov. 1987. *Die Inkongruenz im biblischen Hebräisch*. Wiesbaden: Harrassowitz.

Levinsohn, Stephen H. 2000. "NP References to Active Participants and Story Development in Ancient Hebrew." Working Papers of the Summer Institute of Linguistics, University of North Dakota Session 44.

Matsuda, Kenjirô. 1998. "On the Conservativism of Embedded Clauses." Pages 255–68 in *Historical Linguistics 1997*, edited by Monika S. Schmid, Jennifer R. Austin, and Dieter Stein. Amsterdam: John Benjamins.

Mayer, Rudolf. 1961. "Iranischer Beitrag zu Problemen des Daniel- und Esther- Buches." Pages 127–35 in *Lex tua veritas: Festschrift für Hubert Junker*, edited by H. Gross and F. Mussner. Trier: Paulinus.

van der Merwe, Christo H. J., Jackie A. Naudé, and Jan H. Kroeze. 1999. *A Biblical Hebrew Reference Grammar*. Biblical Languages: Hebrew 3. Sheffield: Sheffield Academic. [= MNK]

Meyer, Charles F. 1992. *Apposition in Contemporary English*. Cambridge: Cambridge University Press.

Millard, A. R. 1977. "The Persian Names in Esther and the Reliability of the Hebrew Text." *Journal of Biblical Literature* 96 (4): 481–88.

Miller[-Naudé], Cynthia L. 1996. *The Representation of Speech in Biblical Hebrew Narrative*. Atlanta: Scholars Press.

———. 1999. "Pivotal Issues in Analyzing the Verbless Clause." Pages 3–17 in *The Verbless Clause in Biblical Hebrew: Linguistic Approaches*, edited by Cynthia L. Miller. Linguistics Studies in Ancient West Semitic 1. Winona Lake, Ind.: Eisenbrauns.

———. 2005. "Ellipsis Involving Negation in Biblical Poetry." Pages 37–52 in *Seeking Out the Wisdom of the Ancients: Essays Offered to Honor Michael V. Fox on the Occasion of His Sixty-Fifth Birthday*, edited by Ronald L. Troxel, Kevin G. Friebel, and Dennis R. Magary. Winona Lake, Ind.: Eisenbrauns.

———. 2007. "Constraints on Ellipsis in Biblical Hebrew." Pages 165–80 in *Studies in Comparative Semitic and Afroasiatic Linguistics Presented to Gene B. Gragg*, edited by C. L. Miller. Chicago: The Oriental Institute of the University of Chicago.

———. 2010. "Vocative Syntax in Biblical Hebrew Prose and Poetry: A Preliminary Analysis." *Journal of Semitic Studies* 55 (2): 347–64.

Miller[-Naudé], Cynthia L., and Ziony Zevit, eds. 2012. *Diachrony in Biblical Hebrew*. Linguistic Studies in Ancient West Semitic 8. Winona Lake, Ind.: Eisenbrauns.

Moore, Carey A. 1967. "A Greek Witness to a Different Hebrew Text of Esther." *Zeitschrift für die alttestamentliche Wissenschaft* 79: 351–58.

———. 1971. *Esther*. Anchor Bible 7B. Garden City, N.Y.: Doubleday.

———. 1982. *Studies in the Book of Esther*. New York: Ktav.

Moreshet, M. 1967. "The Predicate Preceding a Compound Subject in the Biblical Language." *Leshonenu* 31 (4): 251–60. (Hebrew)

Moshavi, Adina. 2010. *Word Order in the Biblical Hebrew Finite Clause*. Linguistic Studies in Ancient West Semitic 4. Winona Lake, Ind.: Eisenbrauns.

Müller, Hans-Peter. 1995. "Ergative Constructions in Early Semitic Languages." *Journal of Near Eastern Studies* 54 (4): 261–71.

Murphy, Roland. 1992. *Ecclesiastes*. Word Biblical Commentary 23A. Dallas: Word Books.

Naudé, J.A. 1999. "Syntactic Aspects of Co-ordinate Subjects with Independent Personal Pronouns." *Journal of Northwest Semitic Languages* 25 (2): 75–99.

Pat-El, Na'ama. 2007. "Some Notes on the Syntax of Biblical Hebrew zeh." *Zeitschrift für Althebraistik* 20: 150-58.

Paton, Lewis Bayles. 1908. *Esther*. International Critical Commentary. Edinburgh: T&T Clark.

Payne Smith, J. 1903. *A Compendious Syriac Dictionary: Founded upon the Thesaurus Syriacus of R. Payne Smith*. Oxford: Clarendon.

Pearce, Laurie E. 2006. "New Evidence for Judeans in Babylonia." Pages 399–411 in *Judah and the Judeans in the Persian Period*, edited by Oded Lipschits and Manfred Oeming. Winona Lake, Ind.: Eisenbrauns.

Pérez Fernández, Miguel. 1997. *An Introductory Grammar of Rabbinic Hebrew*. Translated by John Elwolde. Leiden: Brill.

Pintzuk, Susan. 2003. "Variationist Approaches to Syntactic Change." Pages 509–28 in *The Handbook of Historical Linguistics*, edited by Brian D. Joseph and Richard D. Janda. London: Blackwell.

Polzin, Robert. 1976. *Late Biblical Hebrew: Toward an Historical Typology of Biblical Hebrew Prose*. Missoula, Mont.: Scholars Press.

Pustet, Regina. 2003. *Copulas: Universals in the Categorization of the Lexicon*. Oxford Studies in Typology and Linguistic Theory. Oxford: Oxford University Press.

Qimron, Elisha. 1986. *The Hebrew of the Dead Sea Scrolls*. Harvard Semitic Studies 29. Atlanta: Scholars Press.

———. 1994. *Discoveries in the Judaean Desert X*. Oxford: Clarendon.

Rabin, Chaim. 1970. "Hebrew." Pages 304–24 in *Current Trends in Linguistics* 6, edited by Thomas A. Sebeok. The Hague: Mouton.

Rendsburg, Gary A. 1992. "Kabbir in Biblical Hebrew: Evidence for Style-Switching and Addressee-Switching in the Hebrew Bible." *Journal of the American Oriental Society* 112 (4): 649–51.

Revell, E. J. 1980. "Pausal Forms in Biblical Hebrew: Their Function, Origin and Significance." *Journals of Semitic Studies* 25 (2): 165–79.

———. 1993. "Concord with Compound Subjects and Related Uses of Pronouns." *Vetus Testamentum* 43 (1): 69–87.

Rosenthal, Franz. 2006. *A Grammar of Biblical Aramaic*. 7th ed. Wiesbaden: Harrassowitz.

Roth, Martha T., ed. 1956–2010. *The Assyrian Dictionary of the Oriental Institute of the University of Chicago*. Chicago: The Oriental Institute. [= CAD]

Rothstein, Susan. 1995. "Small Clauses and Copular Constructions." Pages 27–48 in *Small Clauses*, edited by Anna Cardinaletti and Maria Teresa Guasti. San Diego, Calif.: Academic Press.

Sáenz–Badillos, Angel. 1993. *A History of the Hebrew Language*. Translated by John Elwolde. Cambridge: Cambridge University Press.

Screnock, John. 2011. "Word Order in the War Scroll (1QM) and Its Implications for Interpretation." *Dead Sea Discoveries* 18 (1): 29–44.

Segal, M. H. 1927. *A Grammar of Mishnaic Hebrew*. Oxford: Oxford University Press.

Siewierska, Anna. 1988. *Word Order Rules*. London: Croom Helm.

Steiner, Richard C. 2000. "Does the Biblical Hebrew Conjunction *-w* Have Many Meanings, One Meaning, or No Meaning at All?" *Journal of Biblical Literature* 119 (2): 249–67.

Stiehl, Ruth. 1956. "Das Buch Esther." *Wiener Zeitschrift für die Kunde des Morgenlandes* 53: 4–22.

Striedl, H. "Untersuchung zur Syntax und Stilistik des hebräischen Buches Esther." *Zeitschrift für die alttestamentliche Wissenschaft* 14 (1937): 73–108.

Subtelny, Maria E. 2004. "The Tale of the Four Sages Who Entered the Pardes: A Talmudic Enigma from a Persian Perspective." *Jewish Studies Quarterly* 11: 3–58.

Thomason, S. G. 2003. "Contact as a Source of Language Change." Pages 687–712 in *The Handbook of Historical Linguistics*, edited by Brian D. Joseph and Richard D. Janda. London: Blackwell.

Tov, Emanuel, and Frank Polak. 2009. *The Revised CATSS Hebrew/Greek Parallel Text*. Jerusalem.

Waltke, Bruce K., and M. O'Connor. 1990. *An Introduction to Biblical Hebrew Syntax*. Winona Lake, Ind.: Eisenbrauns. [= WO]

Weitzman, Steven. 1996. "The Shifting Syntax of Numerals in Biblical Hebrew: A Reassessment." *Journal of Near Eastern Studies* 55 (3): 177–85.

Wolfram, Walt, and Natalie Schilling-Estes. 2003. "Dialectology and Linguistic Diffusion." Pages 713–35 in *The Handbook of Historical Linguistics*, edited by Brian D. Joseph and Richard D. Janda. London: Blackwell.

Yamauchi, Edwin M. 1980. "The Archaeological Background of Esther." *Bibliotheca Sacra* 137: 99–117.

Young, Ian, Robert Rezetko, and Martin Ehrensvärd. 2008. *Linguistic Dating of Biblical Texts*. 2 vols. London: Equinox.

Zadok, Ran. 2009. "Judeans in Babylonia in Ancient Times." Pages 757–62 in *Encyclopedia of the Jewish Diaspora*, Vol. 2: *Countries, Regions, and Communities*, edited by M. A. Ehrlich. Santa Barbara, Calif.: ABC Clio.

INDEX OF LINGUISTIC ISSUES

In the following index, primary discussions of each linguistic issue are in ***bold****; all other references indicate either where the linguistic phenomenon appears in Esther, where we discuss it in our commentary, or both. Note that a feature may occur without our commenting on it, and that we may discuss a linguistic issue though it does not in fact occur in that verse. The index is intended as a tool and is thus not exhaustive (though we try to include all the references of which we are aware).*